D0781323

The C# Player's Guide

Third Edition

RB Whitaker

Starbound Software

Many of the designations used by manufacturers and sellers to distinguish their products are claimed as trademarks. Where those designations appear in this book, and the author and publisher were aware of those claims, those designations have been printed with initial capital letters or in all capitals.

The author and publisher of this book have made every effort to ensure that the information in this book was correct at press time. However, the author and publisher do not assume, and hereby disclaim any liability to any party for any loss, damage, or disruption caused by errors or omissions, whether such errors or omissions result from negligence, accident, or any other cause.

Copyright © 2012-2017 by RB Whitaker

All rights reserved. No part of this book may be reproduced or transmitted in any form or by any means, electronic or mechanical, including photocopying, recording, or by any information storage and retrieval system, without written permission from the author, except for the inclusion of brief quotations in a review. For information regarding permissions, write to:

RB Whitaker
rbwhitaker@outlook.com

ISBN-10: 0-9855801-3-5
ISBN-13: 978-0-9855801-3-1

Contents at a Glance

Part 3: Object-Oriented Programming

Part 4: Advanced Topics

Part 5: Mastering the Tools

Part 6: Wrapping Up

Table of Contents

Part 2: The Basics

Part 3: Object-Oriented Programming

Part 4: Advanced Topics

Part 5: Mastering the Tools

Part 6: Wrapping Up

Acknowledgements

The task of writing a book is like writing software. When you start, you're sure it's only going to take a few weeks. *It'll be easy*, you think. But as you start working, you start seeing that you're going to need to make changes, and lots of them. You need to rearrange entire chapters, add topics you hadn't even thought about, and you discover that there's not even going to be a place in your book for that chapter called *Muppets of the Eastern Seaboard*.

I couldn't have ever finished this book without help. I'll start by thanking Jack Wall, Sam Hulick, Clint Mansell, and the others who wrote the music for Mass Effect. (You think I'm joking, don't you?) I listened to their music nearly incessantly as I wrote this book. Because of them, every moment of the creation of this book felt absolutely epic.

I need to also thank the many visitors to my game development tutorials site, who provided feedback on the early versions of this work. In particular, I want to thank Jonathan Loh, Thomas Allen, Daniel Bickler, and Mete ÇOM, who went way above and beyond, spending hours of their own personal time, reading through this book and provided detailed critique and corrections. With their help, this book is far more useful and valuable.

I also need to thank my mom and dad. Their confidence in me and their encouragement to always do the best I can has caused me to do things I never could have done without them.

Most of all, I want to thank my beautiful wife, who was there to lift my spirits when the weight of writing a book became unbearable, who read through my book and gave honest, thoughtful, and creative feedback and guidance, and who lovingly pressed me to keep going on this book, day after day. Without her, this book would still be a random scattering of Word documents, buried in some obscure folder on my computer, collecting green silicon-based mold.

To all of you, I owe you my sincerest gratitude.

-RB Whitaker

Introduction

In a Nutshell
- Describes the goals of this book, which is to function like a player's guide, not a comprehensive cover-everything-that-ever-existed book.
- Breaks down how the book is organized from a high-level perspective, as well as pointing out some of the extra "features" of the book.
- Provides some ideas on how to get the most out of this book for programmers, beginners, and anyone who is short on time.

The Player's Guide

This book is not about playing video games. (Though programming is as fun as playing video games for many people.) Nor is it about *making* video games, specifically. (Though you definitely can make video games with C#.)

Instead, think of this book like a player's guide, but for a programming language. A player's guide is a popular kind of book that is written to help game players:

- learn the basics of the game,
- prevent them from getting stuck,
- understand how the world they're playing in works,
- learn how to overcome the obstacles and enemies they face,
- point out common pitfalls they may face and locate useful items,
- and master the tools they're given.

This book accomplishes those same goals for the C# programming language. I'll walk you through the language from the ground up, point out places where people get stuck, provide you with hands-on examples to explore, give you quizzes to ensure you're on the right track, and describe how to use the tools that you'll need to create programs. I'll show you the ins and outs of the many features of C#, describing *why* things work the way they do, rather than just simple mechanics and syntax.

My goal is to provide you with the "dungeon map" to direct you as you begin delving into C#, while still allowing you to mostly explore whatever you want, whenever you want.

I want to point out that this book is intentionally *not* called *Everything you Need to Know about C#,* or *The Comprehensive Guide to C#.* (Note that if books with those titles actually exist, I'm not referring to them specifically, but rather, to just the general idea of an all-encompassing book.) I'm here to tell you, when you're done with this book, you'll still have lots to learn about C#.

But guess what? That's going to happen with *any* book you use, including those all-encompassing books. Programming languages are complex creations, and there are enough dark corners and strange combinations that nobody can learn everything there is to know about them. In fact, I've even seen the people who designed the C# language say they just learned something new about it! For as long as you use C#, you'll constantly be learning new things about it, and that's actually one of the things that makes programming interesting.

I've tried to cover a lot of ground in this book, and with roughly 400 pages, anyone would expect that to be quite a bit. And it is. But there are plenty of other books out there that are 800 or even 1200 pages long. A book so heavy, you'll need a packing mule to carry it anywhere. That, or permanently place it on the central dais of an ancient library, with a single beam of dusty light shining in on it through a hole in the marble ceiling. Instead of all that, the goal of this book is effectiveness and clarity, not comprehensiveness. Something that will fit both on your shelf and in your brain.

It is important to point out that this book is focused on the C# programming language, rather than libraries for building certain specific application types. So while you can build desktop applications, web pages, and computer games with C#, we won't be discussing WPF, ASP.NET, DirectX, or any other platform- or framework-specific code. Instead, we'll focus on core C# code, without bogging you down with those additional libraries at first. Once you've got the hang of C#, heading into one of those areas will be much easier.

How This Book is Organized

This book is divided into six parts. Part 1 describes what you need to get going. You'll learn how to get set up with the free software that you need to write code and make your first C# program.

Part 2 describes the basics of procedural programming—how to tell the computer, step-by-step, what to do to accomplish tasks. It covers things like how information is stored (in variables), how to make decisions, loop over things repeatedly, and put blocks of code that accomplish specific tasks into a reusable chunk called a method. It also introduces the type system of the C# language, which is one of the key pieces of C# programming.

Part 3 goes into object-oriented programming, introducing it from the ground up, but also getting into a lot of the details that make it so powerful. Chapter 20, in my opinion, is the critical point of the book. By Chapter 19, we've introduced all of the key concepts needed to make almost any C# program, including classes, which is the most powerful way C# provides for building your own data types. Chapter 20 contains the task (and solution) to making a simple but complete game of Tic-Tac-Toe, which will put all of the knowledge from the earlier chapters to the test. Everything we do after this chapter is simply fleshing out details and giving you better tools to get specific jobs done faster.

Part 4 covers some common programming tasks, as well as covering some of the more advanced features of C#. For the most part, these topics are independent of each other, and once you've made it past that critical point in Chapter 20, you should be able to do these at any time you want.

Part 5 changes gears, and covers more details about Visual Studio, which you use to create C# programs, additional information about the .NET Platform, and some tools, tricks, and information you can use as you program.

Finally, Part 6 wraps up the book with some larger scale programs for you to try making, a chapter on where to go next as you continue to learn C#, and a glossary of words that are defined throughout the book, which you can use as a reference when you run across a word or phrase that you are unfamiliar with or have forgotten about.

Try It Out!

Scattered throughout the book are a variety of sections labeled *Try It Out!* These sections give you simple challenge problems and quizzes that give you a chance to play around with the new concepts in the chapter and test your understanding. If this were a class, these would be the homework.

The purpose of these *Try It Out!* sections is to help you get some real world practice with the new information. You can't learn to drive a car by reading the owner's manual, and you can't learn to program without writing any code.

I strongly encourage you to spend at least a few minutes doing each of these challenges to help you understand what you're reading and ensure that you've learned what you needed to.

If you have something else you want to explore with the new concepts instead of the challenges I've provided, all the better. The only thing better than playing around with this stuff is doing something with it that you have a personal interest in. If you want to explore a different direction, go for it!

At the end of the book, in Chapter 50, I have an entire chapter full of larger, tougher challenge problems for you to try out. These problems involve combining concepts from many chapters together into one program. Going through some or all of these as you're finishing up will be a great way to make sure you've learned the most important things you needed to.

The most important thing to remember about these *Try It Out!* sections is that the answers are all online. If you get stuck, or just want to compare your solution to someone else's, you can see mine at **starboundsoftware.com/books/c-sharp/try-it-out/**. I should point out that just because your solution is different from mine (or anyone else's) doesn't necessarily mean it is wrong. That's one of the best parts about programming—there's always more than one way to do something.

In a Nutshell

At the beginning of each chapter, I summarize what it contains. These sections are designed to do the following:

- Summarize the chapter to come.
- Show enough of the chapter so that an experienced programmer can know if they already know enough to skip the chapter or if they need to study it in depth.
- Review the chapter enough to ensure that you got what you needed to from the chapter. For instance, imagine you're about to take a test on C#. You can jump from chapter to chapter, reading the *In a Nutshell* sections, and anything it describes that you didn't already know, you can then go into the chapter and review it.

In Depth

On occasion, there are a few topics that are not critical to your understanding of C#, but they are an interesting topic that is related to the things you're learning. You'll find this information pulled out into *In Depth* sections. These are never required reading, so if you're busy, skip ahead. If you're not too busy, I think you'll find this additional information interesting, and worth taking the time to read.

Glossary

As you go through this book, you're going to learn a ton of new words and phrases. Especially if you're completely new to programming in general. At the back of this book is a glossary that contains the definitions for these words. You can use this as a reference in case you forget what a word means, or as you run into new concepts as you learn C#.

Getting the Most from This Book

For Programmers

If you are a programmer, particularly one who already knows a programming language that is related to C# (C, C++, Java, Visual Basic .NET, etc.) learning C# is going to be relatively easy for you.

C# has a lot in common with all of these languages. In fact, it's fair to say that all programming languages affect and are inspired by other languages, because they evolve over time. C# looks and feels like a combination of Java and C++, both of which have roots that go back to the C programming language. Visual Basic .NET (VB.NET) on the other hand, looks and feels quite different from C# (it's based on Visual Basic, and Basic before that) but because both C# and VB.NET are designed and built for the .NET Platform, they have many of the same features, and there's almost a one-to-one correspondence between features and keywords.

Because C# is so closely tied to these other languages, and knowing that many people may already know something about these other languages, you'll see me point out how C# compares to these other languages from time to time.

If you already know a lot about programming, you're going to be able to move quickly through this book, especially the beginning, where you may find very few differences from languages you already know. To speed the process along, read the *In a Nutshell* section at the start of the chapter. If you feel like you already know everything it describes, it's probably safe to skip to the next chapter.

I want to mention a couple of chapters that might be a little dangerous to skip. Chapter 6 introduces the C# type system, including a few concepts that are key to building types throughout the book. Also, Chapter 16 is sort of a continuation on the type system, describing value and reference types. It's important to understand the topics covered in those chapters. Those chapters cover some of the fundamental ways that C# is different from these other languages, so don't skip them.

For Busy People

One of the best parts about this book is that you don't need to read it all. Yes, that's right. It's not all mandatory reading to get started with C#. You could easily get away with only reading a part of this book, and still understand C#. In fact, not only understand it, but be able to make just about any program you can dream up. This is especially true if you already know a similar programming language.

At a minimum, you should start at the beginning and read through Chapter 20. That covers the basics of programming, all the way up to and including an introduction to making your own classes. (And if you're already a programmer, you should be able to fly through those introductory chapters quickly.)

The rest of the book could theoretically be skipped, though if you try to use someone else's code, you're probably going to be in for some surprises.

Once you've gone through those 20 chapters, you can then come back and read the rest of the book in more or less any order that you want, as you have extra time.

For Beginners

If you've never done any programming before, be warned: learning a programming language can be hard work. The concepts in the first 20 chapters of this book are the most important to understand. Take whatever time is necessary to really feel like you understand what you're seeing in these chapters. This gets you all of the basics, and gets you up to a point where you can make your own types using classes. Like with the *For Busy People* section above, Chapter 20 is the critical point that you've got to get to, in order to really understand C#. At that point, you can probably make any program that you can think of, though the rest of the book will cover additional tools and tricks that will allow you to do this more easily and more efficiently.

After reading through these chapters, skim through the rest of the book, so that you're aware of what else C# has. That's an important step if you're a beginner. It will familiarize you with what C# has to offer, and when you either see it in someone else's code or have a need for it, you'll know exactly where to come back to. A lot of these additional details will make the most sense when you have an actual need for it in a program of your own creation. After a few weeks or a few months, when you've had a chance to make some programs on your own, come back and go through the rest of the book in depth.

I Genuinely Want Your Feedback

Writing a book is a huge task, and no one has ever finished a huge task perfectly. There's the possibility of mistakes, plenty of chances to inadvertently leave you confused, or leaving out important details. I was tempted to keep this book safe on my hard drive, and never give it out to the world, because then those limitations wouldn't matter. But alas, my wife wouldn't let me follow Gandalf's advice and "keep it secret; keep it safe," and so now here it is in your hands.

If you ever find any problems with this book, big or small, or if you have any suggestions for improving it, I'd really like to know. After all, books are a lot like software, and there's always the opportunity for future versions that improve upon the current one. Also, if you have positive things to say about the book, I'd love to hear about that too. There's nothing quite like hearing that your hard work has helped somebody.

To give feedback of any kind, please visit **starboundsoftware.com/books/c-sharp/feedback**.

This Book Comes with Online Content

On my website, I have a small amount of additional content that you might find useful. For starters, as people submit feedback, like I described in the last section, I will post corrections and clarifications as needed on this book's errata page: **starboundsoftware.com/books/c-sharp/errata**.

Also on my site, I will post my own answers for all of the *Try It Out!* sections found throughout this book. If you get stuck, or just want something to compare your answers with, you can visit this book's site and see a solution. To see these answers, go to: **starboundsoftware.com/books/c-sharp/try-it-out/**.

The website also contains some extra problems to work on, beyond the ones contained in this book. I've been frequently asked to add more problems to the book than what it currently has. Indeed, this version contains more than any previous version. But at the same time, most people don't actually do these problems. To avoid drowning out the actual content with more and more problems, I've provided additional problems on the website. This felt like a good compromise. These can be found at **starboundsoftware.com/books/c-sharp/additional-problems**.

Additional information or resources may be found at **starboundsoftware.com/books/c-sharp**.

Part 1

Getting Started

The world of C# programming lies in front of you, waiting to be explored. In Part 1 of this book, within just a few short chapters, we'll do the following:

- Get a quick introduction to what C# is (Chapter 1).
- Get set up to start making C# programs (Chapter 2).
- Write our first program (Chapter 3).
- Dig into the fundamental parts of C# programming (Chapters 3 and 4).

The C# Programming Language

In a Nutshell
- Describes the general idea of programming, and goes into more details about why C# is a good language.
- Describes the core of what the .NET Platform is.
- Gives some history on the C# programming language for context.

I'm going to start off this book with a very brief introduction to C#. If you're already a programmer, and you've read the Wikipedia pages on C# and the .NET Framework, skip ahead to the next chapter.

On the other hand, if you're new to programming in general, or you're still a little vague on what exactly C# or the .NET Platform is, then this is the place for you.

I should point out that we'll get into a lot of detail about how the .NET Platform functions, and what it gives you as a programmer in Chapter 44. This chapter just provides a quick overview of the basics.

What is C#?

Computers only understand binary: 1's and 0's. All of the information they keep track of is ultimately nothing more than a glorified pile of bits. All of the instructions they run and all of the data they process are binary.

But humans are notoriously bad at doing anything with a giant pile of 1's and 0's. So rather than doing that, we created programming languages, which are based on human languages (usually English) and structured in a way that allows you to give instructions to the computer. These instructions are called *source code*, and are simple text files.

When the time is right, your source code will be handed off to a special program called a *compiler*, which is able to take it and turn it into the binary 1's and 0's that the computer understands, typically in the form of an EXE file. In this sense, you can think of the compiler as a translator from your source code to the binary machine instructions that the computer knows.

There are thousands, maybe tens of thousands of programming languages, each good at certain things, and less good at other things. C# is one of the most popular. C# is a simple general-purpose programming language, meaning you can use it to create pretty much anything, including desktop applications, server-side code for websites, and even video games.

C# provides an excellent balance between ease of use and power. There are other languages that provide less power and are easier to use (like Java) and others that provide more power, giving up some of its simplicity (like C++). Because of the balance it strikes, it is the perfect language for nearly everything that you will want to do, so it's a great language to learn, whether it's your first or your tenth.

What is the .NET Platform?

C# relies heavily on something called the .NET Platform. It is also commonly also called the .NET Framework, though we'll make a subtle distinction between the two later on. The .NET Platform is a large and powerful platform, which we'll discuss in detail in Chapter 44. You can go read it as soon as you're done with this chapter, if you want.

The .NET Platform is vast, with many components, but two stand out as the most central. The first part is the *Common Language Runtime*, often abbreviated as the *CLR*. The CLR is a software program that takes your compiled C# code and runs it. When you launch your EXE file, the CLR will start up and begin taking your code and translating it into the optimal binary instructions for the physical computer that it is running on, and your code comes to life.

In this sense, the CLR is a middle-man between your code and the physical computer. This type of program is called a virtual machine. We'll get into more of the specifics in Chapter 44. For now, it's only important to know that the .NET Platform itself, specifically the CLR runtime, play a key role in running your application—and in making it so your application can run on a wide variety of computer architectures and operating systems.

The second major component of the .NET Platform is the .NET Standard Library. The Standard Library is frequently called the Base Class Library. The Standard Library is a massive collection of code that you can reuse within your own programs to accelerate the development of whatever you are working on. We will cover some of the most important things in the Standard Library in this book, but it is huge, and deserves a book of its own. More detail on the Standard Library and the Base Class Library can be found in Chapter 44.

Built on top of the .NET Standard Library is a collection of *app models*. An app model is another large library designed for a specific type of application. This includes things like WPF and Windows Forms for GUI applications, ASP.NET for web development, and Xamarin for iOS and Android development. Game frameworks or engines like MonoGame and Unity could also be considered app models, though these are not maintained directly by Microsoft.

This book, unfortunately, doesn't cover these app models to any serious extent. There are two reasons for this. Each app model is gigantic. You could write multiple books about each of these app models (and indeed, there are many books out there). Trying to pack them all into this book would make it a 5000 page book.

Second, the app models are, true to their name, specific to a certain type of application. This means that the things that are important to somebody doing desktop development are going to be wildly different from somebody doing web development. This book focuses on the C# language itself, and the aspects of the .NET Platform that are useful to everybody. Once you've finished this book, you could then proceed on to other books that focus on specific app models. (Those books all generally assume you know C# anyway.)

We will cover how the .NET Platform is organized and how it functions in depth in Chapter 44.

C# and .NET Versions

C# has gone through quite a bit of evolution over its history. The first release was in 2002, and established the bulk of the language features C# still has today.

A little over a year later, in 2003, C# 2.0 was released, adding in a lot of other big and powerful features, most of which will get quite a bit of attention in this book (generics, nullable types, delegates, static classes, etc.)

C# 3.0 expanded the language in a couple of very specific directions: LINQ and lambdas, both of which get their own chapters in this book.

The next two releases were somewhat smaller. C# 4.0 added dynamic typing, as well as named and optional method arguments. C# 5.0 added greatly expanded support for asynchronous programming.

In the C# 5 era, a new C# compiler was introduced: Roslyn. This compiler has a number of notable features: it's open source, it's written in C# (written in the language it's for), and it is available while your program is running (so you can compile additional code dynamically). Something about its construction also allows for people to more easily tweak and experiment with new features, which led to the features added in C# 6.0 and 7.0.

C# 6.0 and 7.0 added a whole slew of little additions and tweaks across the language. While previous updates to the language could usually be summed up in a single bullet point or two, and are given their own chapters in this book, the new features in C# 6.0 and 7.0 are small and numerous. I try to point out what these new features are throughout this book, so that you are aware of them.

Alongside the C# language itself, both Visual Studio and the Standard Library have both been evolving and growing. This book has been updated to work with Visual Studio 2017 and C# 7.0 at the time of publishing.

Future versions will, of course, arrive before long. Based on past experience, it's a safe bet that everything you learn in this book will still apply in future versions.

Installing Visual Studio

In a Nutshell
- To program in C#, we will need a program that allows us to write C# code and run it. That program is Microsoft Visual Studio.
- A variety of versions of Visual Studio exists, including the free Community Edition, as well as several higher tiers that offer additional features at a cost.
- You do not need to spend money to make C# programs.
- This chapter walks you through the various versions of Visual Studio to help you decide which one to use, but as you are getting started, you should consider the free Visual Studio 2017 Community Edition.

To make your own programs, people usually use a program called an *Integrated Development Environment* (IDE). An IDE combines all of the tools you will commonly need to make software, including a special text editor designed for editing source code files, a compiler, and other various tools to help you manage the files in your project.

With C#, nearly everyone chooses to use some variation of Visual Studio, made by Microsoft. There are a few different levels of Visual Studio, ranging from the free Community Edition, to the high-end Enterprise Edition. In this chapter, I'll guide you through the process of determining which one to choose.

As of the time of publication of this book, the latest version is the 2017 family. There will inevitably be future releases, but the bulk of what's described in this book should still largely apply in future versions. While new features have been added over time, the fundamentals of Visual Studio have remained the same for a very long time now.

There are three main flavors of Visual Studio 2017. Our first stop will be to look at the differences among these, and I'll point out one that is most likely your best choice, getting started. (It's free, don't worry!) I'll then tell you how to download Visual Studio and a little about the installation process. By the end of this chapter, you'll be up and running, ready to start doing some C# programming!

Versions of Visual Studio

Visual Studio 2017 comes in three editions: Community, Professional, and Enterprise. While I'm ultimately going to recommend the Community Edition (it's free, and it still allows you to make and sell commercial applications with it) it is worth briefly considering the differences between the three.

From a raw feature standpoint, Community and Professional are essentially the same thing. Enterprise comes with some nice added bonuses, but at a significantly higher cost. These extra features generally are non-code-related, but instead deal with the surrounding issues, like team collaboration, testing, performance analysis, etc. While nice, these extra features are probably not a great use of your money as you're learning, unless you work for a company or attend school at a place that will buy it for you.

Now that I've pushed you away from Enterprise as a beginner, the only remaining question is what to actually use. And to answer that, we need to compare the Community Edition to the Professional Edition.

Community and Professional are essentially the same product with a different license. Microsoft wants to make Visual Studio available to everybody, but they still want to be able to bring in money for their efforts. With the current licensing model, they've managed to do that pretty well.

While Professional costs roughly $500, Community is free. But the license prevents certain people (the ones with tons of money) from using it. While the following interpretation is not legally binding, the general interpretation of the Community license is essentially this:

You can use it to make software, both commercially and non-commercially, as long as you don't fit in one of the following categories:

- You have 5+ Visual Studio developers in your company. (If you're getting it for personal home use or moonlighting projects, you don't count the place you work for. You have 1 developer.)
- You have 250+ computers or users in your company.
- You have a gross income of $1,000,000.

If any of the above apply, you don't qualify for the Community license, and you must buy Professional. But then again, if any of those apply to you, you probably have the money to pay for Professional anyway.

There are a couple of exceptions to that:

- You're a student or educator, using it solely for educational uses.
- You're working solely on open source projects.

In short, for essentially everybody reading this book, you should be able to either use Community, or you're working somewhere that can afford to buy Professional or Enterprise for you.

This makes the decision simple: you will almost certainly want Visual Studio Community for now.

The Installation Process

Visual Studio can be downloaded from **https://www.visualstudio.com/downloads**. This will actually install the Visual Studio Installer, which is a separate program from Visual Studio itself. (It sounds complicated, but the Visual Studio Installer is a powerful and useful product in its own right.)

Once you get the installer downloaded and running, you will see a screen that looks similar to this:

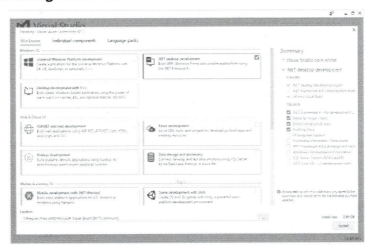

If instead of the above, you see a screen that lists Visual Studio Community, Professional, and Enterprise, choose to install Visual Studio Community (or the option that is the one you need) and you will arrive at this screen.

Visual Studio, with every single bit of functionality, is a lumbering behemoth of a product. Starting with Visual Studio 2017, the product and the installer got a massive rewrite to allow you to install only the components you actually care about. The screen that you see in the previous image is the part of the installer that allows you to choose what components you want.

By default, nothing is checked, which would give you a very barebones Visual Studio. That's probably *not* what you want. Instead, we need to check the items that we want to include.

For this book, you will want to check the box for *.NET desktop development* on the Workloads tab. Feel free to look through the rest of the things and check anything else you might want to play around with at some point.

The installer contains three tabs at the top. The **Individual components** tab lets you pick and choose individual items that you might want a la carte. The **Workloads** tab will pre-select groups of items on the **Individual components** tab, to give you groups of items that are well suited for making specific types of applications. The **Language packs** tab is for choosing languages for Visual Studio. English is included by default, but check the box on other languages if you want to be able to use a different language like French or Russian.

When you have the components you want (at a minimum, **.NET desktop development**) hit the Install button and your selected components will be installed for you.

You may get an icon for Visual Studio on your desktop, but you'll also always be able to find Visual Studio in your Start Menu under "Visual Studio 2017."

Also, if you ever want to modify the components that you've installed (either to remove unused ones or add new ones) you can find "Visual Studio Installer" on your start menu as well, and simply re-run it to modify your Visual Studio settings and add or remove components.

Visual Studio will ask you to sign in with a Microsoft account at some point. If you don't have one, you can follow their instructions to make one.

Starting in the next chapter and throughout the rest of this book, we'll cover all sorts of useful tips and tricks on using Visual Studio. Towards the end of this book, in Part 5, we'll get into Visual Studio in a little more depth. Once you get through the next couple of chapters, you can jump ahead to that part whenever you're ready for it. You don't have to read through the book in order.

This book will use screenshots from Visual Studio 2017 Community. You may see some slight differences depending on which version of Visual Studio you're using and what add-ons you have active. But all of the things we talk about in this book will be available in all editions.

> **Try It Out!**
> **Install Visual Studio.** Take the time now to choose a version of Visual Studio and install it, so that you're ready to begin making awesome programs in the next chapter.

C# Programming on Mac and Linux

If you are interested in doing C# programming on a Mac or on Linux, you're still in luck.

Your first option is Visual Studio Code, which can be grabbed from **https://code.visualstudio.com**. Visual Studio Code is a lightweight version of Visual Studio that runs on Windows, Mac, and Linux. Visual Studio Code is missing a number of significant features that this book talks about, but it does support the basics of editing and compiling your code.

Your second option is Xamarin Studio (**http://xamarin.com/studio**), which works on macOS. Xamarin Studio is a powerful, full IDE similar to Visual Studio. In fact, Microsoft is releasing Visual Studio for Mac, but it is essentially just Xamarin Studio rebranded. (Xamarin is owned by Microsoft, so they're on the same team.)

3

Hello World: Your First C# Program

In a Nutshell

- Start a new C# Console Application by going to **File > New > Project...**, choosing the Console Application template, and giving your project a name.
- Inside of the **Main** method, you can add code to write out stuff using a statement like **Console.WriteLine("Hello World!");**
- Compile and run your program with **F5** or **Ctrl + F5**.
- The template includes code that does the following:
    - **using** directives make it easy to access chunks of previously written code in the current program.
    - The **namespace** block puts all of the contained code into a single collection.
    - The code we actually write goes into the **Program** class in a method called **Main**, which the C# compiler recognizes as the starting point for a program.

In this chapter we'll make our very first C# program. Our first program needs to be one that simply prints out some variation of "Hello World!" or we'll make the programming gods mad. It's tradition to make your first program print out a simple message like this whenever you learn a new language. It's simple, yet still gives us enough to see the basics of how the programming language works. Also, it gives us a chance to compile and run a program, with very little chance for introducing bugs.

So that's where we'll start. We'll create a new project and add in a single line to display "Hello World!" Once we've got that, we'll compile and run it, and you'll have your very first program!

After that, we'll take a minute and look at the code that you have written in more detail before moving on to more difficult, but infinitely more awesome stuff in the future!

Creating a New Project

Let's get started with our first C# program! Open up Visual Studio, which we installed in Chapter 2.

When the program first opens, you will see the Start Page come up. To create a new project, select **File > New > Project...** from the menu bar. (Note you can also search for the Console Application template on the Start Page directly.)

Once you have done this, a dialog will appear asking you to specify a project type and a name for the project. This dialog is shown below:

On the left side, you will see a few categories of templates to choose from. Depending on what version of Visual Studio you have installed and what plugins and extensions you have, you may see different categories here, but the one you'll want to select is the Visual C# category, which will list all C#-related templates that are installed.

Once that is selected, in the list in the top-center, find and select the **Console Application (.NET Framework)** template. The Console Application template is the simplest template and it is exactly where we want to start. For all of the stuff we will be doing in this book, this is the template to use.

As you finish up this book, if you want to start doing things like making programs with a graphical user interface (GUI), game development, smart phone app development, or web-based development, you will be able to put these other templates to good use.

At the bottom of the dialog, type in a name for your project. I've called mine "HelloWorld." Your project will be saved in a directory with this name. It doesn't matter what you call a project, but a good name will help you find it later. By default, Visual Studio tries to call your programs "ConsoleApplication1" or "ConsoleApplication2." If you don't choose a good name, you won't know what each of these do. By default, projects are saved under your Documents directory (Documents/Visual Studio 2017/Projects/).

Finally, press the **OK** button to create your project!

A Brief Tour of Visual Studio

Once your project has loaded, it is worth a brief discussion of what you see before you. We'll look in depth at how Visual Studio works later on (Chapter 45) but it is worth a brief discussion right now.

By this point, you should be looking at a screen that looks something like this:

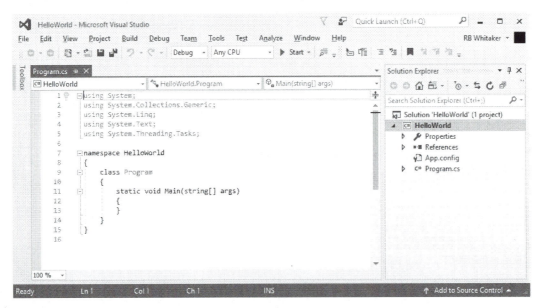

Depending on which version of Visual Studio you installed, you may see some slight differences, but it should look pretty similar to this.

In the center should be some text that starts out with **using System;**. This is your program's source code! It is what you'll be working on. We'll discuss what it means, and how to modify it in a second. We'll spend most of our time in this window.

On the right side is the Solution Explorer. This shows you a big outline of all of the files contained in your project, including the main one that we'll be working with, called "Program.cs". The *.cs file extension means it is a text file that contains C# code. If you double-click on any item in the Solution Explorer, it will open in the main editor window. The Solution Explorer is quite important, and we'll use it frequently.

As you work on your project, other windows may pop up as they are needed. Each of these can be closed by clicking on the 'X' in the upper right corner of the window.

If, by chance, you are missing a window that you feel you want, you can always open it by finding it on either the **View** menu or **View > Other Windows**. For right now, if you have the main editor window open with your Program.cs file in it, and the Solution Explorer, you should be good to go.

Building Blocks: Projects, Solutions, and Assemblies

As we get started, it is worth defining a few important terms that you'll be seeing throughout this book. In the world of C#, you'll commonly see the words *solution*, *project*, and *assembly*, and it is worth taking the time upfront to explain what they are, so that you aren't lost.

These three words describe the code that you're building in different ways. We'll start with a project. A *project* is simply a collection of source code and resource files that will all eventually get built into the same executable program. A project also has additional information telling the compiler how to build it.

When compiled, a project becomes an *assembly*. In nearly all cases, a single project will become a single assembly. An assembly shows up in the form of an EXE file or a DLL file. These two different extensions represent two different types of assemblies, and are built from two different types of projects (chosen in the project's settings).

A *process assembly* appears as an EXE file. It is a complete program, and has a starting point defined, which the computer knows to run when you start up the EXE file. A *library assembly* appears as a DLL file. A DLL file does not have a specific starting point defined. Instead, it contains code that other programs can access and reuse on the fly.

Throughout this book, we'll be primarily creating and working with projects that are set up to be process assemblies that compile to EXE files, but you can configure any project to be built as a library assembly (DLL) instead.

Finally, a *solution* will combine multiple projects together to accomplish a complete task or form a complete program. Solutions will also contain information about how the different projects should be connected to each other. While solutions can contain many projects, most simple programs (including nearly everything we do in this book) will only need one. Even many large programs can get away with only a single project.

Looking back at what we learned in the last section about the Solution Explorer, you'll see that the Solution Explorer is showing our entire solution as the very top item, which it labels "Solution 'HelloWorld' (1 project)." Immediately underneath that, we see the one project that our solution contains: "HelloWorld." Inside of the project are all of the settings and files that our project has, including the Program.cs file that contains source code that we'll soon start editing.

It's important to keep the solution and project separated in your head. They both have the same name and it can be a little confusing. Just remember the top node is the solution, and the one inside it is the project.

Modifying Your Project

We're now ready to make our program actually do something. In the center of your Visual Studio window, you should see the main text editor, containing text that should look identical to this:

```
using System;
using System.Collections.Generic;
using System.Linq;
using System.Text;
using System.Threading.Tasks;

namespace HelloWorld
{
    class Program
    {
        static void Main(string[] args)
        {
        }
    }
}
```

In a minute we'll discuss what all of that does, but for now let's go ahead and make our first change—adding something that will print out the message "Hello World!"

Right in the middle of that code, you'll see three lines that say **static void Main(string[] args)** then a starting curly brace ('{') and a closing curly brace ('}'). We want to add our new code right between the two curly braces.

Here's the line we want to add:

```
Console.WriteLine("Hello World!");
```

So now our program's full code should look like this:

```
using System;
using System.Collections.Generic;
using System.Linq;
using System.Text;
using System.Threading.Tasks;

namespace HelloWorld
{
    class Program
    {
        static void Main(string[] args)
        {
            Console.WriteLine("Hello World!");
        }
    }
}
```

We've completed our first C# program! Easy, huh?

Try It Out!

Hello World! It's impossible to understate how important it is to actually *do* the stuff outlined in this chapter. Simply reading text just doesn't cut it. In future chapters, most of these *Try It Out!* sections will contain extra things to do, beyond the things described in the actual body of the chapter. But for right now, it is very important that you simply go through the process explained in this chapter. The chapter itself is a *Try It Out!* So follow through this chapter, one step at a time, and make sure you're understanding the concepts that come up, at least at a basic level.

Compiling and Running Your Project

Your computer doesn't magically understand what you've written. Instead, it understands special instructions that are composed of 1's and 0's called *binary*. Fortunately for us, Visual Studio includes a thing called a *compiler*. A compiler will take the C# code that we've written and turn it into binary that the computer understands.

So our next step is to compile our code and run it. Visual Studio will make this easy for us.

To start this process, press **F5** or choose **Debug > Start Debugging** from the menu.

There! Did you see it? Your program flashed on the screen for a split second! (Hang on... we'll fix that in a second. Stick with me for a moment.)

We just ran our program in debug mode, which means that if something bad happens while your program is running, it won't simply crash. Instead, Visual Studio will notice the problem, stop in the middle of what's going on, and show you the problem that you are having, allowing you to debug it. We'll talk more about how to actually debug your code in Chapter 48.

So there you have it! You've made a program, compiled it, and executed it!

If it doesn't compile and execute, double check to make sure your code looks like the code above.

Help! My program is running, but disappearing before I can see it!

You likely just ran into this problem when you executed your program. You push **F5** and the program runs, a little black console window pops up for a split second before disappearing again, and you have no clue what happened.

There's a good reason for that. Your program ran out of things to do, so it finished and closed on its own. (It thinks it's so smart, closing on its own like that.)

But we're really going to want a way to make it so that *doesn't* happen. After all, we're left wondering if it even did what we told it to. There are two solutions to this, each of which has its own strengths and weaknesses.

Approach #1: When you run it *without* debugging, console programs like this will always pause before closing. So one option is to run it without debugging. This option is called Release Mode. We'll cover this in a little more depth later on, but the bottom line is that your program runs in a streamlined mode which is faster, but if something bad happens, your program will just die, without giving you a chance to debug it.

You can run in release mode by simply pressing **Ctrl + F5** (instead of just **F5**). Do this now, and you'll see that it prints out your "Hello World!" message, plus another message that says "Press any key to continue..." which does exactly what it says and waits for you before closing the program. You can also find this under **Debug > Start Without Debugging** on the menu.

But there's a distinct disadvantage to running in release mode. We're no longer running in debug mode, and so if something happens with your program while it is running, your application will crash and die. (Hey, just like all of the other "cool" programs out there!) Which brings us to an alternative approach:

Approach #2: Put another line of code in that makes the program wait before closing the program. You can do this by simply adding in the following line of code, right below where you put the **Console.WriteLine("Hello World!");** statement:

```
Console.ReadKey();
```

So your full code, if you use this approach, would look like this:

```
using System;
using System.Collections.Generic;
using System.Linq;
using System.Text;
using System.Threading.Tasks;

namespace HelloWorld
{
    class Program
    {
        static void Main(string[] args)
        {
            Console.WriteLine("Hello World!");
            Console.ReadKey();
        }
    }
}
```

Using this approach, there is one more line of code that you have to add to your program (in fact, every console application you make), which can be a little annoying. But at least with this approach, you can still run your program in debug mode, which you will soon discover is a really nice feature.

Fortunately, this is only going to be a problem with console apps. That's what we'll be doing in this book, but before long, you'll probably be making windows apps, games, or awesome C#-based websites, and this problem will go away on its own. They work in a different way, and this won't be an issue there.

Try It Out!

See Your Program Twice. I've described two approaches for actually seeing your program execute. Take a moment and try out each approach. This will give you an idea of how these two different approaches work. Also, try combining the two and see what you get. Can you figure out why you need to push a key twice to end the program?

A Closer Look at Your Program

Now that we've got our program running, let's take a minute and look at each line of code in the program we've made. I'll explain what each one does so that you'll have a basic understanding of everything in your simple Hello World program.

Using Directives

```
using System;
using System.Collections.Generic;
using System.Linq;
using System.Text;
using System.Threading.Tasks;
```

The first few lines of your program all start with the keyword **using**. A *keyword* is simply a reserved word, or a magic word that is a built-in part of the C# programming language. It has special meaning to the C# compiler, which it uses to do something special. The **using** keyword tells the compiler that there is a whole other pile of code that someone made that we want to be able to access. (This is actually a bit of a simplification, and we'll sort out the details in Chapter 27.)

So when you see a statement like **using System;** you know that there is a whole pile of code out there named *System* that our code wants to use. Without this line, the C# compiler won't know where to find things and it won't be able to run your program. You can see that there are five **using** directives in your little program that are added by default. We can leave these exactly the way they are for the near future.

Namespaces, Classes, and Methods

Below the **using** directives, you'll see a collection of curly braces ('{' and '}') and you'll see the keywords **namespace**, **class**, and in the middle, the word **Main**. Namespaces, classes, and methods (which **Main** is an example of) are ways of grouping related code together at various levels. Namespaces are the largest grouping, classes are smaller, and methods are the smallest. We'll discuss each of these in great depth as we go through this book, but it is worth a brief introduction now. We'll start at the smallest and work our way up.

Methods are a way of consolidating a single task together in a reusable block of code. In other programming languages, methods are sometimes called functions, procedures, or subroutines. We'll get into a lot of detail about how to make and use methods as we go, but the bulk of our discussion about methods will be in Chapter 15, with some extra details in Chapter 28.

Right in the middle of the generated code, you'll see the following:

```
static void Main(string[] args)
{
}
```

This is a method, which happens to have the name **Main**. I won't get into the details about what everything else on that line does yet, but I want to point out that this particular setup for a method makes it so that C# knows it can be used as the starting point for your program. Since this is where our program starts, the computer will run any code we put in here. For the next few chapters, everything we do will be right in here.

You'll also notice that there are quite a few curly braces in our code. Curly braces mark the start and end of code blocks. Every starting curly brace ('{') will have a matching ending curly brace ('}') later on. In this particular part, the curly braces mark the start and end of the **Main** method. As we discuss classes and namespaces, you'll see that they also use curly braces to mark the points where they begin and end. From looking at the code, you can probably already see that these code blocks can contain other code blocks to form a hierarchy.

When one thing is contained in another, it is said to be a *member* of it. So the **Program** class is a member of the namespace, and the **Main** method is a member of the **Program** class.

Classes are a way of grouping together a set of data and methods that operate on that data into a single reusable package. Classes are the fundamental building block of object-oriented programming. We'll get into this in great detail in Part 3, especially Chapters 17 and 18.

In the generated code, you can see the beginning of the class, marked with:

```
class Program
{
```

And later on, after the **Main** method it contains, you'll see a matching closing curly brace:

```
}
```

Program is simply a name for the class. It could have been just about anything else. The fact that the **Main** method is contained in the **Program** class indicates that it belongs to the **Program** class.

Namespaces are the highest level grouping of code. Many smaller programs may only have a single namespace, while larger ones often divide the code into several namespaces based on the feature or component that the code is used in. We'll spend a little extra time detailing namespaces and **using** directives in Chapter 27.

Looking at the generated code, you'll see that our **Program** class is contained in a namespace called "HelloWorld":

```
namespace HelloWorld
{
    ...
}
```

Once again, the fact that the **Program** class appears within the **HelloWorld** namespace means that it belongs to that namespace, or is a member of it.

Whitespace Doesn't Matter

In C#, whitespace such as spaces, new lines, and tabs don't matter to the C# compiler. This means that technically, you could write any program on a single line! But don't do that. That would be a bad idea.

Instead, you should use whitespace to help make your code more readable, both for other people who may look at your code, or even yourself a few weeks from now, when you've forgotten what exactly your code was supposed to do.

I'll leave the decision about where to put whitespace up to you, but as an example, compare the following pieces of code that do the same thing:

```
static void Main(string
[] args) { Console
.WriteLine                                (
            "Hello World!"                    );}
```

```
static void Main(string[] args)
{
    Console.WriteLine("Hello World!");
}
```

For the sake of clarity, I'll use a style like the bottom version throughout this book.

Semicolons

You may have noticed that the lines of code we added all ended with semicolons (';').

This is how C# knows it has reached the end of a statement. A *statement* is a single step or instruction that does something. We'll be using semicolons all over the place as we write C# code.

> ## Try It Out!
> **Evil Computers.** In the influential movie *2001: A Space Odyssey*, an evil computer named HAL 9000 takes over a Jupiter-bound spaceship, locking Dave, the movie's hero, out in space. As Dave tries to get back in, to the ship, he tells HAL to open the pod bay doors. HAL's response is "I'm sorry, Dave. I'm afraid I can't do that." Since we know not all computers are friendly and happy to help people, modify your Hello World program to say HAL 9000's famous words, instead of "Hello World!"

This chapter may have seemed long, and we haven't even accomplished very much. That's OK, though. We have to start somewhere, and this is where everyone starts. We have now made our first C# program, compiled it, and executed it! And just as important, we now have a basic understanding of the starter code that was generated for us. This really gets us off on the right foot. We're off to a great start, but there's so much more to learn!

Comments

Quick Start
- Comments are a way for you to add text for other people (and yourself) to read. Computers ignore comments entirely.
- Comments are made by putting two slashes (**//**) in front of the text.
- Multi-line comments can also be made by surrounding it with asterisks and slashes, like this: **/* this is a comment */**

In this short chapter we'll cover the basics of comments. We'll look at what they are, why you should use them, and how to do them. Many programmers (even many C# books) de-emphasize comments, or completely ignore them. I've decided to put them front and center, right at the beginning of the book—they really are that important.

What is a Comment?

At its core, a *comment* is text that is put somewhere for a human to read. Comments are ignored entirely by the computer.

Why Should I Use Comments?

I mentioned in the last chapter that whitespace should be used to help make your code more readable. Writing readable and understandable code is a running theme you'll see in this book. Writing code is actually far easier than reading it, or trying understanding what it does. And believe it or not, you'll actually spend far more time reading code than writing it. You will want to do whatever you can to make your code easier to read. Comments will go a very long way towards making your code more readable and understandable.

You should use comments to describe what you are doing so that when you come back to a piece of code that you wrote after several months (or even just days) you'll know what you were doing.

Writing comments—wait, let me clarify—writing *good* comments is a key part of writing good code. Comments can be used to explain tricky sections of code, or explain what things are supposed to do. They are a primary way for a programmer to communicate with another programmer who is looking at their code. The other programmer may even be on the other side of the world and working for a different company five years later!

Comments can explain what you are doing, as well as why you are doing it. This helps other programmers, including yourself, know what was going on in your mind at the time.

In fact, even if you know you're the only person who will ever see your code, you should still put comments in it. Do you remember what you ate for lunch a week ago today? Neither do I. Do you really think that you'll remember what your code was supposed to do a week after you write it?

Writing comments makes it so that you can quickly understand and remember what the code does, how it does it, why it does it, and you can even document why you did it one way and not another.

How to Make Comments in C#

There are three basic ways to make comments in C#. For now, we'll only really consider two of them, because the third applies only to things that we haven't looked at yet. We'll look at the third form of making comments in Chapter 15.

The first way to create a comment is to start a line with two slashes: **//**. Anything on the line following the two slashes will be ignored by the computer. In Visual Studio the comments change color—green, by default—to indicate that the rest of the line is a comment.

Below is an example of a comment:

```
// This is a comment, where I can describe what happens next...
Console.WriteLine("Hello World!");
```

Using this same thing, you can also start a comment at the end of a line of code, which will make it so the text after the slashes are ignored:

```
Console.WriteLine("Hello World!"); // This is also a comment.
```

A second method for creating comments is to use the slash and asterisk combined, surrounding the comment, like this:

```
Console.WriteLine("Hi!"); /* This is a comment that ends here... */
```

This can be used to make multi-line comments like this:

```
/* This is a multi-line comment.
   It spans multiple lines.
   Isn't it neat? */
```

Of course, you can do multi-line comments with the two slashes as well, it just has to be done like this:

```
//  This is a multi-line comment.
//  It spans multiple lines.
//  Isn't it neat?
```

In fact, most C# programmers will probably encourage you to use the single line comment version instead of the **/* */** version, though it is up to you.

The third method for creating comments is called XML Documentation Comments, which we'll discuss later, because they're used for things that we haven't discussed yet. For more information about XML Documentation Comments, see Chapter 15.

How to Make Good Comments

Commenting your code is easy; making *good* comments is a little trickier. I want to take some time and describe some basic principles to help you make comments that will be more effective.

My first rule for making good comments is to write the comments for a particular chunk of code as soon as you've got the piece more or less complete. A few days or a weekend away from the code and you may no longer really remember what you were doing with it. (Trust me, it happens!)

Second, write comments that add value to the code. Here's an example of a bad comment:

```
// Uses Console.WriteLine to print "Hello World!"
Console.WriteLine("Hello World!");
```

The code itself already says all of that. You might as well not even add it. Here's a better version:

```
// Printing "Hello World!" is a very common first program to make.
Console.WriteLine("Hello World!");
```

This helps to explain *why* we did this instead of something else.

Third, you don't need a comment for every single line of code, but it is helpful to have one for every section of related code. It's possible to have too many comments, but the dangers of over-commenting code matter a whole lot less than the dangers of under-commented (or *completely* uncommented code).

When you write comments, take the time put in anything that you or another programmer may want to know if they come back and look at the code later. This may include a human-readable description of what is happening, it may include describing the general method (or *algorithm*) you're using to accomplish a particular task, or it may explain why you're doing something. You may also find times where it will be useful to include why you aren't using a different approach, or to warn another programmer (or yourself!) that a particular chunk of code is tricky, and you shouldn't mess with it unless you really know what you're doing.

Having said all of this, don't take it to an extreme. Good comments don't make up for sloppy, ugly, or hard to read code. Meanwhile nice, clean, understandable code reduces the times that you need comments at all. (The code is the authority on what's happening, not the comments, after all.) Make the code as readable as possible first, then add just enough comments to fill in the gaps and paint the bigger picture.

When used appropriately, comments can be a programmer's best friend.

Try It Out!

Comment *ALL* the things! While it's overkill, in the name of putting together everything we've learned so far, go back to your Hello World program from the last chapter and add in comments for each part of the code, describing what each piece is for. This will be a good review of what the pieces of that simple program do, as well as give you a chance to play around with some comments. Try out both ways of making comments (*//* and */* */*) to see what you like.

Part 2

The Basics

With a basic understanding of how to get started behind us, we're ready to dig in and look at the fundamentals of programming in C#.

It is in this part that our adventure really gets underway. We'll start learning about the world of C# programming, and learn about the key tools that we'll use to get things done.

In this section, we cover aspects of C# programming that are called "procedural programming." This means we'll be learning how to tell the computer, step-by-step, how to get things done.

We'll look at how to:

- Store data in variables (Chapter 5).
- Understand the type system (Chapter 6).
- Do basic math (Chapters 7 and 9).
- Get input from the user (Chapter 8).
- Make decisions (Chapter 10).
- Repeat things multiple times (Chapter 12 and 13).
- Create enumerations (Chapter 14).
- Package related code together in a way that allows you to reuse it (Chapter 15).

Variables

In a Nutshell

- You can think of variables as boxes that store information.
- A variable has a name, a type, and a value that is contained in it.
- You declare (create) a variable by stating the type and name: **int number;**
- You can assign values to a variable with the assignment operator ('='): **number = 14;**
- When you declare a variable, you can initialize it as well: **int number = 14;**
- You can retrieve the value of a variable simply by using the variable's name in your code: **Console.WriteLine(number);**
- This chapter also gives guidelines for good variable names.

In this chapter, we're going to dig straight into one of the most important parts of programming in C#. We're going to discuss variables, which are how we keep track of information in our programs. We'll look at how you create them, place different values in them, and use the value that is currently in a variable.

What is a Variable?

A key part of any program you make, regardless of the programming language, is the ability to store information in memory while the program is running. For example, you might want to store a player's score or a person's name, so that you can refer back to it later or modify it.

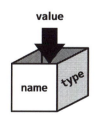

You may remember discussing variables in math classes, but these are a little different. In math, we talk about variables being an "unknown quantity" that you are supposed to solve for. Variables in math are a specific value that you just need to figure out.

In programming, a *variable* is a place in memory where you can store information. It's like a little box or bucket to put stuff in. At any point in time, you can look up the contents of the variable or rewrite the contents of the variable with new stuff. When you do this, the variable itself doesn't need to change, just the contents in the box.

Each variable has a name and a type. The name is what you'll use in your program when you want to read its contents or put new stuff in it.

The variable's *type* indicates what kind of information you can put in it. C# has a large assortment of types that you can use, including a variety of integer types, floating point (real valued) types, characters, strings (text), Boolean (true/false), and a whole lot more.

In C#, types are a really big deal. Throughout this book, we'll spend a lot of time learning how to work with different types, converting from one type to another, and ultimately building our own types from scratch.

In the next chapter, we'll get into types in great detail. For now though, let's look at the basics of creating a variable.

Creating Variables

Let's make our first variable. The process of creating a variable is called *declaring* a variable.

Let's start by going to Visual Studio and creating a brand new console project, just like we did with the Hello World project, back in Chapter 3. Inside of the **Main** method, add the following single line of code:

```
int score;
```

So your code should look something like this:

```
using System;
using System.Collections.Generic;
using System.Linq;
using System.Text;
using System.Threading.Tasks;

namespace Variables
{
    class Program
    {
        static void Main(string[] args)
        {
            int score;
        }
    }
}
```

Congratulations! You've made your first variable! When you declare a variable, the computer knows that it will need to reserve a place in memory for this variable.

As you can see, when you declare a variable, you need to indicate the variable's name and type. This one line has both of those parts on it. The first part you see here is **int**. This is the variable's type. We'll look at the different types that are available in a minute, but for now all we need to know is that the **int** type is for storing integers. (In case you don't remember from math class, integers are whole numbers and their negatives, so 0, 1, 2, 3, 4, ..., and -1, -2, -3, -4, ...) Because we've made a variable that stores integers, we know we could put the number 100 in it, or -75946. But we could *not* store the number 1.3483 (it's not an integer), and we also could not store a word like "hamburger" (it's not an integer either). The variable's type determines what kind of stuff we can put in it.

The second part of declaring a variable is giving it a name. It is important to remember that a variable's name is meant for humans. The computer doesn't care what it is called. (In fact, once you hand it off to the computer, it changes the name to a memory location anyway.) So you want to choose a name that makes sense to humans, and accurately describes what you're putting in it. In math, we often call variables by a single letter (like x), but in programming we can be more precise and call it something like **score** instead.

As always, C# statements end with a ';', telling the computer that it has reached the end of the statement. After this line, we have made a new variable with the name **score** and a type of **int** which we can now use!

Assigning Values to Variables

The next thing we want to do is put a value in the variable. This is called *assigning* a value to the variable, and it is done using the assignment operator: "**=**". The line of code below assigns the value 0 to the score variable we just created:

```
score = 0;
```

You can add this line of code right below the previous line we added.

This use of the equals sign is different than how it is used in math. In math, "=" indicates that two things are the same, even though they may be written in different formats. In C# and many other programming languages, it means we're going to take the stuff on the right side of the equals sign and place it in the variable that is named on the left.

You can assign any integer value to **score**, and you can assign different values over time:

```
score = 4;
score = 11;
score = -1564;
```

You can assign a value to a variable whenever you want, as long as it is after the variable has been declared. Of course, we haven't learned very powerful tools for programming yet, so "whenever you want" doesn't mean much yet. (We'll get there soon, don't worry!)

When we create a variable, we often want to give it a value right away. (The C# compiler is not a big fan of you trying to see what's inside an empty variable box.) While you can declare a variable and assign it a value in separate steps, it is also possible to do both of them at the same time:

```
int theMeaningOfLife = 42;
```

This line creates a variable called **theMeaningOfLife** with the type **int**, and gives it a starting value of 42.

Retrieving the Contents of a Variable

As we just saw, we can use the assignment operator ('=') to put values into a variable. You can also see and use the contents of a variable, simply by using the variable's name. When the computer is running your code and it encounters a variable name, it will go to the variable, look up the contents inside, and use that value in its place.

For example, int the code below, the computer will pull the number out of the **number** variable and write 3 to the console window:

```
int number = 3;
Console.WriteLine(number); // Console.WriteLine prints lots of things, not just text.
```

When you access a variable, here's what the computer does:

1. Locates the variable that you asked for in memory.
2. Looks in the contents of the variable to see what value it contains.
3. Makes a *copy* of that value to use where it is needed.

The fact that it grabs a copy of the variable is important. For one, it means the variable keeps the value it had. Reading from a variable doesn't change the value of the variable. Two, whatever you do with the copy won't affect the original. (We'll learn more about how this works in Chapter 16, when we learn about value and reference types.)

For example, here is some code that creates two variables and assigns the value of one to the other:

```
int a = 5;
int b = 2;

b = a;
a = -3;
```

With what you've learned so far about variables, what value will **a** and **b** have after this code runs?

Try It Out!

Playing with Variables. Take the little piece of code above and make a program out of it. Follow the same steps you did in Chapter 3 when we made the Hello World program, but instead of adding code to print out "Hello World!", add the lines above. Use **Console.WriteLine**, like we did before and print out the contents of the two variables. Before you run the code, think about what you expect to be printed out for the **a** and **b** variables. Go ahead and run the program. Is it what you expected?

Right at the beginning of those four lines, we create two variables, one named **a**, and one named **b**. Both can store integers, because we're using the **int** type. We also assign the value 5 to **a**, and 2 to **b**. After the first two lines, this is what we're looking at:

We then use the assignment operator to take the value inside of **a** and copy it to **b**:

Finally, on the last line we assign a completely new value to **a**:

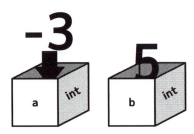

If we printed out **a** and **b**, we would see that **a** is -3 and **b** is 5 by the time this code is finished.

How Data is Stored

Before we move into a discussion about the C# type system, we need to understand a little about how information is stored on a computer. This is a key part of what drives the need for types in the first place.

It is important to remember that computers only work with 1's and 0's. (Technically, they're tiny electric pulses or magnetic fields that can be in one of two states which we label 1 and 0.)

A single 1 or 0 is called a *bit*, and a grouping of eight of them is called a *byte*. If we do the math, this means that a single byte can store up to a total of 256 different states.

To get more states than this, we need to put multiple bytes together. For instance, two bytes can store 65,536 possible states. Four bytes can store over 4 billion states, and eight bytes combined can store over 18 quintillion possible states.

But we need a way to take all of these states and make sense out of them. This is what the type system is for. It defines how many bytes we need to store different things, and how those bits and bytes will be interpreted by the computer, and ultimately, the user.

For example, let's say we want to store letters. Modern systems tend to use two bytes to store letters. Programmers have assigned each letter a specific pattern of bits. For instance, we assign the capital letter 'A' to the bit pattern 00000000 01000001. 'B' is one up from that: 00000000 01000010. Because we're using two bytes, we have 65,536 different possibilities. That's enough to store every symbol in every language that is currently spoken on Earth, including many ancient languages, and still have room to spare.

For each different type of data, we interpret the underlying bits and bytes in a different way. The **int** type that we were using earlier works like this. The **int** type uses four bytes. For brevity, in this discussion, I'm leaving off the first three bytes, which contain all zeros for the small sample numbers we're using here. The value 0 is represented with the bit pattern 00000000. The value 1 is represented with the bit pattern 00000001. 2 is represented with 00000010. 3 is 00000011. This is basically counting in a base two numbering system, or a binary numbering system.

Other types will use their bits and bytes in other ways. We won't get into the specifics about how they all work, as that's really beyond the scope of this book. I'll just point out that the way C# interprets bits and bytes uses the same standard representations as nearly every other language and computer.

Multiple Declarations and Assignments

Our earlier code for creating a variable and for assigning a value to a variable just did one per line. But you can declare multiple variables at the same time using code like this:

```
int a, b, c;
```

If you do this, all variables must be of the same type (**int** in this case). We'll talk about types in more depth in Chapter 6.

You can also assign the same value to multiple different variables all at the same time:

```
a = b = c = 10;
```

Most cases will probably lead you to make and assign values individually, rather than simultaneously, but it is worth knowing that this is an option.

Good Variable Names

Before we go on, let's talk about how to choose good names for your variables. Not everybody agrees on what makes a variable name good. But I'm going to give you the rules I follow, which you'll discover are pretty typical, and not too far off from what most experienced programmers do.

The purpose of a variable name is to give a human-readable label for the variable. Anyone who stumbles across the variable name should be able to instantly know what information the variable contains.

It's easy to write code. It's hard to write code that you can actually go back and read and understand. Like comments, good variable names are an absolutely critical part of writing readable code, and it's not something that can be ignored. Here are my rules:

Rule #1: Meet C#'s Requirements. C# has a few requirements for variable names. All variable names have to start with a letter (a-z or A-Z) or the underscore ('_') character, and can then contain any number of other letters, numbers, or the underscore character. You also cannot name a variable the same thing as one of the reserved keywords that C# defines. These keywords are highlighted in blue in Visual Studio, but includes things like **namespace**, **int**, and **public**. Your code won't compile if you don't follow this rule.

Rule #2: Variable names should describe the stuff you intend on putting in it. If you are putting a player's score in it, call it **score**, or **playerScore**, or even **plrscr** if you have to, but don't call it **jambalaya**, **p**, or **monkey**. But speaking of **plrscr**...

Rule #3: Don't abbreviate or remove letters. Looking at the example of **plrscr**, you can tell that it resembles "player score." But if you didn't already know, you'd have to sit there and try to fill in the missing letters. Is it "plural scar," or "plastic scrabble"? Nope, it is "player score." You just have to sit there and study it. The one exception to this rule is common abbreviations or acronyms. HTML is fine.

Rule #4: A good name will usually be kind of long. In math, we usually use single letters for variable names. In programming, you usually need more than that to accurately describe what you're trying to do. In most cases, you'll probably have at least three letters. Often, it is 8 to 16. Don't be afraid if it gets longer than that. It's better to be descriptive than to "save letters."

Rule #5: If your variables end with a number, you probably need a better name. If you've got **count1** and **count2**, there's probably a better name for them. (Or perhaps an array, which we'll talk about later.)

Rule #6: "data", "text", "number", and "item" are usually not descriptive enough. For some reason, people seem to fall back to these all the time. They're OK, but they're just not very descriptive. It's best to come up with something more precise in any situation where you can.

Rule #7: Make the words of the variable name stand out from each other. This is so it is easier to read a variable name that is composed of multiple words. **playerScore** (with a capital 'S') and **player_score** are both more readable than **playerscore**. My personal preference is the first, but both work.

> ## Try It Out!
> **Variables Quiz.** Answer the following questions to check your understanding. When you're done, check your answers against the ones below. If you missed something, go back and review the section that talks about it.
>
> 1. Name the three things all variables have.
> 2. **True/False.** You can use a variable before it is declared.
> 3. How many times must a variable be declared?
> 4. Out of the following, which are legal variable names? answer, 1stValue, value1, $message, delete-me, delete_me, PI.

Answers: (1) name, type, value. **(2)** False. **(3)** 1. **(4)** answer, value1, delete_me, PI.

The C# Type System

In a Nutshell
- It is important to understand the C# type system.
- Integral types (**int**, **short**, **long**, **byte**, **sbyte**, **uint**, **ushort**, **ulong**, and **char**) store integers with various ranges.
- Floating point types (**float**, **double**, **decimal**) store floating point numbers with various levels of precision and range.
- The **bool** type stores truth values (**true/false**).
- The **string** type stores text.
- Other types will be discussed in future chapters.

An Introduction to the Type System

Now that we understand a bit about how the computer stores information and how raw bits and bytes are interpreted, we can begin to look at the C# type system from a broader perspective.

In C#, there are tons of types that have been defined for you. In addition, as you go through this book, you'll see that C# gives you the option to create and use your own types.

In this introduction to types, we will cover all of the *primitive types*, or *built-in types*. These are types that the C# compiler knows a whole lot about. The language itself makes it easy to work with these types because they are so common. We're going to cover a lot of ground, so as you read this, remember that you don't need to master it all in one reading. Get a feel for what types are available, and come back for the details later.

The 'int' Type

We already saw the **int** type in the last chapter, but it is worth a little more detail here to start off our discussion on types. The **int** type uses 4 bytes (32 bits) to keep track of integers. In the math world, integers can be any size we want. There's no limit to how big they can be. But on a computer, we need to be able to store them in bytes, so the **int** type has to be artificially limited. The **int** type can store numbers roughly in the range of -2 billion to +2 billion. In a practical sense, that's a bigger range than you will need for most things, but it *is* limited, and it is important to keep that in mind.

The 'byte', 'short', and 'long' Types

Speaking of limitations in the size of the **int** type, there are three other types that also store integers, but use a different number of bytes. As a result, they have different ranges that they can represent. These are the **byte**, **short**, and **long** types. The **byte** type is the smallest. It uses only one byte and can store values in the range 0 to 255. The **short** type is larger, but still smaller than **int**. It uses two bytes, and can store values in the range of about -32,000 to +32,000. The **long** type is the largest of the four, and uses 8 bytes. It can store numbers roughly in the range of -9 quintillion to +9 quintillion. That is an absolutely massive range, and it is only in very rare circumstances when that wouldn't be enough.

Type	Bytes	Range
byte	1	0 to 255
short	2	-32,768 to 32,767
int	4	-2,147,483,648 to 2,147,483,647
long	8	-9,223,372,036,854,775,808 to 9,223,372,036,854,775,807

That's four different types (**byte**, **short**, **int**, and **long**) that use a different numbers of bytes (1, 2, 4, and 8, respectively). The larger they are, the bigger the number they can store. You can think of these different types as different sizes of boxes to store different sizes of numbers in.

It is worth a little bit of an example to show you how you create variables with these types. It is done exactly like earlier, when we created our first variable with the **int** type:

```
byte aSingleByte = 34;
aSingleByte = 17;

short aNumber = 5039;
aNumber = -4354;

long aVeryBigNumber = 395904282569;
aVeryBigNumber = 13;
```

The 'sbyte', 'ushort', 'uint', and 'ulong' Types

We've already talked about four different types that store integers of various sizes. Now, I'm going to introduce four additional types that are related to the ones we've already discussed.

But first, we need to understand the difference between *signed types* and *unsigned types*. If a type is signed, it means it can include a + or - sign in front of it. In other words, the values of a signed type can be positive or negative. If you look back at the four types we already know about, you'll see that **short**, **int**, and **long** are all signed. You can store positive or negative numbers. The **byte** type, on the other hand, has no sign. (It is typically assumed that no sign is the equivalent of being positive.)

For each of the signed types we have looked at, we could have an alternate version where we shift the valid range to only include positive numbers. This would allow us to go twice as high, at the expense of not being able to use negative values at all. The **ushort**, **uint**, and **ulong** types do just this. The **ushort** type uses two bytes, just like the **short** type, but instead of going from -32,000 to +32,000, it goes from 0 to about 64,000. The same thing applies to the **uint** and **ulong** types.

Likewise, we can take the **byte** type, which is unsigned, and shift it so that it includes negative numbers as well. Instead of going from 0 to 255, it goes from -128 to +127. This gives us the signed byte type, **sbyte**.

Not surprisingly, we can create variables of these types just like we could with the **int** type:

```
ushort anUnsignedShortVariable = 59485; // This could not be stored in a normal short.
```

We now know of eight total types, all of which are designed to store only integers. These types, as a collection, are known as *integral types* (sometimes "integer types"). We can organize these types in the hierarchy diagram to the right. As we continue our discussion of types throughout this chapter and this

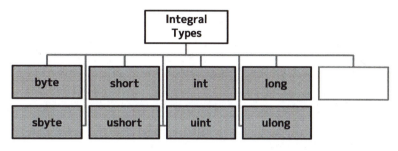

book, we'll continue to expand this chart. You may notice that we're still missing one additional integral type, which we'll discuss shortly.

Each of the types we've discussed use a different number of bytes and store different ranges of values. That means each of them is best suited for storing different types of information. So how do you know what type to use? Here are three things to consider as you're choosing a type for a particular variable:

- Do you need signed values? (Can things be negative?) If so, you can immediately eliminate all of the unsigned types.
- How large can the values be? For example, if you are using a variable to store the population of a country, you know you'll need to use something bigger than a **byte** or a **short**.
- When in doubt, many programmers tend to default to the **int** type. This may be sort of a Goldilocks thing (not too big, not too small, but just about right). As a result, sometimes **int** is overused, but it may be a good starting point, at any rate.

The 'char' Type

We have one more integral type to discuss before we move on. This last type is called the **char** type, and is used for storing single characters or letters, as opposed to numbers.

It is strange to think of characters as an integral type, which are all designed to store integers. Behind the scenes though, each letter can basically be assigned to a single number, which is why it gets lumped in among the integral types. However, when we use the **char** type, the computer will know to treat it as a letter instead, so we'll see it print out the letters instead of numbers. As we'll see later, the close association of the **char** type and the other integral types means that we can do most of the same things with any of these types.

The **char** type is two bytes big, giving it over 64,000 possible values. It's enough to store every letter in every language in the world (including some dead languages and some fictional languages like Klingon) with room to spare. The numeric value assigned to each letter follows the widely used Unicode system.

You can create variables with the **char** type in a way that is very similar to the other types we've seen, though you put the character you want to store inside single quotes:

```
char favoriteLetter = 'c';    // Because C is for cookie. That's good enough for me.
favoriteLetter = '&';
```

Later in this chapter, we'll talk about storing text of any length.

To summarize where we're at with the C# type system, we've learned 9 different integral types, including four for signed integers, four for unsigned integers, and one for characters:

Type	Bytes	Range
byte	1	0 to 255
short	2	-32,768 to 32,767
int	4	-2,147,483,648 to 2,147,483,647
long	8	-9,223,372,036,854,775,808 to 9,223,372,036,854,775,807
sbyte	1	-128 to +127
ushort	2	0 to 65,535
uint	4	0 to 4,294,967,295
ulong	8	0 to 18,446,744,073,709,551,615
char	2	U+0000 to U+ffff (All Unicode characters)

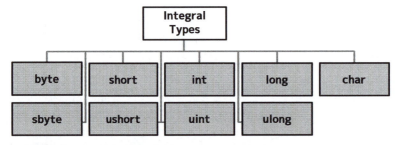

The 'float', 'double', and 'decimal' Types

You're probably sick of integral types by now, so let's expand our discussion to include some additional types to store what are called *floating point numbers* ("real numbers" in the math world). Floating point numbers are able to store not just integer values, but also numbers with a decimal part. For example, the number 1.2 is not an integer and can't be stored by any of the integral types that we've talked about. But it *can* be stored in any of the three floating point types that C# provides.

We'll start off with the **float** type. The **float** type uses four bytes to store floating point numbers. With the **float** type, you get seven digits of precision. The largest values you can store are very large: about 3.4×10^{38}. This is much higher than any of the integral types. But even these floating point types are limited in their own way. Because it only has seven digits of precision, the computer can't tell 1,000,000,000 and 1,000,000,001 apart. (Though it can tell 1000 and 1001 apart.) Of course, maybe you don't care about that kind of a difference either, because it's so small compared to their magnitude. It may be close enough for all practical purposes. Note that the integral values don't have this problem. Within the range that they can store, integral types are always exact.

There is also a limit to how small (as in, "close to zero") the **float** type can store, and that is about $\pm 1.5 \times 10^{-45}$—a very tiny number.

The **double** type uses 8 bytes—twice as many as the **float** type (hence the name "double"). This has 15 or 16 digits of precision, and can store values as small as $\pm 5 \times 10^{-324}$ or as large as $\pm 1.7 \times 10^{308}$. If you thought the **float** type had a huge range, think again. This dwarfs what the **float** type can hold, albeit at the expense of taking up twice as much space.

Creating variables with either of these types is pretty straightforward as well:

```
double pi = 3.14159265358979323846;
float anotherPi = 3.1415926f;
```

Take a close look at those two numbers. Obviously, the **double** version has more digits, which it can handle. But do you see what's hanging out there at the end of the number we've used for the **float**?

There's a letter 'f'.

In code, whenever we write out a value directly it is called a *literal*. When we say **a = 3;** the 3 is an integer literal. Here, when we put 3.1415926, it's a floating point literal. When we use a floating point literal like this, the compiler assumes it is the **double** type. But knowing that the **double** type is a much bigger "box" that uses 8 bytes, we can't just stuff that in a variable that is using the **float** type. It's too big. Sticking the letter 'f' on the end of a floating point literal tells the C# compiler to treat is as a literal of the **float** type, instead of the **double** type. Note that we could use lower case 'f' or capital 'F' and get the same results.

While we're on the subject, I want to point out that if we're working with an integer literal, we can put lower case 'l' or upper case 'L' on the end to indicate that it is a **long** integer literal. Though, I'd recommend that you always use the upper case version ('L') because lower case 'l' and the number '1' look too much alike. So you could do this if you want:

```
long aBigNumber = 39358593258529L;
```

You are also able to stick a 'u' or 'U' on the end of an integer literal to show that it is supposed to be an unsigned integer literal:

```
ulong bigOne = 2985825802805280508UL;
```

Anyway, back to the **float** and **double** types. Both of these types follow standards that have been around for decades (see the IEEE 754 floating point arithmetic standard) and are a native part of many computers' circuitry and programming languages.

C# provides another type, though, that doesn't conform to "ancient" standards. It's the **decimal** type. This type was built with the idea of using it for calculations involving money. Because it doesn't have the same hardware-level support that **float** and **double** have, doing math with it is substantially slower, but it doesn't have the same issues with losing accuracy that **float** and **double** have. This type allows for the range $\pm 1.0 \times 10^{-28}$ up to $\pm 7.9 \times 10^{28}$, but has 28 or 29 significant digits. Essentially, a smaller range overall, but much higher precision.

You can create variables using the **decimal** type in a way that is very similar to all of the other types that we've talked about. Similar to the **float** type, you'll need to put an 'm' or 'M' at the end of any literals that you want to have be treated as the **decimal** type:

```
decimal number = 1.495m;
number = 14.4m;
```

Type	Bytes	Range	Digits of Precision
float	4	±1.0e-45 to ±3.4e38	7
double	8	±5e-324 to ±1.7e308	15-16
decimal	16	±1.0 × 10e-28 to ±7.9e28	28-29

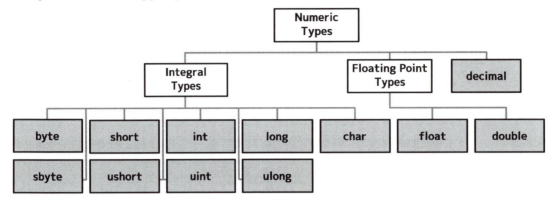

The 'bool' Type

Finally moving away from number-based types, the **bool** type is used to store Boolean or "truth" values. They can either be **true** or **false**. Boolean values are named after Boolean logic, which in turn was named after its inventor, George Boole. At first glance, this type may not seem very useful, but in a few chapters we'll begin to talk about decision making (Chapter 10) and these will become very important.

You can create or assign values to a variable with the **bool** type like this:

```
bool itWorked = true;
itWorked = false;
```

Note that both **true** and **false** are considered Boolean literals.

In many other languages, **bool** is treated like a special case of an integral type, where 0 represents false and 1 represents true. (In fact, in many of those languages, 0 represents false and anything but 0 is true.) While the C# **bool** type uses 0 and 1 to store **true** and **false** behind the scenes, bool values and numbers are completely separated. For example, you cannot assign 1 to a **bool** variable, or **true** to an integer.

While a **bool** type only keeps track of two states, and could theoretically be stored by a single bit, the **bool** type uses up a whole byte, because single bytes are the smallest unit of memory that can be addressed.

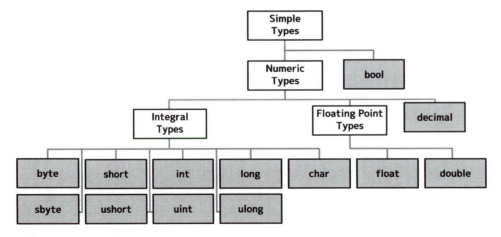

The 'string' Type

The last type we are going to talk about here is the **string** type. Behind the scenes, this type is actually very different from all of the other types that we've discussed so far, but we won't get into the details about why or how until Chapter 16.

The **string** type is used to store text of any length. The name "string" comes from the field of formal languages, where a string is defined as a sequence of symbols chosen from a set of specific symbols. In our case, that set of symbols is the set of all Unicode characters, which we discussed with the **char** type.

To create or assign values to **string** type variables, you follow the same pattern as all of the other types we've seen. String literals are marked with double quotes:

```
string message = "Hello World!";
message = "Purple Monkey Dishwasher";
```

When you see this, you'll probably think back to the Hello World program we made, because we saw a very similar thing there. It turns out, when we used the line **Console.WriteLine("Hello World!");** we were using a **string** there as well!

Try It Out!

Variables Everywhere. Create a new console application and in the **Main** method, create one variable of every type we've discussed here. That's 13 different variables. Assign each of them a value. Print out the value of each variable.

In this section, we've covered a lot of types, and I know it can be a bit overwhelming. Don't worry too much. This chapter will always be here as a reference for you to come back to later.

There are a lot more to types than we've discussed here (beyond the built-in types) but this has given us a good starting point. As we continue to learn C#, we'll learn even more about the C# type system. The following diagram shows all of the types we've discussed so far. You can see that we're still missing a few pieces, but we'll pick those up as we go.

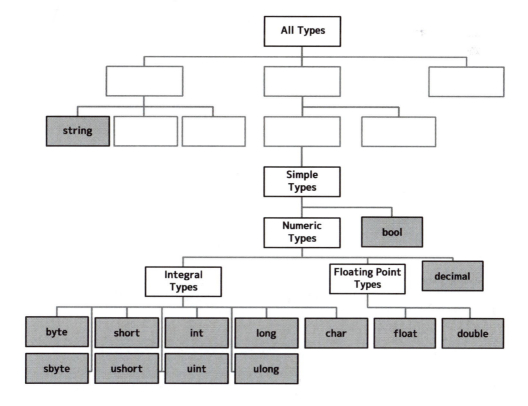

Try It Out!

Types Quiz. Answer the following questions to check your understanding. When you're done, check your answers against the ones below. If you missed something, go back and review the section that talks about it.

1. **True/False.** The **int** type can store any possible number.
2. **True/False.** The **char** type is an integral type.
3. Order the following by how large of numbers they can store, from smallest to largest: **short**, **long**, **int**, **byte**.
4. **True/False.** The **byte** type is a signed type.
5. Which can store higher numbers, **int** or **uint**?
6. What three types can store floating point numbers?
7. Which of the options in question 6 can store the largest numbers?
8. Which of the options in question 6 is considered the most precise?
9. In the following, should **myVariable** have the type **int**, **char**, or **string**, based on the literal value on the right hand side? **[type] myVariable = "8";**
10. What type is used to store true or false values?

Answers: **(1)** false. **(2)** true. **(3)** byte, short, int, long. **(4)** false. **(5)** uint. **(6)** float, double, decimal. **(7)** double. **(8)** decimal. **(9)** Double quotes indicate a string literal. **(10)** bool.

Numeric Literal Variations

Earlier, we talked about the various integral types that C# supports, including **int**, **long**, **uint**, **ulong**, etc. We also talked about how when we write out a number directly in code, it is called a literal. So for example, the 3 below is an integral (integer) literal:

```
int x = 3;
```

Before we walk away from the subject of different variable types in C#, there are a few nifty tricks that we can do when defining numeric literals that are worth mentioning.

Scientific Notation or E Notation

In many scientific and mathematical fields, you sometimes deal with gigantic or tiny numbers. As a programmer, you will sometimes have to deal with these numbers as well. Consider a statement like this: "There are 602,200,000,000,000,000,000,000 hydrogen atoms in a single gram of hydrogen."

That very quickly becomes too big to want to write out. So scientists decided they could (and should) use a different way to write that number out, which is called scientific notation. Using scientific notation, you would write gigantic or tiny numbers with an exponent instead, and shift the decimal point around. Instead of that earlier number, you might write 6.022×10^{23}.

Even that isn't so great in situations where you can't clearly write an exponent as a superscript (which is true in code, as well as other places). So in some cases, this same number is written as 6.022e23, or 6.022E23.

We are quickly veering outside of stuff that is truly relevant for this book, but it is worth mentioning that floating point literals can be written out this way in your C# code, using a small **e** or a capital **E**:

```
double avogadrosNumber = 6.022e23; // The official name of this number.
```

Depending on the field you're working in, you may or may not see this much. It's a different notation that can take a little getting used to. But I think it's safe to say that if you're in a field where this is common, you'll probably get plenty of practice with converting to and from scientific notation, and if you're not in a field like this, you probably won't ever have much of a need to write numbers like this in code.

Binary Literals

Like with scientific notation, there are certain programming scenarios in which it is easier to write out your numbers in binary than in the normal decimal system.

Like with scientific notation, this doesn't apply in all fields. You're more likely to use this if you are dealing with low-level things like device drivers and parsing network packets than if you're making a non-networked game or a simple data manipulation project. Depending on the type of projects you work on, you may never use this, or you may use it frequently.

To write a binary literal, start your number with a **0b**. For example:

```
int thirteen = 0b00001101;
```

There is no requirement to pad the number with leading 0's, though you are allowed to do so, and is somewhat common to show full, complete bytes.

Hexadecimal Literals

We've now talked about how to write things in base 10, which is the normal format. Base 10 has 10 total digits (0 through 9). We have also talked about how to write values out that are in base 2, or binary, with two total digits: 0 and 1.

The final way to write integer literals is by using base 16, or *hexadecimal*, often just called simply *hex*. With a hexadecimal number, you have 16 different digits that you can use. You start at 0, and go through 9 like the normal, standard decimal system. But then the next number greater than 9 is actually the number A. Then B. Letters are used through F. At this point, you finally roll over to the next digit.

So for example, to count in hexadecimal (base 16) you would go: 0, 1, 2, 3, 4, 5, 6, 7, 8, 9, A, B, C, D, E, F, 10, 11, 12, 13, 14, 15, 16, 17, 18, 19, 1A, 1B, 1C, 1D, 1E, 1F, 20, 21... F8, F9, FA, FB, FC, FD, FE, FF, 100, 101...

To write out a literal in hexadecimal, you preface it with **0x**.

```
int theColorMagenta = 0xFF00FF;
```

This example points out one of the times that hexadecimal is sometimes used: to represent colors. On a computer, colors are frequently represented as a byte for the red, green, and blue (and sometimes alpha/transparency) channels. Two hexadecimal "characters" cover a full byte, and so these are frequently used to indicate how bright or how "on" each color channel is, with 00 being completely off and FF being completely on.

In addition to colors, hex is also frequently used when working with low-level byte manipulation and display.

The 0x notation for a hexadecimal number is incredibly common. If you haven't seen it around before, keep your eyes open. Now that you know what it is and what to look for, you'll start seeing it pop up in random places on your computer.

All integer literals—normal, binary, or hexadecimal—will be treated as an **int** if the value can fit into an **int**, then a **uint** if that fails, then a **long**, then a **ulong**. (You can put the 'U' and 'L' characters at the end of any integer literal to automatically promote them to the bigger type.) If you want the literal to fit in a smaller type, like a **byte** or a **short**, you will need to cast to that type (Chapter 9).

The Digit Separator

The last trick is that of the digit separator. When writing long numbers, humans frequently use a special separator character to break apart a large number to make it easier to read and understand. For example, in the USA and other parts of the world, a comma is often used to separate blocks of digits (e.g., 562,988,142) though other parts of the world use periods (e.g., 562.988.142) or spaces (e.g., 562 988 142).

C# 7 has taken a page from many other languages, and has chosen to use the underscore character (_) to be a digit separator for your numeric literals:

```
int bigNumber = 1_000_000_000;
```

You don't need do use digit separators. Ever. This is a C# 7 feature, so C# developers went for 15 years without having this feature and survived. But it can make numbers more readable in some instances.

Interestingly, the digit separator can go almost anywhere in your number. All of the following are allowed:

```
int a =  123_456_789;
int b = 12_34_56_78_9;
int c = 1_2__3___4____5;
double d = 1_000.000_001;
```

You can see that you have a lot of flexibility in terms of how you arrange your digit separators. That's by design. The purpose of the digits separator is to allow the programmer to make numbers easier to read and understand. Different scenarios will dictate different schemes.

For example, you could use the digit separator to separate different bytes in a binary literal:

```
long x = 0b0010010_00100110_00001101_01011111;
```

Or with the hex literals, you might use the digit separator to demarcate related chunks:

```
uint color = 0xFF_FF_D1_00;
```

But there are a few restrictions on where you can place a digit separator. These restrictions generally can be summed up with the principle that you can't place them at the start or end of a literal, nor can it be immediately before or after any special character or symbol within a literal.

These special characters or symbols include the decimal point, the **e** in exponential notation for floating point types, the **0x** and **0b** used for hex and binary literals, or the U's, L's, F's, and M's that indicate specific types (unsigned, long, floats, decimals). So none of the following will actually compile:

```
// COMPILER ERRORS WITH THE DIGIT SEPARATOR!
int a = _1;         // Can't start with an underscore.
int b = 1_;         // Can't end with an underscore.
int c = 0_b_10101;  // Can't place an underscore before or after the 'b' in a binary literal...
int d = 0_xFFDDA0;  // ... or the 'x' in a hex literal.
double e = 1_e3;    // Can't place one before or after the 'e' in exponential notation.
float f = 3.14_f;   // Or around the characters used to mark the type, like the 'f' here...
ulong g = 1_U_L;    // ... or the U or L here.
double h = 1_.3;    // Can't place an underscore immediately before or after the decimal point.
```

Type Inference

As we've seen, in C#, every variable has a type. This type is a key part of a variable. Things of one type can't go into variables of another type without being converted over to it first. Because of that, type names like **int** and **string** will appear all across your code.

The C# compiler is very smart, and has a powerful feature within it called *type inference*. Type inference is the idea that the compiler can infer or determine the type of something based on clues in the code around it.

The compiler will use type inference to make your life easier. We'll see type inference come up again in the future, but our first encounter is here with the **var** keyword.

A variable can be declared using the **var** keyword, instead of one of the other types we've talked about. For example:

```
var message = "Hello World!";
```

This code is identical to the version earlier in the chapter that explicitly stated that it was a **string**.

The compiler is smart enough to pick up on the clues around it that this variable must be a **string**. In particular, this line of code is assigning a string literal ("Hello World!") to the variable, so that really leaves **string** as the only option here.

It's important to point out that **var** does not mean anything can go in the variable. It is not a catch-all. Types are important to C#, and **var** doesn't erase all of that.

In Visual Studio, in places where you use the **var** keyword, you can use the mouse and hover over the **var**. The popup that appears when you do this will state the type that it has inferred.

There are some definite advantages and drawbacks to **var** that are worth pointing out. In terms of advantages, **var** is a very short name, meaning there are few characters to type. Every other type will be as long or longer. This is actually magnified greatly when we start defining our own types in a few chapters. Our own types tend to have longer names. (12 or 20 characters is fairly normal, and 30 or 40 is not uncommon either.) So the brevity is a big selling point.

The real drawback to **var** is that it can reduce code clarity, which is a big deal. The **var message** example doesn't illustrate this very well, but there are plenty of scenarios where the compiler can easily infer the right type, but where the human programmer has a much harder time. Just because the compiler can infer the correct type does not necessarily mean you should make humans infer it as well.

Different programmers have wildly different takes on if and when to use **var**. Some programmers feel you should use **var** whenever you can. Others banish it from their code entirely. Others will only allow it in places where a human can quickly and clearly infer the correct type. These are largely personal preferences. There is not a definitive correct answer.

In this book, I'm going to avoid **var** when possible. That is because there is no compiler in the book to help you infer the types. To eliminate confusion, I will use specific named types.

Basic Math

In a Nutshell
- Arithmetic in C# is very similar to virtually every other programming language out there.
- Addition: **a = 3 + 4;**
- Subtraction: **b = 7 - 2;**
- Multiplication: **c = 4 * 3;**
- Division: **d = 21 / 7;**
- The remainder operator ('%') gets the remainder of a division operation like this: **e = 22 % 7;** In this case, the variable **e** will contain the value 1.
- You can combine multiple operations into one, and use other variables too: **f = 3 * b - 4;**
- Operator precedence (order of operations) and operator associativity are rules that govern which operations happen before others in an expression that contains multiple operations. These rules can be overridden by grouping things in parentheses.
- Compound assignment operators (**+=, -=, /=, *=,** and **%=**) do the desired operation and assign it to the variable on the left. So for instance **a += 3;** is the same as **a = a + 3;**
- Chapter 9 covers additional math stuff.

With a basic understanding of variables behind us, we're ready to get in to some deeper material: math. This math is all pretty easy. The basic arithmetic you learned in elementary school. Computers love math. In fact, it is basically all they can do. (Well, that and push bytes around.) But they do it incredibly fast.

In this chapter, we'll cover how to do basic arithmetic in C#. We'll start with addition and subtraction, move up through multiplication and division, a lesser known operator called the remainder operator, positive and negative numbers, operator precedence and associativity, and conclude with some compound assignment operators, which do math and assign a value all at once.

Operations and Operators

Let's start with a quick introduction to operations and operators. Whether you know it or not, you've been working with operations since you first learned how to add. In math, an operation is a calculation that takes two (usually) numbers and does something with them to get a result. Addition is an example of an operation, as is multiplication. Operations usually have two pieces to them: an operator (like the '+' sign) and operands. *Operand* is just a fancy name for the thing that the operator works on. So if we look at the operation 2 + 3, the numbers 2 and 3 are operands.

Interestingly, not all operators require two operands. Those that do are called *binary operators*. These are probably the ones you are most familiar with. We'll also see some that only need one operand. These are called *unary operators*. C# also has an operator that requires three operands. It's a *ternary operator*. Because of what it does, it won't make sense to discuss it yet. We'll look at it in Chapter 10.

Addition, Subtraction, Multiplication, and Division

Doing the basic operations of addition, subtraction, multiplication, and division is pretty straightforward. Let's start with a simple math problem. The following code adds the numbers 3 and 4 and stores it into the variable called **a**:

```
int a = 3 + 4;
```

The same thing works for subtraction:

```
int b = 5 - 2;
```

While both of the above examples show doing math on the same line as a variable declaration (which is why we see the variable's type listed), all of these operations that we'll look at can be done anywhere, not just when a variable is first declared. So this would work too:

```
int a;          // Declaring the variable a.
a = 9 - 2;      // Assigning a value to a, using some math.
a = 3 + 3;      // Another assignment.

int b = 3 + 1;  // Declaring b and assigning a value to b all at once.
b = 1 + 2;      // Assigning a second value to b.
```

Remember that a variable must be declared before you can use it, as shown in the above code. You can also use any previously existing variables in your math. You don't just have to use numbers:

```
int a = 1;
int b = a + 4;
int c = a - b;
```

Don't rush by that last part too quickly. The fact that you can use variables on the right hand side of an equation is how you'll be able to calculate one thing based on another, step-by-step. As your program is running, the computer will figure out the result of the calculation on the right side of the equals sign and stick that value in the variable on the left.

You can also chain many operations together on one line:

```
int result = 1 + 2 - 3 + 4 - 5 + a - b + c - d;
```

Multiplication and division work in the exact same way, though there's a few tricks we need to watch out for if we do division with integers. We'll look at that more in Chapter 9, but for now, we'll just use the **float** or **double** type for division instead of integers. The sign for multiplication in C# is the asterisk (*****) and the sign for division in C# is the forward slash (**/**).

```
float totalCost = 22.54f;
float tipPercent = 0.18f;                    // Remember, this is the same as 18%
float tipAmount = totalCost * tipPercent;
```

```
double moneyMadeFromGame = 100000;
double totalProgrammers = 4;
double moneyPerPerson = moneyMadeFromGame / totalProgrammers; // We're rich!
```

Below is a more complicated example that calculates the area of a circle based on its radius.

```
// The formula for the area of a circle is pi * r ^ 2
float radius = 4;
float pi = 3.1415926536f;  // The 'f' makes it a float literal instead of a double literal.
float area = pi * radius * radius;

// Using the + operator with strings results in "concatenation".
Console.WriteLine("The area of the circle is " + area + ".");
```

In the above code, we have variables for the radius of a circle, the value of the number π, and the area, which we calculate using a standard formula from geometry class. We then display the results.

Notice that we can use the '+' operator with strings (text) and numbers. This is a cool feature of C#. It knows that you can't technically add a string and a number in a mathematical sense, but there is an intelligent way of handling it. It knows that it can turn the number into a string (the text representation of the number) and then it knows of a way to add or combine strings together: concatenation. It sticks one piece of text at the end of the other to create a new one. If you run this code, you will see that the program outputs, "The area of the circle is 50.26548."

By the way, back in Chapter 3, we defined what a statement was. At this point, it is worth defining another related term: *expression*. An expression is something that evaluates to a single value. Something like **3 + 4** is an expression, because it can get turned into the value 7. **(3 * 2 - 17 + 8 / 4.0)** is also an expression. It's quite a bit more complex, but it can still be evaluated to a single value. You'll see as we go through this book that expressions and statements can get very large.

Try It Out!

Area of a Triangle. Following the example above for calculating the area of a circle, create your own program that calculates the area of a triangle. The formula for this is:

$$A = \frac{1}{2}bh$$

A is the area of the triangle, b is the base of the triangle, and h is the height of the triangle.

You will want to create a variable in your program for each variable in the equation. Print out your results. Run through a few different values for b and h to make sure that it is working. For instance, check to make sure that if b is 5 and h is 6, the result is 15, and that if b is 1.5 and h is 4, you get 3.

The Remainder Operator

Do you remember in elementary school, not too long after you first learned division, how you always did things like: "23 divided by 7 is 3 remainder 2"? Well in programming, calculating the remainder has its own operator. This operator is called the *remainder operator*, though it is sometimes called the *modulo operator*, or *mod* for short. This operator *only* gives you back the remainder, not the division result. The sign for this operator is the percent sign ('**%**'). So it is important to remember that in C#, '**%**' does not mean "percent," it means "get the remainder of."

In Depth

Remainders Refresher. I know some people haven't done much with remainders since elementary school, so as a refresher, remainders work like this. For 23 % 7, we know that 7 goes in to 23 a total of 3 whole times. But since 7 * 3 is 21, there will be two left over. In this case, 2 is our remainder.)

Say you have 23 apples, and 7 people want the apples, this means everyone gets 3, and there are 2 remaining, or left over. This little example would look like this in C#:

```
int totalApples = 23;
int people = 7;
int remainingApples = totalApples % people; // this will be 2.
```

At first glance, the remainder operator seems like an operator that's not very useful, but if you know how to use it, you will find ways to put it to use. For example, the remainder operator can be used to determine if a value is a multiple of another value. If it is, then the remainder operator will give us 0.

```
int remainder = 20 % 4; // This will be 0, which tells us 20 is a multiple of 4.
```

Try It Out!

Remainders. Create a simple program to write out the results of a division operation. Create two integer variables called **a** and **b**. Create a third integer variable called **quotient** (the result of a division) that stores the result of the division of **a** and **b**, and another integer variable called **remainder** that stores the remainder (using the % operator). Write out the results using **Console.WriteLine** or **Console.Write** to write out the results in the following form: if a = 17 and b = 4, print the following:

17/4 is 4 remainder 1

For bonus points check your work. Create another variable and store in it **b * quotient + remainder**. Print this value out as well. This value should be the same as **a** in all cases.

Edit your code to try multiple values for **a** and **b** to ensure it's working like it should.

Unary '+' and '-' Operators

Let's now turn our attention to a couple of unary operators. Remember, these only have one operand that they work on. You've already sort of seen these operators, but it is worth going into them a little bit more. The two operators that we want to talk about here are the unary "**+**" and unary "**-**" operators. (We're using the same sign as addition and subtraction, but it's technically a different operator.) You have probably seen these before in math. They indicate whether the number right after them is positive or negative.

```
// These are the unary '+' and '-' operators. They only work on the number right after them.
int a = +3;
int b = -44;
```

```
// These are the binary '+' and '-' operators (addition and subtraction) that operate on two numbers.
int a = 3 + 4;
int b = 2 - 66;
```

The unary "**+**" and unary "**-**" indicate the sign of the number (+ or -) that they are in front of. Or looking at it a different way, the "**+**" operator will take the value immediately after it and produce a new value that is exactly equal to it, while the "**-**" operator will take the value immediately after it and produce the negative of it as a result. (So **b = -a;** takes the value in **a**, creates a negative version of it, and stores it in **b**.)

Operator Precedence and Parentheses

Perhaps you remember *operator precedence*, a.k.a. "order of operations" from math classes. This is the idea that when many operators appear mixed together in a single expression, some should be done before the others. This same thing applies in the programming world. All C# operators have a certain precedence that determine the order you do things in. C# follows the same rules that you learned in math class. That means, for example, that multiplication, division, and remainder operations happen before addition and subtraction.

If you want your operations to happen in a different order than the default order of operations, you can modify it by enclosing the operations you want done first in parentheses. For instance:

```
// Some simple code for the area of a trapezoid (http://en.wikipedia.org/wiki/Trapezoid)

double side1 = 5.5;
double side2 = 3.25;
double height = 4.6;

double areaOfTrapezoid = (side1 + side2) / 2 * height;
```

In math, if you have an especially complicated formula with lots of parentheses, sometimes square brackets ('[' and ']') and curly braces ('{' and '}') are used as "more powerful" parentheses. In C#, like most programming languages, that's not how it's done. Instead, you put in multiple sets of nested parentheses like below. Be careful with multiple sets of parentheses to ensure everything lines up correctly.

```
// This isn't a real formula for anything. I'm just making it up for an example.
double a =3.2;
double b = -4.3;
double c = 42;
double d = -91;
double e = 4.343;

double result = (((a + b) * (c - 4)) + d) * e;
```

Operators also have a concept called *associativity* which indicate how multiple operations of the same precedence are grouped together. What value will the variable **x** below contain?

```
int x = 5 - 3 - 1; // Is this (5 - 3) - 1`, or 5 - (3 - 1)?
```

Subtraction is left associative (or left-to-right associative), which means you work from left to right. **(5 - 3) - 1** is the correct way to process this, so **x** will have a value of **1**. The opposite of left associativity is right (or right-to-left) associativity.

C# stays true to mathematical rules of precedence and associativity, so there aren't a lot of surprises in this regard. In the very back of the book, in the Tables and Charts section, the Operators table shows all C# operators, as well as their precedence and associativity.

Why the '=' Sign Doesn't Mean Equals

I mentioned in Chapter 5 that the '=' sign doesn't mean that the two things equal each other. Not directly. Instead, it is an *assignment* operator, meaning that the stuff on the right gets calculated and put into the variable on the left side of the '=' sign.

Watch how this works:

```
int a = 5;
a = a + 1; // the variable a will have a value of 6 after running this line.
```

If you've done a lot of math, you may notice how strange that looks. From a math standpoint, it is impossible for a variable to equal itself plus 1. It's nonsense.

But from a programming standpoint, it makes complete sense, because what we are really saying is, "take the value currently in **a** (5), add one to it (to get 6), and assign that value back into the variable **a**." So after running that line, we've taken **a** and added one to it, replacing the old value of 5.

It's important to remember that the '=' sign indicates assignment, rather than equality.

Compound Assignment Operators

It turns out that what I just described (taking the current value of a variable, making a change to it, and updating the variable with the new value) is very common. So much so that there is a whole set of other operators that make it easy to do this. These operators are called *compound assignment operators*, because they perform a math function *and* assign a value all at once.

For instance, here's the compound assignment operator that does addition:

```
int a = 5;
a += 3;            // This is the same as a = a + 3;
```

There are also equivalent ones for subtraction, multiplication, division, and the remainder operator:

```
int b = 7;
b -= 3;    // This is the same as b = b - 3; At this point b would be 4.
b *= 5;    // This is the same as b = b * 5; At this point b would be 20.
b /= 4;    // This is the same as b = b / 4; At this point b would be 5.
b %= 2;    // This is the same as b = b % 2; At this point b would be 1.
```

We've covered a lot of math, and there's still more to come. But before we dig into even more math, we're going to take a little break in the next chapter and do something a little different. We'll look at how to allow the user to type in stuff for you to use in your program. We'll come back and discuss more math related things in Chapter 9.

User Input

In a Nutshell
- You can get input from the user with **Console.ReadLine();**
- Convert it to the type you need with various methods from the **Convert** class. For example, **Convert.ToInt32** converts to the **int** type, **Convert.ToDouble** converts to the **double** type, etc.

In this short chapter, we'll take a look at two additional pieces of code that we'll need to create a simple program that has some actual value.

We'll first learn how to get input from the user through the console window, then how to convert between the data types that we learned about in Chapter 6, so that you can change string-based user input to anything else.

User Input from the Console

We can get input from the user by using a statement like the following:

```
string whatTheUserTyped = Console.ReadLine();
```

This looks a lot like **Console.WriteLine**, which we've been using up to this point. Both **ReadLine** and **WriteLine** are methods. Methods are little blocks of reusable code. We'll get into methods in detail later (Chapter 15). For now, all we need to know is that we can use them to make things happen—read and write lines of text in this particular case. **Console.ReadLine()** will grab an entire line of text from the user (up until the <Enter> key is pressed) and place it in the **whatTheUserTyped** variable.

Converting Types

But simply grabbing the user's input and sticking it in a **string** variable frequently doesn't get the input into the right data type for our needs. For instance, what if we need the user to type in a number? When we put it into a **string**, we can't do math with it. We'll need to convert it to the right type of data first. To convert to the right data type, we're going to use another method that converts any of the built-in data types to another. For example, to convert this string to an integer, we do this:

```
int aNumber = Convert.ToInt32(whatTheUserTyped);
```

There are similar methods for each of the other data types. For instance, **ToInt16** is for the type **short**, **ToBoolean** is for the type **bool**, **ToDouble** is for **double**, and so on. The one for the **float** type is tricky: **ToSingle**. Contrasted with the **double** type, the **float** type is said to have "single" precision.

These **Convert.ToWhatever** methods convert things besides just strings. Any of the built-in types can be converted to any of the other built-in types. For instance, you could do the following to change a **double** to a **float**, or a **bool** to an **int** using the code below:

```
bool b = false;
int i = Convert.ToInt32(b);

double d = 3.4;
float f = Convert.ToSingle(d);
```

A Complete Sample Program

We now know enough to make a program that does something real: getting information from the user, doing basic stuff with it, and printing the results. Our next step is to actually *make* a real program. Even if you've been skipping the *Try It Out!* sections, take a few minutes and do the one below. While most of these *Try It Out!* sections have example code online, as I described in the Introduction, I've actually put my sample code for this particular problem here in the book as well.

Spend some time and actually write the program below. When you've got it complete, or if you get hung up on it, go down and compare what you've got with my code below. (Just because yours is different from the code below, doesn't mean it is wrong. There are always more than one way to get things done.)

Try It Out!

Cylinders: A Complete Program. We're going to create a simple program that will tell the user interesting information about a cylinder. A cylinder is usually defined by a height (**h**) and radius of the base (**r**). Create a program that allows the user to type in these two values. We'll do some math with those values to figure out the volume of that cylinder, as well as the surface area. (Don't worry about the formulas; I'll provide them to you.) The program will then output the results to the user.

The formula for the volume of a cylinder is this:
$$V = \pi r^2 h$$

The formula for the surface area of a cylinder is this:
$$SA = 2\pi r(r + h)$$

In both of these equations, **r** is the radius of the cylinder, **h** is the height of the cylinder, and of course, $\pi \approx 3.1415926$.

Once you've given the program above a shot, take a look at my code to accomplish this task below:

```
using System;
using System.Collections.Generic;
using System.Linq;
using System.Text;
using System.Threading.Tasks;

namespace CylinderCalculator
```

```
{
    class Program
    {
        static void Main(string[] args)
        {
            // Print a greeting message. After all, why not?
            Console.WriteLine("Welcome to Cylinder Calculator 1.0!");

            // Read in the cylinder's radius from the user
            Console.Write("Enter the cylinder's radius: ");
            string radiusAsAString = Console.ReadLine();
            double radius = Convert.ToDouble(radiusAsAString);

            // Read in the cylinder's height from the user
            Console.Write("Enter the cylinder's height: ");
            string heightAsAString = Console.ReadLine();
            double height = Convert.ToDouble(heightAsAString);

            double pi = 3.141592654; // We'll learn a better way to do PI in the next chapter.

            // These are two standard formulas for volume and surface area of a cylinder.
            // You can find them on Wikipedia: http://en.wikipedia.org/wiki/Cylinder_(geometry)
            double volume = pi * radius * radius * height;
            double surfaceArea = 2 * pi * radius * (radius + height);

            // Now we output the results
            Console.WriteLine("The cylinder's volume is: " + volume + " cubic units.");
            Console.WriteLine("The cylinder's surface area is: " + surfaceArea + " square units.");

            // Wait for the user to respond before closing...
            Console.ReadKey();
        }
    }
}
```

Let's look at this a little at a time. The first part, with the **using** directives, is all template code that we discussed in Chapter 3.

The first thing we add is a simple welcome message to the user.

```
// Print a greeting message. After all, why not?
Console.WriteLine("Welcome to Cylinder Calculator 1.0!");
```

This is basically just the Hello World program we did earlier. No surprises here.

Next, we prompt the user to enter the cylinder's radius and height and turn them into the right data type using the things we learned in this chapter:

```
// Read in the cylinder's radius from the user
Console.Write("Enter the cylinder's radius: ");
string radiusAsAString = Console.ReadLine();
double radius = Convert.ToDouble(radiusAsAString);

// Read in the cylinder's height from the user
Console.Write("Enter the cylinder's height: ");
string heightAsAString = Console.ReadLine();
double height = Convert.ToDouble(heightAsAString);
```

The first line is just simple output. We then read in the user's text and store it in a **string**. The third line uses more stuff we learned in this chapter and turns it into the correct data type. I used the **double** type, but **float** or **decimal** would accomplish the same task with no meaningful difference. (You would just use **Convert.ToSingle** or **Convert.ToDecimal** instead.) We repeat the process with the cylinder's height.

We then define the value of PI and use the math operations from the last chapter to calculate the volume and surface area of the cylinder.

```
double pi = 3.141592654; // We'll learn a better way to do PI in the next chapter...

// These are two standard formulas for volume and surface area of a cylinder.
// You can find them on Wikipedia: http://en.wikipedia.org/wiki/Cylinder_(geometry)
double volume = pi * radius * radius * height;
double surfaceArea = 2 * pi * radius * (radius + height);
```

Finally, we output the results to the user, again using stuff from our first Hello World program:

```
// Now we output the results
Console.WriteLine("The cylinder's volume is: " + volume + " cubic units.");
Console.WriteLine("The cylinder's surface area is: " + surfaceArea + " square units.");
```

And finally, we end the program by waiting for the user to press any key:

```
// Wait for the user to respond before closing...
Console.ReadKey();
```

And there we have it! Our first *useful* C# program!

Escape Characters

When working with strings, we often run into things called escape characters. *Escape characters* (or *escape sequences*) are special sequences of characters that have a different interpretation than face value. These escape characters are designed to make it easy to represent things that don't normally appear on the keyboard, or that the compiler would otherwise interpret as a part of the language itself.

For example, how could you print out an actual quotation mark character? **Console.WriteLine(""");** won't work. The first quotation mark indicates the beginning of the string, and the compiler will interpret the middle one as the end of the string. That leaves the third quotation mark, which it can't make sense of.

To handle this, we can take advantage of escape characters. In C#, you start an escape sequence with the backslash character ('\'). Inside of a string literal, you can use a backslash, followed by a quotation mark, to get it to recognize it as a quotation mark that belongs inside of the string, as opposed to one that indicates the end of the string:

```
Console.WriteLine("\"");
```

It is worth pointing out that even though **\"** is visually two characters, it is treated as only one.

C# has many different escape characters that you'll find useful. For example, **\t** is the tab character, and **\n** is the newline character. You can see how this works in the following example:

```
Console.WriteLine("Text\non\nmore\nthan\none\nline.");
```

This will print out:

```
Text
on
more
than
one
line.
```

What happens if you want to print out an actual backslash character? By default, the computer will try to take \ and combine it with the next letter to represent an escape character, since it marks the beginning of an escape sequence. To print out the backslash character, you will need to use two backslashes:

```
Console.WriteLine("C:\\Users\\RB\\Desktop\\MyFile.txt");
```

This will print out:

```
C:\Users\RB\Desktop\MyFile.txt
```

If you find that all of these extra slashes are kind of annoying, you can put the '@' symbol before the text (called a *verbatim string literal*) which tells the computer to ignore escape characters in the string. The following line is equivalent to the previous one:

```
Console.WriteLine(@"C:\Users\RB\Desktop\MyFile.txt");
```

String Interpolation

It's common when you display something to the user to mix together text with some code. Earlier in this chapter, we did this by concatenating the strings and code together with a "+":

```
Console.WriteLine("The cylinder's volume is: " + volume + " cubic units.");
```

C# 6.0 introduced a feature called string interpolation. This feature lets you write this same thing in a much more concise and readable way:

```
Console.WriteLine($"The cylinder's volume is: {volume} cubic units.");
```

String interpolation requires two steps. First, before the string, place a "$". This tells the C# compiler that this isn't just a normal string. It's one that has code embedded within it that needs to be evaluated. Within the string, when you want to use code, you simply surround it with curly braces.

This translates to the same code as our first pass, but this is usually more readable, so it's usually preferred. The curly braces can contain any valid C# expression. It's not limited to just a single variable. That means you can do things like perform some simple math, or call a method, etc. You'll even get Visual Studio auto-completion and syntax highlighting inside the curly braces.

There's obviously a practical limit to how much you can stuff inside the curly braces before it becomes unreadable. At some point, the logic gets complicated and long enough that you lose track of how it's being formatted. At that point, it's better to pull the logic out onto a separate line and store it in a variable.

More Math

In a Nutshell

- Division with integer types uses integer division; fractional leftovers are discarded.
- Casting can convert one type to another type. Many types are implicitly cast from narrow types to wider types. Wider types can be explicitly cast to certain narrower types using the type you want in parentheses in front: **float a = (float)3.4445;**
- Division by zero causes an error (Chapter 30) to be thrown for integer types, and results in infinity for floating point types.
- **NaN**, **PositiveInfinity**, and **NegativeInfinity** are defined for the **float** and **double** types (**float.NaN** or **double.PositiveInfinity**, for example).
- **MaxValue** and **MinValue** are defined for essentially all of the numeric types, which indicate the maximum and minimum values that a particular type can contain.
- π and *e* are defined in the **Math** class, and can be accessed like this: **float area = Math.PI * radius * radius;**
- Mathematical operations can result in numbers that go beyond the range of the type the value is being stored in. For integral types, this results in truncation (and wrapping around). For floating point types, it results in **PositiveInfinity** or **NegativeInfinity**.
- You can use the increment and decrement operators (**++** and **--**) to add one or subtract one from a variable. For example, after the following, **a** will contain a 4: **int a = 3; a++;**

We're back for Round 2 of math. There's so much math that computers can do—in fact, it is *all* computers can do. But this will be our last math-specific chapter. We'll soon move on to much cooler things.

There are still quite a few things we need to discuss. The things we're going to talk about in this chapter are not very closely related to each other. Each section is its own thing. This means that if you already know and understand one topic, you can just jump down to the next.

Here are the basic things we're going to discuss in this chapter. We'll start by talking about doing division with integers ("integer division") and an interesting problem that comes up when we do that. We'll then talk about converting one type of data to another (called *typecasting* or simply *casting*). Next we'll talk about dividing by zero, and what happens in C# when you attempt this. We'll then talk about a few cool special numbers in C#, like infinity, NaN, the number *e*, and π. Then we'll take a look at overflow and underflow, and finish up with incrementing and decrementing numbers.

It's probably not required to read all of this if you're in a rush, but don't skip the section on casting or the section on incrementing and decrementing.

There's a lot to learn here. Don't worry if you don't catch it all your first time. You can always come back later. In fact, having some experience behind you will probably help make it clearer.

Integer Division

Let's start this section off with an experiment to illustrate a specific problem that arises when you do division with integers. In your head, figure out what 7 / 2 is. Got it? Your answer was probably 3.5, or maybe 3 remainder 1. Both are correct.

Now go into C#, and write the following, and see what ends up in **result**:

```
int a = 7;
int b = 2;
int result = a / b;
Console.WriteLine(result);
```

The computer thinks it is 3! Not 3.5, or 3 remainder 1. What we're doing isn't the normal division you learned in elementary school, but rather, a thing called *integer division*. In integer division, there's no such thing as fractional numbers.

Integer division works by taking only the integer part of the result, leaving off any fractional or decimal part. This is true no matter how close it is to the next higher number. For example, 99 / 100 is 0, even though from a math standpoint, it is 0.99, which is really close to 1.

Integer division is used when you do division with any of the integral data types, but *not* when you use the floating point types.

For comparison purposes, check out the following piece of code:

```
int a = 7;
int b = 2;
int c = a / b; // results in 3. Uses integer division.

float d = 7.0f;
float e = 2.0f;
float f = d / e; // results in 3.5. Uses "regular" floating point division.
```

This gets especially tricky when you mix different data types like this:

```
int a = 7;
int b = 2;
float c = 4;
float d = 3;
float result = a / b + c / d;
```

Here, the **a / b** part becomes 3 (like before), but the **c / d** part does floating point division (the normal division) and gives us 1.33333. Adding the two gives us 4.33333.

It is important to keep in mind that integer types will always use integer division. This may seem like a problem, but you can actually leverage integer division to your advantage. The key is to remember when it happens, so that you aren't surprised by it.

If you don't want integer division, you'll need to convert it to floating point values, as we'll discuss in the next section.

Working with Different Types and Casting

Typically, when you do math with two things that have the same type (adding two **int**s for example) the result is the same type as what you started with. But what if you do math with two different types? For example, what if you add an **int** with a **long**? The computer basically only knows how to do math on two things with the same type. So to get around this problem, types can be changed to different types on the fly to allow the operation to be done. This conversion is called *typecasting* or simply *casting*.

There are two types of casting in C#. One is *implicit casting*, meaning it happens for you without you having to say so, while the other is *explicit casting*, meaning you have to indicate that you want to do it.

Generally speaking, implicit casting happens for you whenever you go from a *narrower* type to a *wider* type. This is called a *widening conversion*, and it is the kind of conversion that doesn't result in any loss of information. To help explain, remember that an **int** uses 32 bits, while a **long** uses 64 bits. Because of this, the **long** type can hold all values that the **int** type can handle plus a whole lot more. Because of this, we say that the **int** type is narrower, and the **long** type is wider. C# will happily cast the narrower **int** to the wider **long** when it sees a need, without having to be told. It will implicitly cast from **int** to **long**.

So for instance, you can do the following:

```
int a = 4049;
long b = 284404039;
long sum = a + b;
```

When you do the addition operation, the value is pulled from **a**, implicitly cast into a **long**, and added to **b**.

This is a widening conversion. There's no risk of losing information because the wider type (a **long**) can always contain any value of the narrower type (the **int**). Because there's no risk of losing data, the conversion is safe to do.

Floating point types are considered wider than integral types, so when there's a need, C# will convert integral types to floating point types. For example:

```
int a = 7;
float b = 2; // this converts the integer value 2 to the floating point value 2.0

// The value in `a` below will get implicitly cast to a float to do this division because `b` is a float.
// This results in floating point division, rather than integer division.
float result = a / b;
```

On the other hand, there are also times that we will want to change from a wider type to a narrower type. This is done with an explicit cast, meaning we need to actually state, "Hey, I want to turn this type into another type." Explicit casts usually turn a value from a wider type into a narrower type, which leaves the possibility of data loss.

To do an explicit cast, you simply put the type you want to convert to in parentheses in front of the value you want to convert. For instance, look at this example, which turns a **long** into an **int**:

```
long a = 3;
int b = (int)a;
```

Casting doesn't just magically convert anything to anything else. Not all types can be converted to other types. The compiler will give you an error if you are trying to do an explicit cast to something that it can't do. If you're trying to cast from one thing to another and the compiler won't allow it, the **Convert.ToWhatever()** methods might still be able to make the conversion (Chapter 8).

Casting is considered an operator (the conversion operator) like addition or multiplication, and fits into the order of operations. Casting has a higher precedence than the arithmetic operators like addition and multiplication. For example, if you have the following code:

```
float result = (float)(3.0/5.0) + 1;
```

The following will happen:

1. The stuff in parentheses is done first, taking 3.0 and dividing it by 5.0 to get 0.6 as a **double**.
2. The conversion/casting will be done next, turning the 0.6 as a **double** into a 0.6 as a **float**.
3. To prepare for addition with 0.6 as a **float**, and an integer 1, the 1 will be implicitly cast to a **float**.
4. Addition will be done with the 0.6 as a **float** and the 1.0 as a **float**, resulting in 1.6 as a **float**.
5. The 1.6 as a **float** will be assigned back into the **result** variable.

Try It Out!

Casting and Order of Operations. Using the above as an example, outline the process that will be done with the following statements:

- double a = 1.0 + 1 + 1.0f;
- int x = (int)(7 + 3.0 / 4.0 * 2);
- Console.WriteLine((1 + 1) / 2 * 3);

If this is confusing, try putting the code into Visual Studio and running it. You can try breaking out parts of it into different lines and debug it if you want. (Chapter 48 discusses debugging in depth.)

Division by Zero

You probably remember from math class that you can't divide by zero. It doesn't make sense mathematically. Bad things happen. You rip holes in the fabric of space-time, sucking you into a vortex of eternal doom, where you're forced to turn trees into toothpicks using nothing but one of those plastic sporks that you get at fast food restaurants.

So let's take a moment and discuss what happens when you divide by zero in C#. If you divide by zero with integral types, a strange thing happens. An exception is "thrown." That's a phrase we'll come back to in more detail later when we talk about exceptions (Chapter 30), but for now, it is enough to know that an exception is simply an error. Your program will die instantly if you are running without debugging. On the other hand, if you are running *with* debugging, Visual Studio will activate right at the line that the exception occurred at, allowing you to attempt to fix the problem. (For more information on what to do if this happens, see Chapter 48.)

Interestingly, if you are using a floating point type like **double** or **float**, it doesn't crash. Instead, you'll get the resulting value of **Infinity**. Integer types don't define a value that means **Infinity**, so they don't have this option. We'll look at **Infinity** and other special numbers in the next section.

Infinity, NaN, e, π, MinValue, and MaxValue

Infinity

There are a few special values that are worth discussing. Let's start off by looking at infinity. Both the **double** and the **float** type define special values to represent positive and negative infinity (+∞ and -∞). In the math world, doing stuff with infinity often results in some rather unintuitive situations. For example, ∞ + 1 is still ∞, as is subtracting 1: ∞ - 1 = ∞.

To use these directly, you can do something like the following:

```
double a = double.PositiveInfinity;
float b = float.PositiveInfinity;
```

NaN (Not a Number)

NaN is another special value with the meaning "not a number." Like infinity, this can come up when you do something crazy, like ∞/∞. This can be accessed like this:

```
double a = double.NaN;
float b = float.NaN;
```

E and π

The numbers **e** and **π** are two special numbers that may be used frequently (or not) depending on what you are working on. Regardless of how often you might use them, they're worth knowing about. You can always do what we did a few chapters back, and create a variable to store those values, but why do that when there's already a pre-defined variable that does the same thing?

To use these, we'll use the **Math** class. (We're still going to talk about classes a lot more, starting in Chapter 17.) You can do this with the following code:

```
double radius = 3;
double area = Math.PI * radius * radius;

// You'll likely find more uses for pi than e.
double eSquared = Math.E * Math.E;
```

We don't need to create our own **pi** variable anymore, because it has already been done for us!

MinValue and MaxValue

Finally, let's talk quickly about **MinValue** and **MaxValue**. Most of the numeric types define a **MinValue** and **MaxValue** inside of them. These can be used to see the minimum or maximum value that the type can hold. You access these like NaN and infinity for floating point types:

```
int maximum = int.MaxValue;
int minimum = int.MinValue;
```

Overflow and Underflow

Think about this. A **short** can have a maximum value of up to 32767. So what if we do this?

```
short a = 30000;
short b = 30000;
short sum = (short)(a + b); // The sum will be too big to fit into a short. What happens?
```

First of all, I should point out that when you do math with the **byte** or **short** type, it will automatically convert them to the **int** type. So in the code above, I've had to do an explicit cast to get it back to a **short**.

Try out that code, and print out the **sum** variable at the end and see what you get.

Mathematically speaking, it should be 60000, but the computer gives a value of -5536.

When a mathematical operation causes something to go beyond the allowed range for that type, we get a thing called *overflow*. What happens is worth paying attention to. For integer types (**byte**, **short**, **int**, and **long**), the most significant bits (which overflowed) get dropped. This is especially strange, because the computer then interprets it as wrapping around. This is why we end up with a negative value in our example. You can easily see this happening if you start with the maximum value for a particular type (for example, **short.MaxValue**) and adding 1 to it. You'll end up at the minimum value.

For the floating point types, things happen differently. Because they have **PositiveInfinity** and **NegativeInfinity** defined, instead of wrapping around, they become infinity.

You actually have more control than what is described above. In Chapter 43 we'll revisit this and flesh out overflow a bit more.

Another similar condition called *underflow* that can occur sometimes with floating point types. Imagine you have a very large floating point number. Something like 1,000,000,000,000. A **float** can store that number. Now let's say you have a very small number, like 0.00000001. You can store that as a **float** as well. However, if you add the two together, a **float** cannot store the result: 1,000,000,000,000.00000001.

A **float** just simply cannot be that big *and* that precise at the same time. Instead, the addition would result in 1,000,000,000,000 again. This is perhaps close enough for most things. But still, potentially valuable information is lost. Floating point types have a certain number of digits of accuracy. Starting at the first digit that matters, it can only keep track of so many other digits before it just can't keep track of any more.

Underflow is not nearly as common as overflow; you may never encounter a time where it matters.

Incrementing and Decrementing

Perhaps you've noticed that lots and lots of times in this book, I've added 1 to a value. We've already seen two ways of doing this:

```
int a = 3;
a = a + 1;  // Normal addition operator, and then assign it to the variable.
```

And:

```
int a = 3;
a += 1;   // The compound addition/assignment operator.
```

Here's yet another way of adding 1 to a value:

```
int a = 3;
a++;
```

This is called *incrementing*, and "++" is called the *increment operator*. Before long, we'll see many places where we can use this.

As its counterpart, you can use "--" to subtract one from a number. This is called *decrementing*, and "--" is called the *decrement operator*.

Incidentally, the "++" in the name of the well-known C++ programming language comes from this very feature. C++ was designed to be the "next step" or "one step beyond" the programming language C, hence the name C++. (C, C++, and Java all have the increment operator too.)

The increment and decrement operators can be written in one of two ways. You can write **a++;**, or you can write **++a;**. (Likewise, you can write **a--;** and **--a;**.) With the ++ at the end, it is called *postfix notation*, and with it at the beginning, it is called *prefix notation*.

There's a subtle difference between prefix and postfix notation. To understand the difference, it is important to realize that this operation, like many others, "returns a value." This is a phrase that we'll frequently see later on, but it is a concept we have already been working with. Take the addition operator, for instance. When we do **2 + 1**, the math happens and we're left with a specific result (**3**).

As it happens, using the increment or decrement operators will also return a result, aside from just modifying the variable involved. With postfix notation (**a++;**) the *original* value of **a** is returned. With prefix notation (**++a;**) the new, incremented value is returned. Here's an example:

```
int a = 3;
int b = ++a; // Both 'a' and 'b' will now be 4.

int c = 3;
int d = c++; // The original value of 3 is assigned to 'd', while 'c' is now 4.
```

a++ means, "give me the value in **a**, then increment **a**," while **++a** means, "increment **a** first, then give me the resulting value."

Using this operator to both modify a variable and return a result can be confusing. Even experienced programmers often don't readily remember the subtle differences between postfix and prefix notations without looking it up. It is more common to split the logic across two lines, which sidesteps the confusion:

```
int a = 3;
a++;
int b = a;

int c = 3;
int d = c;
c++;
```

Decision Making

In a Nutshell

- Decision making is the ability for a program to make choices and do different things conditionally.
- The **if** statement is the cornerstone of decision making in C#, and can optionally include **else** statements and **else-if** statements to create more sophisticated behavior:

```
if(condition)
{
    // ...
}
else if(another condition)
{
    // ...
}
else
{
    // ...
}
```

- In an **if** statement's condition block, you can use the operators **==, !=, <, >, <=,** and **>=** to check if something is "equal to", "not equal to", "less than", "greater than", "less than or equal to", or "greater than or equal to" the second side.
- The **!** operator reverses Boolean types.
- The operators **&&** (*and* operator) and **||** (*or* operator) allow you to check multiple things in an **if** statement.
- **if** statements can be nested.

Any program that does real work will have to make decisions. These decisions are made based on whether a particular condition holds true or not. Sections of code can be ran conditionally. The central piece of decision making is a special C# statement called an **if** statement. We'll start by looking at the **if** statement, along with a few related statements. Then we'll look at a variety of ways to compare two values. We'll then look at a few other special operators ("logical operators") that help us make more sophisticated conditions.

The 'if' Statement

Imagine a simple scenario where a teacher is assigning grades and wants to know what grade a student should get based on their test score.

Grading systems vary throughout the world, but a pretty typical one is to give out the letters A, B, C, D, and F, where A represents a very high level of competence, F represents a failure, and B, C, and D represent varying levels in between.

The basic process is for the teacher to take a look at the student's score, and if it's 90 or higher, the student gets an 'A'. If they're lower than that, but still at 80 or higher, then they get a 'B', and so on, down to a failing grade. In order to figure out what grade a student should get, you need to make decisions based on some condition. We do things *conditionally*—meaning it only happens some of the time. We only give *some* students A's, while others get B's, and others fail.

As we start talking about decision making, let's go through the process of building a program that will determine a student's grade, based on their score.

Let's start at the beginning. In C#, decision making will always start with an **if** statement. A simple **if** statement can check if two things are equal, like the code below:

```
if(score == 100)
{
    // Code between the curly braces is only executed when the condition in the parentheses is true.
    Console.WriteLine("Perfect score!");
}
```

That should be fairly straightforward. There are a few parts to a basic **if** statement. We start off by using the **if** keyword. Then in parentheses, we put the condition we're checking for.

There are many ways to define a condition, but for now, we simply use the **==** operator. The **==** operator is called the *equality operator*. It evaluates to **true** when the two things on each side are equal to each other.

We then use the curly braces ('{' and '}') to show a code block that should only be run when the condition is true—the student's score was 100, in this particular case.

So to put this in the context of a complete program, here is what this might look like in your code:

```
using System;
using System.Collections.Generic;
using System.Linq;
using System.Text;
using System.Threading.Tasks;

namespace DecisionMaking
{
    class Program
    {
        static void Main(string[] args)
        {
            // Everything up here, before the if-statement will always be executed.
            int score;

            Console.WriteLine("Enter your score: ");
            string scoreAsText = Console.ReadLine();
            score = Convert.ToInt32(scoreAsText);

            if (score == 100)
            {
                // Code between the curly braces is executed when the condition is true.
                Console.WriteLine("Perfect score! You win!");
```

```
                        }
            // Everything down here, after the if-statement will also always be executed.
            Console.ReadKey();
        }
    }
}
```

Remember back in Chapter 7, that I said the "=" operator doesn't mean equals, like we find in math? Neither does the equality operator ("==") that we see here, though it is much closer. In math, to say that two things are equal is an assertion that the two are exactly equivalent to each other, just written in different forms. The equality operator in C# is a little different, in that it is a check, or a query to see if two things currently have the same value. If they do, the comparison evaluates to **true**, and if not, the comparison evaluates to **false**.

The 'else' Statement

So what if you want to do something in one case, but otherwise, do something else? For instance, what if you want to print out "You win!" if the student got 100, but "You lose!" if they didn't? That's easy to do using an **else** block immediately after the **if** block:

```
if(score == 100)
{
    // This code gets executed when the condition is met.
    Console.WriteLine("Perfect score! You win!");
}
else
{
    // This code gets executed when it is not.
    Console.WriteLine("Not a perfect score. You lose.");
}
```

The thing to remember here (and use it to your advantage) is that one or the other block of code will be executed, but not both. If it does one, it won't do the other, but it will for sure do one of them.

'else if' Statements

You can also get more creative with **if** and **else**, stringing together many of them:

```
if(score == 100)
{
    Console.WriteLine("Perfect score! You win!");
}
else if(score == 99)
{
    Console.WriteLine("Missed it by THAT much."); // Get Smart reference, anyone?
}
else if(score == 0)
{
    Console.WriteLine("You must have been TRYING to get that bad of a score.");
}
else
{
    Console.WriteLine("Ah, come on! That's just boring. Next time get a more interesting score.");
}
```

In this code, one (and only one) of the blocks will get executed, based on the score.

While most of the **if** and **else** blocks that we've looked at so far have had only one statement in them, that's not a requirement. You can have as much code inside of each set of curly braces as you want.

Curly Braces Not Always Needed

So far, our examples have always had a block of code after the **if** or **else** statement, surrounded by curly braces. If you have exactly one statement, then you don't actually need the curly braces. So we could have written the previous code like this:

```
if(score == 100)
    Console.WriteLine("Perfect score! You win!");
else if(score == 99)
    Console.WriteLine("Missed it by THAT much."); // Get Smart reference, anyone?
else if(score == 0)
    Console.WriteLine("You must have been TRYING to get that bad of a score.");
else
    Console.WriteLine("Ah, come on! That's just boring. Next time get a more interesting score.");
```

On the other hand, if you have multiple statements, you will always need the curly braces.

In a lot of cases, if it's just a single line, it can be more readable to leave off the curly braces, which have a tendency to add a lot of mental weight to the code. The code feels lighter without them.

It's important to remember one maintenance problem when you leave off the curly braces. There's a danger that as you make changes to your code later on, you might accidentally add in the new lines and *forget* to add the curly braces. This completely change the way the code is executed, as shown here:

```
if(score == 100)
    Console.WriteLine("Perfect score! You win!");
    Console.WriteLine("That's awesome!");          // Inadvertently executed every time.
```

Remember, whitespace doesn't matter in C#, so even though that last statement *looks* like it belongs in the **if** statement, it actually isn't in there. The middle line will only be executed when the condition is met, but the last line will always be executed, because it isn't in the **if** statement.

Just be careful as you modify **if** statements so that you don't make this mistake. If you're adding a second line to the the **if** statement, make sure you've also added in the curly braces as well.

Relational Operators: ==, !=, <, >, <=, >=

Let's take a look at some better and more powerful ways to specify conditions. So far, we've only used the == operator to check if two things are exactly equal, but there are many others.

The **==** operator that we just saw is one of many *relational operators*, which is a fancy way of saying "an operator that compares two things." There are several others.

For instance, the **!=** operator checks to see if two things are *not* equal to each other. You use this in the same way that we use ==, but it does the opposite:

```
if(score != 100)
{
    // This code will be executed, as long as the score is not 100.
}
```

Then there's the **>** and **<** operators, which determine if something is greater than or less than something else. These work just like they do in math:

```
if(score > 90)
{
    // This will only be executed if the score is more than 90.
    Console.WriteLine("You got an 'A'!");
}
```

```
if(score < 60)
{
    // This will only be executed if the score is less than 60.
    Console.WriteLine("You got an 'F'. Sorry.");
}
```

Of course, you may have noticed that the code above isn't exactly what we set out to do in the original problem statement. We wanted to give an A if they scored *at least* 90. In the above code, 90 doesn't result in an A, because 90 is not greater than 90.

Which brings us to the last two relational operators **>=** and **<=**. These two mean "greater than or equal to" and "less than or equal to" respectively.

```
if(score >= 90)
{
    // This will only be executed if the score is 90 or higher...
    // Subtly different than the above example, because it also picks up 90.
    Console.WriteLine("You got an 'A'!");
}
```

In math, we would use the symbols ≤ and ≥, but since those aren't on the keyboard, C# and most other programming languages will use <= and >= instead.

This gives us everything we need to write the full program we set out to do:

```csharp
using System;
using System.Collections.Generic;
using System.Linq;
using System.Text;
using System.Threading.Tasks;

namespace DecisionMaking
{
    class Program
    {
        static void Main(string[] args)
        {
            int score;

            Console.Write("Enter your score: ");
            string scoreAsText = Console.ReadLine();
            score = Convert.ToInt32(scoreAsText);

            // This if-statement is separate from the rest of them. Not because of the blank
            // line between this statement and the next block, but because that starts all
            // over with a brand new if-statement.
            if (score == 100)
                Console.WriteLine("Perfect score! You win!");

            // This checks each condition in turn, until it finds the first one that
            // is true, at which point, it executes the chosen code block, then jumps down
            // to after the end of the whole if/else code.
            if (score >= 90)
                Console.WriteLine("You got an A.");
            else if (score >= 80)
                Console.WriteLine("You got a B.");
            else if (score >= 70)
                Console.WriteLine("You got a C.");
            else if (score >= 60)
                Console.WriteLine("You got a D.");
            else
                Console.WriteLine("You got an F.");

            Console.ReadKey();
        }
```

```
        }
}
```

Using 'bool' in Decision Making

Remember when we first discussed data types in Chapter 6 that I told you about the **bool** type, and that it would turn out to be useful? We're there now. You can use variables with the **bool** type in making decisions; in fact, it is very common to do so. For instance, check out this block of code, which determines if a player has enough points to pass the level:

```
int score = 45; // Ideally, this would change as the player progresses through the game.

int pointsNeededToPass = 100;

bool levelComplete;

if(score >= pointsNeededToPass)
    levelComplete = true;
else
    levelComplete = false;

if(levelComplete)
{
    // We'll be able to do more here later, as we learn more C#
    Console.WriteLine("You've beaten the level!");
}
```

Note that relational operators *return* or "give back" a **bool** value—meaning you can use a relational operator like **==** or **>** to directly assign a value to a **bool**:

```
int score = 45; // Ideally, this would change as the player progresses through the game.

int pointsNeededToPass = 100;

// The parentheses below are optional.
bool levelComplete = (score >= pointsNeededToPass);

if(levelComplete)
{
    // We'll be able to do more here later, as we learn more C#
    Console.WriteLine("You've beaten the level!");
}
```

> **Try It Out!**
> **Even and Odd.** In Chapter 7, we talked about the remainder operator (%). This can be used to determine if a number is even or odd. If you take a number and divide it by 2 and the remainder is 0, the number is even. If the remainder is 1, the number is odd. Write a program that asks the user for a number and displays whether the number is even or odd.

The '!' Operator

For helping with conditions and conditional logic, C# also has the '**!**' operator, which returns the logical opposite of what is supplied to it. A **true** becomes a **false**, and a **false** becomes a **true**. For instance:

```
bool levelComplete = (score >= pointsNeededToPass);

if(!levelComplete) // If the level is NOT complete...
    Console.WriteLine("You haven't won yet. Better keep trying...");
```

You can also combine this with all of the conditional operators that we've talked about, but the **!** operator has higher precedence than the relational operators, so it happens first. If you want to do the comparison first and then negate it, you have to use parentheses. To illustrate:

```
if(!(score > oldHighScore))
{
}

// That's effectively the same as:
if(score <= oldHighScore)
{
}
```

Conditional Operators: && and || (And and Or)

There are a lot of ways your conditions could become more complicated. For instance, imagine you are making a game where the player controls a spaceship that has both shields and armor, and the player only dies when *both* shields and armor are gone. You will need to check both things, rather than just one.

Here's where conditional operators come in to play. C# has an *and* operator, which looks like this: **&&**, and an *or* operator that looks like this: **||**. (The '|' key is above the **<Enter>** key on most keyboards and requires pushing **<Shift>**.) You can use these to check multiple things at once:

```
int shields = 50;
int armor = 20;

if(shields <= 0 && armor <= 0)
    Console.WriteLine("You're dead.");
```

This can be read as, "if **shields** are less than or equal to zero, and **armor** is less than or equal to zero." With the **&&** operator, both parts of the condition must be true in order for the whole expression to be true.

The **||** operator works in a similar way, though if either one is true, then the whole thing becomes true.

```
int shields = 50;
int armor = 20;

if(shields > 0 || armor > 0)
    Console.WriteLine("You're still alive! Keep going!");
```

One thing worth mentioning is that with either of these, the computer will do *lazy evaluation*. This means that it won't check the second part unless it needs to. So in the example above, the computer will always check to see if **shields** is greater than 0, but it only bothers checking if **armor** is greater than 0 if **shields** is less than or equal to 0.

You can combine lots of these together, and along with parentheses, make some pretty crazy conditions. Anything you want is possible, though readability may quickly become an issue. Which leads us to the next section, which might provide an alternative approach that may be more readable.

Nesting If Statements

You can also put **if** statements (and **if-else** statements) inside of other **if** statements. This is called *nesting* them. For example:

```
if(shields <= 0)
{
    if(armor <= 0)
        Console.WriteLine("Your shields and armor are both zero! You're dead!");
    else
```

```
        Console.WriteLine("Shields are gone, but armor is keeping you alive!");
}
else
{
    Console.WriteLine("You still have shields left. The world is safe.");
}
```

It doesn't have to end there, either. You could nest **if** statements inside of **if** statements inside of **if** statements inside of even more **if** statements. However, the fact that it is doable doesn't necessarily make it a good idea. Lots of nesting means the code is less readable. Use it when there's a need for it (and there will be) but don't overdo it.

> ## Try It Out!
> **Positive or Negative?** One thing that a lot of people have trouble with is doing multiplication when negative numbers are involved. They typically run into trouble when trying to figure out if the result should be positive or negative.
>
> You're going to write a program to help them! But there's a catch. In this example, you're banned from actually doing the multiplication to figure out the answer. (It would be all too easy to take two numbers and multiply them, and then check if the result is greater than or less than zero.) Instead, you will follow the same logic that a human has to follow to get your answer.
>
> When you're multiplying two numbers together, if the two numbers have the same sign (both positive or both negative) the result is positive. If they have different signs, the result is negative.
>
> Write a program that asks the user for two numbers and then, using the rule above, prints out whether the result should be positive or negative.

The Conditional Operator ?:

Now that we know a little about logic, I want to bring up another operator in C#. Remember when we first talked about operators in Chapter 7, how we discussed unary and binary operators? Unary operators only work on one thing, (for example, the negative sign) while binary operators work on two things (addition or subtraction). I'm going to introduce a new operator, which is a ternary operator. This means it operates on *three* parts. This might seem kind of strange to you. It probably ought to. It's not a very normal thing to see in math or programming (though this specific operator is in many languages).

This operator is called the conditional operator, and it works quite a bit like an **if-else** statement. It uses the **?** and **:** characters like this:

```
(boolean condition) ? value if true : value if false
```

A practical example might look like this:

```
Console.WriteLine((score > 70) ? "You passed!" : "You failed.");
```

Everything that you do with the conditional operator could have been done without it. But it is a nice shorthand way to do things that can be very readable. On the other hand, it can also reduce readability, so it isn't *always* a better choice. Just an alternative that you may find helpful.

Switch Statements

In a Nutshell
- **switch** statements are an alternative to **if** statements, especially if they involve a lot of "else if X... else if Y... else if Z..." kind of stuff.
- You can use the following types in a switch statement: **bool**, **string**, and all integral types.
- You can also use enumerations (Chapter 14).
- You can't fall through from one case block to another. You always need a **break** (or **return**) at the end of a block.

In the previous chapter, we looked at basic **if** statements and decision making. C# has another type of statement that is very similar to **if** statements. These statements are called **switch** statements. In this case, think of a switch like a railroad switch, which determines which track a train will travelling down.

We'll take a look at when we'd want to use **switch** statements, how to do them, and then wrap up with a couple of extra details about **switch** statements.

Anything you can do with a **switch** statement can also be done with an **if** statement. While there may be some small performance tradeoffs with using **switch** vs. **if-else** (**switch** is usually considered as fast or faster, depending on the situation) it is usually not enough to overtake readability concerns. It is usually best to pick whichever version produces the most readable code.

The Basics of Switch Statements

It is pretty common to have a variable and want to do something different depending on the value of that variable. For instance, let's say we have a menu with five choices (1-5). The user types in their choice, which we store in a variable. We want to do something different depending on which value they chose.

Using only the tools that we already know, we'd probably think about a sophisticated **if-else** statement. Or rather, an **if/else-if/else-if/else-if/else-if/else** statement. Something like this:

```
int menuChoice = 3;

if (menuChoice == 1)
```

```
      Console.WriteLine("You chose option #1.");
else if (menuChoice == 2)
      Console.WriteLine("You chose option #2. I like that one too!");
else if (menuChoice == 3)
      Console.WriteLine("I can't believe you chose option #3.");
else if (menuChoice == 4)
      Console.WriteLine("You can do better than 4....");
else if (menuChoice == 5)
      Console.WriteLine("5? Really? That's what you went with?");
else
      Console.WriteLine("Hey! That wasn't even an option!");
```

That gets the job done, but this could also be done with a **switch** statement.

To make an equivalent **switch** statement, we'll use the **switch** keyword, and a **case** keyword for each of the various "cases" or options that we have. We'll also use the **break** and **default** keywords, but we'll talk about those more in a second. The **if** statement we had above would look like this as a **switch** statement:

```
int menuChoice = 3;

switch (menuChoice)
{
    case 1:
        Console.WriteLine("You chose option #1");
        break;
    case 2:
        Console.WriteLine("You chose option #2. I like that one too!");
        break;
    case 3:
        Console.WriteLine("I can't believe you chose option #3.");
        break;
    case 4:
        Console.WriteLine("You can do better than 4....");
        break;
    case 5:
        Console.WriteLine("5? Really? That's what you went with?");
        break;
    default:
        Console.WriteLine("Hey! That wasn't even an option!");
        break;
}
```

As you can see, we start out with the **switch** statement, and in parentheses, we put the variable we are going to base our "switch" on.

Then we have a sequence of **case** statements (sometimes called **case** labels), which indicate that if the variable matches the value in the **case** statement, the flow of execution enters the following code block.

It is important to note that the flow of execution will go into exactly one of the **case** labels, so you will never end up in a situation where more than one **case** block gets executed.

At the end of each **case** block, you must put the **break** keyword, which sends the flow of execution back outside of the entire **switch** statement, and down to the next part of the code.

We can also have a **default** label, which indicates where the flow of execution should go if no other case label is a match. The **default** label doesn't *need* to be the last one, but it is typical and good practice to do so. The **default** block works as a sort of catch-all for anything other than the specific situations of the other **case** labels. Note that this is like the final **else** block in our original, giant **if** statement.

Switch statements do not allow arbitrary logic in a case condition. That is, with an **if** statement, we can write something like **if(x < 10)**, there is no equivalent to this for a switch statement. You can't write **case < 10:** or **case x < 10:**. If you want arbitrary logic, then you will have to fall back to an **if** statement instead.

Types Allowed with Switch Statements

In our above example, we see that you can use the **int** type in a **switch** statement. Not all types can be used in a **switch**, but many can. Here's the list of types that can be used: **bool**, **string**, and any of the integral types (including **char**). We haven't talked about enumerations yet (Chapter 14) but those can also be used in a **switch** statement.

No Implicit Fall-Through

C++ and Java have a little trick where if you leave out the **break** statement, you can have one **case** block "fall through" to the next **case** block. But this is banned in C#:

```
switch (menuChoice)    // This DOES NOT work in C#
{
    case 1:
        Console.WriteLine("You chose 1.");
    case 2:
        Console.WriteLine("You chose 2. Or maybe you chose 1.");
        break;
}
```

Because there's no **break** in the **case 1** block, the code there would be executed, and then continue on down into the **case 2** block. This isn't allowed in C#. Every **case** block needs a **break** statement.

The reason for requiring this is that people *accidentally* ended up doing this far more often than they intentionally do it. They leave off the **break** statement by accident, resulting in a bug that is usually tricky to resolve. To prevent this, C# won't allow you to skip the **break** statement and fall through.

However, there is one situation where you *can* do this: multiple case blocks with no code in between it:

```
switch (menuChoice)   // This DOES work in C#
{
    case 1:
    case 2:
        Console.WriteLine("You chose option 1 or 2.");
        break;
}
```

In this case, both 1 and 2 end up in the same case block. While **case 1** doesn't have a **break** statement, it also doesn't need it, because we're simply stating the two are the equal. You can write the same thing with an **if** statement as well, using the || operator.

Try It Out!

Making a Calculator. We're going to make a simple calculator. Ask the user to type in two numbers and then to type in a math operation to perform on the two numbers.

Use a switch statement to handle the different operations in different ways. Allow the user to type in '+' for addition, '-' for subtraction, '*' for multiplication, '/' for division, and '%' for remainder. For bonus points, allow the user to type in '^' for a power. (You can compute this using the Math.Pow method. For example, the following does x^2: **Math.Pow(x, 2);)**

Print out the results for the user to see.

Looping

> ## In a Nutshell
> - **while** loops, **do-while** loops, and **for** loops all allow you to repeat things in various ways.
>
> ```
> while(condition) { /* ... */ }
>
> do { /*... */ } while(condition);
>
> for(initialization; condition; update) { /* ... */ }
> ```
>
> - You can break out of a loop at any time with the **break** keyword and advance to the next iteration of the loop with the **continue** keyword.
> - The **foreach** loop is not discussed here, but will be in the next chapter.

In this chapter we'll discuss yet another very powerful feature in the C# language: loops. Loops allow you to repeat sections of code multiple times. We'll discuss three types of loops in this chapter, and cover a fourth type in the next chapter when we discuss arrays. (It will make a lot more sense there.)

The While Loop

The first kind of loop we're going to talk about is the **while** loop. A **while** loop will repeat certain code over and over, as long as a certain condition is true. While loops are constructed in a way that looks a whole lot like an **if** statement:

```
while( condition )
{
    // This code is repeated as long as the condition is true.
}
```

Let's start with a really simple example that counts to ten:

```
int x = 1;
while(x <= 10)
{
    Console.WriteLine(x);
    x++;
}
```

Let's take a minute and look at what the computer does when it runs into this code. This starts with the variable **x** being 1. The program then checks the condition in the **while** loop and asks, "is **x** less than or equal to 10?" This is true, so the stuff inside the **while** loop gets executed. It writes out the value of **x**, which is 1, then increments **x** (adds 1 to it). When it hits the end curly brace, it has finished the **while** loop and goes back up to the beginning of the loop, checking the condition again. This time however, **x** has changed. It is now 2. The condition is still true (2 is still less than or equal to 10) and the loop repeats again, printing out "2" and incrementing **x** to 3. This will happen 10 times total, until **x** gets incremented to 11. When the program checks to see if 11 is less than or equal to 10, the condition is no longer true, and the flow of execution jumps down past the end of the loop.

One thing to keep in mind is that it is easy to end up with a bug in your code that makes it so the condition of a loop is never met. Imagine if the **x++;** line wasn't there. The program would keep repeating the loop, and each time **x** would still be 1. The program would never end! This problem is common enough to be given its own name: an *infinite loop*. I promise you, by the time you're done making your first *real* program, you will be the proud writer of at least one infinite loop. It happens.

To fix the problem, you may need to pause your program's execution, see where it is getting stuck, close your program, fix the problem in your code, and restart. The process of debugging your program like this is discussed in Chapter 48.

While we're on the subject of infinite loops, I'm going to mention that sometimes people make them on purpose. It sounds strange, I know. But it is easy to do:

```
while(true)
{
    // Depending on what goes in here, you'll never end...
}
```

Depending on what you put inside the loop (like a **break** statement, which we'll discuss in detail later in this chapter) you can actually still get out of the loop.

I've occasionally heard an infinite loop that was done intentionally be called a "forever loop" instead. It's not a term all programmers will be familiar with, but there is some value in distinguishing intentional infinite loops from the accidental ones.

Moving on, here's a more complicated (and more useful) example which repeats over and over until the user enters a number between 0 and 10:

```
int playersNumber = -1;

while(playersNumber < 0 || playersNumber > 10)
{
    // This code will get repeated until the player types in a number between 0 and 10.

    Console.Write("Enter a number between 0 and 10: ");
    string playerResponse = Console.ReadLine();
    playersNumber = Convert.ToInt32(playerResponse);
}
```

One important thing to remember with a **while** loop is that it checks the condition before even going into the loop. So if the condition is not met right from the get-go, it doesn't ever go in the loop. In the example above, it is important that we initialize **playersNumber** to -1, because if we had started it at 0, the flow of execution would have jumped right over the **while** loop block, and the player would have never been able to choose a number.

Like with **if** statements, if you only have one statement inside of a **while** loop (or any of the other loops we'll discuss here) the curly braces are optional.

The Do-While Loop

The next type of loop we'll look at is a slight variation on the **while** loop. It is the **do-while** loop. Remember that a **while** loop will first check the condition to see if it is met, and if not, it could potentially skip the loop entirely. (This isn't a bad thing; it's just something to remember. Most of the time, that's exactly how you want it.)

In contrast, the **do-while** loop will *always* be executed at least once. This is useful if you are trying to set up some stuff the first time through the loop, and you *know* it needs to be executed at least once.

Let's revisit that last example, because it is a prime candidate for a **do-while** loop. Remember, we needed to set up the player's number to -1, to *force* it to go through the loop at least once? Doing this as a **do-while** loop solves the need for that:

```
int playersNumber;

do
{
    Console.Write("Enter a number between 0 and 10: ");
    string playerResponse = Console.ReadLine();
    playersNumber = Convert.ToInt32(playerResponse);
}
while (playersNumber < 0 || playersNumber > 10);
```

To form a **do-while** loop, we put the **do** keyword at the start of the loop, and at the end, we put the **while** keyword. Also notice that you need a semicolon at the end of the **while** line. Everything else is the same, but this time, you don't need to initialize the **playersNumber** variable because we know that the loop will be executed at least once before the condition is checked.

The For Loop

Now let's take a look at a slightly different kind of loop: the **for** loop. **For** loops are very common in programming. They are an easy way of doing counting-type loops, and we'll see how useful they are again in the next chapter with arrays. For loops are a bit more complicated to set up, because they require three components inside of the parentheses, whereas **while** and **do-while** loops only require one. It is structured like this:

```
for(initial condition; condition to check; action at end of loop)
{
    //...
}
```

There are three parts separated by semicolons. The first part sets up the initial state, the second part is the condition (the same thing that was in the **while** and **do-while** loops), and the third part is an action that is performed at the end of the loop. An example will probably make this clearer, so let's do the counting to ten example as a **for** loop:

```
for(int x = 1; x <= 10; x++)
{
    Console.WriteLine(x);
}
```

Note that we can declare and initialize a variable right in the **for** loop like we do here, with **int x = 1;**.

One of the reasons why this kind of loop is so popular is because it separates the looping logic from what you're actually doing with the number. Rather than having the **x++** statement inside of the loop and declaring the variable before the loop, all of that stuff gets packed into the loop control mechanism, making the stuff you're actually trying to accomplish clearer.

One other cool thing to point out is that anything you can do with one type of loop you can do with the other two as well. Often, one type of loop is cleaner and easier to understand than the others, but they can all do the same stuff. If suddenly the C# world ran out of **while** keywords, and all you had left was **for**s, you'd be fine. Because of this, you should pick the looping mechanism that creates the code that is easiest to understand.

Breaking Out of Loops

Another cool thing you can do with a loop is *break* out of it any time you want. Sometimes, as you're working through a loop, you get to a point where you know there's no point in continuing with the loop. You can jump out of a loop whenever you want with the **break** keyword like this:

```
int numberThatCausesProblems = 54;

for(int x = 1; x <= 100; x++)
{
    Console.WriteLine(x);

    if(x == numberThatCausesProblems)
        break;
}
```

This code will only go until it hits 54, at which point the **if** statement catches it and sends it out of the loop. This is not a very practical example, but it is a good illustration of how you might use the **break** command. When we start the loop, we're fully expecting to get to 100, but then we realize at some point that there's a critical problem (or alternatively, we've found the result we were looking for) and we can ignore the rest of the loop.

By the way, this is the kind of thing that makes forever loops actually worth something:

```
while(true)
{
    Console.Write("What is thy bidding, my master? ");
    string input = Console.ReadLine();

    if(input == "quit" || input == "exit")
        break;
}
```

Before we leave the topic of forever loops, I should say that you rarely truly need to write one. We could have restructured the code above to not need it. (By moving the **input** variable outside of the loop and converting the **if** statement to be the condition in the while loop.) But occasionally, the code will be more readable this way, so it is good to know about.

Continuing to the Next Iteration of the Loop

Similar to the **break** command, there's another command that, rather than getting out of the loop altogether, jumps back to the start of the loop and checks the condition again. In other words, it continues on to the next iteration of the loop without finishing the current one.

This is done with the **continue** keyword:

```
for(int x = 1; x <= 10; x++)
{
    if(x == 3)
        continue;
```

```
        Console.WriteLine(x);
}
```

In this code sample, all of the numbers will get printed out with one exception. 3 gets skipped because of the **continue** statement. When it hits that point, it jumps back up, runs the **x++** part of the loop, checks the **x < 10** condition again, and continues on with the next cycle through the loop.

Nesting Loops

Like with **if** statements it is possible to nest loops. And to put **if** statements inside of loops and loops inside of **if** statements. You can go absolutely crazy with all of this control!

Let's go through a couple more complete examples.

I'm going to repeat a really simple example that I remember from when I first started learning to program. (Back then, it was C++, not C#, and we had to walk uphill both ways to school, and define our own **true** and **false**!) The task was to write a loop that would print out the following (you were only allowed to have the '*' character in your program once):

```
**********
**********
**********
**********
**********
```

The code below accomplishes this:

```
for(int row = 0; row < 5; row++)
{
    for(int column = 0; column < 10; column++)
        Console.Write("*");

    Console.WriteLine(); // This makes it wrap around to the beginning of the line.
}
```

Let's try a harder one. If we want to do this:

```
*
**
***
****
*****
******
*******
********
*********
**********
```

The code would be:

```
for(int row = 0; row < 10; row++)
{
    for(int column = 0; column < row + 1; column++)
        Console.Write("*");

    Console.WriteLine();
}
```

Notice how tricky we were, using **row** in the condition of the **for** loop with the **column** variable.

I should probably mention (because I'm sure you're wondering) that programmers seem to love 0-based indexing, meaning we love to start counting at 0. (There's actually a good reason for this, which we'll look at a little bit more when we look at arrays in the next chapter.)

You'll see that I've done this frequently in these samples. I start with **row** and **column** at 0, and go up to the amount I want (10 in this case), but not including it. That does it 10 times. You could do it starting at 1, and use **row <= 10** instead, but what I wrote is more typical of a programmer.

Try It Out!

Print-a-Pyramid. Like the star pattern examples that we saw earlier, create a program that will print the following pattern:

```
    *
   ***
  *****
 *******
*********
```

If you find yourself getting stuck, try recreating the two examples that we just talked about in this chapter first. They're simpler, and you can compare your results with the code included above.

This can actually be a pretty challenging problem, so here is a hint to get you going. I used three total loops. One big one contains two smaller loops. The bigger loop goes from line to line. The first of the two inner loops prints the correct number of spaces, while the second inner loop prints out the correct number of stars.

Try It Out!

FizzBuzz. We now know everything we need to be able to do a popular test problem in programming: the FizzBuzz problem. This is a simple little toy problem that many people who claim to know a particular programming language still seem to struggle with.

If you can complete this problem, you're probably better off than half of the other people in the world who claim to know C#. It's actually a sad state of affairs, because the problem is so simple, but even still, it is a fact than many people who claim to know C# (or another language) can't even write this simple program in it. (Admittedly, they are frequently asked to do this on a whiteboard in a job interview and don't have a compiler to check their work, which makes the problem harder.)

The challenge is to print out all of the numbers from 1 to 100. Except if a number is a multiple of 3, print out the word "Fizz" instead. If the number is a multiple of 5, print out "Buzz". If a number is a multiple of both 3 and 5 (like 15 or 30) then print out "FizzBuzz". For example, "1 2 Fizz 4 Buzz Fizz 7 8 Fizz Buzz…"

A couple of things to remember that seem to derail people: Be sure you're going through the numbers 1-100, not 0-99, and you'll likely use the remainder operator (%) which can be used to determine if something is a multiple of another number.

Still to Come: Foreach

It is worth mentioning that we have one more type of loop to discuss, which we'll do in the next chapter: the **foreach** loop. I only bring that up because a full discussion of loops has to include this type of loop. But the **foreach** loop makes the most sense in conjunction with arrays, which we'll be talking about next.

Arrays

In a Nutshell
- Arrays store collections of related objects of the same type.
- To declare an array, you use the square brackets: **int[] numbers;**
- To create an array, you use the **new** keyword: **int[] scores = new int[10];**
- You can also use collection initializer syntax: **int[] scores = new int[] { 1, 2, 3, 4, 5 };**
- You can access and modify values in an array with square brackets as well:
  int firstScore = scores[0]; and **scores[0] = 44;**
- Indexing of arrays is 0-based, so 0 refers to the first element in the array.
- You can create arrays of anything, including arrays of arrays: **int[][] grid;**
- You can also create multi-dimensional arrays: **int[,] grid = new int[5, 4];**
- You can use the **foreach** loop to easily loop through an array and do something with each item in the array: **foreach(int score in scores) { /* ... */ }**

In this chapter, we'll take a look at arrays. Arrays are a variable type that allows us to group multiple items of the same type together into a single collection. This chapter discusses how to make and use arrays, a few samples of using them, how to make multi-dimensional arrays, and then wrap up with a discussion of the last type of loop that we didn't discuss in the previous chapter.

What is an Array?

An *array* is a way of keeping track of a group of many related things of the same type in a single collection. Imagine that you have a high score board in a game, with 10 high scores on it. Using only the tools we know so far, you could create one variable for every score that you want to keep track of. For example:

```
int score1 = 100;
int score2 = 95;
int score3 = 92;
// Keep going to 10...
```

That's one way to do it. But what if you had 10,000 scores? All of a sudden, creating that many variables to store scores becomes overwhelming.

This brings us to arrays. Arrays are perfect for keeping track of things like this, since they could store 10 scores or 10,000 scores in a way that is both easy to create and easy to work with.

Creating Arrays

Declaring an array is very similar to declaring any other variable. You give it a type and a name, and you can initialize it at the same time if you want. You declare an array using square brackets (**[** and **]**).

```
int[] scores;
```

The square brackets here indicate that this is an array, not just a single **int.** This declares an array variable which can contain multiple **int**s. Like with all other types that we've discussed so far, this is basically just a named location in memory to stick stuff. To actually *create* a new array and place it in the variable, use the **new** keyword and specify the number of elements that you'll have in the array:

```
int[] scores = new int[10];
```

In the first example, we had not yet assigned a value to the array variable. We had just declared it, reserving a spot for it. In this second example, our array now exists and has room for 10 items in it.

Once we have set a size for an array, we can't change it. You can change the individual values in the array (we're still coming to that) but not the size. You can, however, create a new array with a different size, copy the values over into part of the new, larger array, and then assign that back in to your array variable. The variable itself doesn't care how large the array is specifically.

On the other hand, if you truly want resizable collections, you should use the **List** type, which we'll talk about in Chapter 25.

By the way, this is the first time we're seeing the **new** keyword, but it won't be the last. We use this keyword to create things that aren't just simple primitive data types. We'll see this come back in a big way later, when we start looking at classes in Chapter 17.

Arrays aren't limited to **int**s. You can make arrays of anything. For example, here's an array of **string**s:

```
string[] names = new string[10];
```

(For those coming from a C++ background, you may be wondering if there is a **delete** keyword, and when and how to clean things up. While C++ requires you to clean up memory that you are no longer using with **delete**, C# doesn't require or even allow this. C# uses managed memory, and uses garbage collection to clean up things that are no longer in use. We'll look at this in more detail in Chapter 16.)

Getting and Setting Values in Arrays

Now that we have an array declared and created, we can assign values to specific spots in the array. To access a specific spot in the array, we use the square brackets again, along with what is called a *subscript* or an *index*, which is a number that tells the computer which of the *elements* (things in an array) to access. For example, to put a value in the first spot of an array, we would use the following:

```
scores[0] = 99;
```

You can see here that the first spot in the array is number 0. It is very important to remember that array indexing is 0-based. If you forget about 0-based indexing, and start with 1, you'll run into what are called "off-by-one" errors, because you're on the wrong number.

You can access any value in an array by using the same technique:

```
int fourthScore = scores[3];
int eighthScore = scores[7];
```

If you try to access something beyond the end of the array (for example, **scores[54]** in an array with only 10 items in it), your program will crash, telling you the index was out of the bounds of the array.

Side Note

0-based Indexing. I know it seems kind of strange if you're new to programming, but there's a very good reason for 0-based indexing. The array itself has a specific spot in memory—a specific memory address. This address is called the base address.

For any particular array, the size of each slot in the array may be a different size based on the size of the type you're putting into the array. An array of **int**s will have slots that are 4 bytes big, since **int**s are 4 bytes. An array of **long**s will have slots that are 8 bytes big.

Because the computer knows the base memory address, and how big each slot is, it is easy for it to calculate the memory location of any particular index in the array using the simple formula:

$$address = base + index \times size$$

If we didn't use 0-based indexing (perhaps using 1-based indexing instead) the math here would become more complicated.

More Ways to Create Arrays

There are a couple of other ways of initializing an array that are worth discussing here. You can also create an array by giving it specific values right from the get-go, by putting the values you want inside of curly braces, separated by commas:

```
int[] scores = new int[10] { 100, 95, 92, 87, 55, 50, 48, 40, 35, 10 };
```

When you create an array this way, you don't even need to state the number of items that will be in the array (the '10' in the brackets, in this case). You can leave that out:

```
int[] scores = new int[] { 100, 95, 92, 87, 55, 50, 48, 40, 35, 10 };
```

In fact, because of type inference, in these cases, you can even leave off the type name as long as all of the items are the same literal type:

```
int[] scores = new [] { 100, 95, 92, 87, 55, 50, 48, 40, 35, 10 };
```

Array Length

We can tell how long an array is by using the **Length** property. We haven't talked about properties at all yet (we will cover them in depth in Chapter 19), but the code for doing this is useful enough and simple enough that it is worth taking the time to point out. For instance, the code below grabs an array's **Length** property and uses it to print out the length of an array:

```
int totalThingsInArray = scores.Length;
Console.WriteLine("There are " + totalThingsInArray + " things in the array.");
```

Some Examples with Arrays

Now that we know the basics of how arrays work, let's look at a couple of examples using arrays.

Minimum Value in an Array

In our first example, we'll calculate the minimum value in an array, using a **for** loop.

The basic process will require looking at each item in the array in turn. We'll create a variable to store the value that we know is the minimum that we've seen so far. As we go down the array, if we find one that is less than our current known minimum, we update the known minimum to the new one.

```
int[] array = new int[] { 4, 51, -7, 13, -99, 15, -8, 45, 90 };

int currentMinimum = Int32.MaxValue; // We start high, so that any element in the array will be lower.

for(int index = 0; index < array.Length; index++)
{
    if(array[index] < currentMinimum)
        currentMinimum = array[index];
}

// At this point, currentMinimum contains the minimum value in the array.
```

Average Value in an Array

Let's try a similar but different task: finding the average value in an array. We'll follow the same basic pattern as in the last example, but this time we're going to total up the numbers in the array. When we're done doing that, we'll divide by the total number of things in the array to get the average.

```
int[] array = new int[] { 4, 51, -7, 13, -99, 15, -8, 45, 90 };

int total = 0;

for (int index = 0; index < array.Length; index++)
    total += array[index];

float average = (float)total / array.Length;
```

> ### Try It Out!
> **Copying an Array.** Write code to create a copy of an array. First, start by creating an initial array. (You can use whatever type of data you want.) Let's start with 10 items. Declare an array variable and assign it a new array with 10 items in it. Use the things we've discussed to put some values in the array.
>
> Now create a second array variable. Give it a new array with the same length as the first. Instead of using a number for this length, use the **Length** property to get the size of the original array.
>
> Use a loop to read values from the original array and place them in the new array. Also print out the contents of both arrays, to be sure everything copied correctly.

Arrays of Arrays and Multi-Dimensional Arrays

You can have arrays of anything. **int**s, **float**s, **bool**s. Even arrays of arrays! This is one way that you can create a matrix. (A matrix is simply a grid or table of numbers with rows and columns.)

To create an array of arrays, one option is to use the following notation:

```
int[][] matrix = new int[4][];
matrix[0] = new int[4];
matrix[1] = new int[5];
matrix[2] = new int[2];
matrix[3] = new int[6];
```

```
matrix[2][1] = 7;
```

Notice that each of my arrays within the main array has a different length. You could of course make them all the same length (there's a better way to do this that we'll see in a second). When each array within a larger array has a different length, it is called a *jagged array*. If they're all the same length, it is often called a *square array* or a *rectangular array*.

There's another way to work with arrays of arrays, assuming you want a rectangular array (which is often the case). This is called a *multi-dimensional array*.

To do this, you put multiple indices inside of one set of square brackets like this:

```
int[,] matrix = new int[4, 4];
matrix[0, 0] = 1;
matrix[0, 1] = 0;
matrix[3, 3] = 1;
```

It is worth briefly describing how you might go about looking at each element in these more complicated arrays. For an array of arrays, or a jagged array, this might look like this:

```
int[][] matrix = new int[4][];
matrix[0] = new int[2];
matrix[1] = new int[6];
// Continue filling in values for the jagged array...

for(int row = 0; row < matrix.Length; row++)
{
    for(int column = 0; column < matrix[row].Length; column++)
        Console.Write(matrix[row][column] + " "); // Each item in the row separated by spaces

    Console.WriteLine(); // Rows separated by lines
}
```

Or with a multi-dimensional array:

```
int[,] matrix = new int[4,4];
// Fill in contents for multi-dimensional array

// Note: GetLength gives back the size of the multi-dimensional array for a specific index.
for(int row = 0; row < matrix.GetLength(0); row++)
{
    for(int column = 0; column < matrix.GetLength(1); column++)
        Console.Write(matrix[row, column] + " ");

    Console.WriteLine();
}
```

The 'foreach' Loop

To wrap up our discussion of arrays, let's go back to what was mentioned in the last chapter about loops. There's one final type of loop that works really well when working with collections such as arrays. This type of loop is called the **foreach** loop (as in, "do this particular task for each element in the array").

To use a **foreach** loop, you use the **foreach** keyword with an array, specifying the name of the variable to use inside of the loop:

```
int[] scores = new int[10];

foreach (int score in scores)
    Console.WriteLine("Someone had this score: " + score);
```

Inside of the loop, you can use the **score** variable. One key thing to note is that inside of the loop, you have no way of knowing what index you are currently at. (You don't know if you are on **scores[2]** or **scores[4]**.) In many cases, that's no big deal. You don't care what index you're at, you just want to do something with each item in the array.

If you need to know what index you're at, your best bet is to use a **for** loop instead:

```
int[] scores = new int[10];

for(int index = 0; index < scores.Length; index++)
{
    int score = scores[index];
    Console.WriteLine("Score #" + index + ": " + score);
}
```

Compared to a **for** loop, a **foreach** loop has a tendency to be more readable. There is not as much overhead clutter inside of the parentheses. Also, in many cases the first thing you do a **for** loop is use the index to get the correct item out of the array. This is bypassed with a **foreach** loop.

But **foreach** loops are somewhat slower, simply as a result of their internal mechanics. If you're discovering that a particular **foreach** loop is taking way more time than you'd like, converting it to a **for** loop is an easy way to get a little extra speed out of it.

This leaves us with a final question: when can **foreach** loops be used? The short answer (which won't make much sense just yet) is that it can be used on anything that implements the **IEnumerable** interface. We haven't talked about interfaces at all yet, but virtually every container or collection across the .NET Platform uses it. That means that **foreach** can be used on almost anything that has multiple items in it.

Try It Out!

Minimum and Averaging Revisited. Earlier in this chapter, I presented code to go through an array and find the minimum value contained in it. I also presented code to average the values in an array. Using that code as a starting point, rewrite them to use **foreach** loops instead.

Enumerations

In a Nutshell
- Enumerations are a way of defining your own type of variable so that it has specific values.
- Enumerations are defined like this: **public enum DaysOfWeek { Sunday, Monday, Tuesday, Wednesday, Thursday, Friday, Saturday };**
- Enumerations are usually defined directly in a namespace, outside of any classes or other type definitions.
- The fact that an enumeration can only take on the values that you explicitly listed means that you won't end up with bad or meaningless data (unless you force it by casting).
- You can assign your own numeric values to the items in an enumeration: **public enum DaysOfWeek { Sunday = 5, Monday = 6, Tuesday = 7, Wednesday = 8, Thursday = 9, Friday = 10, Saturday = 11 };**

Enumerations (or *enumeration types*, or *enums* for short) are a cool way to define your own type of variable. This is the first of many ways we'll see to create your own.

The word *enumeration* comes from the word *enumerate*, which means "to count off, one after the other," which is the intent of enumerations. We'll start by looking at the kinds of situations where enumerations might be useful. We'll then look at how to create your own enumeration and use it. We'll take a look at a few additional important features of enumerations before wrapping up the chapter.

The Basics of Enumerations

Let me start off with an example of when enumerations may be used. Let's say you are keeping track of something that has a known, small, specific set of possible values that you can use—for instance, the days in the week. One way you could do this is to assign numbers to each of these in your head. Sunday would be 1, Monday would be 2, Tuesday would be 3, and so on. Your code could look something like this:

```
int dayOfWeek = 3;

if(dayOfWeek == 3)
    Console.WriteLine("It's Tuesday!");
```

For the sake of readability, you might decide to create a variable to store each of these days:

```
int sunday = 1;
int monday = 2;
int tuesday = 3;
int wednesday = 4;
int thursday = 5;
int friday = 6;
int saturday = 7;

int dayOfWeek = tuesday;

if(dayOfWeek == tuesday)
    Console.WriteLine("It's Tuesday!");
```

This kind of situation is exactly what enumerations are for. You create an enumeration, and list the possible values it can have.

When we create an enumeration, we're defining a new type. We've discussed a wide variety of types before, but this is the first experience we'll have creating our own type. When we define a new type, we put them directly inside of the namespace. You use the **enum** keyword, give your enumeration a name, and list the values that your enumeration can have inside of curly braces:

```
public enum DaysOfWeek { Sunday, Monday, Tuesday, Wednesday, Thursday, Friday, Saturday };
```

Remember, enumerations are placed directly inside of the namespace (outside of other classes or types you might have, including the **Program** class that we've been using). This is shown in context below:

```
using System;
using System.Collections.Generic;
using System.Linq;
using System.Text;
using System.Threading.Tasks;

namespace Enumerations
{
    // You define enumerations directly in the namespace.
    enum DaysOfWeek { Sunday, Monday, Tuesday, Wednesday, Thursday, Friday, Saturday };

    public class Program
    {
        static void Main(string[] args)
        {
        }
    }
}
```

Alternatively, enumerations can be defined in their own file. We'll see how to do this when we learn about classes in Chapter 18.

Inside of your **Main** method, you can now create variables that have your new **DaysOfWeek** type, instead of just the built-in types that we've been working with. We've defined a brand new type! Creating a variable with your new type works just like any other variable:

```
DaysOfWeek today; // Indicate the type, and give it a name.
```

To assign it a value, you will use the '.' operator (usually read "dot operator", but more formally called the "member access operator"). We'll discuss the '.' operator more later, but for now what you need to know is that it is used for *member access*. This means that you use the '.' operator to use something that is a part of something else. The values are a part of the enumeration, so we use this operator.

```
today = DaysOfWeek.Tuesday;
```

This works like any other variable, even for things like comparison in an **if** statement:

```
DaysOfWeek today = DaysOfWeek.Sunday;

if(today == DaysOfWeek.Sunday)
{
    // ...
}
```

Why Enumerations are Useful

There's a very good reason to use enumerations. Let's go back to where we first started this chapter—doing days of the week with the **int** type. Remember how we had defined **dayOfWeek = 3;** which meant Tuesday? What if someone put **dayOfWeek = 17;**? As far as the computer knows, this should be valid. After all, **dayOfWeek** is just an **int** variable. Why not allow it to be 17? But for what we're doing, 17 doesn't make any sense. We are only using 1 through 7.

Enumerations force the computer (and programmers) to use only specific, named ("enumerated") values. It prevents tons of errors, and makes your code more readable. For example, **dayOfWeek = DaysOfWeek.Sunday** is immediately clear what it means, while **dayOfWeek = 1** is not.

Underlying Types

Before moving on, it is worth looking at a couple of additional details about enumerations. Under the surface, C# is simply wrapping our enumeration around an *underlying type*. By default, this underlying type is the **int** type, though it is possible to choose a different integer type. Enumerations are, at their core, just numbers, though done in a way that ensures that only the *right* numbers can be used. When you create an enumeration, each item you list is assigned a number, starting at 0. In the enumeration that we created, Sunday has a value of 0, Monday is 1, and so on.

This means that you can cast to and from an **int** like this:

```
int dayAsInt = (int)DaysOfWeek.Sunday;
DaysOfWeek today = (DaysOfWeek)dayAsInt;    // Both of these require an explicit cast.
```

By default, enumerations make sure that only *valid* values are used. However, if you use an explicit cast to convert an invalid number to an enumeration, you can break this:

```
DaysOfWeek today = (DaysOfWeek)17; // Legal, but a bad idea...
```

Because of this, you should be very cautious about casting to an enumeration type.

Assigning Numbers to Enumeration Values

When you create an enumeration, you can additionally assign it specific values if you want:

```
enum DaysOfWeek { Sunday=5, Monday=6, Tuesday=7, Wednesday=8, Thursday=9, Friday=10, Saturday=11 };
```

> **Try It Out!**
> **Months of the Year.** Using the **DaysOfWeek** enumeration as an example, create an enumeration to represent the months of the year. Assign them the values 1 through 12. Write a program to ask the user for a number between 1 and 12. Check to be sure that they gave you a value in the right range and use an explicit cast to convert the number to your month enumeration. Then, using a **switch** statement or **if** statement to print out the full name of the month they entered.

Methods

In a Nutshell
- Methods are a way of creating a chunk of reusable code.
- You can return stuff from a method by putting the return type in the method definition, and then using the **return** keyword inside of the method anywhere you want to return a value.
- Parameters are passed to a method by listing them in parentheses after the method's name.
- Methods can share the same name ("overloading") as long as their signatures are different.
- Recursion is where you call a method from inside itself, and requires a base case to prevent the flow of execution from continuing into deeper and deeper method calls.

Think about how much code goes into a program like *Microsoft Word* or a game like the latest *Assassin's Creed*. They're enormous! Especially when compared to the little programs that we've been making so far.

How do you think you could manage all of that code? Where would you look if there was a bug?

As programmers, we've learned that when you have a large program, the best way to manage it is by breaking it down into smaller, more manageable pieces. This even gives us the ability to reuse these pieces. This basic concept of breaking things down into smaller pieces is called *divide and conquer*, and it is one we'll see over and over again.

C# provides us with a feature that allows us to break down our program into small manageable pieces. These small, reusable building blocks of code are called *methods*. Methods are sometimes called *functions*, *subroutines*, or *procedures* in other programming languages.

The concept of a method is to take a piece of your code and place it inside of a special block and give it a name, allowing you to run it from anywhere else in your program. We can re-run ("invoke" or "call") a method as many times as we want, which means we don't have to retype it, saving ourselves time.

In this chapter, we'll look at how to create and use methods, as well as how to get data to and from a method. We'll also look at *overloading* methods, which is giving two or more methods the same name. We'll then revisit the **Console** and **Convert** classes from earlier chapters, armed with the new knowledge we have about methods. We'll wrap up our discussion about methods with a quick look at a powerful (but sometimes confusing) trick that you can use with methods called *recursion*.

Creating a Method

Let's get started by creating our first method. If you start with a brand new project, you'll start with code that looks like this:

```csharp
using System;
using System.Collections.Generic;
using System.Linq;
using System.Text;
using System.Threading.Tasks;

namespace Methods
{
    public class Program
    {
        static void Main(string[] args)
        {
        }
    }
}
```

If you remember from the Hello World program we made back in Chapter 3, this template code already defines a method (the **Main** method) for us. At the time, we only had a basic idea of what a method was, but we know more now. You can see from the template code that the **Main** method is contained inside of a class called **Program**. (We're still getting to classes.) When it comes down to it, we've already been using a method, without even really thinking about it.

All methods belong to a type. A class is one specific example of a type. Most of the types we create will be classes, but methods can belong to the handful of other types that we will look at over the course of this book. Because the method belongs to the class, it is a *member* of that class.

When we create a method, we need to place it inside of a type. They can't just be floating around on their own. For now, we've already got the **Program** class where our **Main** method is, which is a perfect spot for our new methods.

So let's go ahead and make our first method. Let's make a method that simply prints out the numbers 1 through 10. This new method looks like the following:

```csharp
static void CountToTen()
{
    for(int index = 1; index <= 10; index++)
        Console.WriteLine(index);
}
```

Placing this in the rest of our program might look like this:

```csharp
using System;
using System.Collections.Generic;
using System.Linq;
using System.Text;
using System.Threading.Tasks;

namespace Methods
{
    public class Program
    {
        static void Main(string[] args)
        {
        }

        static void CountToTen()
        {
```

```
            for (int index = 1; index <= 10; index++)
                Console.WriteLine(index);
        }
    }
}
```

This code won't do anything yet. Remember, our program will run everything in the **Main** method by default, and we have nothing in the **Main** method for the time being. Before we're done, we'll need to have our **Main** method "call" our newly created **CountToTen()** method, but we'll do that in a second. First, let's discuss the piece of code that we've just added.

There are just a few pieces in play here. The first piece is the **static** keyword. We'll talk about this a little more when we start creating our own classes. (See Chapter 18.) For now, we'll assume that it's just needed for what we're doing.

The second thing we added is the keyword **void**. We'll talk more about this in a second, when we discuss returning stuff from a method, but basically, the **void** keyword tells us our method doesn't produce any results.

The next part is the method's name: **CountToTen**. Like with variables, you can name your method all sorts of things. Giving methods descriptive names will make it easier to explain what it does. While it is not required, the standard convention in C# is to have method names start with an upper case letter, while variables usually start with a lower case letter.

Next we have the parentheses. Right now, there's nothing inside of our parentheses, but we'll soon see that we can put stuff in here, allowing us to hand stuff off to a method.

Lastly, we have a set of curly braces where we put the *body* or *implementation* of the method. This is where we put the code that the method executes when called. Up until now, we have been putting all of our code in the body of the **Main** method. As of this chapter, we'll start putting our code in the body of different methods to organize our code into separate, reusable tasks.

We can see that in the body of our method, we have a simple **for** loop. Any of the code that we've written before can go inside of a method, including loops, **if** statements, math, and variable declarations.

The order that methods appear within a class doesn't matter. In the example above, we could have put **CountToTen** above **Main** and it wouldn't have made a difference. The C# compiler is smart enough to scan through your file and find all of the methods that exist in it.

Calling a Method

Now that we've got our method created, we want to be able to use it. Doing this is really easy. Inside of your **Main** method, you do the following:

```
CountToTen();
```

So your complete code would look like this:

```
using System;
using System.Collections.Generic;
using System.Linq;
using System.Text;

namespace Methods
{
    public class Program
    {
        static void Main(string[] args)
        {
```

```
            CountToTen();
        }

        static void CountToTen()
        {
            for (int index = 1; index <= 10; index++)
                Console.WriteLine(index);
        }
    }
}
```

Now you can run your program (which automatically starts in the **Main** method) and see that it jumps over to the **CountToTen** method and does everything inside of it. When it reaches the end of a method, it goes back to where it came from. So looking at this code:

```
using System;
using System.Collections.Generic;
using System.Linq;
using System.Text;

namespace Methods
{
    public class Program
    {
        static void Main(string[] args)
        {
            Console.WriteLine("I'm about to go into a method.");

            DoSomethingAwesome();

            Console.WriteLine("I'm back from the method.");
        }

        static void DoSomethingAwesome()
        {
            Console.WriteLine("I'm inside of a method! Awesome!");
        }
    }
}
```

This will result in the following output:

```
I'm about to go into a method.
I'm inside of a method! Awesome!
I'm back from the method.
```

It is also worth mentioning that you can call a method from inside of any other method, so you can go crazy creating and calling methods all over in your program. (In fact, that's essentially what software engineering is! Creating and calling methods in a way that minimizes the craziness.)

Returning Stuff from a Method

Methods are created to do some specific task. Often, that task involves figuring something out, and we want to be able to know the results. A method has the option of giving something back. (How generous of them!) This is called *returning* something. (Even if it doesn't return anything, like the first method we wrote a second ago, people still talk about "returning from a method.")

So far, all of the methods we've looked at haven't returned anything. We've always been using the **void** keyword. This means that the method doesn't return anything. By changing that, our method can return something. To do this, instead of the **void** keyword, we simply place a different type there, like **int**, **float**, or **string**. This makes it so our method can (and must) return a value of that particular type.

Then inside of the method, we use the **return** keyword to return a specific value. This is followed by the value we want to return. A very simple example of returning a value is this:

```
static float GetRandomNumber()
{
    return 4.385f; // Obviously very random.
}
```

You can see that we start off by stating the return type (**float** in this case, meaning we're going to return something of the type **float**), and inside of the method, we simply use the **return** keyword, along with the actual value we want to return. Obviously, this is not a very useful example, but it illustrates the point.

Let's do something more practical. In this book, there have been many times that we've done things like ask the user to type in a number. The code below creates a method that asks the user for a number between 1 and 10, and keeps asking until they finally give us something that works. At that point, we'll return the number the user gave us.

```
static int GetNumberFromUser()
{
    int usersNumber = 0;

    while(usersNumber < 1 || usersNumber > 10)
    {
        Console.Write("Enter a number between 1 and 10: ");
        string usersResponse = Console.ReadLine();
        usersNumber = Convert.ToInt32(usersResponse);
    }

    return usersNumber;
}
```

If your method returns nothing (**void**), you don't need a **return** statement. But if it *does* return something, we're required to have a **return** statement.

If a method returns something, we can grab the value returned by the method and do something with it, like put it in a variable or do some math with it. For instance, the code below will take the value that is returned by the **GetNumberFromUser** method and store it in a variable:

```
int usersNumber = GetNumberFromUser();
```

As it turns out, we've been doing stuff like that all along! But now we can better understand what's going on. For instance, when we've written things like **string usersResponse = Console.ReadLine();**, we're just calling a method (**ReadLine**) that belongs to the **Console** class and getting the value returned by it!

While the **return** statement is often the last line in a method, it doesn't have to be. For instance, you can have an **if** statement in the middle of a method that returns "early" before the end of the method:

```
static int CalculatePlayerScore()
{
    int livesLeft = 3;
    int underlingsDestroyed = 17;
    int minionsDestroyed = 4;
    int bossesDestroyed = 1;

    // If the player is out of lives, they lose all of their points.
    if(livesLeft == 0)
        return 0;

    // Otherwise, the player gets 10 points per underling destroyed, 100 points
    // per minion, and 1000 points per boss.
    return underlingsDestroyed*10 + minionsDestroyed*100 +  bossesDestroyed*1000;
}
```

If your method's return type is **void**, you don't *need* the **return** keyword anywhere, but it can still be used alone to return early:

```
static void DoSomething()
{
    int aNumber = 1;

    if(aNumber == 2)
        return;

    Console.WriteLine("This only gets printed if the 'return' statement wasn't executed.");
}
```

As soon as a **return** statement is hit, the flow of execution *immediately* goes back to where the method was called from—nothing more gets executed in the method.

You can't make the return type of a method be **var**. You must always explicitly state the type.

Passing Stuff to a Method

Sometimes, we want a method to do stuff with certain pieces of information. We can hand stuff off to a method by putting what we want it to work with inside of the parentheses. Earlier, we made a method that was called **CountToTen**, which simply printed out the numbers 1 through 10. We can create an alternate method that requires you to supply a number to count to. The method could then be used to count to 10, 25, 1000, or anything else.

To do this, we need a way to hand off information for the method to use. This is done by putting a list of variables inside of the parentheses when we're defining the method. Our modified version of the **CountToTen** method, which works for any number, might look like this:

```
static void Count(int numberToCountTo)
{
    for(int current = 1; current <= numberToCountTo; current++)
        Console.WriteLine(current);
}
```

Where you define the method, you identify the variable's type and give it a name to use throughout the method. This particular kind of variable is called a *parameter*. The variable **numberToCountTo** is a parameter.

When you call a method that has a parameter, you "pass in" or hand off a value to the method by putting it in the parentheses:

```
Count(5);
Count(15);
```

This code, in conjunction with the example before it, will first print out the numbers 1 through 5, and then it will print out the numbers 1 through 15.

Like with the return value, a parameter must have an explicit type. You cannot use **var**.

Passing in Multiple Parameters

You can also create a method that passes in multiple parameters. All of the parameters listed—everything inside of the parentheses—is called the *parameter list*. The code below is a simple example of passing two numbers into a **Multiply** method that multiplies them together, and returns the result:

```
static int Multiply(int a, int b)
{
```

```
     return a * b;
}
```

Having multiple parameters like this is extremely common. There's a technical limit to how many parameters you can have (just over 65,500) but the practical limit is far lower. Most programmers will start complaining about the number of parameters a method has well before you even reach 10. If you need that many parameters, you should spend some time trying to come up with an approach that lets you break the task down into smaller tasks, where each task requires fewer pieces of data to work on.

Try It Out!

Reversing an Array. Let's make a program that uses methods to accomplish a task. Let's take an array and reverse the contents of it. For example, if you have 1, 2, 3, 4, 5, 6, 7, 8, 9, 10, it would become 10, 9, 8, 7, 6, 5, 4, 3, 2, 1.

To accomplish this, you'll create three methods: one to create the array, one to reverse the array, and one to print the array at the end.

Your **Main** method will look something like this:

```
static void Main(string[] args)
{
    int[] numbers = GenerateNumbers();
    Reverse(numbers);
    PrintNumbers(numbers);
}
```

The **GenerateNumbers** method should return an array of 10 numbers. (For bonus points, change the method to allow the desired length to be passed in, instead of just always being 10.)

The **PrintNumbers** method should use a **for** or **foreach** loop to print out each item in the array.

The **Reverse** method will be the hardest. Give it a try and see what you can make happen. If you get stuck, here's a couple of hints:

Hint #1: To swap two values, you will need to place the value of one variable in a temporary location to make the swap:

```
// Swapping a and b.
int a = 3;
int b = 5;

int temp = a;
a = b;
b = temp;
```

Hint #2: Getting the right indices to swap can be a challenge. Use a **for** loop, starting at 0 and going up to the length of the array / 2. The number you use in the **for** loop will be the index of the first number to swap, and the other one will be the length of the array minus the index minus 1. This is to account for the fact that the array is 0-based. So basically, you'll be swapping **array[index]** with **array[arrayLength – index – 1]**.

Method Overloading

One cool, but potentially confusing thing that you can do with methods is create multiple methods with the same name. This is called *method overloading* or simply *overloading*.

While two methods can have the same name, they can't have the same *signature*. A method's signature is defined as the combination of the method name and the types and order of the parameters that get passed in. Note that this does *not* include the parameters' names, just their types.

To help illustrate what a method signature is, take the following example:

```
static int Multiply(int a, int b)
{
    return a * b;
}
```

This has a signature that looks like this: **Multiply(int, int)**.

You can only overload a method if you use a different signature. So for example, the following works:

```
static int Multiply(int a, int b)
{
    return a * b;
}

static int Multiply(int a, int b, int c)
{
    return a * b * c;
}
```

This works because the two multiply methods have a different number of parameters, and as a result, a different signature. We could also define a **Multiply** method that has no parameters (**int Multiply()**), or one parameter (**int Multiply(int)**), though in this particular case, I can't imagine how either of those two methods would do multiplication with zero or one thing. (Hey, it's just an example!) Likewise, you could define a **Multiply** method with eight or ten parameters, if there was a need for it.

Also, you can have the same number of parameters, if their types are different:

```
static int Multiply(int a, int b)
{
    return a * b;
}

static double Multiply(double a, double b)
{
    return a * b;
}
```

This works because the two **Multiply** methods each have their own signature (**Multiply(int, int)** and **Multiply(double, double)**).

The following does not work:

```
static int Multiply(int a, int b)
{
    return a * b;
}

static int Multiply(int c, int d) // This won't work. It has the same signature.
{
    return c * d;
}
```

The magic of method overloading is that you can have many methods that do very similar work on different types of data (like the **int** multiplication and the **double** multiplication above) without needing a completely different method name. With different signatures, the C# compiler can easily determine which of the overloaded methods to use.

You should only overload methods when you are trying to do the exact same kind of thing with different kinds of data. If two methods have the same name, they should perform essentially the same task. If you know what one does, it should be obvious what the other does, even if it uses slightly different data. If that's not the case, you should use a different method name altogether to avoid confusion.

Revisiting the Convert and Console Classes

With a basic understanding of how methods work in C#, it is worth a second discussion about some of the classes that we've already been using. For instance, in the **Console** class, we've done things like this:

```
Console.WriteLine("Hello World!");
```

With our new knowledge of methods, we can see that there is a **Console** class, which has a method named **WriteLine** that we call. The **WriteLine** method has one parameter, which is a **string**. We pass in the string "Hello World!" and the method runs off and does its job.

This is a perfect example of *why* we use methods. Because someone already made a **WriteLine** method that writes stuff to the console window, we don't need to write it ourselves, nor do we need to worry about how it actually goes about its job. All we care about is that it does it, and that it is easy to use. This frees us up to worry about the more unique or interesting parts of our programs.

We see similar things with the **Convert** class, which we have used several times as well:

```
int number = Convert.ToInt32("42");
```

The **Convert** class has a ton of methods that let you convert many types to other types. In the example above, we see a method called **ToInt32**, which takes a **string** as a parameter. This class uses method overloading extensively, because it has a **ToInt32** method that takes a **string**, one that takes a **double**, one that takes a **short**, and so on.

XML Documentation Comments

In Chapter 4, we introduced the idea of comments. I mentioned that there is one additional way to do comments that we couldn't really talk about back then. We're ready to discuss it here.

It is a good idea to add a comment by a method to describe what it does. This way, when you or somebody else wants to use it, they can easily figure out what it does, and how to make it work. This is especially important because methods are *designed* to be reused.

You can add comments to a method using any of the methods we discussed in Chapter 4, but there is one additional way that works really well if you are trying to describe what a method does. (By the way, this also applies to classes, structs, enumerations, and other things that we'll discuss shortly.) This additional way is called XML documentation comments.

Let's say you have a **Multiply** method like we were talking about a second ago:

```
public static int Multiply(int a, int b)
{
    return a * b;
}
```

To add XML documentation comments, go just above the method, and type three forward slashes: ///

As soon as you hit that third forward slash, Visual Studio will pop in a big comment that looks like this:

```
/// <summary>
///
/// </summary>
```

```
/// <param name="a"></param>
/// <param name="b"></param>
/// <returns></returns>
```

This is your XML documentation comment. In between the **<summary>** and **</summary>** lines, you can add a description of what the method does. In between the **param** tags, you can describe what each parameter of your method does, and in the **returns** tags, you can add what the return value should be. A completely filled in example of this might look like this:

```
/// <summary>
/// Takes two numbers and multiplies them together, returning the result.
/// </summary>
/// <param name="a">The first number to multiply</param>
/// <param name="b">The second number to multiply</param>
/// <returns>The product of the two input numbers</returns>
```

The nice thing about adding in an XML documentation comment is that Visual Studio's IntelliSense will immediately start showing it as we work on our code (Chapter 45).

The Minimum You Need to Know About Recursion

There's one additional trick people use with methods that I think is worth bringing up here. It's kind of a complicated trick, so right now you don't need to master it. But it is worth mentioning, so you know what it is when it comes up, and so you can start thinking about how it might be useful.

The trick is called *recursion*, and it is where you call a method from inside itself. Here's a trivial example (which happens to break when you run it):

```
static void MethodThatUsesRecursion()
{
    MethodThatUsesRecursion();
}
```

This example is going to break on you because it just keeps going into deeper and deeper method calls. Eventually, it will run out of memory to make more method calls, and the program will crash.

The problem with this first example, is that there is no *base case*. Recursion always needs a state where it doesn't call itself again, and each time it calls itself, it should be getting closer and closer to that base case. If not, it will never get to a point where it is done, and can start returning from the method calls back up to the starting point.

One of the classic examples of when you could use recursion is the mathematical factorial function. Perhaps you remember from math classes that factorial, written as an exclamation mark by a number, means to take it and multiply it by all smaller numbers. For example, **7!** means **7 * 6 * 5 * 4 * 3 * 2 * 1**.

72! would be **72 * 71 * 70 * 69 * ... * 3 * 2 * 1**. (With factorial, by the way, you really quickly run into the overflow issues that we were talking about back in Chapter 9.)

In this case, we know that **1!** is **1**. This can serve as a base case. The factorial of any other number can be thought of as the number multiplied by the factorial of the number smaller than it. **7!** is the same as **7 * 6!**.

This sets up a great opportunity for recursion:

```
static int Factorial(int number)
{
    // We establish our "base case" here. When we get to this point, we're done.
    if(number == 1)
        return 1;
```

```
    return number * Factorial(number - 1);
}
```

Try It Out!

The Fibonacci Sequence. If you're up for a good challenge involving recursion, try out this challenge. The Fibonacci sequence is a sequence of numbers where the first two numbers are 1 and 1, and every other number in the sequence after it is the sum of the two numbers before it. So the third number is 1 + 1, which is 2. The fourth number is the 2nd number plus the 3rd, which is 1 + 2. So the fourth number is 3. The 5th number is the 3rd number plus the 4th number: 2 + 3 = 5. This keeps going forever.

The first few numbers of the Fibonacci sequence are: 1, 1, 2, 3, 5, 8, 13, 21, 34, 55, ...

Because one number is defined by the numbers before it, this sets up a perfect opportunity for using recursion.

Your mission, should you choose to accept it, is to create a method called **Fibonacci**, which takes in a number and returns that number of the Fibonacci sequence. So if someone calls **Fibonacci(3)**, it would return the 3rd number in the Fibonacci sequence, which is 2. If someone calls **Fibonacci(8)**, it would return 21.

In your **Main** method, write code to loop through the first 10 numbers of the Fibonacci sequence and print them out.

Hint #1: Start with your base case. We know that if it is the 1st or 2nd number, the value will be 1.

Hint #2: For every other item, how is it defined in terms of the numbers before it? Can you come up with an equation or formula that calls the **Fibonacci** method again?

16

Value and Reference Types

In a Nutshell
- Your program's memory is divided into several sections including the stack and the heap.
- The stack is used to keep track of your program's state and local variables.
- The heap is used to store data that is accessible anytime from anywhere.
- The CLR manages memory in the heap for you. It cleans up dead memory using garbage collection.
- Value types store their data directly inside of the variable. Reference types store a reference to a location in the heap, where the rest of the data is stored.
- Value types have value semantics, which means that when you assign one variable the contents of another, the entire contents of the variable are copied, so you get a complete copy in the other variable. Reference types have reference semantics, which means when you assign one variable to another, only the reference is copied, and the two are referencing the same object. Changes to one affects the other.

We're going to change gears a little and spend a chapter in pure learning mode, instead of coding mode. We're going to discuss a few topics that are going to be important to understanding types and how classes work. This chapter is probably the most technical chapter in the book, but trust me when I say it is both important and useful.

The Stack and the Heap

When your program first starts, the operating system gives it a pile of memory for it to work with. Your program splits that up into several areas that it uses for different things, but most of it is used by two sections for storing data as your program runs. These two sections are the *stack* and the *heap*. The stack and the heap are used for slightly different things, and they're organized in different ways.

The stack is used to keep track of the current state of the program, including all of the local variables that you have. The stack behaves like a stack of containers. Whenever we enter a method, we place a new container on the top of the stack. These containers on the stack are called *frames*. All of the local variables (including parameters) for a particular method go in a single frame.

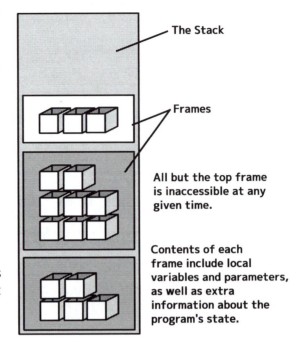

The Stack

Frames

All but the top frame is inaccessible at any given time.

Contents of each frame include local variables and parameters, as well as extra information about the program's state.

Additionally, a frame will include information to keep track of the program's current state of execution, like what line of code the program was at just before entering the new method. In fact, one of the primary purposes of the stack is to keep track of the program's current state of execution.

Like with a stack of containers, you can readily access the contents of the frame on the top of the stack, but you can't really get to the containers lower down. When we return from a method, the top frame is taken off the stack and discarded, and we go back down to the frame beneath it.

Interestingly, the debugger that is built into Visual Studio *can* inspect the entire stack, including the buried frames, and show them to you. (This is called a *stack trace*.)

The heap, on the other hand, is not concerned at all about keeping track of the program's state. Instead, it is only focused on storing data. The heap is organized in a way where it is easy to get access to things any time you need. It's easy for the program to grab some space in the heap and start using it to store the information it needs. There's not necessarily any logical organization to what gets stored where on the heap, so it is easy to think of it as just a pile of individual blocks of data.

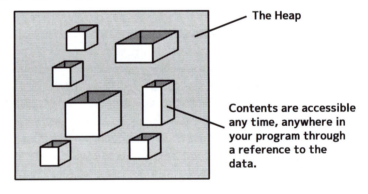

The Heap

Contents are accessible any time, anywhere in your program through a reference to the data.

If you have a multi-threaded application (Chapter 39) each thread will have its own stack, but all threads in the program will share the same heap.

Memory Management and Garbage Collection

A program needs to manage the memory it is using. In particular, it needs to clean up old memory that is no longer being used. For the stack, this is easy. Any time it returns from a method, it knows it can throw the top frame away and reuse that space immediately.

The heap is a little more complicated. Back in the day, when you put stuff in the heap, you needed to remember it, and when you were done using it you had to tell the computer you were done with it. This would allow you to reuse that space again.

If you were putting something on the heap for just a moment, and then getting rid of it right after, this was easy to do. But this was not so simple when what you were putting on the heap needed to stay there a while before being cleaned up. It was very easy to forget that it was even there, and even if you remembered, it was usually all too easy to fail to free that memory correctly. You'd end up with garbage in the heap that you no longer wanted, but the computer didn't know it could reuse. This is called a memory leak, and if you had one (or many) then your program was eventually going to run out of space and die.

Fortunately for us, C# uses an approach where the .NET Platform manages your heap's memory for you. If you're starting to run low on memory for your program, a part of the .NET Platform called the *garbage collector* will run through and get rid of any old, unused stuff on your heap, freeing it up to be reused. If you've never had to manage your own program's memory, it may be hard to see this, but garbage collection is a huge deal, and it saves you lots of time, worry, and customer complaints.

References

Since data on the heap is sort of scattered about rather than structured like the stack is, you will need a way to keep track of the variable or data you are interested in.

Outside of C#'s automatic memory management, you would access things in the heap using a *pointer*, which is special variable type that stores a memory address in the heap, rather than the actual data. You can then use this memory address to hunt down the data you want from the heap as needed.

With C#, the heap's memory is managed for you. This "managed"-ness primarily means two things to you. First, when objects on the heap are no longer in use (nothing in your program can reach it anymore) the runtime's garbage collector will automatically free up the memory for you. Second, the garbage collector will move things around from one memory location to another to keep things organized and ensure that there are always large, contiguous blocks of memory available for the next memory allocation.

Because the garbage collector can move stuff around on you, pointers containing a raw memory address won't work for you. The data may get moved to a different memory location without you even knowing.

Instead, C# uses a thing called a *reference*, which is conceptually similar to a pointer, but the reference to the data is also maintained for you by the garbage collector. Even when data gets moved around in memory, the reference will still be able to get you to the data you want.

It is helpful to think of a reference as an arrow pointing you to a specific item or variable within the heap. But technically speaking, references are more of a unique identifier that tells the computer where to find the rest of the data within the heap.

Value Types and Reference Types

In C#, all types are divided into two broad categories: value types and reference types. With our discussion on the stack vs. the heap, and what we now know about references, we're ready to dig into the difference between these two. This is one of the biggest stumbling blocks or misunderstandings for both new programmers and experienced programmers, so take the time to make sure you understand how these two different categories of types work.

Value and reference types are one of the biggest things that make C# stand out from C++, Java, and other programming languages, which do things in a completely different way.

Here is the key difference: with a value type, the actual contents of the variable live where the variable lives. With a reference type, the contents of the variable live on the heap, and the variable itself contains only a reference to the actual content.

Go back and read that last paragraph again a time or two to make sure you understand it.

It turns out we have already been using both value and reference types. The **string** type is a reference type, and arrays are references as well (though the contents of the array can be either reference or value types). All of the simple types that we've discussed before, as well as enumerations (Chapter 14) are all value types.

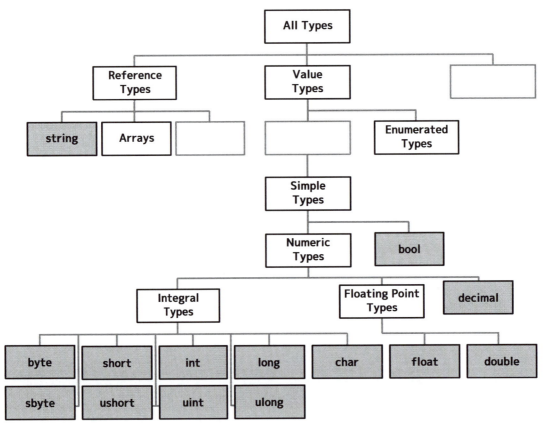

As we get started with Part 3 of this book, we're going to learn how you can create your own custom value or reference types, and finish filling in our type system diagram.

Let's pick this apart a little more and get into some details and examples. We'll start with reference types. Look at the following code:

```
string message = "Hello!";
```

Since the **string** type is a reference type, the actual "Hello!" text will always be stored in the heap, and the **message** variable will simply contain a reference to that text. As a local variable or parameter, the **message** variable will be stored on the stack somewhere, and contain a reference to that actual text on the heap.

Depending on how things are set up, reference type variables can also live on the heap, so you could have references from one part of the heap pointing to other parts of the heap. This would be the case if you have an array of **string**s, both of which are reference types. For instance, look at the following:

```
string[] messages = new string[3] { "Hello", "World", "!" };
```

This might look like this:

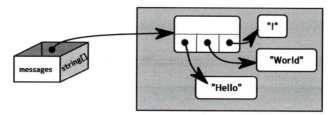

A local **messages** variable on the stack has a reference to the **string** array, but that actual array lives on the heap. Within that array, each item contains another reference to other parts of the heap—the **string**s that go in the array in this case. Taking this further, it is entirely possible to have huge networks of references spread throughout the heap.

On the other hand, value types are stored entirely at the place that the variable exists. If they're local variables or parameters, this means they're stored entirely on the stack. We've seen this with nearly all of the built-in types that we've been working with so far, like **int** and **double**. The variable doesn't contain a reference, just the actual value.

This still holds true, even when the value type is defined on the heap. Value typed variables will always contain their data right there where the variable is at. Arrays give us a great example of how this works. Let's say you had an array of value types, like this: **int[] numbers = new int[3] { 2, 3, 4 };**. This would end up looking something like this:

Note that the items in the array don't point to elsewhere like they did with our **string** array earlier. The numbers exist right where the variable exists.

That covers the basics of *how* value and reference types work. In a minute, we'll come back and take a look at what that means for us, when we talk about value and reference semantics. But first, a little bit of a detour to cover something else that we need to know about reference types.

Null: References to Nothing

One interesting thing about reference types is that you can have them reference nothing at all. This is called a *null reference*. Assigning a reference type a value of null can be done with the **null** keyword:

```
string message = null;
int[] numbers = new int[] { 2, 4, 6, 8 };
numbers = null;
```

With the middle line, we create a new array, which is placed on the heap, and then we immediately reassign **numbers** to **null**. At this point, the **numbers** variable isn't referencing that array anymore, and since nothing else is referencing it either, it has become inaccessible, and isolated on the heap. Because it is inaccessible, eventually it will be garbage collected.

If a reference type has a value of **null**, it means there's no data at the other end. If you inadvertently try to actually do something with it, your program is going to crash:

```
int[] numbers = null;
numbers[3] = 6;        // This crashes, since numbers doesn't reference anything.
```

To address this, you can do a simple check to see if a reference type is **null** first:

```
if(numbers != null)
    numbers[3] = 6;
```

Value types cannot be assigned a value of **null**.

Checking for null is incredibly common. While the approach above covers you in all cases, C# 6 introduced a new pair of operators that allow you to check for null using much more concise syntax. For more information on this other syntax, see the section called *Simple Null Checks: Null Propagation Operators* in Chapter 43.

Value and Reference Semantics

If the only difference between value and reference types was whether they stored their data "on site" or off elsewhere in the heap, I wouldn't normally worry about that kind of detail for an introductory book like this. However, there's more to it. Because of this difference, we get different behavior.

Reference types have what's called *reference semantics*, and value types have *value semantics* or *copy semantics*. Let's compare these two with an example, using the **int** type (a value type) and an array of **int**s (the array is a reference type, even though it contains things that are value types). Let's say you have the following code:

```
int a = 3;
int b = a;
b++;
```

We've created two variables with the **int** type. We place the value 3 inside **a**. We then assign the contents of **a** to **b**. Doing this means reading the contents of **a** (which is 3) and putting that value into **b**. Next, we modify **b** by incrementing it so **b** is now 4. But **a** is still the original value of 3. When we assign the contents of **a** to **b**, we made a new copy for **b**. Whatever happens with the **b** variable won't affect the original **a** variable.

Interestingly, the exact same thing happens with reference types, but because the variable contains only a reference instead of the actual value, we get different behavior entirely. Take a look at this example:

```
int[] a = new int[] { 1, 2, 3 };
int[] b = a;
b[0] = 17;
Console.WriteLine(a[0]); // This will print out 17.
```

When we create our array, the entire contents of the array are placed in the heap. While **a** may be stored on the stack, it will contain a reference to the array out in the heap. When we assign the value of **a** to the variable **b**, we read the value from **a**, which is a reference, and copy it into **b**. But copying a reference gives **b** a reference to the same object on the heap. At this point, both of our variables are referencing the same array in the heap. We then modify that array by going through the **b** variable, but since the two things reference the same memory location in the heap, **a** has been modified as well.

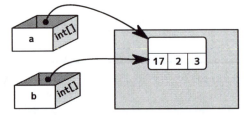

This same thing happens as you send things to methods as parameters. For value types, the value is copied over to the parameter. Inside the method, we have a copy of the data. Changing the variable there won't affect the original, back in the calling method.

With reference types, while you're still technically passing a copy of the variable's contents, it is a copy of a reference, so inside of the method, the parameter is referencing the exact same thing on the heap. Making changes to it inside of the method affects the thing back in the calling method.

This is often done intentionally, handing an array or other reference type to a method with the specific task of modifying it in some way. But of course, if you hand a reference type to a method, expecting it to remain unchanged, and the method makes changes, you'll be in for a surprise.

This can be a useful thing or a liability, but it *is* a fact. You have to understand the differences between value types and reference types, or it will come back to haunt you repeatedly. Surprisingly, there are a lot of talented programmers who claim to know C# that haven't figured this heap vs. stack and value vs. reference type stuff yet. If you don't understand these differences, you will be constantly running into strange problems that just don't seem to make sense.

Try It Out!

Value and Reference Types Quiz. Answer the following questions to check your understanding. When you're done, check your answers against the ones below. If you missed something, go back and review the section that talks about it.

1. **True/False.** Anything on the stack can be accessed at any time.
2. **True/False.** The stack keeps track of local variables.
3. **True/False.** The contents of a value type can be placed in the heap.
4. **True/False.** The contents of a value type are *always* placed in the heap.
5. **True/False.** The contents of reference types are *always* placed in the heap.
6. **True/False.** The garbage collector cleans up old, unused space on both the heap and stack.
7. **True/False.** You can assign **null** to value types.
8. **True/False.** If **a** and **b** are reference types, and both reference the same object, modifying **a** will affect **b** as well.
9. **True/False.** If **a** and **b** are value types with the same value, modifying **a** will affect **b** as well.

Answers: (1) False. **(2)** True. **(3)** True. **(4)** False. **(5)** True. **(6)** False. **(7)** False. **(8)** True. **(9)** False.

Part 3

Object-Oriented Programming

C# is an object-oriented programming language, meaning that the code we write is typically organized into little blocks that are modeled after real-world objects. We define what kind of data those objects have and what those objects can do.

The object-oriented aspect of C# is a key part of the language. Without knowing how to create and use classes, our understanding of the language is far from complete.

Part 3 is all about designing and building your own types in C#. Building your own reusable types and assembling them together is how you'll be able to make truly amazing software.

We'll dig straight to the heart of object-oriented programming. We'll look at the following:

- Introduce what object-oriented programming is about (Chapter 17).
- Discuss how to make your own classes (Chapter 18) and structs (Chapter 21).
- Create easy access to data in your own custom types with properties (Chapter 19).
- A single chapter devoted to a large Try It Out problem: Tic-Tac-Toe (Chapter 20).
- Make classes that are special types of other classes with inheritance (Chapter 22).
- Making special types that can do the same tasks in their own way (Chapters 23 and 24).
- Make generic types (Chapters 25 and 26).

Object-Oriented Basics

In a Nutshell
- Object-oriented programming is a programming style where you create chunks of code that are modeled after real world objects.
- Classes in C# define what an entire "class" of objects can do (what all players can do, or what any car can do), including what kind of data it stores and the tasks that it can do.
- Classes are reference types.
- Creating a class is the most powerful way C# has of defining your own new types.
- You can create a new object with something like this: **Random random = new Random();**. This creates a new **Random** object, which is used to generate random numbers.

We've worked with a lot of different types so far: **int**, **string**, arrays, etc. We even learned how to define our own simple enumeration types. The next step in our journey is to begin to work with and make our own custom types from scratch. Custom types are defined by assembling data that defines the information that the type has, as well as methods that operate on that data. These custom-made types form the fundamental building block of "object-oriented programming." This chapter will primarily focus on concepts of this important programming style, and get us some practice with using classes and objects. We'll begin making our own class types in the next chapter.

Object Classes and Object Instances

Over the many years that people have been programming, we've come to learn that one of the best ways to structure code is to mimic the way the real world works. It helps to break things down into manageable pieces, and presents an intuitive way for programmers to work with their code. This concept of making our code mimic real-world objects is called *object-oriented programming*.

Read that last paragraph again. It's important.

In object-oriented programming, there are two ways of thinking about the objects that exist. The first is to think in terms of categories or types of objects. For example, in the real world, we have houses, and cars, and planets. These are all general categories of objects. Or we could say that these are "classes" of objects.

Additionally, there are specific occurrences or "instances" of these object classes. This house, that house, the White House, and that weird house that is painted pink on the next block over.

Each category or class of objects have certain properties in common, or share certain functionality. For example, when talking about a house, we know all houses have a size or a color. Each specific house will have its own unique size measurement or color, but we know all houses will have a size measurement and a color of some sort.

Here is another example that might be more applicable in a game development scenario. An Asteroids clone needs to deal with asteroids. We know all asteroids in the game will have a position in the game world and a size. Each individual asteroid will have its own unique position and its own unique size. We can talk about asteroids in the general sense (the entire class of asteroid-type things) and we can also talk about specific asteroids. One over here is at (60, 121) and has a size of 15, and another one over here is at (542, 97) and has a size of 5.

With object-oriented programming, we can define a blueprint for a specific type or category of object by defining a *class*. This is a new, custom type that we make, similar to when we made our own enumeration types.

These class definitions allow us to specify what data a particular class of object has in common. If we were defining an **Asteroid** class for example, we would probably want to indicate that asteroids have a position and a size.

In addition to data, a class definition will also allow us to define behavior that all things that belong to the class can perform. Continuing with the Asteroids game theme, if we had a **Ship** class that represented what the player controlled, this might include the ability to **Fire** a bullet, or **Warp** to a different location. These behaviors are defined as methods (Chapter 15), and they can use and also modify the data that belongs to the class.

Based on a class definition, we can then create specific instances of the class within our programs. For example, our Asteroids clone could create a dozen different instances of the **Asteroid** class and different locations and with different sizes. And it could then create one or two **Ship** instances for a one or two player game. Each instance has its own position. Each ship can warp or fire separately from the others, but because all ships "belong to" the same Ship class or category, we know they all have the capability to fire or warp. Different instances of a class are independent of each other. They have their own set of data and asking them to perform an action or method is for a specific instance, rather than for the whole class of objects. But if two instances are of the same class, we know we can interact with them in the same way because they share the same blueprint.

People frequently use the term *instance* and *object* interchangeably to mean a specific occurrence, with its own unique data.

These two concepts—the idea that classes of objects share the same blueprint, and that unique instances of a certain type are independent of other instances of the same type but can be interacted with in the same way—form the foundation of object-oriented programming.

Working with an Existing Class

We will soon turn our attention to defining our own classes, but before we do, let's start by using a simple class that already exists: the **Random** class. The **Random** class lets you create random numbers. For example, you could use this class to simulate rolling dice, or to shuffle a deck.

> **In Depth**
>
> **Computers and Randomness.** Generally speaking, random numbers on a computer aren't truly random. They are actually chosen using an algorithm that simply *appears* random. They need to be initialized, starting with a number chosen by the programmer. This number is called a seed. If you start with the same seed, you will get the same sequence of random numbers, over and over again.
>
> Since the vast majority of the time, this is not something you want, programmers will often seed the random number generator with the current time, accurate to the millisecond. This makes it so that a different sequence is generated every time you run the program.
>
> The **Random** class that we're using here will automatically seed the random number generation with the current time, but you can also specify a seed if you would like.

We can use the **Random** class in a way that is very similar to any other type:

```
Random random = new Random();
```

In this case, we specify **Random** as our variable's type and give our variable a name (**random**). Like with any other variable, we can assign a value by using the assignment operator (=).

But after that, we'll see a couple of things that we haven't really seen. You can see the **new** keyword there. This tips us off to the fact that we're going to create a new instance of the **Random** class—an object with the **Random** type.

The **Random()** part might look like a method call to you, and it kind of is. In fact, it is a special kind of method called a *constructor*. A constructor is placed in a class and describes how to create or build a new instance of that type. This particular constructor has no parameters (hence the empty parentheses) but it is possible to have constructors with parameters, like any other method.

When that line is finished executing, our variable called **random** will contain a reference to a brand new instance with the type **Random**.

Using an Instance

Now that we have a working object, we can do stuff with it. If you remember, an object has state, and it has behaviors. In the specific case of the **Random** object we just created, internally, it is keeping track of its state, but it doesn't expose any of that to us.

So while we can't modify a **Random** object's state, we can use its behaviors, defined by its methods. A different type might expose some of its state and provide methods that allow us to request changes to that state (like our **Ship**'s **Fire** and **Warp** methods).

We can access our object's behaviors through the methods it has defined in it. For starters, there's the **Next** method. We call this method by using the dot operator ("."):

```
Random random = new Random();
int aRandomNumber = random.Next();
```

The dot operator is used for member access. In other words, to access something that belongs to something else. Here, we use it to say, "Look in **random** to find the method called **Next**." Things that belong to an object, like variables and methods, are called *members* of the type and are accessible with the dot operator.

The **Next** method is overloaded (Chapter 15), so there are multiple versions of the **Next** method, including one that lets us choose a range to use:

```
Random random = new Random();
int dieRoll = random.Next(6) + 1; // Add one, because Next(6) gives us 0 to 5.
```

The **Random** class also has a **NextDouble** method, which returns floating point numbers between 0 and 1. This allows you to do things like random probabilities and so on.

Once you have created an object like this, you can use any of its methods in any order, at any time.

Try It Out!

Die Rolling. Tons of games use dice. The **Random** class gives us the ability to simulate die rolling. Many games give the player the task of rolling multiple six-sided dice and adding up the results.

We're going to write a program that makes life easier for the player of a game like this. Start the program off by asking the player to type in a number of dice to roll. Create a new **Random** object and use the **Random.Next** method to simulate that many die rolls. Add the total up and print the result to the user. (You should only need one **Random** object for this.)

For bonus points, keep looping and handle new numbers until they enter "quit" or "exit."

The Power of Objects

Classes are a core part of object-oriented programming languages like C#. In fact, you could argue they are *the* core part. Classes and instances are the fundamental building blocks of programming in these languages. In C#, all of your code will belong to a particular class (or another custom-made type). In fact, all of the code we've been writing so far has been inside of a **Program** class! (Starting in the next chapter though, we're going to be building our own classes, and putting code elsewhere.)

Classes of objects and specific instances of objects are an idiom borrowed from the real world, which is something programmers have plenty of experience with. This idiom allows you to build large programs by breaking the sum total of the functionality down into smaller pieces that each do a very small subset of the total. By modeling pieces of your program after real-world objects or conceptual components to a solution, it becomes easier to see how a vast program made up of many small pieces is combined together in the right way to get the desired behavior.

Classes are Reference Types

Anything that is defined as a class is a reference type. This means that everything we learned in Chapter 16 about reference types applies to classes. For example, you can assign **null** to it:

```
Random random = null;
```

And two variables that are assigned the same reference *will* affect each other, because they use reference semantics:

```
Random random1 = new Random();
Random random2 = random1;
// random1 and random2 are actually referencing the same Random object now.
```

And like all reference types, this applies even as you pass the contents of a variable to a method as a parameter. If you pass an instance of a class to a method, the parameter inside of the method will reference the exact same instances as whatever was passed in. This means changing the object from inside of the method will affect variables that reference the same instance in the calling method, for better or worse.

```
public static void Main(string[] args)
{
    Random random = new Random();
    DoSomething(random);
}

public static void DoSomething(Random r)
{
    // The variable 'r' references the same instance as 'random' in Main. Two references, same instance.
    Console.WriteLine(r.Next());
}
```

Making Your Own Classes

In a Nutshell
- Classes typically go in their own file (though C# doesn't require it).
- Anything that is a part of a class (or other type) is called a member. This includes instance variables, methods, and constructors.
- Variables can be added to a class—these are called instance variables.
- You can add as many constructors to a class as you want.
- You can add methods to a class, which operate on the instance variables that the class has.
- A **private** method or instance variable is only visible from inside the class.
- A **public** method or instance variable can be seen from anywhere, inside or outside the class.
- This chapter also covers scope, name hiding, and the **this** keyword.

In the previous chapter we learned the basics of classes and instances. We'll now start to make our own classes in this chapter.

The ability to create your own classes is very important. As you write your own programs in C#, you will make many, many classes. That's because building your own classes allows you to break your whole program into manageable pieces that you can work with.

While we cover a lot of ground in this chapter, this is the end of the beginning. By the end of this chapter, you will know enough of the fundamentals to program in C#! While there is more to cover, it is possible to write almost any program you want after this chapter.

Creating a New Class

We're now ready to create our very first class. Remember from the last chapter that a class works as a blueprint for what an entire class or category of things can do and keep track of. Through this chapter, we'll create and use a simple **Book** class, which can be used to represent a book in a program.

While you are allowed to put multiple classes in a single file, it is a good idea to put each new class into its own file. This helps keep your files to a manageable size, and makes it easier to find things.

Our first step is to create a new file inside of our project. To do this, in the Solution Explorer, right-click on your project. The very top level item in the Solution Explorer is your *solution*, which is simply a collection of related projects. That's not the one you want. Your solution probably only has one project right now, and it likely has the same name as the solution. So in most cases, this means you'll be clicking on the second item in your Solution Explorer. After right-clicking, choose **Add > Class...**.

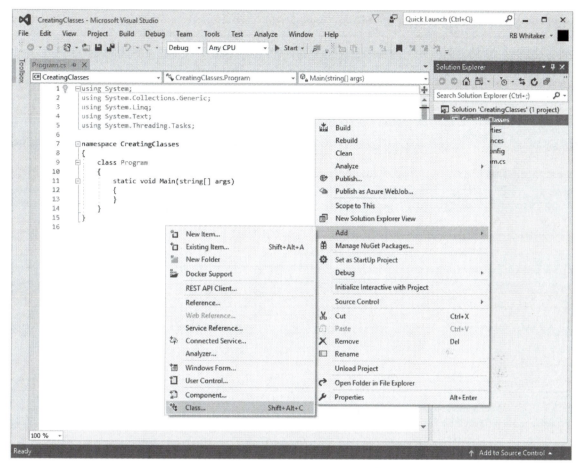

This will bring up the **Add New Item** dialog, with the Class template already selected. At the bottom, type in the name of your new class. I've called mine **Book.cs**, so my class will be called **Book**. Press the **Add** button, and your new file will be created.

When your new file is created, you'll see that Visual Studio generated some template code for you. **Book.cs** will contain code that looks something like this:

```
using System;
using System.Collections.Generic;
using System.Linq;
using System.Text;
using System.Threading.Tasks;

namespace CreatingClasses // Your namespace will likely be different here.
{
    class Book // Whatever name you chose will appear here as the class name.
    {
    }
}
```

The class that was generated for us is completely empty. Our task now will be to fill in the class with the things it needs. Anything that is a part of a class is called a *member* of the class. As we define a new class, we will be adding three main types of members to it: the data it has (as variables), the things it can do (methods), and ways to initialize new instances of the class (constructors). We'll now go through the process of adding each of these to our new class.

Instance Variables

The first thing we'll do is add variables to store the data that this object class will have for each instance. The variables we place in a class define what type of data any instance of the class will have. The class serves as the blueprint for all instances of the type. While we define what data instances of the class should have, each instance will actually get its own copy of the variables and data to work with, rather than sharing the data across all instances. (Though there's a way to do that too.)

Because of this, the variables that we add directly to a class are called *instance variables*.

For our simple **Book** class, we're going to keep track of the book's title, author, number of pages, and the word count. There is undoubtedly more information we could store about a book (publisher, publication date, etc.) but these four pieces of data are enough to illustrate the point.

Instance variables are made by placing them directly in the class, not in a method like we've done before:

```
using System;
using System.Collections.Generic;
using System.Linq;
using System.Text;
using System.Threading.Tasks;

namespace CreatingClasses
{
    class Book
    {
        private string title;
        private string author;
        private int pages;
        private int wordCount;
    }
}
```

Each instance variable above starts with the **private** modifier, which we'll discuss in a second. The rest is just like creating any other variable—we state the type of variable, followed by its name. (Note that you can't use **var** for instance variables. You must explicitly specify the type.)

These variables are a little different from what we've seen up until now, in terms of how they're used. All of our earlier variables have been either *local variables* or *parameters*, both of which can only be used within the scope of a single method. (Parameters are defined as a part of the method's signature, and are filled in by the calling method, whereas local variables are not. *Instance variables* on the other hand belong to the instance as a whole. These can be used from any method (including constructors) across the entire class. They aren't limited to just a single method.

Access Modifiers: private and public

Let's go back to that **private** keyword. Everything in a class has an *accessibility level*. An accessibility level indicates where it can be accessed from. The **private** keyword makes it only accessible (both to retrieve and set new values) from inside the class. Anything outside of the class doesn't even know it exists.

By contrast, the **public** accessibility level means that it can be seen or used from anywhere, including outside of the class. We could have made these variables **public**. The problem with doing this is that it makes it too easy for "outsiders" to modify our class's data in ways that shouldn't be allowed. For example, somebody could intentionally or accidentally modify **wordCount** to be negative, which is meaningless.

A class should protect the integrity of its own data. This is a concept called *encapsulation*. In general, a class should keep its internal data private but then allow for public mechanisms to request the current state of that data or to request applying new values for that data. This allows our class itself, through those mechanisms, to act as a gatekeeper, and make sure that only reasonable changes are performed.

By the way, if you don't put an access modifier, these variables would be **private** by default; **private** is the default accessibility level for all members of a class. Because of this, it wasn't technically necessary to use **private** in this case, but I think it's a good idea to put it in anyway, to make it obvious.

Constructors

Now that we've got instance variables ready, our second step is to indicate how you can create new instances of our class. This is done by adding in special methods called constructors.

When making constructors, we want to think about what we need to do to get our newly created instance into a valid starting state. This is usually determined in large part by the instance variables that our class contains. We frequently want constructors that will allow users of the class to supply initial values for these instance variables.

For instance, it probably doesn't make sense to create a book without a title. The same thing probably holds true for an author as well. So we'll probably want to make a constructor that allows the user to specify both of these as parameters. The code below adds a constructor that does this to our **Book** class:

```csharp
using System;
using System.Collections.Generic;
using System.Linq;
using System.Text;
using System.Threading.Tasks;

namespace CreatingClasses
{
    class Book
    {
        private string title;
        private string author;
        private int pages;
        private int wordCount;

        public Book(string title, string author)
        {
            this.title = title;
            this.author = author;
        }
    }
}
```

You can see from the above code that constructors look very much like methods, but with a few subtle differences. The first key difference here is that a constructor *must* share the same name as the class, while a normal method is forbidden from doing this. (This is, in fact, the way that the C# compiler distinguishes the two.)

The second difference is that constructors do not (and cannot) specify a return type. Not even **void**. By contrast, methods are required to specify a return type.

You can also see that we've made our constructor **public**, instead of **private** like our instance variables. By making this **public**, it allows code outside of the class to be able to create instances of the **Book** class. Had we made it private, it could only be reachable from inside the class. Since we nearly always want to be able to create instances of a class from outside the class, constructors will usually be public, though this isn't a requirement by any means.

In all other regards, a constructor is the same as a method. You can put any arbitrary code in there, like we've done with other methods, including things like loops and **if** statements. The constructor is also allowed to have parameters, like any other method. The variables defined by the parameters are usable throughout the method.

By the way, if you don't put any constructors in your class, the C# compiler will put one in for you. That constructor is parameterless. This is called the *default parameterless constructor*. Placing any other constructor of your own in a class will prevent the default parameterless constructor from being added automatically. If you wrote the default parameterless constructor by hand, it would look like this:

```
public Book()
{
}
```

The body of our constructor probably brings up some additional questions. Specifically, what is that **this** thing doing in there? To answer that question, we're going go through a series of important concepts that shape how both constructors and normal methods work when placed inside of a class.

Variable Scope

With the introduction of instance variables that live directly inside of a class (contrasted with local variables and parameters, that all live within a single method) we need to talk about an important concept called *scope* or *variable scope*. The scope of a variable refers to the places in the code that a variable is accessible.

There are generally three main "levels" of scope that we concern ourselves with:

- If something has *class scope*, it means it is accessible across an entire class.
- If something has *method scope*, it means it is accessible across an entire single method, but not before the line on which it is declared.
- If something has *block scope* or *inner block scope*, then it is accessible within just a section of a method. A **for** loop or **foreach** loop, for example, can declare a variable for use in the loop itself. These variables "go out of scope" at the end of the loop.

While not perfect, as a general rule, you can let the curly braces be your guide.

Here is a simple example of scope:

```
public void DoSomething()
{
    int a = 0;

    for(int x = 0; x < 10; x++)
        Console.WriteLine(x);

    x = -5;  // This won't compile--the variable 'x' is "out of scope".
}
```

In this method, the variable **a** has method scope, but the variable **x** has block scope. The **a** variable on the other hand can be used throughout the method, because it has method scope. The variable **x** can be used within the loop itself, but not after the loop. It won't even compile. It has fallen out of scope.

Interestingly, we can create a second **for** loop, reusing the same variable name (**x**) for a different variable, and the two won't conflict:

```
public void DoSomething()
{
    for(int x = 0; x < 10; x++)
        Console.WriteLine(x);

    for(int x = 50; x < 60; x++)
        Console.WriteLine(x);
}
```

Going back to our **Book** constructor, each of the four instance variables that we've defined in the class have class scope. They are accessible throughout the class, including from within the constructor. The **title** and **author** parameters defined at the top of the **Book** class, by contrast, have method scope.

Name Hiding

Related to the previous topic on variable scope, in some cases, it is possible for a nested scope to name something the same as something in the broader parent scope that contains it. Our constructor here is a perfect example of this. We had an instance variable called **author** that has class scope, and we created a parameter by the same name that has method scope.

When this happens, the variable in the smaller scope "hides" the variable in the larger scope. This is a situation called *name hiding*. That is, while both the class-level **author** variable and the method-level **author** variable both officially exist, within the context of the constructor, the local **author** variable hides the class-level **author** variable, making it inaccessible through direct means.

What do we do about this?

Well one solution is to just always name local variables and parameters something different than the class-level instance variable.

If you choose to solve this problem this way, I strongly recommend establishing a naming convention. I've seen people be inconsistent about names like this and it causes a great deal of pain. For example, if you make **bookAuthor** and **title** your class-level variables, but **author** and **theTitle** your method-level variables, you're going to always be confused about which variable belongs to the class and which are local to the method.

Many C# programmers will prefix the class-level instance variables with either an "**m_**" or just a plain "**_**". (In this case, the "m" is for "member".) In other words, we could make our instance variables **m_author**, **m_title**, etc.

This approach solves our name hiding problem by simply avoiding name hiding systematically. The only real drawback to this is that placing "**m_**" or even just "**_**" does have an impact on readability, especially when you're literally reading it out loud. (This is more common than you might think, because of how often programmers will discuss code in pairs or groups.) "Em underscore title" is a whole lot more to say than just simply "title". But in the grand scheme of things, this isn't so bad.

There is another solution to this problem though. There is a way that we can directly reference things in the class scope, regardless of what local variables might be hiding it. We'll discuss this in the next section.

The 'this' Keyword

At any point in time, you can get access to the current instance and the things in the class scope with the **this** keyword that our constructor illustrated. **this** is a special reference to the current instance that a method or constructor is running in. It's a quick and easy way to reach up into the class scope and work with instance variables and even methods that belong to the class.

This allows us to sidestep nearly all name hiding issues, and is what I showed in our constructor:

```
public Book(string title, string author)
{
    this.title = title;
    this.author = author;
}
```

Because there is a local variable called **title** that name hides the class-level **title** variable, when we refer directly to **title**, it will always refer to the method-level title variable. But if we start with "**this.**", then we can reach back up to the class-level directly, and reference the **title** instance variable.

This is a clean and simple way to avoid name hiding problems while still giving all variables simple, easy to understand names.

Multiple Constructors

A class can have as many constructors as you want to place in it.

Keep in mind that the goal of a constructor is to ensure that new instances of the class are put into a valid starting state. This state can be modified later through method calls, but the constructor should ensure that it always starts in a "safe" state.

As an example, it might make sense with our **Book** class to provide a second constructor that allows the user to additionally specify the pages and word count. If we wanted to add this, we might include a second constructor that looks like this:

```
public Book(string title, string author, int pages, int wordCount)
{
    this.title = title;
    this.author = author;
    this.pages = pages;
    this.wordCount = wordCount;
}
```

Methods

The last major category of things to add to a class is an appropriate set of methods. Methods allow outside code to make requests of the instance. There is no limit to what these requests can entail. It just depends on what the class is capable of and what other pieces of the system will need from it.

A few possibilities include things like requesting the current state of some part of its data, a request to change the current state of its data to a new value, or asking it to perform some sort of task.

In this section, we'll tackle three simple methods, one in in each of those categories. But a full-fledged **Book** class might want many more methods than this. A class doesn't really have a limit to the number of methods it has (or constructors or instance variables for that matter) but at some point, as the number gets bigger and bigger, it is probably a sign that the class is responsible for too much, and should be broken down into smaller pieces.

The three methods we'll add here are:

1.   A method to retrieve the current title for a book.
2.   A method to specify a new title for the book.
3.   A method that supplies the text of the book and updates the word count accordingly.

This is obviously not a comprehensive list of all methods our **Book** class could possibly ever want. It is merely illustrative of how you add methods to a class.

The following code shows a possible implementation for these three methods:

```
using System;
using System.Collections.Generic;
using System.Linq;
using System.Text;
using System.Threading.Tasks;

namespace CreatingClasses
{
    class Book
    {
        private string title;
        private string author;
        private int pages;
        private int wordCount;

        public Book(string title, string author)
        {
            this.title = title;
            this.author = author;
        }

        public Book(string title, string author, int pages, int wordCount)
        {
            this.title = title;
            this.author = author;
            this.pages = pages;
            this.wordCount = wordCount;
        }

        public string GetTitle()
        {
            return title;
        }

        public void SetTitle(string title)
        {
            this.title = title;
        }

        public void AssignWordCountFromText(string text)
        {
            wordCount = text.Split(' ').Length;
        }
    }
}
```

We've made all of these methods **public**, which means they can be called from both inside and outside the **Book** class. If somebody has a **Book** instance, then they'll be able to invoke these methods on it. This was by design here, but we can have private methods as well, which can be called only from inside the class. In this case, these become utility methods of the class itself.

You'll also notice that we have a method that starts with **Get** and another that starts with **Set**. These retrieve ("get") the value of some piece of data (**title** in this particular case) and request a new value be assigned to the data. These are called "getters" and "setters", and they're a very common thing to see in a class. (So much so that we'll talk about a more powerful way of doing this in Chapter 19). While we only made a **GetTitle** and **SetTitle**, you can easily imagine having a **GetAuthor** and **SetAuthor**, a **GetPages** and a **SetPages**, and so on.

You can see that for the **GetTitle** and **SetTitle** methods above, they simply pass through to the instance variable. In this case, you might be tempted to say, "Let's just make **title** public, and let people just directly read from or write to that variable." The syntax there would definitely be cleaner. But remember that classes should protect their own data. This protection means keeping the instance variables private in most scenarios, and providing alternative means (getters and setters) to make requests instead. This allows us to change our logic (for example, preventing you from setting the title to **null**) without breaking any code that uses the method.

You may have noticed that these methods are missing the **static** keyword that we've been using in the past. In the next section, we'll learn what **static** means and why we didn't use it here.

The 'static' Keyword

In the past, we've been putting **static** on the methods we create, but in the previous section, we specifically skipped it. So what does **static** actually mean?

In object-oriented programming, we have classes, which define general behavior for an entire category of objects, and then we have instances, which are individual occurrences of the category.

If something is marked **static**, then it means it belongs to the class as a whole—it is shared across all instances. In fact, in Visual Basic.NET, C#'s evil twin language, they actually use the keyword **Shared** for this concept instead, which is a much better way of describing this concept, in my opinion.

While we've been using **static** quite a bit in the past, now that we're introducing classes, we're going to stop using it in most places. In most cases, we don't actually want to make things **static** and share them across all instances of the class.

The **static** keyword can be applied to any class member, which slight variations in meaning or usage. The rest of this section will discuss the various ways to use **static** and its implications.

Static Variables

For a class-level variable, marking it with **static** means that rather than every instance have its own variable as defined by a template, there is only a single variable that is shared by all instances and owned by the class as a whole. Because it is shared, if one instance changes the value of the variable, it will affect all other instances as well. Applying static to a class-level variable means it is no longer an instance variable, but a *static class variable*, or *class variable* for short. It belongs to the class as a whole, not to any particular instance of it.

Static Methods

If a method is **static** then it can be accessed through the class name directly, rather than through any particular instance of the class, since it belongs to the class as a whole, instead of an instance. To illustrate, here is how you use a "normal" non-static method:

```
Book book = new Book("Rendezvous with Rama");
book.AssignWordCountFromText("Sooner or later, it was bound to happen.");
```

We have an actual instance of the **Book** class (stored in the **book** variable) and to invoke the normal non-static method, we use the dot operator and call the method from the instance itself.

But if a method is static, then we don't use an instance. We access it through the class as a whole. We saw this with the **Console** class:

```
Console.WriteLine("Hello World!");
```

WriteLine is a static method, so we don't need to create an instance of the **Console** class. We just invoke the method directly from the class itself.

There is a time and place for both static and non-static methods. While we've been mostly doing static methods up to this point, normal non-static methods are going to become the new normal. But that doesn't completely negate the usefulness of static methods.

A static method does not have access to instance variables, nor can it invoke instance methods.

Static Classes

You can also apply the **static** keyword to a class. If you do this, then it can't contain any instance variables or methods. Everything inside it must be **static**. Furthermore, if a class is **static**, then you can't create an instance of it either. The compiler will enforce all of this. The **Console**, **Convert**, and **Math** classes are all static classes. In this sense, static classes are simply a way to group a related collection of utility code.

Static Constructors

While far less useful than some of the other static things we've talked about, it is also possible to make a **static** constructor. While normal constructors are meant to get a brand new instance into a valid starting state, a **static** constructor is meant to get the class as a whole into a valid starting state. This largely only applies in cases where you have a bunch of **static** class variables that need to be initialized. (Note that you can only have one static constructor in a class.) Here is an example:

```
public class Something
{
    public static int sharedNumber;

    static Something()
    {
        sharedNumber = 3;
    }
}
```

When your class is first used, the CLR runtime that is executing your code will pause for a second and look to see if a class has a **static** constructor. If it does, it will run it (once and never again during the application's lifetime).

Using Our Class

Now that we've created a **Book** class and walked through some of the nuances of creating a class, we should also look at how to actually use our new class. We saw some of this in the last chapter. Our **Book** class is used similarly to the **Random** class we saw there. In your **Main** method, you can create an instance of your **Book** class, and work with it like this:

```
Book book = new Book("Harry Potter", "J.K. Rowling");

// Changed my mind. Let's use the full name.
book.SetTitle("Harry Potter and the Half-Blood Prince.");

// Now I forgot. What was the title again?
Console.WriteLine(book.GetTitle());
```

This is a simple, almost trivial example, but it grows and expands from here. We can use our newly created class like any other type of data. We create a new instance any time we need to represent a new book in our system. For any instance, we can call its methods to make requests and interact with it.

Our system will begin to grow. More class definitions will define additional pieces of the larger system. Instances of the different classes can be combined together to form a cohesive whole, where each class and each instance is only concerned with a tiny piece of the complete puzzle.

The 'internal' Access Modifier

In addition to making things public and private, we can also make things have an "internal" accessibility level by applying the **internal** access modifier. The **internal** modifier is similar to **public**. It means it can be used inside and outside of the class. By contrast though, it indicates that it is only accessible in the assembly it is defined in. We talked about assemblies back in Chapter 3, but the general idea is that if something is internal, then it is only accessible in the project that it is defined in.

This is important because things placed directly in a namespace (like a class) default to the **internal** accessibility level if nothing else is specified. When we made the **Book** class in a new file, our class definition looked like this:

```
class Book // Or any other name...
{
```

This class has the internal accessibility level. If you want to be able to use the class outside of the project where it is defined, you will have to specifically mark it with the **public** access modifier:

```
public class Book
{
```

(I'd also recommend explicitly stating that a class is **internal** if you truly mean for it to be internal, rather than ever just leaving it off and being implicitly **internal**.)

You can also make class members like instance variables and methods **internal** as well, if the situation is right.

So when do you use which accessibility level?

The short answer is, you should make everything as restricted (**private** over **internal**, and **internal** over **public**) as possible while still allowing things to get done.

The longer answer is a bit more nuanced. Data that belongs to a class should generally be protected by the class, and so class-level variables should usually be made **private**.

When it comes to deciding between **public** and **internal**, it all comes down to how widely used you expect the class to be. If you think a class is reusable across many projects, then you might as well make it **public** from the beginning. If you mean for the type to be used only inside a single project, it should be **internal**. The same rule applies to methods as well.

Class Design and Software Engineering

This chapter has described the basics of building classes. Defining new types like this is *the* key aspect of building large products. But while the basic rules of designing and building classes is straightforward, mastering class design and using it to build complicated software takes a lifetime to master.

The rest of this book will continue to provide you with new tools and techniques for building more powerful and more interesting classes. But the real learning will take place over the next weeks, months, and even years as you get more practice and experience with building larger systems out of individual classes and instances.

As you begin to explore class design, you will sometimes make mistakes and organize your code into the wrong set of classes. It's OK to get the design wrong. No matter how much experience you have with class design, and no matter how many rules and "best practices" you've learned, you will still sometimes get it wrong.

A good programmer will be able to recognize when they've accidentally structured their code into the wrong classes and will refactor and rearrange it so that it is better. As you get more practice, this will become rarer, but it will never go away completely.

By the time you've written 10000 classes, you will have become quite skilled at designing classes.

Try It Out!

Designing and Building Classes. Try creating the two classes below, and make a simple program to work with them, as described below.

Create a Color class:

- On a computer, colors are typically represented with a red, green, blue, and alpha (transparency) value, usually in the range of 0 to 255. Add these as instance variables.
- A constructor that takes a red, green, blue, and alpha value.
- A constructor that takes just red, green, and blue, while alpha defaults to 255 (opaque).
- Methods to get and set the red, green, blue, and alpha values from a **Color** instance.
- A method to get the grayscale value for the color, which is the average of the red, green and blue values.

Create a Ball class:

- The **Ball** class should have instance variables for size and color (the **Color** class you just created). Let's also add an instance variable that keeps track of the number of times it has been thrown.
- Create any constructors you feel would be useful.
- Create a **Pop** method, which changes the ball's size to 0.
- Create a **Throw** method that adds 1 to the throw count, but only if the ball hasn't been popped (has a size of 0).
- A method that returns the number of times the ball has been thrown.

Write some code in your **Main** method to create a few balls, throw them around a few times, pop a few, and try to throw them again, and print out the number of times that the balls have been thrown. (Popped balls shouldn't have changed.)

Try It Out!

Classes Quiz. Answer the following questions to check your understanding. When you're done, check your answers against the ones below. If you missed something, go back and review the section that talks about it.

1. **True/False.** Classes are reference types.
2. (Classes/Instances) define what a particular type of thing can do and store, while a/an (class/instance) is a specific object that contains its own set of data.
3. Name three types of members that can be a part of a class.
4. **True/False.** If something is static, it is shared by all instances of a particular type.
5. What is a special type of method that sets up a new instance called?
6. Where can something **private** be accessed from?
7. Where can something **public** be accessed from?
8. Where can something **internal** be accessed from?

Answers: (1) True. **(2)** Classes, instance. **(3)** Instance variables, methods, constructors. **(4)** True. **(5)** Constructor. **(6)** Only within the class. **(7)** Anywhere. **(8)** Anywhere inside of the project it is contained in.

Properties

In a Nutshell
- Properties provide a cleaner approach to creating getters and setters for instance variables.
- You can create a property with code like the following:

```csharp
public int Score
{
    get
    {
        return score;
    }
    set
    {
        score = value;
        if (score < 0)
            score = 0;
    }
}
```

- Not all properties need both a setter and a getter.
- Getters and setters can have different accessibility levels.
- Auto-implemented properties can be created that allow you to quickly define a simple property with default behavior (**public int Score { get; set; }**).
- Auto-implemented properties can have a default value: **public int Score { get; set; } = 10;**

In the last chapter, we saw how it is common to have an instance variable and then getter and setter methods that allow outside code to retrieve and request new values for the variable. This leads to lots of **GetSomething** and **SetSomething** methods. This is so common that C# provides a very powerful feature that makes it easy to access the value of an instance variable called *properties*. This chapter will discuss why properties are so helpful, and several ways to create them.

The Motivation for Properties

Imagine you are creating a simple class to represent a player in a video game, which looks like this so far:

```
using System;
using System.Collections.Generic;
using System.Linq;
using System.Text;
using System.Threading.Tasks;

namespace Properties
{
    class Player
    {
        private int score;
    }
}
```

Let's say that you want to be able to have something outside of the class be able to get and set the value of the player's score.

In the last chapter, we learned a way to accomplish this might be by creating a **GetScore** and a **SetScore** method. These two methods can do any special checking that they might need (like ensuring that the score being set isn't negative). This might look like this:

```
public int GetScore()
{
    return score;
}

public void SetScore(int score)
{
    this.score = score;
    if(this.score < 0)
        score = 0;
}
```

But the need for getter and setter methods is extremely common, and making getter and setter methods is a little cumbersome. Plus, using these methods (e.g., **player.SetScore(10);**) is rather wordy.

It is tempting to just make our **score** instance variable **public** instead of **private**. Then you could simply say **player.score = 10**. That would be very convenient, except for one problem: now the instance variable is public, and outsiders can intentionally or accidentally put bad data in there. The **SetScore** method kept the data protected.

C# has a feature that solves all of these issues, creating a clean way to get or set the value of an instance variable without publicly exposing it. This feature is called a *property*.

Creating Properties

A property is simply an easy way to create get and set methods, while still maintaining a high level of readability. Instead of the two methods that we showed in that last example, we could do this instead:

```
public int Score
{
    get
    {
        return score;
    }
    set
    {
        score = value;
        if (score < 0)
            score = 0;
    }
}
```

This creates a **Score** property. We can see that it is **public**, so anyone can use it (though we could also use **private** if we had wanted). We also specify the type of the property, which in this case is an **int**. Then we give it a name.

We then use the **get** and **set** keywords to show what should happen when someone tries to read the value of the property or set the value of the property. The code inside of the curly braces is nearly the same code that was in the **GetScore()** and **SetScore(int)** methods.

With a normal setter method (like **SetScore**) we would normally have a single parameter that is the new value being set. In a property, we can't list parameters. Instead, we're given exactly one, which we can access with the keyword **value**. This takes on the value that the caller is trying to set. The type of **value** is the same type as the property. We can call our property using something like this:

```
Player player = new Player();
int currentScore = player.Score;
player.Score = 50;
```

When we try to read from the **Score** property, the code inside of the property's **get** block is executed and returned. When we assign a value to the **Score** property, the code inside of the **set** block gets executed. In this case, the value **50** gets put into the **value** keyword inside of the **set** block.

Properties are the best of both worlds. Outsiders get nice clean syntax for getting or setting the data, but the data isn't exposed publicly, and is funneled through our logic that allows us to do a sanity check on the request, rather than blindly allowing outside code to directly manipulate the data.

Interestingly, properties are just syntactic sugar. Behind the scenes, the C# compiler is just turning these back into normal methods.

Whenever we have a property that gets or sets the value of a specific instance variable, that instance variable is called a *backing field* of the property. In our example above, the **Score** property uses the **score** instance variable as its backing field.

Properties are not required to have a backing field. Let's look at another example where a property does not have a backing field:

```
using System;
using System.Collections.Generic;
using System.Linq;
using System.Text;
using System.Threading.Tasks;

namespace Properties
{
    class Time
    {
        private int seconds;

        public int Seconds
        {
            get
            {
                return seconds;        // Seconds is the backing field here...
            }
            set
            {
                seconds = value;
            }
        }

        public int Minutes
        {
```

```
        get
        {
            return seconds / 60; // But there's no 'minutes' backing field here.
        }
    }
}
```

You can see here that we have a **seconds** instance variable, along with a **Seconds** property that uses it as a backing field. (By the way, using lower case names for instance variables, and upper case names for the matching property is very common.)

In addition, we also have a **Minutes** property that doesn't have a backing field at all. Instead, we just do some other work—in this case, return the number of seconds divided by 60.

Another thing this example shows us is that we don't necessarily need both **set** and **get** blocks for a property. You can have one or the other or both. If you only have a **get** block, then the property is *read-only*, because you can't set it. This is the case with the **Minutes** property we just saw. If you have only a **set** block, the property would be write-only. (Though write-only properties are rarely actually useful.)

Different Accessibility Levels

So far, our properties have all been public. This means that both the getter and the setter are accessible to everyone. However, it is possible to make the two have different accessibility levels from each other. For example, we might want the getter to be public, so that everyone can read it, while making the setter private, so that it can only be changed from within the class.

To make this happen, you can specify an access modifier before the **get** or **set** keywords, like this:

```
public int Score
{
    get // This is public by default, because the property is marked 'public'.
    {
        return score;
    }
    private set // This, however, is now private.
    {
        score = value;
    }
}
```

Auto-Implemented Properties

You will probably find yourself making a lot of things that look something like this:

```
private int score;

public int Score
{
    get
    {
        return score;
    }
    set
    {
        score = value;
    }
}
```

If you have no extra logic that you need to perform in the getter or setter, C# has a feature called an auto-implemented property that does this same thing with far less effort:

```
public int Score { get; set; }
```

This creates a backing field behind the scenes, and simple **get** and **set** code. You won't have direct access to the backing field in this case. This is a nice shorthand way to create very simple properties.

Read-Only Auto-Implemented Properties

You can also create read-only auto-implemented properties. These can only be written to in a constructor (or with a default value, which we'll look at next). After that, their value cannot be changed:

```
public class Vector2
{
    public double X { get; }
    public double Y { get; }

    public Vector2(double x, double y)
    {
        X = x;
        Y = y;
    }
}
```

It may seem a little odd to restrict a property from being written to. But making all data of a type be read-only after creation (making the type "immutable") has certain advantages. For instance, you know that if you've got a shared copy of the object that nobody is going to change its values without you knowing because they simply can't be changed. Immutability is a broader topic than just read-only properties, and we'll discuss it again later through this book.

The key point to remember here is that you can make your auto-implemented property read-only by simply having only a getter with no setter. This causes it to be writeable while the object is being created, but not afterwards.

Default Values

For an auto-implemented property, you can also assign a default value to the property:

```
public class Vector2
{
    public double X { get; set; } = 0;
    public double Y { get; set; } = 0;
}
```

Of course, the default value of any number will always be 0, so in this case we haven't actually changed anything, but it conveys the idea and the syntax correctly.

You can also supply default values for the read-only properties we just described in the last section.

A default value is assigned before the constructor actually runs. That means that the default value will already be set by the time the constructor begins, and setting a new value in the constructor will overwrite the default value.

Object Initializer Syntax

When you're using an object with properties, you can set values for the properties one at a time. You frequently do this just after creating a new object. For example:

```
Book book = new Book();
book.Title = "Frankenstein";
book.Author = "Mary Shelley";
```

But C# provides a way to set properties like this more concisely, using a thing called *object initializer syntax*. This syntax looks like this:

```
Book book = new Book() { Title = "Frankenstein", Author = "Mary Shelley" };
```

The properties all get set on the same line as the object is created. This is frequently more readable than the earlier option, but not in all cases. Choose the one that makes your code most readable for any given situation.

Going a bit further, if you use object initializer syntax and you use a parameterless constructor, the parentheses are (weirdly) optional.

```
Book book = new Book { Title = "Frankenstein", Author = "Mary Shelley" };
```

> **Try It Out!**
> **Playing with Properties.** At the end of the last chapter, we created a couple of classes as practice. Go back to those classes and add properties for the various instance variables that they have. While doing so, make sure you try at least one auto-implemented property.

Anonymous Types

Now that we understand properties, we can introduce a more advanced (but only occasionally used) concept called an *anonymous type*: a class that doesn't have an actual formal name. To create an instance of an anonymous type, you use the **new** keyword, and then make use of the object initializer syntax that we just looked at:

```
var anonymous = new { Name = "Steve", Age = 34 };
Console.WriteLine($"{anonymous.Name} is {anonymous.Age} years old.");
```

This code creates a new instance of an unnamed class with two properties: **Name** and **Age**.

Since an anonymous type is anonymous and doesn't have a name, a variable that stores one of these must use the **var** type, as shown above.

It's also worth pointing out that you can only specify properties for an anonymous type at creation time. You can't add more after creation. It is a fixed, unchangeable type, just like any other class we make, just without the name.

You can't use an anonymous type anywhere that a type name is required. This includes return values and parameter types. That means anonymous types can only be used inside of a single method, and can't be passed into another, or returned from one.

Giving types names is usually greatly preferred. But on occasion, you have something simple and short-lived enough (contained to a single method or smaller) where an anonymous type could be a decent solution. We'll see a few places where this is the case as we continue through this book. Notably, query expressions (Chapter 38) are a common place to use anonymous types.

Tic-Tac-Toe

In a Nutshell
- This chapter contains a single big project: making a functioning game of Tic-Tac-Toe, including defining the requirements for the game and my own solution to use as a reference.

We now have all of the knowledge needed to start tackling some larger programs. That is what we will do in this chapter: make a working game of Tic-Tac-Toe. This particular problems is notably more complicated than the *Try It Out!* problems we've done so far.

If this book were a course, this would be the mid-term project. If this book were a game, this would be the Mini-Boss.

Because this is larger than what we've done so far, it's OK if it takes longer to sort through the details and get it working. (I don't think you'd be wasting your time if you even spent up to 20 hours working through this problem if you're new to programming.)

My solution to this problem is included, along with an analysis of *why* I did it the way I did, right here in this chapter. Feel free to peek through what I've done as you're working on your own solution to get some ideas or help.

Your solution doesn't need to be the same as mine to be correct. I've just made a *possible* solution. Yours will inevitably be very different in at least one major way, and slightly different in many more minor ways. As long as you've satisfied the requirements for the Tic-Tac-Toe game listed below, you're in good shape, even if it doesn't match my solution.

You can also download the complete source code for my solution from the book's website here: **http://starboundsoftware.com/books/c-sharp/try-it-out/tic-tac-toe**.

Requirements

The following list contains the requirements for Tic-Tac-Toe:

- The game is console-based. (No requirements for a GUI.)
- Two human players take turns using the same keyboard.

- The players are able to designate which square they want to play in next using the keyboard.
  - ○ One possible approach would be to number the squares in the 3x3 board with the digits 1 through 9, like the number pad on the keyboard. If a player enters the number 7, then the top left corner of the board is chosen.
- The game should ensure that only legal moves are made.
  - ○ You cannot play in a square that already has something.
  - ○ The wrong player cannot take a turn.
  - ○ If the player makes an illegal move, the board should remain unchanged.
- The game needs to be able to detect when either player wins, or when a draw ("cat") happens (the board is full).
- Upon detecting that the game is over the outcome is displayed to the user.
- Only a single round of play is required.

You might consider something like the following for display of the state of a game:

```
   | x |
---+---+---
   | o | x
---+---+---
 o |   |
```

> **Try It Out!**
> **Tic-Tac-Toe.** Create a Tic-Tac-Toe game that meets the requirements listed in this section. You should spend a minimum of 20 minutes on this problem (no matter how stuck you get). This is a much bigger problem than any other *Try It Out!* so far, so plan on it taking more time. If you find yourself stuck beyond recovery, read ahead and see if part or all of my solution can help you get unstuck enough to continue on.

High-Level Design

A Tic-Tac-Toe game is not a huge project compared to some, but it is large enough we can't (or at least shouldn't) dump it all into a single class.

Our first task is to start identifying individual pieces or components in our system that we can turn into classes. As a general rule, each class we make should have only a single responsibility. It should be doing only a single thing.

So what kinds of data structures is our game going to need? And what sort of algorithms is our game going to need?

Here is the high-level breakdown of what I identified myself as candidates for being turned into classes in the system:

A *State* Enumeration. Not a class per se, but a type that needs to exist. It makes sense to me to create an enumeration that lists the states that a single square can be in: **X**, **O**, and **Undecided** (empty). This will be a helpful building block in the rest of our game.

A *Position* Class. It made sense to me to make a simple class that could be used to represent a location on the board, with **Row** and **Column** properties.

A *Board* Class. This class is the fundamental, central data structure for the game as a whole. It contains a 3x3 array of **State** values to represent the board, along with ways to request the current state of a position on the board and request placing a new value on the board. In my particular implementation, I also kept track of whose turn it was and made sure that only the right player could take a turn at any point in time.

*A **Player** Class.* A class that is designed to translate input from the player into a board position to play on. In our particular case, this will be handling keyboard input, but it isn't a big stretch to imagine creating alternate variations of the player that can handle mouse input, a computer AI, or even receiving instructions over a network. This class will have only one method that will basically be something like: **public Position GetPosition(Board currentState)**.

*A **WinChecker** Class.* This class has the responsibility of analyzing a board and determining if it has resulted in a win for a player or not yet. It will have a method that looks like this: **public State Check(Board currentState)**. It will also have a **public bool IsDraw(Board currentState)** that returns whether the game has reached a draw. The board itself could probably technically have a method that does these things, but I elected to pull this logic out into a separate class.

*A **Renderer** Class.* This class has the responsibility of drawing the game's current state, including displaying the final results of the game when it is over. The **Board** class could have a method that does this too, but once again, I chose to pull it out so that I could swap the rendering mechanism (perhaps for a GUI) without affecting any other part of the code.

*A **Driver** Program.* The last piece we'll need is something that can assemble a functioning game out of all of these pieces and tie them all together to make it work. This is logic that could technically be done in yet another class, but in this particular case, I've chosen to do this in the **Main** method in the default **Program** class.

Refactoring and Iterative Design

Having enumerated the classes that I put into my own Tic-Tac-Toe implementation, I should state that this is the *final* design, not the initial one. It didn't change drastically, but I did rearrange some pieces and handle things in different ways than I initially imagined.

Changing the design as you go is not only allowed, it is required. No design will survive first contact with the codebase. The act of writing code teaches you things about the solution that you hadn't considered. Always be prepared to change your code as you go.

This process of reshaping and reforming the code is called *refactoring*, and is a key part of software development. Your initial design will never be quite right. Plan on going through several iterations to refine your design, even though that sometimes means working on code refactoring instead of adding new features. It is just part of life as a software developer.

The Full Solution

We now shift away from the high level design to the specifics of each type in our Tic-Tac-Toe game. Each of the following sections starts with the code I made for the piece indicated by its title. Following that is a brief description on some of the complexities as well as a bit of information on why I implemented it the way I did.

The State Enumeration

The following is the code for the **State** enumeration:

```
public enum State { Undecided, X, O };
```

This enumeration is straightforward, and just lists the options available. I put **Undecided** first because that makes it the default value, which simplifies the board initialization later on.

The Position Class

The following is the code for the **Position** class:

```
public class Position
{
    public int Row { get; }
    public int Column { get; }

    public Position(int row, int column)
    {
        Row = row;
        Column = column;
    }
}
```

This class is also quite simple. It just defines **Row** and **Column** properties. I have intentionally made this class immutable—everything in it is read-only, once it gets past creation time. Immutability has a number of advantages, including knowing that you can be certain nobody is going to modify it after the fact. (They can create a new instance to place in a variable, but cannot modify an instance.)

This class doesn't bother verifying that the row and column are legitimate locations on the board. It wouldn't be unreasonable to do so, but I opted not to.

The Board Class

The **Board** class is substantially trickier:

```
public class Board
{
    private State[,] state;
    public State NextTurn { get; private set; }

    public Board()
    {
        state = new State[3, 3];
        NextTurn = State.X;
    }

    public State GetState(Position position)
    {
        return state[position.Row, position.Column];
    }

    public bool SetState(Position position, State newState)
    {
        if (newState != NextTurn) return false;
        if (state[position.Row, position.Column] != State.Undecided) return false;

        state[position.Row, position.Column] = newState;
        SwitchNextTurn();
        return true;
    }

    private void SwitchNextTurn()
    {
        if (NextTurn == State.X) NextTurn = State.O;
        else NextTurn = State.X;
    }
}
```

The central aspect of this class is the **State[,] state** instance variable. Everything else is built around that. (The other property in this class is the **NextTurn** property, which determines whose turn is next.)

Since we don't want other parts of the system to be able to reach in and directly manipulate the current state of the board, we provide a getter and setter method for the state of any spot on the board. I would have used a property, but I needed to know what position on the board we were asking about. Properties don't support supplying a parameter like that, so I had to fall back to plain getter and setter methods with the position supplied directly as a parameter.

The **SetState** method is somewhat tricky. If you are trying to go out of turn, it rejects you. If you are trying to play in a square that is already filled, it rejects you. Besides just setting the new state, this method also does maintenance work to make sure that it flips the next turn over to the other player.

The WinChecker Class

The **WinChecker** class has the logic to determine if (a) either X or O has won, and (b) if the board is full, resulting in a draw:

```
public class WinChecker
{
    public State Check(Board board)
    {
        if (CheckForWin(board, State.X)) return State.X;
        if (CheckForWin(board, State.O)) return State.O;
        return State.Undecided;
    }

    private bool CheckForWin(Board board, State player)
    {
        for (int row = 0; row < 3; row++)
            if (AreAll(board, new Position[] {
                        new Position(row, 0),
                        new Position(row, 1),
                        new Position(row, 2) }, player))
                return true;

        for (int column = 0; column < 3; column++)
            if (AreAll(board, new Position[] {
                        new Position(0, column),
                        new Position(1, column),
                        new Position(2, column) }, player))
                return true;

        if (AreAll(board, new Position[] {
                    new Position(0, 0),
                    new Position(1, 1),
                    new Position(2, 2) }, player))
            return true;

        if (AreAll(board, new Position[] {
                    new Position(2, 0),
                    new Position(1, 1),
                    new Position(0, 2) }, player))
            return true;

        return false;
    }

    private bool AreAll(Board board, Position[] positions, State state)
    {
        foreach(Position position in positions)
            if (board.GetState(position) != state) return false;

        return true;
    }
}
```

```
    public bool IsDraw(Board board)
    {
        for (int row = 0; row < 3; row++)
            for (int column = 0; column < 3; column++)
                if (board.GetState(new Position(row, column)) == State.Undecided) return false;

        return true;
    }
}
```

This code isn't quite as bad as it looks. The bulk of it is in checking to see if a win has been reached along the rows, the columns, and then the diagonals. This same logic is reused for both X and O, so it is called from the main **Check** method for each player. I pulled out the logic to actually iterate through all positions to see if they're equal to a separate method (**AreAll**).

The **IsDraw** method at the bottom simply computes whether there the board is a draw or not yet, which is defined as it not being a draw if we can find a single cell that isn't full. If we can't, it is a draw.

The Renderer Class

The following code is for the **Renderer** class:

```
public class Renderer
{
    public void Render(Board board)
    {
        char[,] symbols = new char[3, 3];
        for (int row = 0; row < 3; row++)
            for (int column = 0; column < 3; column++)
                symbols[row, column] = SymbolFor(board.GetState(new Position(row, column)));

        Console.WriteLine($" {symbols[0, 0]} | {symbols[0, 1]} | {symbols[0, 2]} ");
        Console.WriteLine("---+---+---");
        Console.WriteLine($" {symbols[1, 0]} | {symbols[1, 1]} | {symbols[1, 2]} ");
        Console.WriteLine("---+---+---");
        Console.WriteLine($" {symbols[2, 0]} | {symbols[2, 1]} | {symbols[2, 2]} ");
    }

    private char SymbolFor(State state)
    {
        switch(state)
        {
            case State.O: return 'O';
            case State.X: return 'X';
            default: return ' ';
        }
    }

    public void RenderResults(State winner)
    {
        switch (winner)
        {
            case State.O:
            case State.X:
                Console.WriteLine(SymbolFor(winner) + " Wins!");
                break;
            case State.Undecided:
                Console.WriteLine("Draw!");
                break;
        }
    }
}
```

There are two public methods in this, and one utility method. **Render** builds a 3x3 array of what symbols should be used for each slot in the display, then uses a heavy dose of string interpolation to draw the board. **RenderResults** just prints out who won. They both draw on the **SymbolFor** utility method, which simply converts a **State** to a **char**. Interestingly, this allows me to change the symbols for X and O in only one place. (We could play 1's and 0's instead of X's and O's, for example.)

The Player Class

The following is the code for the **Player** class:

```
public class Player
{
    public Position GetPosition(Board board)
    {
        int position = Convert.ToInt32(Console.ReadLine());
        Position desiredCoordinate = PositionForNumber(position);
        return desiredCoordinate;
    }

    private Position PositionForNumber(int position)
    {
        switch (position)
        {
            case 1: return new Position(2, 0); // Bottom Left
            case 2: return new Position(2, 1); // Bottom Middle
            case 3: return new Position(2, 2); // Bottom Right
            case 4: return new Position(1, 0); // Middle Left
            case 5: return new Position(1, 1); // Middle Middle
            case 6: return new Position(1, 2); // Middle Right
            case 7: return new Position(0, 0); // Top Left
            case 8: return new Position(0, 1); // Top Middle
            case 9: return new Position(0, 2); // Top Right
            default: return null;
        }
    }
}
```

In a nutshell, this simply gets a number from the user (ignoring bad input) and then converts a digit to a **Position** object. The positions are arranged like the number pad on a keyboard.

It is worth noting that the **GetPosition** method never actually uses the **board** parameter it is given, and could have been skipped. I opted to include it, partly because I'm thinking about how we could extend the game to include other types of players, especially a computer AI player. An AI would definitely make use of this parameter, since it can't see the screen to make its decisions. Structuring my **Player** class and its **GetPosition** method this way allows me to switch to a completely different implementation of **Player** without requiring the rest of the program to change how they interact with it. (We haven't talked about interfaces yet (Chapter 24) but I'd be using one here if we had.

The Driver Program

The last part is the driver program, which assembles everything else together and runs the game:

```
public class Program
{
    static void Main(string[] args)
    {
        Board board = new Board();
        WinChecker winChecker = new WinChecker();
        Renderer renderer = new Renderer();
        Player player1 = new Player();
        Player player2 = new Player();

        while(!winChecker.IsDraw(board) && winChecker.Check(board) == State.Undecided)
        {
            renderer.Render(board);
```

```
            Position nextMove;
            if (board.NextTurn == State.X)
                nextMove = player1.GetPosition(board);
            else
                nextMove = player2.GetPosition(board);

            if (!board.SetState(nextMove, board.NextTurn))
                Console.WriteLine("That is not a legal move.");
        }

        renderer.Render(board);
        renderer.RenderResults(winChecker.Check(board));

        Console.ReadKey();
    }
}
```

The first block of lines sets up the pieces of our game: a board, a win checker, a renderer, and two players.

The second piece is the "game loop" that makes our game tick. It draws the board, asks for a move from the current player, and updates the board. When the game has become a draw or a win for somebody, the loop ends, the results are displayed, and the program terminates.

This could have been a separate class, and would probably make sense to do so if we wanted to be able to play multiple rounds or configure rounds differently (like giving the player the option of playing a two-player game with two humans, or a one player game against the computer).

Wrapping Up

This covers my implementation of this Tic-Tac-Toe problem. The full solution can be found on the book's website if you want to download and run it: **http://starboundsoftware.com/books/c-sharp/try-it-out/tic-tac-toe**.

Again, my solution is one *possible* solution. It is not meant to be definitive, only to help you get unstuck if you run into problems, or illustrate a second alternative approach.

21

Structs

In a Nutshell
- A *struct* or *structure* is similar to a class in terms of the way it is organized, but a struct is a value type, not a reference type.
- Structs should be used to store compound data (composed of more than one part) that does not involve a lot of complicated methods and behaviors.
- All of the simple types are structs.
- The primitive types are all aliases for certain pre-defined structs and classes.

A few chapters ago we introduced classes. These are complex reference types that you can define and build from the ground up. C# has a feature call *structs* or *structures* which look very similar to classes organizationally, but they are value types instead of reference types.

In this chapter, we'll take a look at how to create a struct, as well as discuss how to decide if you need a struct or a class. We'll also discuss something that may throw you for a loop: all of the built-in types like **bool**, **int**, and **double**, are actually all aliases for structures (or a class in the case of the **string** type).

Creating a Struct

Creating a struct is very similar to creating a class. The following code defines a simple struct, and an identical class that does the same thing:

```
struct TimeStruct
{
    private int seconds;

    public int Seconds
    {
        get { return seconds; }
        set { seconds = value; }
    }

    public int CalculateMinutes()
    {
        return seconds / 60;
```

```
        }
}

class TimeClass
{
    private int seconds;

    public int Seconds
    {
        get { return seconds; }
        set { seconds = value; }
    }

    public int CalculateMinutes()
    {
        return seconds / 60;
    }
}
```

You can see that the two are very similar—in fact the same code is used in both, with the single solitary difference being the **struct** keyword instead of the **class** keyword.

Structs vs. Classes

Since the two are so similar in appearance, you're probably wondering how the two are different.

The answer to this question is simple: structs are value types, while classes are reference types. If you didn't fully grasp that concept back when we discussed it in Chapter 16, it is probably worth going back and taking a second look.

While this is a single difference in theory, this one change makes a world of difference. For example, a struct uses value semantics instead of reference semantics. When you assign the value of a struct from one variable to another, the entire struct is copied. The same thing applies for passing one to a method as a parameter, and returning one from a method.

Let's say we're using the struct version of the **TimeStruct** we just saw, and did this:

```
public static void Main(string[] args)
{
    TimeStruct time = new TimeStruct();
    time.Seconds = 10;

    UpdateTime(time);
}

public static void UpdateTime(TimeStruct time)
{
    time.Seconds++;
}
```

In the **UpdateTime** method, we've received a copy of the **TimeStruct**. We can modify it if we want, but this hasn't changed the original version, back in the **Main** method. We've modified a copy, and the original still has a value of 10 for **seconds**.

Had we used **TimeClass** instead, handing it off to a method copies the reference, but that copied reference still points the same actual object. The change in the **UpdateTime** method would have affected the time variable back in the **Main** method.

Like I said back when we were looking at reference types, this can be a good thing or a bad thing, depending on what you're trying to do, but the important thing is that you are aware of it.

Interestingly, while we get a copy of a value type as we move it around, it doesn't necessarily mean we've completely duplicated everything it is keeping track of. Let's say you had a struct that contained within it a reference type, like an array, as shown below:

```
struct Wrapper
{
    public int[] numbers;
}
```

And then we used it like this:

```
public static void Main(string[] args)
{
    Wrapper wrapper = new Wrapper();
    wrapper.numbers = new int[3] { 10, 20, 30 };
    UpdateArray(wrapper);
}

public void UpdateArray(Wrapper wrapper)
{
    wrapper.numbers[1] = 200;
}
```

We get a copy of the **Wrapper** type, but for our **numbers** instance variable, that's a copy of the reference. The two are still pointing to the same actual array on the heap.

Tricky little things like this are why if you don't understand value and reference types, you're going to get bit by them. If you're still fuzzy on the differences, it's worth a second reading of Chapter 16.

There are other differences that arise because of the value/reference type difference:

- Structs can't be assigned a value of **null**, since **null** indicates a reference to nothing.
- Because structs are value types, they'll be placed on the stack when they can. This could mean faster performance because they're easier to get to, but if you're passing them around or reassigning them a lot, the time it takes to copy them could slow things down.

Another big difference between structs and classes is that in a struct, you can't define your own parameterless constructor. For both classes and structs, if you don't define any constructors at all, one still exists: a default parameterless constructor. This constructor has no parameters, and is the simplest way to create new objects of a given type, assuming there's no special setup logic required.

With classes, you can create your own parameterless constructor, which then allows you to replace the default one with your own custom logic. This cannot be done with structs. The default parameterless constructor creates new objects where everything is zeroed out. All numbers within the struct start at 0, all **bool**s start at false, all references start at **null**, etc. While you can create other constructors in your struct, you cannot create a parameterless one to replace this default one.

Deciding Between a Struct and a Class

Despite the similarities in appearance, structs and classes are made for entirely different purposes. When you create a new type, which one do you choose? Here are some things to think about as you decide.

For starters, do you have a particular need to have reference or value semantics? Since this is the primary difference between the two, if you've got a good reason to want one over the other, your decision is basically already made.

If your type is not much more than a compound collection of a small handful of primitives, a struct might be the way to go. For instance, if you want something to keep track of a person's blood pressure, which consists of two integers (systolic and diastolic pressures) a struct might be a good choice. On the other hand, if you think you're going to have a lot of methods (or events or delegates, which we'll talk about in Chapters 32 and 33) then you probably just want a class.

Also, structs don't support inheritance which is something we'll talk about in Chapter 22, so if that is something you may need, then go with classes.

In practice, classes are far more common, and probably rightly so, but it is important to remember that if you choose one way or the other, and then decide to change it later, it will have a huge ripple effect throughout any code that uses it. Methods will depend on reference or value semantics, and to change from one to the other means a lot of other potential changes. It's a decision you want to make consciously, rather than just always defaulting to one or the other.

Prefer Immutable Value Types

In programming, we often talk about types that are *immutable*, which means that once you've set them up, you can no longer modify them. (As opposed to mutable types, which you can modify parts of its data on the fly.) Instead, you would create a new copy that is similar, but with the changes you want to make. All of the built-in types (including the **string** type, which is a reference type) are immutable.

There are definite benefits to making both value and reference types immutable, but especially so with structs. This is because we think of value types like structs as a cohesive specific value. Because it has value semantics (copies of the whole thing are made, rather than just making a second reference to the same actual bytes in memory) we end up duplicating value types all over the place.

If we aren't careful, with a mutable, changeable value type, we might think we're modifying the original, but are instead modifying the original.

For example, what will the following code output?

```
struct S
{
    public int Value { get; set; }
}

class Program
{
    static void Main(string[] args)
    {
        S[] values = new S[10];          // New array of structs with default values is created here.
        S item = values[0];              // Danger! Copy is made here.
        item.Value++;                    // Copy is modified here.
        Console.WriteLine(values[0].Value); // Original, unmodified value is printed here.
    }
}
```

It actually prints out 0. This might come as a surprise. This is because the line that says **S item = values[0];** produces a copy for the assignment. So when you do **item.Value++**, you are modifying the copy, not the original. (This would not be true if **S** were a class instead of a struct.)

If we make **S** immutable so you can't modify its **Value** property at all, then the only way to produce a new version with the correctly incremented value would be to create a new **S** object, populated with the correct value at construction time. (You would want to define a constructor that allows you to specify value at creation time if you do this.)

At this point, that **item.Value++** line would have to become **item = new S(item.Value + 1);**, and the error becomes much more obvious to spot.

Making things in general immutable has many benefits, but for structs, you should definitely have a preference for making them immutable. (Sometimes the overhead performance cost associated with creating lots of objects will supersede the usefulness of immutable types, for example.)

The Built-In Types are Aliases

Back in Chapter 6, we took a look at all of the primitive or built-in types that C# has. This includes things like **int**, **float**, **bool**, and **string**. In Chapter 16, we looked at value types vs. reference types, and we discovered that these primitive types are value types, except for **string**, which is a reference type.

In fact, more than just being value types, they are actually structs! This means that everything we've been learning about structs also applies to these built-in types.

Even more, all of the primitive types are *aliases* for other structs (or class, in the case of the **string** type).

We've been working with things like the **int** type. But behind the scenes the C# compiler is simply changing this over to a struct that is defined in the same kind of way that we've seen here. In this case, it is the **Int32** struct (**System.Int32**).

So while we've been writing code that looks like this:

```
int x = 0;
```

We could have also used this:

```
Int32 x = new Int32();
Int32 y = 0;            // Or combined.
int z = new Int32();    // Or combined another way. It's all the same thing.
int w = new int();      // Yet another way...
```

The following table identifies the aliases for each of the built-in types:

Primitive Type	Alias For:
bool	System.Boolean
byte	System.Byte
sbyte	System.SByte
char	System.Char
decimal	System.Decimal
double	System.Double
float	System.Single
int	System.Int32
uint	System.UInt32
long	System.Int64
ulong	System.UInt64
object	System.Object
short	System.Int16
ushort	System.UInt16
string	System.String

With only a few of exceptions, the "real" struct name is the same as the keyword version, just with different capitalization. Keywords in C# are all lowercase by convention, but nearly everybody will capitalize type names, which explains that difference.

You'll also see that instead of **short**, **int**, and **long**, the structs use **Int** followed by the number of bits they use. It explicitly states exactly how many bits are in each type, which gives some clarity.

Additionally, **float** becomes **Single** rather than **Float**. Technically, **float**, **double**, and **decimal** are all floating point types. But **double** has twice the bits as **float**, so the term "single" is a more specific (and therefore technically more accurate) name for it. The C# language designers stuck with **float** because that's the keyword that is used for this data type in many other languages.

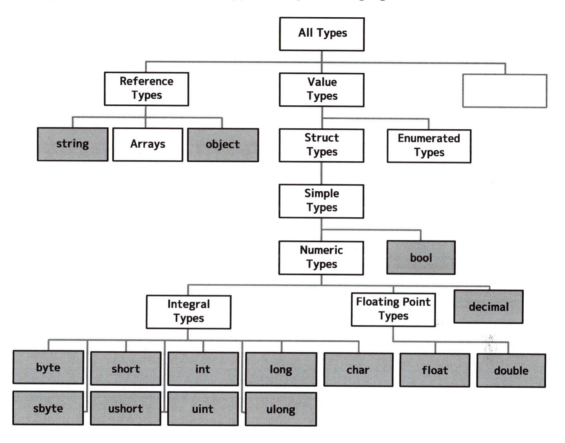

Try It Out!

Structs Quiz. Answer the following questions to check your understanding. When you're done, check your answers against the ones below. If you missed something, go back and review the section that talks about it.

1. Are structs value types or reference types?
2. **True/False.** It is easy to change classes to structs, or structs to classes.
3. **True/False.** Structs are always immutable.
4. **True/False.** Classes are never immutable.
5. **True/False.** All primitive/built-in types are structs.

Answers: (1) Value types. **(2)** False. **(3)** False. **(4)** False. **(5)** False. string and object are reference types.

Inheritance

> **In a Nutshell**
> - Inheritance is a way to reuse classes by expanding them into more specific types of classes. For instance, a **Square** class can be derived from (or inherit from) a **Polygon** class, giving it all of the features that the **Polygon** class has.
> - Any class can be used as a base class, except for sealed classes.
> - To indicate a class is derived from another, you use the colon followed by the base class name. For example class **Square : Polygon { /* ... */ }.**
> - The **protected** access modifier means that anything within the class can use it, as well as anything in any derived class.

Imagine that you are trying to keep track of geometric polygons, like triangles, rectangles, squares, pentagons, and so on. You can probably imagine creating a **Polygon** class that stores the number of sides the polygon has, and maybe a way to represent the positions of the vertices (corners) of the polygon.

Your **Polygon** class could be used to represent any of these polygons, but let's imagine that for a square, you want to be able to do some extra things with it. For example, you might want to create one using only a size (since the width and height are the same length in a square), or maybe you want to add a method that returns the area of the square.

One approach would be to create a **Square** class that duplicates everything in the **Polygon** class, plus adds the extra stuff you want as well. The problem with this is that now you have two entirely different classes, and if you want to make a change in the way people work with polygons, you'll also need to make a change in the way they work with squares. More than that, while you could create an array of polygons (**Polygon[] polygons**) you couldn't put squares in that list, even though in your head, they *are* polygons, and should be able to be treated as polygons.

After all, a square is just a special type of a polygon.

And in fact, that is getting right to the heart of what we're going to discuss in this chapter. A square is a polygon, but more specifically, it is a special type of polygon that has its own special things. Anything a polygon can do, a square can do too, because a square is a polygon.

This is what programmers call an *is-a relationship*, or an *is-a-special-type-of relationship.* It is so common that object-oriented programming languages have a special way to facilitate this kind of thing.

This is called *inheritance*. Inheritance allows us to create a **Polygon** class, and a **Square** class that is based on **Polygon**, This makes it *inherit* (or reuse) everything from the **Polygon** class that it is based on. Any changes we make to the **Polygon** class will also be automatically changed in the **Square** class.

Classes support inheritance, but structs and other types do not. It is a key difference between the two.

Base Classes

A *base class* (or *superclass* or *parent class*) is any normal class that happens to be used by another for inheritance. In our discussion, the **Polygon** class would be a base class.

For instance, we could have a class that looks like this:

```
using System;
using System.Collections.Generic;
using System.Linq;
using System.Text;

namespace Inheritance
{
    // Nothing special about this class. It will be used as the base class.
    class Polygon
    {
        public int NumberOfSides { get; set; }

        public Polygon()
        {
            NumberOfSides = 0;
        }

        public Polygon(int numberOfSides)
        {
            NumberOfSides = numberOfSides;
        }
    }
}
```

Derived Classes

A *derived class* (or *subclass*) is one that is based on, and expands upon another class. In our example, the **Square** class is a derived class that is based on the **Polygon** class. We would say that the **Square** class is *derived* from the **Polygon** class.

You can create a derived class just like any other class with one small addition to indicate which class is its base class. To indicate that the **Square** class is derived from the **Polygon** class, we use the colon (':') and name the base class:

```
class Square : Polygon   // Inheritance!
{
    //...
}
```

Inside of the class, we simply indicate any new stuff that the **Square** class has that the **Polygon** class doesn't have. Our completed **Square** class might look like this:

```
using System;
using System.Collections.Generic;
using System.Linq;
```

```
using System.Text;

namespace Inheritance
{
    class Square : Polygon
    {
        public float Size { get; set; }

        public Square(float size)
        {
            Size = size;
            NumberOfSides = 4;
        }
    }
}
```

So now a square will have a **Size** property, but in addition, it inherits instance variables, properties, and methods that were in the **Polygon** class. So the **Square** class also has a **NumberOfSides** property that it inherits from the **Polygon** class.

One other thing that we should mention here is that a class can inherit from a class that inherits from another class. You're allowed to have as many layers of inheritance as you want. (Though deep hierarchies have their own set of problems.)

Using Derived Classes

Derived classes are just like any other class, and can be used as a type just like any other class. From a basic perspective, there's nothing special about how you use them:

```
Polygon polygon = new Polygon(3); // a triangle
Square square = new Square(4.5f); // a square, which is a polygon with 4 sides of length 4.5.
```

But here's the interesting thing. Because the computer knows that a **Square** is just a special type of **Polygon**, you can actually use the **Square** type anywhere that you could use a **Polygon** type. After all, a **Square** is a **Polygon**!

```
Polygon polygon = new Square(4.5f);
```

As the program is running, when we're using the **polygon** variable, we only have access to the stuff that a **Polygon** has. So we can check to see the **NumberOfSides** it has. But as the program is running, we can only treat it as a **Polygon**. There's a chance that it is a **Square** (or another derived class), but the computer won't assume it is. So we won't be able to automatically use stuff created in the **Square** class in this particular case. Because our variable uses the **Polygon** type, we can only work with the things the **Polygon** type defines.

While we can put a **Square** in a variable with the **Polygon** type, you can't go the other way around. You can't assign a **Polygon** object to a variable with the type **Square**, like this:

```
Square square = new Polygon(3);  // Does not compile.
```

This is because while all squares are polygons, not all polygons are squares.

Checking an Object's Type and Casting

As I just described, it is possible to be actually using an instance of a derived type like the **Square**, but only know that it is a **Polygon**. Sometimes we want to be able to figure out what type an object is specifically, and work with it differently.

It is possible to check to see if an object is a specific type, with the **is** keyword and casting:

```
Polygon polygon = new Square(4.5f);

if (polygon is Square)
{
    Square square = (Square)polygon;
    // We can now do what we want with the square.
}
```

The 'as' Keyword

In addition to casting, there is another way we can convert one object type to another. This is done by using the **as** keyword, which looks like this:

```
Polygon polygon = new Square(4);
Square square = polygon as Square;
```

There are a couple of differences between using the **as** keyword and casting, and it turns out, using the **as** keyword in this type of a situation is usually a better choice.

To fully understand this, let's assume that in addition to the **Polygon** and **Square** classes we've been looking at, there is a **Triangle** class as well. Let's say we have a variable with the **Polygon** type, and assign it a new **Triangle** instance, but then we inadvertently try to turn it into a **Square**:

```
Polygon polygon = new Triangle();
Square square = (Square)polygon;
```

In this case, the program will crash, giving us an error that says it was an invalid cast. On the other hand, if we used the **as** keyword, instead of crashing, we would get **null**, which we can then respond to:

```
Polygon polygon = new Triangle();
Square square = polygon as Square;

if(square != null)
{
    // ...
}
```

Using Inheritance in Arrays

In light of what we've just been discussing, it is worth mentioning that you can create an array of the base class and put any derived class inside of it. This is just like what we already saw with variables that weren't arrays, so it shouldn't be too surprising:

```
Polygon[] lotsOfPolygons = new Polygon[5];
lotsOfPolygons[2] = new Square(2.1f);
lotsOfPolygons[3] = new Triangle();
```

In any case where a base class can be used, you can always substitute a derived class.

Constructors and Inheritance

I mentioned earlier that in a derived class, all properties, instance variables, and methods are inherited. Constructors, on the other hand, are not.

You can't use the constructors in the base class to create a derived class. For instance, our **Polygon** class has a constructor that takes an **int** that is used for the polygon's number of sides. You can't create a **Square** using that constructor. And for good reason. Remember, constructors are special methods that are designed to outline how to build new instances of a particular type. With inheritance, a constructor in the base class doesn't have any clue how to set up the new parts of the derived class. To create an instance of a class, you must use one of the constructors that are defined in that specific class.

When a derived class defines a constructor, it needs to call one of the constructors from the base class. By default, a constructor in the derived class will use the base class's parameterless constructor. (Remember, if you don't define any constructor yourself, a default parameterless constructor will be created for you.) If the base class doesn't have a parameterless constructor, or if you would like a constructor in the derived class to use a different one, you will need to indicate which constructor to use. This is done by using a colon and the **base** keyword along with the parameters for the constructor we want to use, like this:

```
public Square(float size) : base(4) // Uses the Polygon(int numberOfSides) constructor in the base class.
{
    Size = size;
}
```

The 'protected' Access Modifier

In the past, we discussed the **private** and **public** access modifiers. To review, remember that **public** meant anyone could get access to the member (variable, method, property, etc.), while **private** means that you only have access to it from inside of the class that it belongs to.

With inheritance we add another option: **protected**. If a member of the class uses the **protected** accessibility level, then anything inside of the class can use it, as well as any derived class. It's a little broader than **private**, but still more restrictive than **public**.

If the **Polygon** class made the **NumberOfSides** property **protected** instead of **public**, then you could access it from anywhere in the **Polygon** class, as well as the **Square** class, and any other derived class, but not from outside of those.

The Base Class of Everything: object

Without specifying any class to inherit from, any class you make still is derived from a special base class that is the base class of everything. This is the **object** class. All classes are derived from this class by default, unless you state a different class. But even if you state a different class as the base class, that class will be derived from the **object** class. If you go up the inheritance hierarchy, everything always gets back to the **object** class eventually.

You can use this type in your code using the **object** keyword (which is an alias for **System.Object**). Remember what I said earlier about how you can store a derived class in a base type like the code below?

```
Polygon polygon = new Square(4.5f);
```

You can also put it in the **object** type:

```
object anyOldObject = new Square(4.5f);
```

Since the **object** type is the base class for all classes, any and every type of object can be stored in it.

Sealed Classes

There may come a time where you want to prevent a class from being inherited. This might happen if you want to ensure that no one derives anything from a specific class.

You can use the **sealed** keyword to make it so nothing can inherit from a specific class by adding it to your class definition:

```
sealed class Square : Polygon
{
    // ...
}
```

Sealing a class can also result in a performance boost.

Partial Classes

A class can be split across multiple files or sections using the **partial** keyword:

```
public partial class SomeClass
{
    public void DoSomething()
    {
    }
}

public partial class SomeClass
{
    public void DoSomethingElse()
    {
    }
}
```

Even if the two parts are in different files, they'll be combined into one when you compile your program. You can also use the **partial** keyword on structs and interfaces (Chapter 24).

While you can use partial classes to split up a very large class into more manageable files, this is not the purpose of partial classes. In those cases, you should look for ways to split it into multiple classes.

The real purpose of partial classes is to split along "owner" boundaries. For example, UI frameworks will frequently have a GUI design tool, where you drag and drop buttons, checkboxes, etc. onto an editable canvas. The design tool might then be responsible for one part, leaving another part for the programmer to work in. The design tool won't ever accidentally overwrite stuff the programmer did, or vice versa.

Partial Methods

While practical uses are very limited, you can also have partial methods. These are interesting because a partial method is defined in one portion of the class, but is then *optionally* implemented elsewhere.

The code below illustrates how this works, though like with any partial class, in practice, the two pieces likely live in separate files, unlike the code below shows:

```
public partial class SomeClass
{
    partial void Log(string message);
}

public partial class SomeClass
{
    partial void Log(string message)
    {
        Console.WriteLine(message);
    }
}
```

It shouldn't be a surprise to hear that partial methods can only go inside partial classes or structs.

It also shouldn't be a surprise that the signatures must match (same number of parameters and same type of parameters in the same order, as well as the same method name and return type).

What might be a little weird is that you cannot put an access modifier (like **public** or **private**) on the method—they are implicitly private, and can't be changed from that.

Also noteworthy is that their return type *must* be **void**. That is related to what a partial method does, which we'll discuss in just a moment.

Remember that partial methods are optionally implemented. That means that the following code will *also* compile:

```
public partial class SomeClass
{
    partial void Log(string message);
}

public partial class SomeClass
{
    // Intentionally missing implementation of Log.

    public void DoStuff()
    {
        Log("I did stuff."); // But invoking the partial method anyway.
    }
}
```

Does that seem weird? It probably should. At least a little.

What if it is never implemented, but gets called somewhere, like in the code above? What happens then?

This is where the purpose of partial methods comes into play: if a partial method is not implemented, then it gets cut out at compile time. Any place that invokes it is skipped by the compiler. Flat out removed.

The purposes for this are rather limited. It requires a scenario in which parts of the class are defined by one thing (typically some auto-generated partial class from Visual Studio) and wants to be able to expect certain methods are available to call, but where it doesn't want another thing (typically you, the programmer) to be *required* to implement it. You will rarely encounter the need for a partial method, and virtually never need to write both pieces of the partial method.

C# Does Not Support Multiple Inheritance

Some object-oriented programming languages (C++, for example) allowed you to choose more than one base class to derive from. There are some benefits to this, because it allows one type of object to have an *is-a* relationship with more than one other type. For example, you could have a **PocketKnife** class that is-a **Knife** and is-a-really-crappy **Saw**, among other things.

Unfortunately, having multiple inheritance complicates things, and leads to situations where it is ambiguous how the class should behave. Because of this, C# does not to allow multiple inheritance. You must pick only one base class.

You can sometimes mimic multiple inheritance by using interfaces, which we'll talk about in Chapter 24.

> **Try It Out!**
> **Inheritance Quiz.** Answer the following questions to check your understanding. When you're done, check your answers against the ones below. If you missed something, go back and review the section that talks about it.
>
> 1. **True/False.** A derived class adds functionality on to a base class.
> 2. **True/False.** Everything that is in a base class can be accessed by the derived class.
> 3. **True/False.** Structs support inheritance.
> 4. **True/False.** All classes are derived from the **object** class.
> 5. **True/False.** A class can be a derived class and a base class at the same time.
> 6. **True/False.** You can prevent a class from being used as a base class.

Answers: (1) True. **(2)** False. Not private members. **(3)** False. **(4)** True. **(5)** True. **(6)** True.

23

Polymorphism, Virtual Methods, and Abstract Classes

In a Nutshell
- Polymorphism means that you can create derived classes that implement the same method in different ways from each other. This allows different classes to do the same task in their own custom way.
- A method in a base class can be marked **virtual**, allowing derived classes to use the **override** keyword and provide an alternative implementation.
- Classes can be marked as **abstract**, making it so you can't actually create an instance of the class. You have to create an instance of a derived class instead.
- In an **abstract** class, you can mark methods as **abstract** as well, and then leave out the method implementation. Derived classes will need to provide an implementation for any abstract methods.
- The **new** keyword, when attached to a method, means that a new method is being created, unrelated to any methods in the base class with the same name, resulting in two methods with the same name, with the one in the base class being hidden.

In the last chapter, we talked about how it is possible to create a class that is based on another, adding more stuff to it. It turns out inheritance lets us do a lot more than just add new things to an existing class. In this chapter, we'll look at how a derived class can provide its own implementation for a method that was defined in the base class, allowing it to handle the same task in its own way.

Polymorphism

"We do things differently around here." Maybe you've heard people say things like that before. What they're implying is they do the same kind of thing as somebody else, but it is done in a better way.

Take a web search for instance. Everybody knows about Google, but there are plenty of other web-based search engines, like Bing and Yahoo! Search. All of them do the same basic task, but each of them do it in their own way. You give them a word, they go off and dig around in their notes that's they've been furiously taking as they frantically searched for the end of the Internet, and give you back a list of anything that could be useful.

This is an excellent example of something programmers call *polymorphism*, a fancy Greek word meaning "many forms." Polymorphism is a feature that allows derived classes to *override* or change the way the base class does things, and do them in their own way. Alternatively, instead of changing the way the base class does things, the base class may not even *have* a way to do things, forcing derived classes to find their own way to do things. But when all is said and done, these derived classes will have a different way of doing things from the base class and from each other. The fact that these classes can do the same task differently (while still calling the same method) is what gives us "many forms" and polymorphism.

In the last chapter, with our basic inheritance model, derived classes could only add things to a type. With polymorphism, we can do more than just add stuff. We can also alter how the derived class will handle the things the base class supplies.

Going with our search engine example, we might have a **SearchEngine** class like this:

```
class SearchEngine
{
    public virtual string[] Search(string findThis)
    {
        return new string[0]; // I'm terrible at searching... I give up.
    }
}
```

Our **SearchEngine** class happens to define a single method. Here in the base class, we've provided a default (and terrible) implementation of the **Search** method.

You'll also notice the **virtual** keyword. This is what gives derived classes permission to change the way this method works. If you want to allow a derived class to change the way a method is used, you simply need to stick this on your method. (This also can be used for properties, as well as indexers and events, which we haven't discussed yet.)

In a derived class, we now have the option to provide an alternative implementation for the method:

```
class GoogleSearch : SearchEngine
{
    public override string[] Search(string findThis)
    {
        // Google Search is, of course, way better than 3 hard-coded results like this...
        return new string[] {
            "Here are some great results.",
            "Aren't they neat?",
            "I found 1.2 billion things, but you will only look at the first 10." };
    }
}
```

To change the implementation for the derived class, we simply create a new copy of the method, along with our new custom-made implementation, and add in the **override** keyword.

If the base class didn't use the **virtual** keyword for a method you want to override, you can't override it. The **virtual** keyword is the base class's way of saying "I give you permission to do something different with this method," while the **override** keyword is the derived class's way of saying "You gave me permission, so I'm going to use it and take things in a different direction."

You don't *need* to override virtual methods, you're just *allowed* to. And if a class has more than one virtual method, you can override some and not others.

Naturally, you can make any number of derived classes that do things their own way:

```
class RBsSearchEngine : SearchEngine
{
    public override string[] Search(string findThis)
    {
        return new string[] {
                "I found something.",     // Thanks EDI
                "I found this for you."   // Thanks SIRI
            };
    }
}
```

Here's where it gets interesting. Because our derived classes **RBsSearchEngine** and **GoogleSearch** are inherited from the **SearchEngine** class, we can use them anywhere a **SearchEngine** object is required:

```
SearchEngine searchEngine1 = new SearchEngine(); // The plain old original one.
SearchEngine searchEngine2 = new GoogleSearch();
SearchEngine searchEngine3 = new RBsSearchEngine();
```

But now we can use that **Search** method, and depending on the *actual* type, the various implementations will be called:

```
string[] defaultResults = searchEngine1.Search("hello");
string[] googleResults = searchEngine2.Search("hello");
string[] rbsResults = searchEngine3.Search("hello");
```

We'll get different results for each of these methods, because each of these three types define the method differently. The default **SearchEngine** class provides a default implementation of the method but the **GoogleSearch** and **RBsSearchEngine** "alter the deal" and override the original implementation, swapping it out for their own. The CLR is smart enough to know which method to use at the right time.

This type of setup, where calling the same method signature results in different methods actually being executed, is the crux of polymorphism. Polymorphism means "many forms," and in this situation, we can see that calling the same method results in different behaviors or forms.

Revisiting the 'base' Keyword

Last chapter, when we looked at creating constructors in a derived class, we saw the **base** keyword, which lets you access the constructors from the base class. We can also use the **base** keyword elsewhere to access non-private things from the base class, including its methods and properties.

While most of the time, you can directly access things in the base class without actually needing to use the **base** keyword, when you override a method, you'll be able to use the **base** keyword to still get access to the original implementation of the method.

This is convenient for the cases in which you want to override a method by doing everything the old method did, and then a little more. For example:

```
public override string[] Search(string findThis)
{
    // Calls the version in the base class.
    string[] originalResults = base.Search(findThis);

    if(originalResults.Length == 0)
        Console.WriteLine("There are no results.");
```

```
    return originalResults;
}
```

Abstract Base Classes

Let's go back to our **SearchEngine** example. The **SearchEngine** class indicates that any and every **SearchEngine** type object has the ability to search. But looking back at our code, our base **SearchEngine** class didn't do anything intelligent. We provided a dummy implementation that didn't do anything besides waste time writing useless code.

In cases like this, instead of providing a dummy implementation, we have an option to provide no implementation whatsoever. With no implementation or body for a method, the method in question becomes *abstract*.

To accomplish this in code, we need to add the keyword **abstract** to our class, as well as to any methods that we wish to keep unimplemented in the base class:

```
public abstract class SearchEngine
{
    public abstract string[] Search(string findThis);
}
```

When a class is abstract, it is allowed to include abstract methods. Abstract methods cannot go inside of regular, non-abstract classes. When a class is marked **abstract**, you can't create any instances of that class directly. Instead, you need to create an instance of a derived class that isn't abstract.

So with the code above, you won't be able to actually create an instance of **SearchEngine**. Instead, you'd need to create an instance of one of the derived classes, like **GoogleSearch** or **RBsSearchEngine**.

In the code above, you can also see that the method is marked with **abstract** as well. In this case, the method doesn't need a method body, and isn't even allowed to have one. Instead of providing an implementation in curly braces below it, you simply put a semicolon at the end of the line.

Abstract classes can also have as many virtual or normal methods as you want.

In a derived class, to provide an implementation for an abstract method, you use the **override** keyword in the exact same way as we did with virtual methods.

The 'new' Keyword with Methods

There's one other topic that a lot of people seem to get tangled up with all of this **override** and **virtual** stuff, and that is putting the **new** keyword on a method.

You are allowed to use the **new** keyword on a method like this:

```
public new string[] Search(string findThis)
{
    //...
}
```

When you use the **new** keyword like this, what you are saying is, "I'm making a brand new method in the derived class that has absolutely nothing to do with any methods by the same name in the base class." In this example, this **Search** method is completely unrelated to the **Search** method in the **SearchEngine** class.

This is usually a bad idea because it means that you now have two unrelated methods with the same name and same signature. This name conflict *can* be resolved, but it is best to just avoid it altogether.

People often get this **new** keyword confused with overriding virtual and abstract methods for two reasons. One, it looks similar. The **new** keyword here gets used in the exact same way as **override**. Second, if you forget to put anything in at all (**new** or **override**) when you use the same method signature, you'll get a compiler warning that tells you to add the **new** or **override** keyword. (Or in some cases, it only mentions the **new** keyword.) People see the warning and think, "Hmm... I guess I should add the **new** keyword to get the warning to go away."

The bottom line is, you rarely want to use the **new** keyword. It's just not what you're looking for. If you really are trying to make a new unrelated method, consider using a different name instead.

Try It Out!

Polymorphism Quiz. Answer the following questions to check your understanding. When you're done, check your answers against the ones below. If you missed something, go back and review the section that talks about it.

1. **True/False.** Polymorphism allows derived classes to provide different implementations of the same method.
2. **True/False.** The **override** keyword is used to indicate that a method in a derived class is providing its own implementation of a method.
3. **True/False.** The **new** keyword is used to indicate that a method in a derived class is providing its own implementation of a method.
4. **True/False.** Abstract methods can be used in a normal (non-abstract) class.
5. **True/False.** Normal (non-abstract) methods can be used in an abstract class.
6. **True/False.** Derived classes can override methods that were **virtual** in the base class.
7. **True/False.** Derived classes can override methods that were **abstract** in the base class.
8. **True/False.** In a derived class, you can override a method that was neither **virtual** nor **abstract** in the base class.

Answers: (1) True. **(2)** True. **(3)** False. **(4)** False. **(5)** True. **(6)** True. **(7)** True. **(8)** False.

Interfaces

In a Nutshell
- Interfaces define the things that something makes available to the outside world.
- Interfaces in C# define a set of methods, properties, events, and indexers that any class that uses the interface are required to provide.
- Interfaces are built in way that looks like classes or structs: **public interface InterfaceName { /* Define members in here. */ }**
- Members of an interface are implicitly **public** and **abstract**, and are required to be so.
- A class indicates that it implements an interface in the same way it shows it has a base class: **public class AwesomeClass : InterfaceName { /* Implementation Here */ }**
- You can implement multiple interfaces at the same time. You can also implement interfaces and declare a base class at the same time.

In this chapter, we'll cover a feature of C# called an interface, which outlines certain things that something provides. Interfaces are a fairly straightforward concept compared to some of the things we've been looking at in the last few chapters. We'll outline what an interface does, how to create one, and how to set up a class or struct to use one.

What is an Interface?

At a conceptual level, an interface is basically just the boundary it shares with the outside world. Your TV, for instance, probably has several buttons on it (and if it is really old, maybe even a dial or two). Each of these things allows the outside world to interact with it. That's its interface.

Interfaces are everywhere in the real world. They point out to users of the object how it can be used or controlled and also provides feedback on its current status. A couple of examples are in order here.

Cars (all vehicles in general) have a specific interface that they present to their users (the driver). While there are some nuances and details that we'll skip over, the key components are a steering wheel, a gas pedal, and a brake pedal. A car will also provide certain bits of feedback information to the driver on the dashboard, including the vehicle's ground speed and engine speed, as well as its fuel level.

Likewise, the keys on a piano are an interface that a pianist can access to make music. While pianos come in different forms (grand pianos, upright pianos, player pianos, electronic keyboards, etc.) they present a similar interface to the user of the system.

Let's take a moment and pick out a few key principles that apply to interfaces in the real world, like the car and keyboard interfaces. We'll soon see that C# interfaces provide these same key principles.

1. Interfaces define how outside users make requests to the system. By rotating the steering wheel on a car clockwise, we're making a request to turn the vehicle to the right. By pressing Middle C key on the piano's keyboard, we're asking the piano to make a sound at a particular pitch.
2. Interfaces define the ways in which feedback is presented to the user.

This interface defines how other objects can interact with the car, without prescribing the details of how it works behind the scenes. For example, in very old cars, this was all done in a purely mechanical way. Newer cars have things like power steering, and perform some of their feedback to the user digitally. And consider an electric car, which has a "gas" (acceleration) pedal but drives the vehicle using an electric motor instead of a gas motor.

You can even go to an amusement park and find bumper cars and speedway/raceway type rides that use an identical interface to control vehicles. One of the nice things about this shared interface is that as soon as you understand how to use one object through the interface, you generally understand how to use all objects that share the same interface.

Interfaces work both ways. When something presents a particular interface to the user, the user assumes that it's capable of doing the things the interface promises. When you've got a brake pedal in a car, you assume it will let you stop the vehicle quickly. When the brake pedal doesn't fulfill the promised interface, bad things happen. It's why it is frustrating when an elevator has a "Close Door" button, that doesn't actually close the door. The elevator presents an interface that promises the ability to close the door, but fails to actually do so.

The broader lesson here is that interfaces define a specific set of functionality. Users of the interface can know what to expect of the object from the interface, without having to know the details of how the object actually makes it work, and in fact, as long as the interface remains intact, the details on the inside could be swapped out and the user wouldn't have to change anything.

C# has a construct called an *interface* that fills the same role as these interfaces in the real world. It defines a set of members (specifically methods, properties, events (Chapter 33) and indexers (Chapter 35)) that any type claiming to have the interface must provide.

Creating an Interface

Creating an interface is very similar to creating a class or a struct. As an example, let's say our program has a need to write out files (see Chapter 29) but you want to write to lots of different file formats. We can create a different class to handle the nuances of each file type. But they are all going to be used in the same way as far as the calling code is concerned. They all have the same interface.

To model this, we can define an interface in C# for file writers. It is worth pointing out that Visual Studio has a template for creating new interfaces. This can be accessed by going to the Solution Explorer and right-clicking on the project or folder that you want to add the new interface to, and choosing **Add > New Item**, bringing up the Add New Item dialog box. In the list of template categories on the left side, choose **Visual C#**, which will show the list of all C# templates in the middle of the dialog. Up near the top, you'll see a template called **Interface**. This will get you set up with a new interface in a manner similar to how the **Class** template got us set up with a new class.

Interfaces are structured in a way that looks very much like a class or struct, but instead of the **class** or **struct** keyword, you will use the **interface** keyword:

```
using System;
using System.Collections.Generic;
using System.Linq;
using System.Text;
using System.Threading.Tasks;

namespace AwesomeProgram
{
    public interface IFileWriter
    {
        string Extension { get; }

        void Write(string filename);
    }
}
```

You can also see that all of the members of our interface have no actual implementation. They look like the abstract methods that we talked about in the last chapter. But also notice that we didn't use the **abstract** keyword here. Nor do we say that it is **public** (or **private** or **protected** for that matter). All members of an interface are public and abstract by default, and cannot be altered into anything else. You cannot add a method body, nor can you use a different accessibility level.

I also want to point out that I started the name of my interface with the capital letter **I**. It is incredibly common in the C# world to start names of interfaces with the letter I. People do this because it makes it easy to pick out what things are interfaces, and what things are classes. Not everyone does this, and you don't need to either if you don't want, but it is fairly widespread so expect to encounter it.

Using Interfaces

Now we can go ahead and create classes that use this interface. For example, we might create a **TextFileWriter** class, which knows how to write to a text file. Because we want it to do the things that any **IFileWriter** can do, we'll want to signify that this class implements the **IFileWriter** interface that we just defined. This can be done like this:

```
using System;
using System.Collections.Generic;
using System.Linq;
using System.Text;

namespace AwesomeProgram
{
    public class TextFileWriter : IFileWriter
    {
        public string Extension
        {
            get { return ".txt"; }
        }

        public void Write(string filename)
        {
            // Do your file writing here...
        }
    }
}
```

To make a class use or *implement* an interface, we use the same notation that we used for deriving from a base class. We use the colon (':') followed by the name of the interface that we're using.

If a class implements an interface like this, we are required to include an implementation for all of the members that the interface specifies. The class can also include a lot more than that, but at a minimum, it will need to implement the things in the interface. Note, however, that you do not use the **override** keyword when implementing an interface method.

In most ways, an interface will work in the same way that a base class does. For instance, we can have an array of our **IFileWriter** interface, and put different implementations of **IFileWriter** in it:

```
IFileWriter[] fileWriters = new IFileWriter[3];
fileWriters[0] = new TextFileWriter();
fileWriters[1] = new RtfFileWriter();
fileWriters[2] = new DocxFileWriter();

foreach(IFileWriter fileWriter in fileWriters)
    fileWriter.Write("path/to/file" + fileWriter.Extension);
```

Multiple Interfaces and Inheritance

As I mentioned at the end of the Chapter 24, C# doesn't allow you to inherit from more than one base class. However, you are allowed to implement more than one interface. Having your type implement multiple interfaces just means your type will need to include all of the methods for all of the interfaces that you are trying to implement.

In addition to implementing multiple interfaces, you can also still derive from a base class (and only one). C# limits you to a single base class because allowing two or more base classes tends to make the language, the overall structure of your code much more complicated and unintuitive.

To indicate that a class should implement more than one interface, list the interfaces you want after the class name, separated by commas, in any order. (But base classes *must* come first.)

```
public class AnyOldClass : RandomBaseClass, IInterface1, IInterface2
{
    // ...
}
```

> **Try It Out!**
> **Interfaces Quiz.** Answer the following questions to check your understanding. When you're done, check your answers against the ones below. If you missed something, go back and review the section that talks about it.
>
> 1. What keyword is used to define an interface?
> 2. What accessibility level are members of an interface?
> 3. **True/False.** A class that implements an interface does not have to provide an implementation for all of the members of the interface.
> 4. **True/False.** A class that implements an interface is allowed to have other members that aren't defined in the interface.
> 5. **True/False.** A class can have more than one base class.
> 6. **True/False.** A class can implement more than one interface.

Answers: (1) interface. **(2)** Public. **(3)** False. **(4)** True. **(5)** False. **(6)** True.

Using Generics

In a Nutshell
- Generics in C# are a way to create type-safe classes and structs without needing to commit to a specific data type at design time.
- When you create an instance of a type that uses generics, you must fill in the generic type parameters in angle brackets ('<' and '>'): **List<string> listOfStrings = new List<string>();**
- This chapter also covers some of the details of using the **List** class, the **IEnumerable** interface, and the **Dictionary** class, all of which use generics.

In this chapter, we'll take a look at a powerful feature in C# called *generics*. We'll start by taking a look at why generics even exist in the first place, looking at the actual problem they solve. We'll then look at a few classes that come with .NET Platform that use generics. These classes are the **List** and **Dictionary** classes, as well as the **IEnumerable<T>** interface. These types have many uses, and as we make software, we'll definitely be putting them and other generic types to good use.

We'll look at how to make your own generic classes in the next chapter.

The Motivation for Generics

Before we can really discuss generics, we need to discuss why they exist in the first place. So I'm going to start by having you think about the underlying problem that generics solve.

Let's say you wanted to make a class to store a list of numbers. While an array could do this, perhaps we could make a class that wraps an array and creates a new larger one when we run out of space, making it a "growable" list. (Note that there is a **List** class that already does this. You should use this and not write your own. But for now, pretend it doesn't exist. We'll revisit **List** before the end of this chapter.)

Imagine what you'd need to do to make a class to accomplish this task. For example:

```
public class ListOfNumbers
{
    private int[] numbers;

    public ListOfNumbers()
```

```
    {
        numbers = new int[0];
    }

    public void AddNumber(int newNumber)
    {
        // Add some code in here to make a new array, slightly larger
        // than it already was, and add your number in.
    }

    public int GetNumber(int index)
    {
        return numbers[index];
    }
}
```

This isn't complete, but you get the idea. You make the class and use the **int** type all over the place.

But now let's say you want a list of **string**s. Isn't it a shame that you can't use your **ListOfNumbers** class, and put **string**s in it?

So what now? Any ideas?

I suppose we could make a very similar class called **ListOfStrings**, right? It would end up looking basically the same as our **ListOfNumbers** class, only with the **string** type instead of the **int** type. In fact, we could go crazy making all sorts of **ListOf...** classes, one for every type imaginable. But that's kind of annoying, because we could have almost a limitless number of those classes. Lists of **int**s, lists of **string**s, lists of lists....

Maybe there's another way. What if we simply made a list of **object**s? Remember how **object** is the base class of everything?

We could create just a simple **List** class that uses the **object** type:

```
public class List
{
    private object[] objects;

    public List()
    {
        objects = new object[0];
    }

    public void AddObject(object newObject)
    {
        // Add some code in here to make a new array, slightly larger
        // than it already was, and add your object in.
    }

    public object GetObject(int index)
    {
        return objects[index];
    }
}
```

Now we can put any type of object we want in it. We only need to create one class (just the **List** class) for any type of object we want.

This might seem to work at first glance, but it's got a few problems as well. For instance, any time you want to do anything with it, you'll need to cast stuff to the type you're working with. If we have a list has only **string**s, when we want to call the **GetObject** method, we'll need to cast it like this:

```
string text3 = (string)list.GetObject(3);
```

Casting takes time to execute, so it slows things down a bit. Worse than that, this is less readable.

There's a bigger problem here though. Let's assume we're sticking **string**s in our list. We can cast all we want, but since it's a list of **object**s, we could theoretically put *anything* in the list, not just **string**s.

There's nothing preventing us from accidentally putting something else in there. After all, the compiler can't tell that there's anything wrong with saying **list.AddObject(new Random())** even though we intended it to be a list for only **string**s. We could try to be extremely careful and make sure that we don't make that mistake, but there are no guarantees. And even if we are careful ourselves, other people using the code might make that mistake.

We can never know for sure what type of object we're pulling out. We'll always have to check and make sure that it's the type we think it is, because it might *possibly* be something else. Programmers have a name for this by the way. They say it isn't *type safe*. Type safety is where you always know what type of object you are working with.

Type safety wasn't a problem in our first approach because we weren't using **object**. We were using a specific type, like **string**. We knew exactly what we were working with, so we could ensure that we were using the right thing all the time. There was no need for casting, and no possibility of mistakes.

So we've got two bad choices here. Either we make lots of type safe classes of lists, one for each kind of thing we want to put in it, or we make a single class of plain old **object**s that isn't type safe, but doesn't require making lots of different versions.

Here is where generics come in to save the day, fixing this tricky dilemma for us.

What are Generics?

Generics are a clever way for you to define special *generic* types (classes or structs) which save a spot to place a specific type in later. It is a template of sorts, where some types used within your class are filled in when the class gets used, not when the class gets defined.

The template is filled in with the actual types to use when the generic type is used, not when the type is defined. At one time you'll say, "This time I need a list of **int**s," and another time you'll say, "Now I want a list of **Hamburger** objects."

In short, generics provide a way to define type-safe classes, without having to actually commit to any particular type when you create the class.

In the next chapter, I'll show you how to actually create your own generic types, but right now, we'll start by taking a look at a few generic types that already exist in the .NET Standard Library that you'll find very useful. We'll start with the **List** class, which is the "official" version of what we've been describing up until now in this chapter. Then we'll look at a generic interface (**IEnumerable**) which is an interface that allows you to look at all items in a collection, one at a time, and is used by nearly all collection classes. Finally, we'll look at the **Dictionary** class, which is a bit more advanced and shows off a few more of the features that generics offer.

The List Class

The .NET Platform already includes an implementation of a generic **List** class, which is a growable, ordered collection of items (unlike arrays, which can't be resized). The **List** class is a great, simple example that shows us how to use generics in general, but it is also just a useful class to know about, and you'll use it frequently as you do C# programming. For both of these reasons, we'll start our discussion on generics with the **List** class.

This class is called **List**, so you might think you can create a list like this:

```
List listOfStrings = new List(); // This doesn't quite work...
```

But that doesn't quite work. This is because the **List** class uses generics, and has a *generic type parameter*. Having generic type parameters is what makes a type generic. What it means is that we are going to need to fill in some types to be used when we attempt to use it. These generic type parameters are filled in by specifying the types to use inside of angle brackets ('<' and '>'). For a list of **string**s, you do this:

```
List<string> listOfStrings = new List<string>();
```

You now have a list containing strings!

I should point out that the **List<T>** generic type (as well as **IEnumerable<T>** and **Dictionary<K, V>** that we'll talk about next) are all in the System.Collections.Generic namespace, so if your file doesn't have a **using** directive at the top of the file for that, you'll want to add it (Chapter 27). (By default, it is included though.)

With a generic type like this, the generic type parameter gets filled in across the class. In the above case, we've filled in the **string** type in many places for this particular instance, and the compiler will be able to ensure only strings are used to interact with this particular **List** instance.

As an example, the **List** class has an **Add** method, which allows you to put new items in the list:

```
listOfStrings.Add("Hello World!");
```

Because we've specified that we're using **string** for the type parameter, the signature of this **Add** method now requires that we give it a **string**. If we had made it a **List<int>**, then the **Add** method would require that it be given an **int**. Yet the generic **List** class was only defined once. We've gotten the best of both worlds: type safety, but without needing to make lots of different class definitions.

Let's look at a few more examples of using the **List** class.

If adding items to the end isn't what you need, you can use the **Insert** method, which allows you to supply the index to add the item at, pushing everything else back:

```
listOfStrings.Insert(0, "text3");
```

Remember that indices typically start at 0, so the above code inserts at the front of the list.

You can also get an item out of the list using the **ElementAt** method.

```
string firstItem = listOfStrings.ElementAt(0);
```

You can also use the square brackets (**[** and **]**) with the **List** class to get and set values at specific indexes, just like an array. (This is done through an indexer, which we'll see in Chapter 35.) For example:

```
string secondItem = listOfStrings[1]; // Get a value.
listOfStrings[0] = "New Value!";       // Set a value.
```

Also, the **RemoveAt** method allows you to remove items from the list:

```
listOfStrings.RemoveAt(2);
```

While we're talking about deleting stuff, you can remove *everything* from the list with the **Clear** method:

```
listOfStrings.Clear();
```

While arrays have the **Length** property to determine how many items are in the array, the **List** class has a **Count** property instead. (There's no **Length** property; the inconsistency is rather unfortunate.)

```
int itemsInList = listOfStrings.Count;
```

If we're using a **List**, but we want to get a copy of the contents as an array, there's an easy way to do this. There's a **ToArray** method that will make this conversion for us, copying our generic **List** instance into an array of the appropriate type:

```
List<int> someNumbersInAList = new List<int>();
someNumbersInAList.Add(14);
someNumbersInAList.Add(24);
someNumbersInAList.Add(37);

int[] numbersInArray = someNumbersInAList.ToArray();
```

We are also able to loop over all of the items in a **List**, just like with arrays:

```
List<int> someNumbersInAList = new List<int>();
someNumbersInAList.Add(14);
someNumbersInAList.Add(24);
someNumbersInAList.Add(37);

foreach(int number in someNumbersInAList)
{
    // ...
}
```

Since the **List** class is generic, you can create an instance of the **List** class using any other type you want. And when you do, all of the methods like **Add** and **ElementAt** will work *only* for the type that you are using, keeping it type safe like we wanted.

Using Collection Initializer Syntax

When we first introduced arrays, we also discussed *collection initializer syntax* (or simply a *collection initializer*) that allowed us to set up an array using simplified syntax:

```
int[] numbers = new int[] { 1, 2, 3, 4, 5 };
```

We can do this same thing with the **List<T>** class as well. The earlier code that added multiple items to a list could be simplified using collection initializer syntax:

```
List<int> someNumbersInAList = new List<int>() { 14, 24, 37 };
```

This trick works on anything that implements the **IEnumerable<T>** interface (see the next section) and has an **Add** method. The C# compiler simply turns that into calls to **Add**.

The IEnumerable<T> Interface

One of the generic types that you'll encounter the most is the **IEnumerable<T>** interface. If you recall from the chapter on enumerations, the definition of the world "enumerate" means to count off, one-by-one, each item in a group or collection. This is essentially what the **IEnumerable<T>** interface is for. It allows a collection to give others the ability to look at each item contained in it, one at a time.

Nearly every collection class that you encounter in the .NET world will implement this interface. In that sense, it serves as the base or lowest level of defining a collection. Both the **List** class and **Dictionary** class that we'll see next implement it. Even arrays implement **IEnumerable<T>**.

IEnumerable<T> provides the foundation for all sorts of interesting and important features in C#. In Chapter 13 when we were talking about arrays and the **foreach** loop, we saw that if something implements **IEnumerable<T>**, it can be used in a **foreach** loop. And **IEnumerable<T>** is used as the foundation for LINQ queries, which we'll talk about in Chapter 38.

All sorts of things implement **IEnumerable<T>**. If all you care about is the ability to do something with each item in a collection, you can get away with treating it as simply an **IEnumerable<T>**:

```
IEnumerable<int> numbers = new int[3] { 1, 2, 3 };
```

You'll see some methods returning **IEnumerable<T>** if they don't want you to know the actual concrete type being used (it could be an array or a **List** or something else) and if they want you to have the ability to loop through the items, but not modify the collection.

The Dictionary Class

To wrap up our introduction on using generics, let's look at another generic class that is slightly more complex than **List**: the **Dictionary** class. This class isn't quite as versatile as the **List** class, but you'll definitely find uses for it, so it is a good choice to look at.

Let's start by describing what the **Dictionary** class actually is. A physical dictionary has a set of words that you use to look up a definition that belongs to each word. One piece of information is used to look up another piece of information.

The **Dictionary** class does this same thing. We use one piece of information (the *key*) to store and look up another piece of information (the *value*). So it is a mapping of key/value pairs. Because the class is generic, we're not limited to **string**s. We can use any type that we want.

For example, let's look at how you could use a **Dictionary** to create a phone book. Since **Dictionary** is a generic class, we can use it with any type we want. In the case of a phone book, we might use a string name for the key to look up our own custom-made **PhoneNumber** class. (Though these are just examples, and we could use anything else too.)

The **Dictionary** class has *two* generic type parameters, one for the key and one for the value. That tells us we can pick our own type for both keys (we're not just limited to strings) and also for values. For this sample, we'll use **string** for the keys and **PhoneNumber** for the values:

```
Dictionary<string, int> phoneBook = new Dictionary<string, int>();
```

The **Dictionary** class allows us to use the indexing operator ('[' and ']') to get or set values in it:

```
phoneBook["Gates, Bill"] = new PhoneNumber("5550100");
phoneBook["Zuckerberg, Mark"] = new PhoneNumber("5551438");

PhoneNumber billsNumber = phoneBook["Gates, Bill"];
```

When you go to use a generic type, you fill in values (type names) for each of the generic type arguments it defines. Most generic types will have one or two generic type parameters that you can fill in, but there isn't a limit on the number of generic type arguments that a type can have.

As you can see from the above example, when you fill in the generic type arguments with specific types, you can mix and match. There's no requirement for them to all be **string** or anything of that nature.

There is quite a bit more that the **Dictionary** class can do, though we won't get into the details here. Feel free to explore and see what else is there.

Try It Out!

Generics Quiz. Answer the following questions to check your understanding. When you're done, check your answers against the ones below. If you missed something, go back and review the section that talks about it.

1. Describe the problem generics address.
2. How would you create a list of **string**s, using the generic **List** class?
3. How many generic type parameters does the **Dictionary** class have?
4. **True/False**. When a generic class has multiple type parameters, they must all match.
5. What method is used to add items to a **List** object?
6. Name two methods that cause items to be removed from a **List**.

Answers: (1) Type safety without creating many similar types. **(2)** List<string> strings = new List<string>(); **(3)** Two: the key type and the value type. **(4)** False. **(5) Add**. **(6) RemoveAt** and **Clear**.

Making Generic Types

In a Nutshell
- You can create your own class that uses generics by placing the generic type in angle brackets after the class definition: **public class PracticeList<T> { /* ... */ }**.
- Using single capital letters for generic types is common, so **T** is a common in generic classes.
- You can have multiple generic types: **public class PracticeDictionary<K, V> { /* ... */ }**.
- When you include generic type parameters in a type definition, you can use that type name as a placeholder throughout the type (return types, parameter types, instance variable types, etc.) to indicate where it will be used.
- Placing constraints on a generic type variable restrict the kinds of types that can be used, but you know more about the generic type and can do more with it.

In the last chapter, we saw how to use a generic type. In this chapter we will look at how to define your own generic types. Classes, structs, and interfaces can all use generic type parameters.

In this chapter, we'll outline how to make our own generic **PracticeList** class. While the **List** class already exists (we saw it in the previous chapter) this is a good, simple example that will help us see how to make generic types. Obviously, you should use the **List** class and not the one we make here for "real" programs.

Try It Out!
Building Your Own Generic List Class. To help you get a hold of the idea of generics, follow through the contents of this chapter and build your own **PracticeList** class that uses generics.

Creating Your Own Generic Types

To add generic type parameters to a type, you add the generic type parameter names to the type's definition, as shown below:

```
using System;
using System.Collections.Generic;
using System.Linq;
using System.Text;
```

```
using System.Threading.Tasks;

namespace Generics // Your namespace might be different.
{
    public class PracticeList<T>
    {
    }
}
```

You can see that this is the same as a normal class, with the exception of having that **<T>** in there. This is what allows the class to use generics.

This gives a name (**T**) to our generic type parameter. This type can then be used across the type for return types, method parameter types, instance variable types, property types, etc. We'll see examples of this very soon, in the upcoming sections.

Generic type names can be any legal identifier, but two patterns are common: using single capital letters (**T**, **K**, **V**, etc.), and using some simple name, prepended with a **T** (like **TKey** and **TValue**). In places that need just a single generic parameter, most people tend to just use **T**.

If you want multiple generic type arguments, you can simply place them in the same place by naming them inside the angle brackets, separated by commas. For example: **<TKey, TValue>**.

Using Your Generic Type in Your Class

Now that we've created a class with a generic type parameter, we can use this type throughout our class. For instance, since this is a list, we probably want to store the items of our list somewhere. So we can add the following as an instance variable:

```
private T[] items;
```

We create a **private** array called **items**, but you'll see that the type of that array is **T**—our generic parameter type, rather than a "real" type. So whenever someone uses our **PracticeList** class, they'll choose what type to use, and the type they choose will go in here. If they create a **new PracticeList<int>()** then this will become an array of **int**s (**private int[] items**) for that instance.

We probably also want a constructor that will set up our array to have 0 items in it to start:

```
public PracticeList()
{
    items = new T[0];
}
```

This is straightforward enough. We create a new array that uses our generic type parameter **T** with 0 items in it. Yes, having an array with 0 items in it is pretty worthless, but we'll expand it as we add items.

How about a method that returns the item in the list at a particular index?

```
public T GetItem(int index)
{
    return items[index];
}
```

In this case, the return type is our generic type parameter **T**. If we had a **PracticeList<int>**, then this would return an **int**. If it was a **PracticeList<double>**, it would return a **double**.

How about a method that adds an item to the list? This is a little more complicated because it needs to resize the array (technically making a new slightly larger array and then copying the items over to the new array).

```
public void Add(T newItem)
{
    // Make a new bigger array with room to store the new item.
    T[] newItems = new T[items.Length + 1];

    // Copy all of the old items over to the new array.
    for (int index = 0; index < items.Length; index++)
        newItems[index] = items[index];

    // Put the new item at the end.
    newItems[newItems.Length - 1] = newItem;

    // Update our instance variable to hold this new array instead of the old array.
    items = newItems;
}
```

Once again, we are putting our generic type parameter to use. This time, it is used as an input to the method (we only want to be able to add items of the type that matches the list) and also to create the new array that we copy everything to.

Our completed class will look something like this:

```
using System;
using System.Collections.Generic;
using System.Linq;
using System.Text;
using System.Threading.Tasks;

namespace Generics
{
    public class PracticeList<T>
    {
        private T[] items;

        public PracticeList()
        {
            items = new T[0];
        }

        public T GetItem(int index)
        {
            return items[index];
        }

        public void Add(T newItem)
        {
            T[] newItems = new T[items.Length + 1];

            for (int index = 0; index < items.Length; index++)
                newItems[index] = items[index];

            newItems[newItems.Length - 1] = newItem;

            items = newItems;
        }
    }
}
```

Generic Type Constraints

So far, our generic type parameters reserve a spot for another type to be used, and literally any type can be placed in it. This allows people to use anything they want for the generic type in question. It's usually a good thing.

But it does have one problem: within the generic type, you know next to nothing about the objects that it is using. The only thing you can guarantee is that it is an **object**, so the only members you use with instances of the generic type are ones that belong to **object** (**Equals**, **ToString**, **GetHashCode**, etc.)

Many scenarios don't require us to do anything specific with our generic type parameters. For example, a collection just needs to keep track of it. It doesn't have to interact with it. In these cases, the above limitation is not a problem.

But if you do need to be able to do some work with the generic type parameter, you may find that you want to constrain what actual types can be used for the generic type parameter. If you do this, then you limit what types can be filled in at the time of use, but you also know much more about your generic type. As an example, the following shows how you would require that the generic type parameter must be filled in by something that implements the **IComparable** interface:

```
public class PracticeList<T> where T : IComparable
{
    //...
}
```

If we put a generic type constraint in place like this, we will no longer be able to make instances of **PracticeList** where the type parameter is filled in with something that doesn't implement **IComparable**. But in exchange, we could now use **IComparable** methods within the class, because we can be certain that **T** is at least that.

Multiple constraints for a single type can be added by separating them with commas, and if you have multiple generic types, you can specify type constraints for each of them using a new **where** keyword.

```
public class PracticeDictionary<K, V> where K : SomeBaseClass, SomeRandomInterface
                                      where V : SomeOtherInterface
{
    //...
}
```

You can also specify a parameterless constructor constraint, which requires that the type used has a public parameterless constructor. This is done by adding **new()** as a constraint:

```
public class PracticeList<T> where T : new()
{
    //...
}
```

With this, we know that our type parameter **T** has a parameterless constructor and we can invoke it:

```
T newObject = new T();
```

Interestingly, you cannot add "parameterful" constructor constraints. (You can't say **where T : new(int)**, or anything like that.)

You can also specify that a type must be a value or reference type with the struct or class constraint:

```
public class PracticeList<T> where T : class       // Must be a reference type.
{
    //...
}
```

Or:

```
public class PracticeList<T> where T : struct       // Must be a value type.
{
    //...
}
```

You can also indicate that one type parameter must be derived from another type parameter:

```csharp
public class GenericClass<T, U> where T : U
{
    //...
}
```

Generic Methods

In addition to generic classes, you can have individual methods that use generics as well. These can be a part of any class or struct, generic or regular. Like with generic classes, this is useful when you want to have a set of methods that are identical, except for the type that it works on. To do this, you simply list the generic type parameters after the method name but before the parentheses like this:

```csharp
public T LoadObject<T>(string fileName) { ... }
```

Like with classes, you can use as many generic type parameters as you want, apply generic constraints, and also use the generic type parameters in the method's parameter list and return type:

```csharp
public T Convert<T, U>(T item) where T : class
{
    // ...
}
```

To use a generic method, you would do the following:

```csharp
Person person = LoadObject<Person>("person1.txt");
```

The Default Operator

C# includes an operator that will produce the default value for any specific type. This looks like this:

```csharp
int value = default(int);
```

In short, the default value for a type is as close to 0 in meaning as possible. Specifically:

- For all of the integer and floating point types, that's a value of 0.
- For **bool**, it's false.
- For a **char**, it is the character whose numeric value is 0—that is the NULL control character.
- For an enum, it will be a 0. This applies even if you've assigned non-zero values to all of your enum members.
- For a class, including **string** and arrays, it will be **null**.
- For a struct, each element will take on the default value for its type.

The default operator is useful when you are using generics and need to assign a value to a variable of a generic type. If you don't know much about the generic type, then it's hard to do this. For example, if you don't know if something is a value or reference type, then you can't do something like this:

```csharp
T returnValue = null;
```

You can't assign it null, because it might not be a reference type. Likewise, you can't assign it a value of 0 or anything else.

In these cases, all you can do is assign it the default value:

```csharp
T returnValue = default(T);
```

Unfortunately, this sounds more useful than it actually probably is. If you didn't know enough to assign it a real value in the first place, then you still won't know what was created by the **default** operator. You aren't going to be able to do anything with it (short of returning it) once it has been created. There is also no way in C# to define what the default value should be for your class (or struct) either.

So I bring this up because it is an actual operator and keyword in the C# language, and because it does have its uses, but it is not the most powerful of tools you'll find.

In most cases, you will probably want to use the generic type constraints from earlier in this chapter, or come up with a different strategy for creating actual objects rather than using the default value. (There are many approaches to this, though this subject is beyond the scope of this book. But if you do a web search for "creational patterns" you'll find a number of approaches for getting objects of different types created that go far beyond C#'s default operator.)

Try It Out!

Making Generics Quiz. Answer the following questions to check your understanding. When you're done, check your answers against the ones below. If you missed something, go back and review the section that talks about it.

1. How do you indicate that a class has a generic type parameter?
2. **True/False.** Generic classes can only have one generic type parameter.
3. **True/False.** Generic type constraints limit what can be used for the generic type.
4. **True/False.** Constraints let you use the methods of the thing you are constraining to.

Answers: (1) In angle brackets by the class name. **(2)** False. **(3)** True. **(4)** True.

Part

Advanced Topics

We've covered much of the C# language. Much of the things you might want to do, you can do now, and much of what you see you'll be able to understand.

In Part 4, we'll look topic-by-topic at more advanced features of the C# language, and tackle some common tasks that you will likely need to do before too long. This includes:

- More about namespaces and **using** directives (Chapter 27).
- More about methods (Chapter 28).
- Reading from and writing to files (Chapter 29).
- Handling errors using exceptions (Chapter 30).
- Patterns (Chapter 31).
- Delegates (Chapter 32).
- Events (Chapter 33).
- Overloading operators (Chapter 34) and creating indexers (Chapter 35).
- Creating extension methods for existing types (Chapter 36).
- Lambda expressions (Chapter 37) and query expressions (Chapter 38).
- Multi-threading your application (Chapters 39 and 40).
- Dynamic objects (Chapter 41).
- Unsafe (unmanaged) code (Chapter 42).
- A quick pass at a few other features in C# that are worth knowing a bit about (Chapter 43).

Do not feel like you need to read these chapters in order, or even right away. Feel free to jump around and read them as you feel you have a need for these topics.

Namespaces and Using Directives

In a Nutshell

- Namespaces are collections of (usually related) types that are assigned a name collectively.
- A type's fully qualified name is the combination of the namespace name and the type name. You can always use a type's fully qualified name.
- **using** directives indicate which namespace to look in for unqualified type names.
- Name collisions are when the compiler is aware of two different types with the same name. They can be resolved by either using fully qualified names or by using an alias.
- A **using static** directive can be added for any static class, allowing you to use the method without needing the class name: **using static System.Console;** and later: **WriteLine(x);**

Back in Chapter 3, when we made our Hello World program, we first saw **using** directives and the **namespace** keyword. At the time, I mentioned that there's more to understanding these two closely related concepts, but that it was a discussion for another day. That day has arrived!

In this chapter, we'll take a look at what a namespace is, and look in-depth at the use of type names, spread throughout your program. We'll then look at what **using** directives actually do. All of this will give you a much better idea of what is going on with these two important parts of your code.

Namespaces

In a program, it is possible to have two types with the exact same name. Consider this: How many **Point** classes do you think exist out there in the world?

Lots. OpenGL libraries (a very common 3D graphics library) will often have one, every UI framework (like Windows Forms and WPF) has one. The list goes on and on.

You might be thinking, why can't they all just use the same class? Reuse code, and all of that good software engineering mumbo-jumbo.

That's a good thought. In theory. But each of these different libraries needs different things from their **Point** class. Some want it in 2D, others want it in 3D. Some want to use **float**s while others want **double**s. And they each want their **Point** class to be able to do different things. They're fundamentally different types, which just happen to have the same name.

And here's where namespaces come in to play.

A *namespace* is simply a grouping of names.

Usually, people will put related code in the same namespace, so you can also think of a namespace as a module or package for related code. Namespaces are a little like last names. They separate one type with a certain name from other types with the same name.

Fully Qualified Names

Looking back at that **Point** class, the Windows Forms **Point** class is in the **System.Drawing** namespace. The WPF version is in the **System.Windows** namespace. The namespace allows you to distinguish which of the two you have.

When combined, the namespace name and the class name is called a *fully qualified name*. **System.Drawing.Point** is a fully qualified name, as is **System.Windows.Point**. There's no mistaking which of the two you mean.

Up until now, we haven't been using fully qualified names. But we could have been. For example, every place that we've used the **Math** class, we could have used the fully qualified name **System.Math**. We could have written it **System.Math.PI** and **System.Math.Sin(1.2)**.

Using Directives

You can always use a fully qualified name, but in most cases, that's just too much typing, and it tends to make your code less readable.

In any particular file, we have the ability to point out a namespace and say, "I'm using the stuff in that namespace, so if I don't use a fully qualified name, that's where you'll find it." This is done by putting in a **using** directive, which we've been doing since the beginning.

At the top of a file, we can list all of the names of the namespaces that we will be frequently using. With a **using** directive for **System** (**using System;**) we can use the name of anything in the **System** namespace without needing to use the fully qualified name. (This particular **using** directive, along with a few others, is added to our file for us when we create a new file in Visual Studio.)

This is the reason that we've been able to get away with just saying **Math.PI** all along, instead of **System.Math.PI**. Our program already had a **using System;** statement at the top of the file.

The Error 'The type or namespace X could not be found'

If you try to use the unqualified name for a type, leaving out the namespace, and you don't have an appropriate **using** directive, you'll run into the following error:

```
The type or namespace 'X' could not be found (are you missing a using directive or an assembly reference?)
```

This lists two possible causes for the problem: missing a **using** directive or missing an assembly reference. The first part of that is usually what's happening. (Missing assembly references are covered in Chapter 46.) This can easily be solved by simply adding the appropriate **using** directive. (Or use the fully qualified name instead.)

There are two ways you can add a missing **using** directive. First, you could scroll up to the top of the file and manually type in a **using** directive for the right namespace. That works, but it has a few small problems. If you don't know what namespace you actually need, you have to hunt around the Internet to figure it out, which takes time and pulls you away from whatever task you were doing.

There's a shortcut that is much easier.

To illustrate, I've gone into my program and deleted the **using System;** statement in my program, so that C# doesn't know what to do with **Math** anymore.

Once you type something like this:

```
double pi = Math.PI;
```

Visual Studio will underline **Math** in red, because it doesn't know what to do with it:

```
class Program
{
    static void Main(string[] args)
    {
        double pi = Math.PI;
    }
}
```

When this happens, use the mouse to hover over the underlined word, and two extra pieces of UI will pop up: a lightbulb icon and a message describing the error with a link to show possible fixes.

```
class Program
{
    static void Main(string[] args)
    {
        double pi = Math.PI;
    }
}
```
The name 'Math' does not exist in the current context

Show potential fixes (Ctrl+.)

By either clicking on the lightbulb or clicking the link to show potential fixes, you'll get a list of ways this (or any other) problem could be resolved.

```
class Program
{
    static void Main(string[] args)
    {
        double pi = Math.PI;
    }
}
```
using System;
System.Math
Generate variable 'Math'
Generate type 'Math'

CS0103 The name 'Math' does not exist in the current context
using System;
using System.Collections.Generic;
...
Preview changes

Clicking on **using System;** will automatically add a **using** directive for you. (Clicking on the second option there will automatically change your code to use the fully qualified name.)

This makes it so you don't have to memorize or hunt down the namespace that things are in because Visual Studio figures it out for you. You don't even need to leave what you were working on to do it.

There's a keyboard shortcut to get this to pop up: **Ctrl + .** (the period key).

If you are using a type name that is in multiple namespaces, the little drop down box may have multiple choices in it. If so, you'll need to be sure to choose the right one. Accidentally choosing the wrong one is a quick way to a wasted hour and a bad headache.

Name Collisions

On a few rare occasions, you'll add **using** directives for two namespaces that both contain a type with the same name. This is called a *name collision* because the unqualified name is ambiguous. In this case, even though you have **using** directives for an unqualified name, it still can't figure it out.

One solution to this is to just go back to fully qualified names. That tends to be my preferred solution. It keeps things clear and unambiguous. But there's another way to deal with name collisions: aliases.

Using Aliases to Solve Name Collisions

You can also use an alias to solve the problem of a name collision. An alias is a way to create a new name for an existing type name. You can think of it like a nickname.

To illustrate, imagine you have the following code, which won't compile because **C** is a name collision:

```
using N1;
using N2;

namespace N1
{
    public class C { }
}

namespace N2
{
    public class C { }
}

namespace NamespaceExample
{
    class Program
    {
        static void Main(string[] args)
        {
            C c = new C(); // Compiler can't tell if you're using N1.C or N2.C.
        }
    }
}
```

You can define an alias with the **using** keyword (yes, there's a lot of uses for the **using** keyword):

```
using CFromN1 = N1.C;
```

This line is placed among your other using directives, though most people put namespace aliases after normal **using** directives:

```
using N1;
using N2;
using CFromN1 = N1.C; // The name here is arbitrary. You could even reuse the name 'C'.

namespace N1
{
    public class C { }
}

namespace N2
{
    public class C { }
}

namespace NamespaceExample
{
    class Program
```

```
    {
        static void Main(string[] args)
        {
            CFromN1 c = new CFromN1();
        }
    }
}
```

When the compiler is resolving unqualified type names, an alias like this will always take precedence over looking through the things contained in a normal **using** directive, which helps resolves name collisions.

Avoiding name collisions in the first place is preferred. But failing that, you'll have to choose between using fully qualified type names and aliases. Both have pros and cons, and both are commonly used.

Static Using Directives

In Chapter 18, we discussed static classes. For a static class, there is a variation on **using** directives that allow you to make the members of that class available without even needing the class name. That is done by using a *static using directive.* (Ironically, the syntax reverses the ordering of those words.) As an example of this, the following code creates a static **using** directive for both **System.Math** and **System.Console**, which makes it so you can refer to **Console.WriteLine** as just **WriteLine**, **Math.PI** as just **PI**, etc.:

```
using static System.Math;
using static System.Console;

namespace StaticUsingDirectives
{
    public static class Program
    {
        public static void Main(string[] args)
        {
            double x = PI;
            WriteLine(Sin(x));
            ReadKey();
        }
    }
}
```

This is a bit of a double-edged sword. On one hand, it's more concise, which is a good thing. On the other hand, when people see a "bare" method reference (like **WriteLine**) the first assumption is that it lives elsewhere in the class, which isn't necessarily true with a static using directive. So use it when it makes things easier to understand, and avoid it when it makes things harder to understand.

Try It Out!

Namespaces Quiz. Answer the following questions to check your understanding. When you're done, check your answers against the ones below. If you missed something, go back and review the section that talks about it.

1. **True/False. using** directives make previously inaccessible code accessible.
2. **True/False. using** directives make it so you do not need to use fully qualified names.
3. **True/False.** Two types are allowed to have the same name.
4. **True/False.** A name collision is when two types have the same name.
5. Name two ways to resolve a name collision.
6. What **using** directive would need to be added so that you can use **System.Math**'s **Abs** (absolute value) method as **Abs(x)** instead of **Math.Abs(x)**?

Answers: **(1)** False. **(2)** True. **(3)** True. **(4)** True. **(5)** Use fully qualified names or aliases. **(6)** using static System.Math;

Methods Revisited

In a Nutshell
- Local functions can be defined inside of another method.
- Parameters can be made optional by providing a default value for the parameter: **public void DoSomething(int x = 6) { ... }**
- When calling a method, you can name your parameters: **DoSomethingElse(x: 4, z: 2, y:1);** When doing this, you can put the parameters in any order.
- By using the **params** keyword, methods can have a variable number of parameters.
- The **ref** and **out** keyword can be used on a method parameter to pass the actual variable, rather than just the contents of the variable, allowing the called method to modify the contents of variables in the calling method.

We first looked at methods in Chapter 15. We'll now take a second look at methods and discuss a few more advanced features, because we're ready for it now.

Local Functions

We've spent a lot of time defining methods that belong directly to a class, struct or other type. As it turns out, we can actually define a method directly inside of another method.

To clarify, we should probably formalize our terminology here. Generally speaking, a *function* is a section of reusable code that optionally takes inputs (parameters) and optionally produces ("returns") a result.

A *method* is a specific sub-type of function that is owned by a class or other type. As a member of a class, the method also has access to class-level instance variables and the other functions or methods defined in the class. All methods are functions, but not all functions are methods.

Some other languages allow "bare" functions that live outside of any class or type. They're just defined at the top level. These functions would not be considered methods because they aren't members of a class. C# does not allow these types of functions.

But C# does allow you to define *local functions*, which are defined inside of *another* method or function, rather than directly inside of a class or other type. Here is a simple example:

```
public class Program
{
    public static void Main(string[] args)
    {
        int Add(int a, int b)
        {
            return a + b;
        }

        Console.WriteLine(Add(1, 1));
        Console.WriteLine(Add(2, 2));
        Console.WriteLine(Add(3, 7));
    }
}
```

The syntax is mostly the same as you'd expect from a normal method. There are a few caveats worth mentioning. You can't specify an accessibility modifier (like **public** or **private**). Local functions are actually *more* constrained than **private**. They are only accessible within the scope of a single method. You also can't make a local function **static**.

You can define local functions anywhere within another method. The code above defined it at the start of the method. You could alternatively define it at the end, or in the middle. No matter where you put it, you can call the method from anywhere else inside of the method just fine. So this code compiles as well:

```
void AnyMethod()
{
    int Subtract(int x, int y) { return x - y; }

    Console.WriteLine(Add(1, 2) + " " + Subtract(6, 4)); // Outputs "3 2"

    int Add(int a, int b) { return a + b; }
}
```

This code has two local functions: a **Subtract** method at the top and an **Add** method at the bottom, with code that calls both in the middle.

But while you can place them anywhere within a method and call them from anywhere else in the method, you will be doing yourself a big favor if you pick some convention (like always putting local functions first) rather than just scattering them randomly throughout the parent method.

Local functions can be used to separate out logical chunks of a larger method without making those chunks accessible to any other part of the class. (If you want the rest of the class to be able to reuse it, make it a private method in the class instead.) A local function can be invoked repeatedly from inside the containing method, so it allows for code reuse without making it accessible beyond the method.

Optional Parameters

Let's say you are making a method that simulates a die roll by picking a random number between 1 and the number of sides on the die. Suppose your class contained something like this:

```
private Random random = new Random();

public int RollDie(int sides)
{
    return random.Next(sides) + 1;
}
```

It's entirely possible that 99% of the time, you're going to be passing in 6 for the **sides** parameter. It will be kind of annoying to always need to say **RollDie(6)**. C# provides a way to specify a default value for a parameter, making it optional as long as you're OK with the default. Doing this is pretty easy:

```
public int RollDie(int sides = 6)
{
    return random.Next(sides) + 1;
}
```

With this code, you can now call **RollDie()** and the value of 6 will be used, or you can still fall back to putting a value in if you would like:

```
RollDie();   // Uses the default value of 6.
RollDie(20); // Uses 20 instead of the default.
```

While you can have as many optional parameters as you want, and can mix and match them with non-optional parameters, all optional parameters must come at the end after all of the "normal" parameters.

Named Parameters

Occasionally, you'll go to use a method, but you don't remember what order the parameters are in. This is especially true when the method requires several parameters of the same type. As an example, look at the method below, which takes an input value and clamps it to a particular range, returning the result:

```
public int Clamp(int value, int min, int max)
{
    if(value < min) { return min; } // Bump the value up to the min if too low.
    if(value > max) { return max; } // Move the value down to the max if too high.
    return value;                   // Otherwise, we're good with the original value.
}
```

When you go to use this method, you might see something that looks like this:

```
Clamp(20, 50, 100);
```

When you see this, you always need to do a little digging to figure out what's going on. Is it going to clamp the value of 100 to the range 20 to 50? Or clamp the value of 20 to the range 50 to 100?

To avoid this ambiguity, C# allows you to supply names for parameters. This is done by putting the parameter name, followed by a colon, followed by the value for that parameter:

```
Clamp(min: 50, max: 100, value: 20);
```

With named parameters, it is very clear what value belongs to which parameter. Furthermore, as long as the compiler can figure out where everything goes, this allows you to put the parameters in any order, making it so that you don't need to worry about the official ordering, as long as they all have a value.

When you call a method, you can use regular unnamed parameters, or named parameters, but all regular parameters must come first, and each variable must be assigned to only once.

You can also combine optional parameters with named parameters.

One side effect of this feature is that parameter names are now a part of your program's public interface. Changing a parameter's name, can break code that calls the method using named parameters.

Variable Number of Parameters

Let's say you want to average some numbers together. We can write a method to average two numbers:

```
public static double Average(int a, int b)
{
    return (a + b) / 2.0;
}
```

What if you want to average three numbers? You could write a similar method for that:

```
public static double Average(int a, int b, int c)
{
    return (a + b + c) / 3.0;
}
```

What if you wanted 5? Or 10? You could keep adding more and more methods, but it gets unwieldy fast.

C# provides a way to supply a variable number of parameters to a method, by using the **params** keyword with an array variable:

```
public static double Average(params int[] numbers)
{
    double total = 0;

    foreach (int number in numbers)
        total += number;

    return total / numbers.Length;
}
```

To the outside world, the **params** keyword makes it look like you can supply any number of parameters:

```
Average(2, 3);
Average(2, 5, 8);
Average(41, 49, 29, 2, -7, 18);
```

However, behind the scenes, the C# compiler will turn these into an array to use in the method call.

It is also worth pointing out that you can directly pass in an array to this type of method:

```
int[] numbers = new int[5] { 5, 4, 3, 2, 1 };
Average(numbers);
```

You can combine a **params** argument with other parameters, but the **params** argument must be the last one, and there can be only one of them.

The 'out' and 'ref' Keywords

Back in Chapter 16, we talked about value and reference semantics. We looked at how whenever you pass something into a method as a parameter, the contents of the variable are copied. With value types, this meant we got a complete copy of the original data. For reference types, we got a copy of the reference, which was still pointing to the same object in the heap.

Methods have the option of handing off the actual variable, rather than copying its contents, by using the **ref** or **out** keyword. Doing this means that the called method is working with the *exact same variable* that existed in the calling method.

This sort of creates the illusion that value types have been turned into reference types, and sort of takes reference types to the next level, where it feels like you've got a reference to a reference.

To do this, you add either the **ref** keyword or the **out** keyword to a particular parameter.

```
public void MessWithVariables(out int x, ref int y)
{
    x = 3;
    y = 17;
}
```

We can then call this code like this:

```
int banana = 2;
int turkey = 5;

MessWithVariables(out banana, ref turkey);
```

At the end of this code, the **banana** variable will contain a value of 3, and the **turkey** variable will contain a value of 17.

If you look at this code, you'll see that you need to put **out** or **ref** when you call the method as well. There's a good reason for this. Handing off the actual variables from one method to another is a risky game to play. By requiring these keywords in both the called method and the calling method, we can ensure that the variables were handed off intentionally.

There is a small difference between using **ref** and **out**, and that difference has to do with whether the calling method or the called method is responsible for initializing the variable. With the **ref** keyword, the calling method needs to initialize the variable before the method call. This allows the called method to assume that it is already initialized. These are sometimes called *reference parameters*.

With the **out** keyword, the compiler ensures that the called method initializes the variable before returning from the method. These are sometimes called *output parameters*.

Using reference or output parameters does a couple of things. Because we're passing the actual variable, instead of just the contents of the variable, value types won't need to be completely copied when passed into a method. This can speed things up because it could save us from copying a lot of value types.

You can also use this to get back multiple values from a method. You can technically only return one value from a method, but additional values can be returned as an output parameter instead. (More on this later in this chapter.)

Sending the actual variable to a method, instead of just the contents of the variable is a dangerous thing to do. We're giving another method control over our variables, and if used carelessly, it causes a lot of trouble. Use it sparingly and wisely.

Inline Declarations for Output Parameters

It is possible to simultaneously declare a variable for an output parameter in the same location as the method invocation. To illustrate, look at the **double.TryParse** method, which illustrates a pretty common use of an output parameter:

```
if (double.TryParse("3.14", out double newValue))
    return newValue * newValue;
else return double.NaN;
```

The **double.TryParse** method takes a string and parses it (analyzes the text to determine the numeric value that matches the text representation), but it does so conditionally. It returns a **bool** that indicates whether it was successful or not. If it can't parse it (for example, if the string contained "Jabba the Hutt" instead of "3.14") then rather than blowing up on us, it will simply return **false**, rather than **true**. Since the return value is used to indicate whether it was successful or not, the method does not return the parsed value. Instead, it gives that back via the output parameter.

Our earlier example showed declaring the variable on a separate line. While that's always an option, this last example shows that an output parameter can also be defined inline, which tends to produce cleaner code. (This is a C# 7 feature, so if you're using an older version, you will need to declare the variable on an earlier line.)

Ref Return Types and Ref Local Variables

In addition to using **ref** on parameters, **ref** can also be used for local variables and return values.

Consider a scenario from the game development world. While there are many ways you can structure your game, let's say you have a game where the state of the game is represented as a collection of many starships. Suppose you declare a **Ship** struct that looks like this (being a **struct** instead of a **class** is important here):

```
public struct Ship
{
    public double X { get; set; }
    public double Y { get; set; }
    public int PlayerIndex { get; set; }
}
```

And then suppose you've defined your game's current state along these lines:

```
public class GameState
{
    private Ship[] ships;

    public Ship GetShip(int index) // BROKEN!
    {
        return ships[index];
    }
}
```

(Please note that I'm not saying this is the best way to organize your game's code. I'm not even suggesting it's a *good* way. But it does serve to illustrate the point.)

What problem do you get when you attempt to use a value returned from that **GetShip** method to adjust a ship's position?

The issue goes back to the difference between value types and reference types. Note that **Ship** is a struct, which means it has value semantics. When we call **GetShip**, a **Ship** instance is returned, but it's a copy (because of the value semantics) of the intended one.

If somebody tries to modify the ship using code like this, it will fail:

```
Ship ship = gameState.GetShip(2);
ship.X += 0.1;
```

Instead of modifying the one in the game state's **ships** array, we are modifying a copy.

An easy way around this is to use a **ref** return value, which passes the result back by reference, instead of by value, in a manner similar to what we saw with a **ref** parameter or an **out** parameter:

```
public class GameState
{
    private Ship[] ships;

    public ref Ship GetShip(int index)
    {
        return ref ships[index];
    }
}
```

This can then be called like so:

```
ref Ship ship = ref gameState.GetShip(2);
ship.X += 0.1;
```

Like before, you will need the **ref** keyword on both sides of the method (where we return the value, as well as where we store the value when it comes back). This helps establish a clear understanding that you are messing with somebody else's data—that you have a reference to something that will modify somebody else's data. If that is the intent, you're fine. If it's not the intent, the **ref** keyword should make that obvious very quickly.

You'll also note that the local variable that stores the returned value must also be marked with **ref** as well. So **ref** return types and **ref** local variables go hand-in-hand. You'll see them together frequently.

There are other options here. We could have made **Ship** a class instead of a struct. This would have immediately given us reference semantics in all cases. That would have probably made this particular sample simpler.

We also could have simply asked the **GameState** class to do the ship position change through a method instead. Something like **void GameState.MoveShip(int shipIndex, double xAmount, double yAmount)**.

Like usual, choose the one that produces the most understandable and maintainable code.

Try It Out!

Methods Revisited Quiz. Answer the following questions to check your understanding. When you're done, check your answers against the ones below. If you missed something, go back and review the section that talks about it.

For questions 1-3, consider the following code: **void DoSomething(int x, int y = 3, int z = 4) { ... }**

1. Which parameters are optional?
2. What values do **x, y**, and **z** have if called with **DoSomething(1, 2);**
3. What values do **x, y**, and **z** have if called with the following: **DoSomething(x : 2, z : 9);**
4. **True/False.** Optional parameters must be after all required parameters.
5. **True/False.** A parameter that has the **params** keyword must be the last parameter.
6. Given the method **void DoSomething(int x, params int[] numbers) { ... }** which of the following are allowed?
    a.   **DoSomething();**
    b.   **DoSomething(1);**
    c.   **DoSomething(1, 2, 3, 4, 5);**
    d.   **DoSomething(1, new int[] { 2, 3, 4, 5 });**
7. **True/False.** Parameters that are marked with **out** result in handing off the actual variable passed in, instead of just copying the contents of the variable.
8. **True/False.** Parameters that are marked with **ref** result in handing off the actual variable passed in, instead of just copying the contents of the variable.
9. **True/False.** Parameters that are marked with **out** must be initialized inside the method.
10. **True/False.** Parameters that are marked with **ref** must be initialized inside the method.

Answers: **(1)** y and z. **(2)** x=1,y=2,z=4. **(3)** x=2,y=3,z=9. **(4)** True. **(5)** True. **(6)** b, c, d. **(7)** True. **(8)** True. **(9)**True. **(10)** False.

Returning Multiple Values

Generally speaking, methods should only return one value. Returning multiple values is a sign that the method might be doing too much and should be broken down into multiple different methods. But there are certain scenarios where multiple return values are legitimately needed.

One example of this is wanting to be able to compute both the quotient and remainder of an integer division operation. Perhaps you remember doing this in school, where 26 / 5 is 5 remainder 1. In this case, we can compute both the quotient (plain old 26 / 5, which results in 5 because of integer division) and the remainder using the **%** operator (26 % 5 is 1). We could make a method to compute both the quotient and the remainder as a pair.

We're going to use the problem above—the simultaneously computing the division and remainder together—as a sample for the rest of this section. But having said that, the **Math** class actually has a static method (**Math.DivRem**) that does this very thing. In other words, you don't need to write your own. You can reuse the existing method.

Output Parameters

One way to return multiple values is with output parameters, as discussed in the previous section. The syntax with **ref** and **out** is kind of ugly, but it does give you an easy way to pass values back out using a parameter to do so.

```
public static int DivRem(int dividend, int divisor, out int remainder)
{
    remainder = dividend % divisor;
    return dividend / divisor;
}
```

This is used like this:

```
int division = DivRem(26, 5, out int remainder);
Console.WriteLine(division + " remainder " + remainder);
```

Custom Return Type

Traditionally, return values are meant for values computed by the method, while parameters are meant for values provided to the method. So using a parameter as output goes against the conceptual pattern.

As an alternative to using output parameters, you can take multiple values and package them up into a single type (a class or struct, though this is a good fit for a struct). Perhaps something like this:

```
public struct DivRemResults
{
    public int Division { get; }
    public int Remainder { get; }

    public DivRemResults(int division, int remainder) { Division = division; Remainder = remainder; }
}
```

With a custom return type, our **DivRem** method might look like this:

```
public static DivRemResults DivRem(int divisor, int dividend)
{
    return new DivRemResults(divisor / dividend, divisor % dividend);
}
```

Our calling code would then look more like this:

```
DivRemResults results = DivRem(26, 5);
Console.WriteLine(results.Division + " remainder " + results.Remainder);
```

This version uses return values and parameters more traditionally, but it does require creating a unique type (like **DivRemResults**) any time you do this.

Using Tuples

A variation on the last option is to use a class (or struct) that can use generics to store these one-off classes. The .NET Platform has one such class (technically a group of similarly named classes) that can do this for you: the **Tuple** classes.

There is not just a single **Tuple** class, but a whole family of them. The **Tuple** classes are simple generic containers for a specific number of items. There is a 2-item tuple (**Tuple<T1, T2>**) a 3-item tuple (**Tuple<T1, T2, T3>**) and so on, up to 7 items.

Since these are generic, you can substitute in whatever type you need. So rather than creating the **DivRemResults** class in the last section, we could have used a **Tuple<int, int>**:

```
public static Tuple<int, int> DivRem(int divisor, int dividend)
{
    return new Tuple<int, int>(divisor / dividend, divisor % dividend);
}
```

Which could be called like this:

```
Tuple<int, int> results = DivRem(26, 5);
Console.WriteLine(results.Item1 + " remainder " + results.Item2);
```

In theory, you could almost get away with using **Tuple** for pretty much all of your data in your program. In practice, that's a bad idea. Aside from the usefulness of being able to add your own methods, properties, etc., the naming going on inside the **Tuple** classes is awful. The type name, **Tuple**, tells you nothing about what kind of data it stores, and the properties for each individual item in the tuple (**Item1**, **Item2**, etc.) is worse. Giving names to your data is extremely beneficial, and **Tuple** doesn't allow that.

There are places where it will make more sense to make custom classes with good names, while other places might be better off just using **Tuple**. There is a place for both of these options.

ValueTuples and Language-Level Support of Tuples

Our final option for returning multiple values is a new feature of C# 7. Some changes were made to the language that give new syntax for creating and working with tuples. Of greatest importance is that the language now (mostly) has a way to directly return multiple values, or at least the appearance of that. Behind the scenes, a tuple is being created and returned instead, like we saw in the last section.

This language-level support for tuples was not applied to the existing **Tuple** classes, but to new **ValueTuple** structs instead. The language designers felt that it would be better to do multiple return values with a value type (hence the **ValueTuple** structs) instead of with a reference type (like the older **Tuple** classes).

Overall, **ValueTuple** functions the same as **Tuple**, just as a struct (value type) instead of a class (reference type). There are multiple versions with a different number of arguments, all of which are generic.

There is a rather significant catch to the **ValueTuple** structs. Your project does not reference the thing that contains **ValueTuple** by default. It has to be added before anything in this section will work.

Adding references to other packages like this is discussed in Chapter 46. In fact, that chapter specifically uses this **ValueTuple** package as its example. You should feel free to jump ahead and read Chapter 46 (or anything in Part 5, for that matter) whenever you want, including right now, so that you can get your hands on **ValueTuple** to explore and use it in your projects in the future. Specifically, you will want to read the section called "*NuGet Packages*", which will walk you through adding the System.ValueTuple package.

The simplest way to use the **ValueTuple** structs is just like the **Tuple** classes that we saw in the last section:

```
public static ValueTuple<int, int> DivRem(int divisor, int dividend)
{
    return new ValueTuple<int, int>(divisor / dividend, divisor % dividend);
}
```

Which could be called like this:

```
ValueTuple<int, int> results = DivRem(26, 5);
Console.WriteLine(results.Item1 + " remainder " + results.Item2);
```

But what's really cool is the language level support for creating and working with **ValueTuple**s. Consider this code:

```
public static (int division, int remainder) DivRem(int divisor, int dividend)
{
    return (divisor / dividend, divisor % dividend);
}
```

Which can be invoked like this:

```
(int division, int remainder) = DivRem(26, 5);
Console.WriteLine(division + " remainder " + remainder);
```

This code is functionally the same as our earlier code, just with better, cleaner syntax. In the **DivRem** method, we can get a **ValueTuple<int, int>** created by simply placing our two **int** values in parentheses.

Similarly, our return type is specified as **(int division, int remainder)**, which is also a shorthand way of indicating we return a **ValueTuple<int, int>**. Perhaps more importantly, this actually allows us to override the names of the tuple members from **Item1** and **Item2** to **division** and **remainder**.

You can also see on the other side that even though it is technically a **ValueTuple** being returned, we can immediately unpack it into separate, named variables: **(int division, int remainder)**. These names don't have to match the names provided by the method definition, but probably frequently will.

You can omit the names of the return types if you want:

```
public static (int, int) DivRem(string value)
```

If you do this, you can still unpack it to named local variables after returning, like we did before, though in this case, if you store the results in a **ValueTuple** directly, the names of the items will be **Item1** and **Item2**.

Furthermore, you're allowed to use the nice language-level syntax for working with **ValueTuple** on one side of the return, but keep it as a **ValueTuple** on the other side as shown below:

```
ValueTuple<int, int> results = DivRem(26, 5);
Console.WriteLine(results.Item1 + " remainder " + results.Item2);
```

Same the other way around. If you define **DivRem** like this:

```
public static ValueTuple<int, int> DivRem(int divisor, int dividend)
```

You can still use this code:

```
(int division, int remainder) = DivRem(26, 5);
Console.WriteLine(division + " remainder " + remainder);
```

Using **ValueTuple**s is a convenient and powerful way to return multiple values from a method. In most cases, this will probably be the best option if you find yourself truly needing to return multiple values.

ValueTuples do not eliminate the usefulness of the previous options we discussed. It's a great option, but every option listed earlier will be easier to read or better in different scenarios. Pick the one that least to the most understandable and most maintainable code.

And always remember: needing to return multiple values is frequently an indication that a method is doing too much. Before plotting how to return multiple values, first make sure that it's the right move.

Reading and Writing Files

In a Nutshell
- The **File** class is a key part to any file I/O.
- You can write out data to a file all in one go, using **File.WriteAllText** or **File.WriteAllLines**.
- You can read the full contents of a file all at once using **File.ReadAllText** or **File.ReadAllLines**.
- You can read/write a file a little at a time by getting a **FileStream** object from **File.OpenRead** or **OpenWrite**, and wrap that in a **TextReader/TextWriter** or **BinaryReader/BinaryWriter**.
- You need to ensure that unmanaged resources are cleaned up when using **FileStream**s.

Working with files is a very common task in programming. Reading from and writing to files is often called *file input* and *file output* respectively, or simply *file I/O*.

There is a collection of types that will make it very easy to work with files. In this chapter, we'll look at how to write to a file or read from a file all in one step. We'll then look at how to work with files doing a little reading or writing at a time, in both text and binary formats.

The File Class

Writing the File

There are two simple ways to write a bunch of stuff to a file all at once. These ways are defined in the **File** class, which is going to be the starting point for all of our file I/O.

To write a bunch of text to a file, we can use the **File** class's static **WriteAllText** method:

```
string informationToWrite = "Hello persistent file storage world!";
File.WriteAllText("C:/Place/Full/Path/Here.txt", informationToWrite); // Can also be a relative path.
```

Note that the **File** class is in the **System.IO** namespace which isn't included by default, so you'll have to add a **using** directive (**using System.IO;**) in as we described back in Chapter 27.

Alternatively, we can take an array of **string**s and write them out to a file, with each item in the array placed on its own line in the file, using the **WriteAllLines** method:

```
string[] arrayOfInformation = new string[2];
arrayOfInformation[0] = "This is line 1";
arrayOfInformation[1] = "This is line 2";
File.WriteAllLines("C:/Place/Full/Path/Here2.txt", arrayOfInformation); // Can also be a relative path.
```

Both of these require the path (absolute or relative) to the file to write to, along with the text to write out.

Reading the File

Reading a file back in is just as easy:

```
string fileContents = File.ReadAllText("C:/Place/Full/Path/Here.txt");
string[] fileContentsByLine = File.ReadAllLines("C:/Place/Full/Path/Here2.txt");
```

This does the same thing, but in reverse. In the first part, the entire contents of the file are "slurped" into the **fileContents** variable. On the second line, the whole thing is pulled in as an array of **string**s, where each line in the file is a different item in the **string** array.

Assembling and Parsing File Contents

Using **File.ReadAllText** or **File.ReadAllLines** is simple and easy to work with, but your work doesn't usually end there. A **string**, or an array of **string**s is often not the final format of our information.

As an example, let's say you have a file that contains high scores for a game. Our file might look like the following, with a header line and each entry on a separate line below that, with values separated by commas. (This format is called a CSV file, and can actually be created in Excel, as well as a text editor.)

```
Name,Score
Arwen,2778
Gimli,140
Bilbo,129
Aragorn,88
```

Let's say we have a matching **HighScore** class that we created with a **Name** property and a **Score** property:

```
public class HighScore
{
    public string Name { get; set; }
    public int Score { get; set; }
}
```

To go from our program's internal representation (e.g., **HighScore[]**) to a file, we might this:

```
public void SaveHighScores(HighScore[] highScores)
{
    string allHighScoresText = "Name,Score\n";
    foreach(HighScore score in highScores)
        allHighScoresText += $"{score.Name},{score.Score}\n"; // String interpolation again.

    File.WriteAllText("highscores.csv", allHighScoresText);
}
```

To read the file back in and reassemble your high scores list, you could read in the entire text of the file, then *parse* (the process of breaking something into smaller, more meaningful components) the text and turn it back into our list of high scores. The following code reads in the high scores file we just created and turns it back into a high scores list:

```
public HighScore[] LoadHighScores(string fileName)
{
    string[] highScoresText = File.ReadAllLines(fileName);
```

```
HighScore[] highScores = new HighScore[highScoresText.Length];

for (int index = 1; index < highScoresText.Length; index++)
{
    string[] tokens = highScoresText[index].Split(',');

    string name = tokens[0];
    int score = Convert.ToInt32(tokens[1]);

    highScores[index] =new HighScore() { Name = name, Score = score };
}

    return highScores;
}
```

The **Split** method is going to be our friend when we read stuff from a file. This breaks one string into smaller strings, splitting it where it runs into a particular character (the commas in this case).

The **Convert** class has lots of different methods to convert to different types, so pick the ones you need to convert the incoming strings into the types that you need.

Text-Based Files

We can also work with text files without doing it all at once, giving us more control over the process.

Writing the File

We'll start with the **File** class again, but this time, instead of writing out the entire file all at once, we'll just open the file for writing. In doing so, we'll end up with a **FileStream** object, which we'll wrap in a **TextWriter** object to simplify the process, and use that to write out stuff as needed.

```
FileStream fileStream = File.OpenWrite("C:/Place/Full/Path/Here3.txt");
StreamWriter writer = new StreamWriter(fileStream);

writer.Write(3);
writer.Write("Hello");

writer.Close();
```

The **OpenWrite** method returns a **FileStream** object. We could use **FileStream** directly, but it is very low level, and requiring work with individual bytes. Since we don't want to spend our lives pushing bytes around, we wrap the **FileStream** object in a **StreamWriter** object, which works at a higher level. We can then ask it to directly write **string**s, **int**s, and other things with the **Write** method.

When we're done writing, we call the **Close** method to release any connections we have to the file.

Reading the File

Reading a file this way is actually more troublesome than writing it was. The problem is that when we write stuff out to a file, there's no real way to know how it was structured. We lose our context when we write to a file this way. We could fall back to **File.ReadAllLines** (and that's preferred in many cases). But it is worth showing how you could use **StreamReader** to mirror how we write our file out in the first place.

```
FileStream fileStream = File.OpenRead("C:/Place/Full/Path/Here3.txt");
StreamReader reader = new StreamReader(fileStream);

char nextCharacter = (char)reader.Read();        // Read a single character at a time.

char[] bufferToPutStuffIn = new char[2];         // Read multiple characters at a time.
reader.Read(bufferToPutStuffIn, 0, 2);
string whatWasReadIn = new string(bufferToPutStuffIn);

string restOfLine = reader.ReadLine();           // Read a full line at a time.
```

```
reader.Close();
```

We start by opening the file, this time with the **OpenRead** method. We then wrap the **FileStream** object in a **TextReader**, and then we're ready to start reading.

To read in a single character, you can use the **Read()** method. It returns an **int**, so you'll need to cast it to a **char**. (-1 is returned if the end of the file has been reached.)

There is another overload of the **Read** method that allows you to read in many characters at once, if you know how many you want to read in. You can see from the above example that to do this, you need to create a **char** array to store the characters in. (The 0 and 2 that are passed in to **Read** are the spot in the buffer to start writing at and the number of characters to read total.) This **char** array can then be turned into a **string**, as the example shows.

The **TextReader** class has a few other methods that you may find valuable, so if you really want to go this route, take a look at what other methods it has.

When we're done, we call the **Close** method to make sure that we are no longer connected to the file.

Binary Files

Instead of writing a text-based file, another choice is to write a binary file. In binary format, you won't be able to open the file in a simple text editor and make sense of it.

Binary files have a couple of advantages. First, binary files usually take up less space than text-based files. Second, the data is "encrypted" to some extent. (I'm using that term very loosely here, since this isn't true encryption.) Since it isn't text, people can't just open it and read it. It sort of protects your data.

Writing the File

You'll see that this is very similar to the text-based version in the previous section. The code to write to a binary file is the same, with the exception of using a **BinaryWriter** instead of a **StreamWriter**:

```
FileStream fileStream = File.OpenWrite("C:/Place/Full/Path/Here4.txt");
BinaryWriter writer = new BinaryWriter(fileStream);

writer.Write(3);
writer.Write("Hello");

writer.Close();
```

Like before, we open a **FileStream** that's connected to the file we want with **OpenWrite**. This time though, we wrap it in a **BinaryWriter** instead of a **TextWriter**.

We then do as many **Write** calls as needed. When done, we call **Close** to release our file connection.

Reading the File

Reading a binary file is actually quite a bit simpler to work with than the text-based version was.

```
FileStream fileStream = File.OpenRead("C:/Place/Full/Path/Here4.txt");
BinaryReader reader = new BinaryReader(fileStream);

int number = reader.ReadInt32();
string text = reader.ReadString();

reader.Close();
```

In this scenario, data is read in through **BinaryReader**'s various **ReadBlah** methods (**ReadInt32**, **ReadString**, etc.). When done, we call **Close** to release our hold on the file.

30

Error Handling and Exceptions

In a Nutshell

- Exceptions are C#'s built-in error handling mechanism.
- Exceptions package up information about a problem in an object. They are "thrown" from the method that discovered the problem. The exception goes up the call stack until it is handled by something or until it reaches the top of the call stack unhandled, and kills the program.
- If you know you are running code that could potentially cause a problem, you wrap it in a **try-catch** block, putting the type of exception in the parentheses of the **catch** block: **try { /* exception thrown here? */ } catch(Exception e) { /* handle problem here */}**
- You can catch **Exception** or any type derived from **Exception** (e.g., **FormatException**). Catching a more specific type will catch only that type of error, letting others be handled elsewhere.
- You can string together multiple catch blocks, going from most specific to least specific types of exceptions: **try { } catch(FormatException e) { /* handle format errors here */ } catch(Exception e) { /* handle all other errors here */ }**
- You can create your own types of exceptions by deriving from the **Exception** class.
- If your code discovers a problem, you can start an exception with the **throw** keyword: **throw new Exception("An error has occurred.");**
- Exception filters allow you to catch an exception only if certain conditions are met, letting others go on to another catch clause: **catch(Exception e) if(e.Message == "Message")**

We've spent the entirety of this book so far pretending that everything in our program went according to plan. But that never happens in real life. Sometimes a method is running, trying to do its job, when it discovers that something has gone terribly wrong.

As an example, think back to Chapter 15, where we looked at a method that was designed to get a number from the user that was between 1 and 10. That initial version of the code looked like this:

```
static int GetNumberFromUser()
{
    int usersNumber = 0;

    while(usersNumber < 1 || usersNumber > 10)
    {
        Console.Write("Enter a number between 1 and 10: ");
        string usersResponse = Console.ReadLine();
        usersNumber = Convert.ToInt32(usersResponse);
    }

    return usersNumber;
}
```

This code works perfectly, as long as the user enters a number. But what if they enter "asdf" instead?

When we get to the point where we call **Convert.ToInt32**, things fall apart. We're asking it to do something that is an exception to the normal circumstances: turn text that has nothing to do with numbers into a number. Not surprisingly, **Convert.ToInt32** is going to fail at this task. If we don't find a way to successfully handle this error, it will ultimately bring down our whole application.

C# provides a powerful way to trap or "catch" these errors and recover from them gracefully. C# uses an approach called *exception handling*. It is similar to many other languages, like C++, Java, and VB.NET.

How Exception Handling Works

When an error occurs, the code that discovered the problem will package up all of the information it knows about the problem into a special object called an *exception*. These exceptions are either an instance of the **Exception** class or a class derived from the **Exception** class.

Since the method that discovered the error does not know how to recover from it (otherwise it would just handle it itself, without creating an exception), it takes this **Exception** object and *throws* it up to the method that called it, hoping it knows how to resolve the issue. When this happens, it is important to know that once an exception is thrown, the rest of the method will not get executed.

Hopefully, the calling method will know what to do in the event that this particular problem occurs. If it does, it will *catch* the exception, and find a way to recover from the problem. If this method isn't able to provide a solution, the exception bubbles up to the next method, farther and farther up the call stack.

If the exception makes it all the way back to the top of the call stack (usually the **Main** method) without catching and handling the exception, the program will crash and terminate. This is called an *unhandled exception*. Clearly, you want to avoid unhandled exceptions whenever possible, but from a practical standpoint, some inevitably get missed.

In debug mode, Visual Studio intercepts these unhandled exceptions at the last minute. This is actually really convenient. Worst case scenario, this works a little like an autopsy. You'll be able to dig around and see what the actual conditions were when the problem occurred, so that you can know what changes you need to make to fix the problem. In some cases, you can even make the needed change and tell the program to continue running, which might be successful after your fix. This is like being able to change a flat tire on a car as it is still racing down the highway. (Debugging is the focus of Chapter 48.)

Through the rest of this chapter, we'll look at what C# code you need to catch exceptions, handle different types of exceptions in different ways, and how to throw your own exceptions if you discover a problem yourself. Lastly, we'll discuss the **finally** keyword, and how it ties in to exception handling.

Catching Exceptions

Before we can catch exceptions, we have to be aware that they could occur. In other words, we need to know that what we're doing may cause problems that we could handle and recover from.

To catch exceptions, we take potentially dangerous code and place it in a **try** block. After the **try** block, we place a **catch** block that identifies the exceptions we can handle, and how to resolve them.

Going back to our earlier example of getting a number between 1 and 10 from the user, there are two potential problems that could arise. First, as we already discussed, the user could type in text instead. Second, they could type in a number that is so large that it can't actually be converted into something that fits into an **int**.

To catch these errors, we can add in code that looks like this:

```
static int GetNumberFromUser()
{
    int usersNumber = 0;

    while(usersNumber < 1 || usersNumber > 10)
    {
        try
        {
            Console.Write("Enter a number between 1 and 10: ");
            string usersResponse = Console.ReadLine();
            usersNumber = Convert.ToInt32(usersResponse);
        }
        catch(Exception e)
        {
            Console.WriteLine("That is not a valid number. Try again.");
        }
    }

    return usersNumber;
}
```

Inside of the **try** block, we put the potentially dangerous code. After the **try** block is a **catch** block that handles the exception if it goes wrong. This particular **catch** block will catch any and all exceptions that occur, because the type specified in the **catch** block is **Exception**, which serves as the base class of all exception types. In general, any code in this book can go in either the **try** or the **catch** block.

In this particular case, we "handle" the exception by simply telling the user that what they entered didn't make any sense. Because the **usersNumber** variable wasn't ever updated, it will still be 0, and the **while** loop will cause the flow of execution to loop back around and ask for another number.

In the code above, the information about the exception is captured in a variable named **e** that has the type **Exception**. You can use that variable inside of the **catch** block as needed. It's just a normal variable.

If you don't actually use the variable in the catch block, you can actually leave the variable name off:

```
try
{
    //...
}
catch(Exception) // this Exception variable has no name
{
    //...
}
```

Without a name, you can't actually use the exception variable, but it leaves the name available for other things, and you won't get the compiler warning that says, "The variable **e** is declared but never used."

Handling Different Exceptions in Different Ways

I mentioned earlier that exceptions are packaged up into an instance of the **Exception** class (or a derived class). Different types of exceptions are represented with different classes derived from **Exception** (and nearly always include **Exception** in the name). With our earlier examples of catch blocks, we catch every type of exception without fail. That catch block will catch them all, regardless of what the actual error was. (I like to call this "Pokémon exception handling.") In most cases, it is better to handle different types of errors in different ways—you will nearly always have different courses of action to different types of errors. For example, the following code handles three different types of errors in three different ways:

```
try
{
    int number = Convert.ToInt32(userInput);
}
catch (FormatException e)
{
    Console.WriteLine("You must enter a number.");
}
catch (OverflowException e)
{
    Console.WriteLine("Enter a smaller number.");
}
catch (Exception e)
{
    Console.WriteLine("An unknown error occured.");
}
```

When you do this, only *one* of the **catch** blocks will actually be executed. Once the exception is handled, it will skip the rest of the **catch** blocks. So if a **FormatException** is thrown, it enters the first **catch** block and run the code there to fix the problem, but the **catch(Exception e)** block will *not* get executed, even though the exception was technically of the type **Exception**. It was already handled.

Doing this makes it so you can handle different types of exceptions in different ways. You just need to be sure to put the more specific type—the derived type—before the more general, base type. If your first block was the **catch(Exception e)** block, it would catch everything, and nothing would ever get into the **FormatException** or **OverflowException** blocks. So ordering is important.

You don't need to catch all exceptions that might come up. You can build your **catch** blocks in a way that some are handled while others are allowed to propagate further up the call stack, possibly to a **catch** block in another method, or possibly to the point where it kills the program. A single **try/catch** block does not have to handle all possible errors that could occur.

Throwing Exceptions

It's time to look at the other side of this equation: creating and throwing exceptions yourself! Don't get carried away with throwing exceptions. If the method that discovers a problem knows the solution to the problem, don't bother throwing anything. Just handle the problem and continue on. To generalize that statement, the closer you handle an error to the place it was detected the better.

To throw an exception, simply use the **throw** keyword with an instance of some **Exception** class:

```
public void CauseTrouble()  // Always up to no good...
{
    throw new Exception("Just doing my job!");
}
```

It kind of feels like the **return** statement, but it throws exceptions instead of returning a value. You create the **Exception** object, just like any other object, with the **new** keyword, and away it goes.

You're not limited to using the **Exception** class. (It's preferable not to.) There are many options already defined. For instance, here's a small list of some common exceptions and what they're for:

- **NotImplementedException**: Used to indicate that a method hasn't been implemented yet. Visual Studio will frequently put this in when you use it to automatically generate a method.
- **IndexOutOfRangeException:** Used when you access an index beyond the size of a collection.
- **InvalidCastException:** Used when you try to cast to a type that wasn't the right kind of object.
- **FormatException:** Used when text was not in the right format for converting to something else.
- **NotSupportedException:** You tried to do an operation that wasn't supported. For instance, make a method call at a time that didn't allow it.
- **NullReferenceException:** A reference type contained **null** instead of an actual object.
- **StackOverflowException:** You see this when you run out of space on the stack. This is usually a result of recursion that went bad.
- **DivideByZeroException:** You tried to divide by zero and got caught.
- **ArgumentNullException:** One of the arguments or parameters that you gave to a method was **null**, but the method requires something besides **null**.
- **ArgumentOutOfRangeException:** An argument contained a value that the method couldn't intelligently deal with (e.g., it required a number between 1 and 10, but you gave it 13).

If you can't find an existing exception type that fits, you can create your own. All you need to do is create a class that is derived from **Exception** or from another exception class. This will look something like this:

```
public class AteTooManyHamburgersException : Exception
{
    public int HamburgersEaten { get; set; }

    public AteTooManyHamburgersException(int hamburgersEaten)
    {
        HamburgersEaten = hamburgersEaten;
    }
}
```

With this class, you can now say:

```
throw new AteTooManyHamburgersException(125);
```

And:

```
try
{
    EatSomeHamburgers(32);
}
catch(AteTooManyHamburgersException e)
{
    Console.WriteLine($"{e.HamburgersEaten} is too many hamburgers.");
}
```

As a general rule, you should throw different exception types whenever the calling code would want to handle the errors in different ways. If your method could fail in two different ways, you should be throwing two different exception types. This allows people to use different **catch** blocks to handle them differently. If there's no good pre-made exception type for you to use, make your own.

I bring this up because it is really easy to get lazy and start always throwing just the plain old **Exception** type. Don't get lazy; use the right exception types, even if that means creating your own.

The 'finally' Keyword

When you throw an exception, the flow of execution stops going through the method immediately. What if you had done something with significant side effects, like having a file open?

If everything had gone according to plan, you would have been able to close the file in an intelligent way, but since a problem came up and an exception is being thrown, that cleanup code wouldn't ever be executed, leaving our file open. The **finally** keyword allows us to address this problem.

At the end of a **try-catch** block, you can have a **finally** block (making it a **try-catch-finally** block). The code inside of the **finally** section will get executed no matter what. If it ran through the **try** block without errors, it will get executed. If it ran into a **return** statement, it will get executed. If there was an exception, it will get executed (just before jumping up to the calling method with the exception).

Here's an example of how this works:

```
try
{
    // Do some stuff that might throw an exception here
}
catch (Exception)
{
    // Handle the exception here
}
finally
{
    // This code will always get execute, regardless of what happens in the try-catch block.
}
```

This is important, so let me repeat myself: the stuff in the **finally** block gets executed no matter how you leave the **try-catch** block. Error, return statement, reaching the end. It doesn't matter.

Related to this, you're not allowed to put **return** statements inside of **finally** blocks. We may already be returning when we hit the **finally** block, or we may be in the process of handling an exception. Allowing return statements here just doesn't make any sense, so it's banned.

This brings up an interesting point. **finally** blocks are not just for exception handling. It does have plenty of value in those situations, but it can also be used by itself, with no mention of throwing or catching exceptions:

```
private static int numberOfTimesMethodHasBeenCalled = 0;

public static int RandomMethod(int input)
{
    try
    {
        if(input == 0) return 17;
        if(input == 1) return -2;
        if(input == 2) return -11;

        return 5;
    }
    finally
    {
        numberOfTimesMethodHasBeenCalled++;
    }
}
```

In this case, no matter how we return from the method, the code in the **finally** block will always get executed. (There's a lot of better ways to write this particular code, but it illustrates the point.)

Exception Filters

Sometimes, exception types are not quite fine-grained enough. For example, some libraries will reuse the same exception class, but include an error code or use different text in the **Message** property of the exception to indicate subtly different errors. If all of these errors are the same type, it gets harder to separate out the different error types to handle (or not handle) in different ways.

One option is to catch the exception, check for certain conditions and handle the things you want, and then rethrow anything left over:

```
try
{
    throw new Exception("Message");
}
catch(Exception e)
{
    if (e.Message == "Message") { Console.WriteLine("I caught an exception."); }
    else { throw; }
}
```

The above is called "rethrowing the exception." It allows you to throw the exact same exception that was caught, with one caveat. The exception's stack trace ends up changing, so that its location now refers to the location where it was rethrown, rather than where it was thrown from originally. This can make it tough to track down the original problem.

The other way to handle this is with exception filters. Exception filters allow you to add a bit of code to a catch block that can be used to filter whether an exception is actually caught or not. The syntax is similar to an if-statement, but uses the **when** keyword instead:

```
try
{
    throw new Exception("Message");
}
catch(Exception e) when (e.Message == "Message")
{
    Console.WriteLine("I caught an exception.");
}
```

This approach is preferable to filtering by placing an if-statement inside of the catch block. The exception filter syntax is usually clearer, and does not cause the exception's stack trace to be changed.

Some Rules about Throwing Exceptions

When you are throwing exceptions, there are a few guiding principles that you should try to follow. Throwing exceptions can really do some crazy things to the flow of execution in your program, and so we want to take care to prevent bad things from happening when you do so.

At a bare minimum, you should not leave resources open that were opened before the exception was thrown. They should be closed or cleaned up first. This can usually be handled in a **finally** clause. But at a minimum, make sure that your program is still in a safe state.

Second, you want to revert back to the way things were before the problem occurred, so that once the error has been handled, people know the system is still in a valid state. A **finally** block can do this too.

Lastly, if you can avoid throwing an exception in the first place, that is what you should do.

Pattern Matching

In a Nutshell
- A pattern is a syntactic element that allows for conditional execution of code.
- A pattern has four parts:
  - An input value.
  - A rule or condition that determines whether the pattern is a "match" or not.
  - A section of code that is executed when the pattern is a match.
  - An output value or result that is produced from the pattern.
- C# supports three patterns:
  - The constant pattern, which matches when the input equals a specific constant.
  - The type pattern, which matches when the input is of a specific type.
  - The var pattern, which always matches.
- C# allows you to use patterns in two places: switch statements and with the **is** keyword.

C# 7 introduced a concept called *pattern matching*. It is a concept that has been floating around in other languages (primarily functional programming languages like F#) for a while, and C# has it now as well.

This chapter outlines what patterns are at a conceptual level, identifies the patterns that are available in C#, and illustrates where patterns can be used in C#: switch statements and with the **is** keyword.

Contrasted with Regular Expressions

Before diving into patterns, I want to disambiguate the C# language feature of patterns and pattern matching with another useful tool called *regular expressions*, which are also sometimes referred to as patterns or pattern matching. A C# pattern is not the same thing as a regular expression. The two are conceptually related, and C# is capable of doing regular expression searches, but the two are different.

While regular expressions are not on topic for this book (it's a whole other mini-language) a brief overview is probably in order. It's a useful (if not complicated) tool for performing text searches. They are defined by a special syntax or language where you specify a pattern to look for (like a valid email address, a phone number, a credit card, etc.) which can then be applied to strings to detect those patterns in it. They're a powerful tool, and if you end up doing a lot of text searching, it will be worth your time to learn it.

C# is quite capable of using regular expressions. There's a whole namespace that handles regular expression searching (System.Text.RegularExpressions). Microsoft has a pretty good overview of this here: **https://msdn.microsoft.com/en-us/library/ms228595.aspx**.

If you're not familiar with regular expressions but want to be, here's a pretty good website that could serve as a starting point: **http://www.regular-expressions.info/quickstart.html**.

But enough about regular expressions. That's not what this chapter is about.

The Pattern Concept

A *pattern* is a small syntactic element—a small chunk of code—that allows for conditional execution of some code based on a rule or logical condition.

There are four major pieces to the pattern concept:

1. **An input.** Patterns operate on some input data that will be evaluated for a match.
2. **A rule.** Patterns are defined by some sort or rule. This is a chunk of logic that can be executed, and boils down to a **true** or **false** value that indicates whether the pattern was a *match* or not. A match means that the rule evaluated to **true** for the given input.
3. **An action.** A pattern will provide some specific additional logic—an action, a return value, or a side effect—that is to be performed only when the rule matches.
4. **An output.** When a rule matches, the action is executed and an output is produced.

The following diagram illustrates how these pieces work together:

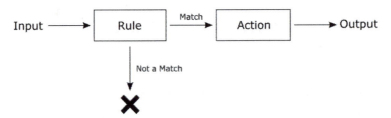

That's all fairly abstract. The coming examples should help illustrate the point more clearly.

As of C# 7, there are only three patterns that are available, and only two places where patterns can be used. Though even just that small sampling of patterns is enough to begin to illustrate the power of patterns, and give us a glimpse into the future of C#.

Available Patterns

There are three patterns available in C# 7. In this section, we will cover those patterns briefly. But those patterns will probably make a lot more sense when we actually put them to use in the next section. So we'll skip some of the details until after the practical examples later on.

The Constant Pattern

The simplest pattern is the *constant pattern*. When you see this pattern, it will show up as a compile-time constant, like **0.0**, **42**, **null**, **true**, etc. This pattern will evaluate to true—that is, it will "match"—when the input equals the constant specified.

The Type Pattern

The second pattern is called the *type pattern*. This is a pattern that matches when the input is of a specific type. This pattern has the form **T x**, where **T** is some type name, and **x** is some variable name. For example, all of the following could be a valid fit for the type pattern: **int n**, **string message**, or **Point p**. It looks a bit like a variable declaration (and in some senses kind of *is* a variable declaration) but the context will make it clear if something is a variable declaration or the type pattern. When the type pattern matches, it produces a new variable with the type and name specified, which can be used afterwards.

This pattern is a little more useful than the constant pattern, and does a little better job of illustrating the value of patterns in the first place. This is probably single most useful pattern that C# has.

We'll see practical uses of this pattern in a minute.

The Var Pattern

The final pattern is the *var pattern*, or the *variable pattern*. This pattern will be written with the **var** keyword and a variable name, similar to the type pattern. For example, **var n**, **var message**, or **var p**.

Unlike the type pattern, the var pattern *always* evaluates to **true**, and essentially just copies the input value into a new variable with the name supplied in the pattern. Because of this, the var pattern is often called a wildcard pattern, because it will always be a match.

Using Patterns in C#

Having introduced the three patterns in C#, it's time to get into some more practical examples, and look at how we would actually use these patterns. C# allows patterns to be used in two places: switch statements (Chapter 11) and with the **is** keyword (Chapter 22). We'll look at examples of both of these.

Patterns in Switch Statements

The first place we'll look at is with switch statements. Back in Chapter 11, when we first saw switch statements, we looked at code that used the constant pattern in switch statements. Consider the code below, which gets a value back from some method and prints out different results based on that value:

```
int number = GetNumberFromSomewhere();
switch(number)
{
    case 0:
        Console.WriteLine("The number was 0");
        break;
    case 1:
        Console.WriteLine("The number was 1");
        break;
}
```

The code marked above (the **0** and the **1**) are both actually uses of the constant pattern. A switch statement is actually just a way to evaluate patterns one after another, until one of them matches.

Let's extend our example and make it so it is operating on an **object**, rather than an **int**. This will allow us to also apply the type pattern and the var pattern as well.

```
object value = GetValueFromSomewhere();
switch(value)
{
    case 0:
        Console.WriteLine("The value was the number 0");
        break;
    case 1:
        Console.WriteLine("The value was the number 1");
        break;
    case int number:
        Console.WriteLine("The value was another number: " + number);
        break;
    case string text:
        Console.WriteLine("The value was the following text: " + text);
        break;
```

```
    case var unknownType:
        Console.WriteLine("The value was of an unknown type: " + value.ToString());
        break;
}
```

This example goes much further in illustrating exactly how patterns work. Each element after a case label is a different pattern.

In the first two case statements, they are constant patterns, where the constant is 0 and 1 respectively.

In the next two case statements, we use the type pattern (**int number** and **string text**). Remember, with the type pattern, the pattern will only match if the input is of the correct type. Before the switch statement, we only know that **value** is of type **object**. We don't know which (if any) derived type it might be. It could be an **int**, a **string**, a **double**, or anything else. If it turns out to be an **int**, then that third case statement (**case int number**) will be a match, and that block will be executed. The input value is placed in an **int** type variable called **number**. The block of code for that case statement can then use that variable.

In the event that the value is not an **int**, the third case statement will not match, and the next case statement will be evaluated. That one is another type pattern, this time looking for **string**s. If the value is a string, then it will match and the value will be put into a **string** typed variable named **text**.

If all four of the first switch statements fail, it falls down to the last one, which is the var pattern. Remember that the var pattern *always* matches, which makes it kind of a default value. (Speaking of that, we could have used a **default:** label here like we did in Chapter 11 with the same functionality.) Because it always matches, this block will be entered if none of the earlier case statements were a match. Like before, you can see that our **unknownType** variable is usable in the code block that follows it. The **unknownType** variable will have the same type as the input value (**object** in this case).

If you put other case statements after this var pattern, they would never execute. That is because only one block in the case statement will run. Since the var pattern always matches and the case expressions are evaluated in order, the var pattern will gobble up everything that makes it that far.

On a related note, the type pattern matches with any value of the correct type. So if we had put the **case int number** before the **case 0** and **case 1**, it would have matched first, and nothing would have gotten in to the constant patterns.

The general rule in a switch statement is that you should progress from more specific patterns to more general patterns.

Patterns with the 'is' Keyword

The second place that patterns can be used is with the **is** keyword. We already saw one way that you can use the **is** keyword, which is a direct way to check that something is of a specific type like so:

```
if(someVariable is Point)
{
    // ...
}
```

You may notice this is *almost* the type pattern, but not quite. (Using a type with no variable name is not a pattern and can't be used in switch statements, for example. It's a unique feature of the **is** keyword.)

But using the type pattern with the **is** keyword looks pretty similar:

```
if(someVariable is Point p) // Using the type pattern.
{
    Console.WriteLine(p.X + ", " + p.Y);
}
```

In fact, this is a very useful way to do the task of both checking if something is a specific type and if so, getting it into a variable of that type. The type pattern performs the check and the transformation to the new type in a single step. Without patterns, you would have to do both of those things as separate operations, perhaps something more like this:

```
if(someVariable is Point) // Not using a pattern
{
    Point p = (Point)someVariable; // Casting is required to transform the type.
    Console.WriteLine(p.X + ", " + p.Y);
}
```

Or maybe this code, which uses the **as** keyword instead:

```
Point p = someVariable as Point; // Using the as keyword,
if(p != null)                    // which requires a null check.
    Console.WriteLine(p.X + ", " + p.Y);
```

You can see that the earlier version that uses the type pattern is way more succinct and understandable.

The type pattern is the most useful pattern with the **is** keyword, but the other patterns could be used here as well. For example, here is the constant pattern:

```
if(someVariable is null) { /* ... */ }
```

We could have used the **==** operator instead with the same functionality (and **==** works for things that aren't compile time constants as well.) You may find you prefer one syntax over the other in different cases. Like usual, prefer the one that makes the code the most understandable and easy to work with.

The var pattern also works with the **is** keyword, though because it always matches, it isn't very practical:

```
if(someVariable is var x) // var pattern works, but...
    Console.WriteLine(x); // this could have been `Console.WriteLine(someVariable);` instead.
```

Expect Patterns to Expand

Patterns are a new concept in C# 7, but they've been around in other programming languages for quite a while. Because patterns are so new, the current stuff only really gives you a small taste of what patterns could be in future versions of the language.

You should expect patterns to expand in future versions of C#, both in regard to the types of patterns available as well as the places that patterns can be used.

Try It Out!

Patterns Quiz. Answer the following questions to check your understanding. When you're done, check your answers against the ones below. If you missed something, go back and review the section that talks about it.

1. Name the four parts to a pattern.
2. Name three patterns that are available in C#.
3. Name two places that a pattern can be used in C#.
4. **True/False.** The type pattern always matches.
5. **True/False.** The var pattern always matches.

Answers: (1) input, rule, action, output. **(2)** constant, type, and var patterns. **(3)** Switch statements, **is** keyword. **(4)** False. **(5)** True.

Delegates

> **In a Nutshell**
> - A delegate type can store methods directly, allowing you to treat methods like an object.
> - To create a delegate, you use the **delegate** keyword, like this: **public delegate float MathDelegate(float a, float b);**. This delegate can now be used to keep track of any method with the same return type and the same parameter list.
> - You can then use a delegate in a way that is very similar to a variable: **MathDelegate mathOperation = Add;**
> - You can also call the method that is being stored in the delegate variable: **float result = mathOperation(5, 7);**

Delegates: Treating Methods like Objects

We've done just about everything you can think of with variables. We've put numbers in them, words in them, and true/false values in them. We've created enumerations to define all possible values a variable can take on, and we've created structs and classes to store complicated variables with multiple parts, including methods to operate on that data.

Now we're going to take it a step further. What if we had a type of variable that we could put a method in? What if we could assign a method to a variable and pass it around, just like we've done with all of our other types of data? C# has this feature, and it is called a *delegate*. Treating methods like data may seem kind of strange at first, but there are many good uses for it.

Creating a Delegate

Having laid out the background, it is time to take a look at how you'd actually create a delegate. Not all methods are interchangeable with others. With regular data, when we have this problem, we simply use different data types. Methods have similar limitations, and delegates will have to account for that. When we create a delegate, we're going to say, "This type of delegate can store any method that has these parameters, and this return type."

Setting up a delegate is relatively straightforward. Defining a delegate is considered defining a new type, and as such, it is typically placed directly inside of a namespace, like we do with classes and structs.

This will probably make more sense with an example, so let's do that by creating a **MathDelegate**, which can be used to keep track of any method that can take two **int**s as input, and return an **int**. This could be used for things like an **Add** method, which takes two numbers, adds them together, and returns the result. Or a **Multiply** method, which takes the two numbers and multiplies them.

So to start, we'd create a brand new file for our delegate with a matching name. (If we're going to call our delegate **MathDelegate**, we'd call the file MathDelegate.cs, like usual.) In that file, to create a delegate, we'd simply put something like the following in there:

```
public delegate int MathDelegate(int a, int b);
```

So our whole MathDelegate.cs file should look something like this:

```
using System;
using System.Collections.Generic;
using System.Linq;
using System.Text;
using System.Threading.Tasks;

namespace Delegates
{
    public delegate int MathDelegate(int a, int b);
}
```

Looking at this, you can probably see that this has a lot of similarities to declaring a method, with the exception of adding in the **delegate** keyword. As we'll soon see, we'll be able to create variables that use this delegate type (**MathDelegate**) to store any method that has this same parameter list and return type. (That is, requires two **int** parameters and returns an **int**.)

Using Delegates

The first thing we need to use a delegate is some methods that match the delegate's requirements: two **int** parameters and returns an **int**. I've gone back to my main **Program** class, where the **Main** method is located, and created these three methods, all of which match the requirements of the delegate:

```
public static int Add(int a, int b)
{
    return a + b;
}

public static int Subtract(int a, int b)
{
    return a - b;
}

public static int Power(int baseNumber, int exponent)
{
    return (int)Math.Pow(baseNumber, exponent);
}
```

To create a delegate-typed object, we simply create a variable with a delegate type, like the **MathDelegate** type we just created. Like with a normal variable, we can assign it a value, but in this case, that value will be the name of a method that matches the delegate:

```
MathDelegate mathOperation = Add;

int a = 5;
```

```
int b = 7;

int result = mathOperation(a, b);
```

On the last line, you see we can also use the variable, invoking whatever method it happens to be storing at that particular point in time. Doing this looks like a normal method call, except that it "delegates to" or hands off execution to whatever method happened to be stored in the delegate variable at the time.

If you've never seen anything like this before, it may look kind of strange. But I hope you can start to imagine how delegates could be helpful, allowing you to dynamically change which method is called at runtime. As we move through the next few chapters, we'll see how they can be used as a part of events (Chapter 33), lambda expressions (Chapter 37), and query expressions (Chapter 38). They will be the foundation for a lot of really powerful features in C#.

The Delegate and MulticastDelegate Classes

Now that we've got a basic understanding of C#'s syntax when dealing with delegates, it's time to look under the hood and see what the C# compiler does with a delegate that you define. This will help explain some of the nuances of delegates, and should help you see delegates from another perspective.

A delegate is just syntactic sugar around a class. The .NET Platform defines a **Delegate** class. When you create a delegate, the C# compiler will turn it into a class that is derived from **Delegate**. Specifically, it will be derived from **MulticastDelegate**, which is derived from **Delegate**.

You are not allowed to create a class that directly derives from either of these manually (**class MyClass : MulticastDelegate** is not legal code). Only the compiler is allowed to derive from these special classes.

The **Delegate** and **MulticastDelegate** classes define the core functionality of delegates. On top of that, the C# language itself heaps a thick slab of magic and a pile of syntactic sugar on top to provide programmers with cleaner syntax for working with delegates.

The key thing to learn from this is that it's just a class, like the many other classes that we've now dealt with. This has several implications that are worthy of mention:

- You can declare a new delegate type anywhere you can declare a new class.
- A variable that stores a delegate can contain **null**.
- Before invoking the delegate, you should check for **null** first if there is any possibility that the variable actually contains a **null** reference.

When you create a delegate type, the class that the C# compiler will generate is derived from **MulticastDelegate**. As an example, the **MathDelegate** delegate we made in the last section is converted into something that looks like this:

```
public class MathDelegate : System.MulticastDelegate
{
    // Constructor
    public MathDelegate(Object object, IntPtr method);

    // This key method matches the definition of the delegate.
    public virtual int Invoke(int a, int b);

    // Two methods to allow the code to be called asynchronously.
    public virtual IAsyncResult BeginInvoke(int a int b);
    public virtual void EndInvoke(IAsyncResult result);
}
```

The constructor defined there allows the system to create a new instance of this delegate class. The second parameter of the constructor, with the type **IntPtr**, references the method that you're trying to put into the delegate. If the method is an instance method (not static) the **object** parameter will contain the instance it is called with. If you create a delegate from a static method, this will be **null**.

Earlier, we had code that did this:

```
MathDelegate mathOperation = Add;
```

The compiler will roughly translate this into something like this:

```
MathDelegate mathOperation = new MathDelegate(null, Add);
```

That's just an approximation, and there's a lot of hand waving in there. I'm completely skipping over the part where the compiler turns the method name of **Add** into an actual **IntPtr**, but that information just isn't available at the C# language level. It's only known by the compiler.

Earlier, we called the delegate method by simply using parentheses and putting our parameters inside:

```
int result = mathOperation(3, 4);
```

In this case, the C# compiler will turn this into a call to the **Invoke** method it created:

```
int result = mathOperation.Invoke(3, 4);
```

Written this way, it's a little easier to see why you might want to check for **null** before invoking the method, just in case the **mathOperation** variable is **null**.

While most C# programmers like the first version of calling a delegate (without the **Invoke**) the second version is both legal (the C# compiler will let you directly call **Invoke** if you want) and is also preferred by some C# programmers. So feel free to use it if it seems preferable or more readable to you.

We'll see more of this syntactic sugar in the next section when we look at chaining.

Delegate Chaining

With a name like "multicast," you'd imagine there'd be a way to have a delegate work with multiple methods. And you're right!

Things get a little complicated when our delegate returns a value, so let's come up with another example instead of the **MathDelegate** we were looking at earlier. This time, one that doesn't return a value. It just does something with some input.

Let's design a really basic logging framework. We can start with a simple **LogEvent** class that has a **Text** property. Obviously, a real logging framework would probably have quite a bit more than this, but let's keep it simple. We're just trying to do some delegate stuff here.

```
public class LogEvent
{
    public string Text { get; }
    public LogEvent(string text)
    {
        Text = text;
    }
}
```

We'll also define a simple delegate type to handle or process these **LogEvent**s in various ways:

```
public delegate void LogEventHandler(LogEvent logEvent);
```

We could easily imagine all sorts of things we could do with an event handler method. Writing things to the console is an obvious first choice. We could also write them to a file or to a database. If we added a

Severity property to our **LogEvent** class, we might even set something up so that if a **Fatal** level log event came in, we'd send an email somewhere.

Let's just stick with the low hanging fruit here and write a method that can write a **LogEvent** to the console and another one that can write it to a file:

```
private static void LogToConsole(LogEvent logEvent)
{
    Console.WriteLine(logEvent.Text);
}

private static void LogToFile(LogEvent logEvent)
{
    File.AppendAllText("log.txt", logEvent.Text + "\n");
}
```

These don't have to be static of course, but since they don't rely on any instance variables or methods, I've made them static.

The first method simply writes to the console, which we've done a million times now.

The second one writes to a file using the static **AppendAllText** method on the **File** class. It writes to a file called **log.txt**, and since it's a relative path, you'll find it right next to the application's EXE file. I also stuck a new line character ('\n') at the end of that so that each log event will show up on its own line. In the case of the console version, **WriteLine** always appends a new line character at the end by default anyway, so we don't need to do that there.

OK, on to the good stuff. Multicast delegates.

Before, when we wanted the delegate to use just a single method, we assigned it the method like this:

```
LogEventHandler logHandlers = LogToConsole;
```

So how do we get a second method in there as well?

The easiest way is with the **+=** operator:

```
LogEventHandler logHandlers = LogToConsole;
logHandlers += LogToFile;
```

Now when we invoke the delegate, both methods in the delegate will be called:

```
logHandlers(new LogEvent("Message"));
```

Since both the **LogToConsole** method and **LogToFile** method have been added to the delegate, both things will happen, and we'll get the message pumped to the console and to the file.

Taking a particular method out of a delegate is simply a matter of using the **-=** operator:

```
logHandlers -= LogToFile;
```

It's useful to keep in mind that what we're doing here with the **+=** and **-=** operators is syntactic sugar, built around some static methods that belong to the **Delegate** class. These methods are the **Combine** and **Remove** methods respectively. The following two lines of code are functionally equivalent:

```
logHandlers += LogToFile;
logHandlers = (LogEventHandler)Delegate.Combine(logHandlers, new LogEventHandler(LogToFile));
```

Likewise, the following two lines are also equivalent and remove a method from the delegate chain:

```
logHandlers -= LogToFile;
logHandlers = (LogEventHandler)Delegate.Remove(logHandlers, new LogEventHandler(LogToFile));
```

Generally speaking, the simplified version using += or -= is clearer and simpler, so it is preferred.

Side Effects of Delegate Chaining

Adding multiple methods to a delegate literally creates a chain of objects, linked together by references. (If you're familiar with the concept of a linked list, that's essentially how it's implemented.) This has a couple of side effects that are worth noting.

The first thing is a multicast delegate's return value. Earlier, we sidestepped that question by using a delegate with a **void** return type, but it should be stated that the return value of a multicast delegate is the result of the final method. All of the other results are completely ignored. This makes multicast delegates somewhat less useful for non-**void** return values. In practice, multicast delegates are generally only used for signatures with a **void** return type anyway. (You can technically go digging into a delegate's invocation list and gather return values, but there is no easy way to do that, so it's rarely done.)

The second catch is in exception handling. If a method invoked by a delegate throws an exception, none of the handlers further down the chain will be invoked. For this reason, you should do everything you can to avoid throwing exceptions in methods that get attached to a delegate.

The Action and Func Delegates

You can make your own delegate types whenever you need to, but in practice, this is rare. Included with the .NET Platform is a collection of delegates that are already defined for you. These delegates are generic, so they are very flexible, and cover most situations. These are the **Action** and **Func** delegates.

The **Action** delegates all have a **void** return type, while the **Func** delegates have a generic return type. There's a whole set of these that are each a little different. For instance, there's the plain old simple **Action** delegate, which looks like this:

```
public delegate void Action();
```

Then there's a version that has one generic parameter, two generic parameters, three generic parameters, and so on, up to 16. (That's crazy talk, right there!)

```
public delegate void Action<T>(T arg);
public delegate void Action<T1, T2>(T1 arg1, T2 arg2);
public delegate void Action<T1, T2, T3>(T1 arg1, T2 arg2, T3 arg3);
```

So as an example, if your method has a **void** return type, and requires two **int**s as parameters, you could use the **Action** delegate with two parameters, putting **int** in for both type parameters:

```
Action<int, int> myDelegate = MethodThatRequiresTwoInts;
myDelegate(3, 4);
```

If you need to return something, you can use one of the **Func** delegates instead. These have a similar pattern, but return a value (of a generic type):

```
public delegate TResult Func<TResult>();
public delegate TResult Func<T, Result>(T arg);
public delegate TResult Func<T1, T2, Result>(T1 arg1, T2 arg2);
```

Again, this goes up to 16 input type parameters, plus the generic result parameter. So instead of our little **MathDelegate** that we made, we could have used **Func<int, int, int>** instead:

```
Func<int, int, int> mathOperation = Add;
int a = 5;
int b = 7;
int result = mathOperation(a, b);
```

Events

In a Nutshell
- Events allow one section of code to notify other sections that something has happened.
- Events rely on delegates to do their work.
- To create an event inside of a class, you would use code similar to this: **public event EventHandler PointChanged;**. In this case, **EventHandler** is the name of the delegate event handlers must use, and **PointChanged** is the name of the event.
- You raise events by first checking to make sure that there are event handlers attached then raising the event: **if(PointChanged != null) { PointChanged(this, EventArgs.Empty); }**
- Attach methods to an event with the **+=** operator: **PointChanged += HandlerMethod;**
- Detach methods from an event with the **-=** operator: **PointChanged -= HandlerMethod;**

One of the coolest things about C# is a feature called events. Events allow classes to notify others when something specific happens. This is extremely common in GUI-based applications where there are things like buttons and checkboxes. These things have the ability to indicate when something of interest happens, like the button was pressed, or the user checked the checkbox other objects can be notified of the change and can handle the event in whatever way they need to.

User interfaces are not the only use for events. Any time that you have one class that has interesting things happening, other classes will want to know about it. Events are very useful in these situations. It keeps the two classes separated and allows the "client" or listener to attach itself to events generated by another object when they're interested, and detach itself when it doesn't care anymore.

This is similar to how we use things like Twitter or an RSS reader to subscribe to blogs. When there is something out there with updates that we are interested in, we subscribe to it. While we're subscribed, we see any new updates they have. When we discover that what we were paying attention to was sacked by llamas and there won't be any more notifications that we care about, we unsubscribe and move on. The blog or Twitter account will continue making notifications for the sake of anyone still listening.

The advantage of this kind of a model is that the object that is raising events doesn't need to know or care about who is attached or listening to any particular event, nor is it responsible for getting listeners registered or unregistered. The listener makes its own decisions about when to start and stop listening.

In the previous chapter, we talked about delegates. Delegates are going to be a key part of events, so it is important to understand the basics of how they work before jumping into events.

Defining an Event

Our first step will be to create an event. Let's say we have a class that represents a point in two dimensions. So it has an x-coordinate and a y-coordinate. This class might look like this:

```csharp
using System;

namespace Events
{
    public class Point
    {
        private double x;
        private double y;

        public double X
        {
            get { return x; }
            set { x = value; }
        }

        public double Y
        {
            get { return y; }
            set { y = value; }
        }
    }
}
```

To define an event inside a class, we'll need to add a single line of code as a member of the class:

```csharp
public event EventHandler PointChanged;
```

So now our code should look like this:

```csharp
using System;

namespace Events
{
    public class Point
    {
        private double x;
        private double y;

        public double X
        {
            get { return x; }
            set { x = value; }
        }

        public double Y
        {
            get { return y; }
            set { y = value; }
        }

        public event EventHandler PointChanged;
    }
}
```

Like other members (properties, methods, and instance variables) we can use **public**, **internal**, **protected**, or **private** for events, though events are usually **public** or **internal**.

The **event** keyword is what makes this particular member an event that others can attach to.

We also specify the delegate type of methods that can be attached to the event. Remembering how delegates work, this means that all listener methods will be required to have a specific set of parameters, as well as a specific return type (though with events, it is almost invariably **void**). In this case, we use the **EventHandler** delegate, which is a pre-defined delegate specifically made for really simple events. This delegate has a return type of **void** and has two parameters, an **object**, which is the "sender" of the event, and an **EventArgs** object. The **EventArgs** object stores some basic information about the event itself.

Any delegate type can be used here. You're not just limited to **EventHandler**.

Raising an Event

Now that we have an event, we need to add in code to *raise* the event in the right circumstances.

Don't add this into your code quite yet, but consider the following code, which raises an event:

```
if(PointChanged != null)
    PointChanged(this, EventArgs.Empty);
```

This little bit of code is pretty simple. We check to see if the event is **null**. If the event is **null**, there are no event handlers attached to the event. (In a second, we'll see how to attach event handlers.) Raising an event with no event handlers results in a **NullReferenceException**, so we need to check this before we raise the event.

Once we know the event has event handlers attached to it, we can raise the event by calling the event with the parameters required by the delegate—in this case, a reference to the sender (**this**) and an **EventArgs** object (though we're just using the static **EventArgs.Empty** object in this case).

While this code to raise an event can technically go anywhere, I usually put it in its own method. It is very common to name these methods the same as the event, but with the word "On" at the beginning: **OnPointChanged**, in our particular case.

So we can add the following method to our code:

```
public void OnPointChanged()
{
    if(PointChanged != null)
        PointChanged(this, EventArgs.Empty);
}
```

When we detect that the conditions of the event have been met, we call this method to raise the event.

In this particular case, since we want to raise the event any time the point changes, we'll want to call this method when the value of **X** or **Y** gets set. To accomplish this, we'll add a method call to the setters of both of these properties:

```
public double X
{
    get { return x; }
    set
    {
        x = value;
        OnPointChanged();
    }
}

public double Y
{
    get { return y; }
    set
```

```
    {
        y = value;
        OnPointChanged();
    }
}
```

Our completed code, including everything to add and raise the event, looks like this:

```
using System;

namespace Events
{
    public class Point
    {
        private double x;
        private double y;

        public double X
        {
            get { return x; }
            set
            {
                x = value;
                OnPointChanged();
            }
        }

        public double Y
        {
            get { return y; }
            set
            {
                y = value;
                OnPointChanged();
            }
        }

        public event EventHandler PointChanged;

        public void OnPointChanged()
        {
            if(PointChanged != null)
                PointChanged(this, EventArgs.Empty);
        }
    }
}
```

Attaching and Detaching Event Handlers

Now that we've got our **Point** class set up with an event for whenever it changes, we need to know how to attach a method as an event handler for the event we've created.

The way we attach something to an event is by giving the event a method to call when the event occurs. The method we attach is sometimes called an event handler. Because events are based on delegates we'll need a method that has the same return type and parameter types as the delegate we're using—**EventHandler** in this case. The **EventHandler** delegate we're using requires a **void** return type, and two parameters, an **object** that represents the sender (the thing sending the event) and an **EventArgs** object, which has specific information about the event being raised.

Anywhere that we want, we can create a method to handle the event that looks something like this:

```
public void HandlePointChanged(object sender, EventArgs eventArgs)
{
```

```
    // Do something intelligent when the point changes. Perhaps redraw the GUI,
    // or update another data structure, or anything else you can think of.
}
```

It is a simple task to actually attach an event handler to the event. Again, the following code can go anywhere you need it to go, where the method is in scope (accessible):

```
Point point = new Point();

point.PointChanged += HandlePointChanged;

// Now if we change the point, the PointChanged event will be raised and HandlePointChanged is called.
point.X = 3;
```

The key line there is the one that attaches the handler to the event: **point.PointChanged += HandlePointChanged;**. The += operator can be used to add the **HandlePointChanged** method to our event. If you try to attach a method that doesn't match the needs of the event's delegate type, you'll get an error when you go to compile your program.

You can attach as many event handlers to an event as you want. In theory, all event handlers attached to an event will be executed. However, if one of the event handlers throws and exception that isn't handled, the remaining handlers won't get called. For this reason, event handlers shouldn't throw any exceptions.

It is also possible to detach event handlers from an event, which you should do when you no longer care to be notified about the event. This is an important step. Without detaching old event handlers, it's easy to end up with tons of event handlers attached to a method, or even the *same* event handler attached to an event multiple times. In the best case scenario, things slow down a lot. In the worst case scenario, things may not even function correctly.

Note that you rarely want the same event handler method attached to an event more than once, but this is allowed. The method will be called twice, because it is attached twice.

To detach an event, you simply use the -= operator in a manner similar to attaching events:

```
point.PointChanged -= HandlePointChanged;
```

After this executes, **HandlePointChanged** will not be called when the **PointChanged** event occurs.

Common Delegate Types Used with Events

When using events, the event can use any delegate type imaginable. Having said that, there are a few delegate types that seem to be most common, and those are worth a bit of attention.

The first common delegate is one of the **Action** delegates, which we talked about in the last chapter. For instance, if you want an event that simply calls a parameterless void method when the event occurs (a simple notification that something happened, without including any data to the listener) you could use plain old **Action**:

```
public event Action PointChanged;
```

You could subscribe the method below to that event:

```
private void HandlePointChanged()
{
    // Do something in response to the point changing.
}
```

If you need to get some sort of information to the subscriber, you could use one of the other variants of **Action** that has generic type parameters. For example, we might want to pass in the point that changed to the subscribers. So we could change the event declaration to use the generic **Action** that has an extra type parameter to include the point:

```
public event Action<Point> PointChanged;
```

Then we subscribe to the event with a method like this:

```
private void HandlePointChanged(Point pointThatChanged)
{
    // Do something in response to the point changing.
}
```

Using different versions of **Action**, we can pass any number of parameters to the event handlers.

Another common option is a delegate that works along these lines:

```
public delegate void EventHandler(object sender, EventArgs e);
```

In this example, we get a reference to the sender, who initiated the event, as well as an **EventArgs** object, which stores any interesting information about the event inside it. In other cases, you may be interested in using a more specialized type, derived from **EventArgs**, with even more information.

In this case, instead of using your own special delegate, you can use the **EventHandler<TEventArgs>** event handler. (To use this, you must use **EventArgs** or another type that is derived from it.)

So let's say you have an event that is keeping track of a change in a number, and in the notification process, we want to see the original number and what it was changed to. We can make a class derived from the **EventArgs** class like this:

```
public class NumberChangedEventArgs : EventArgs
{
    public int Original { get; }
    public int New { get; }
    public NumberChangedEventArgs(int originalValue, int newValue)
    {
        Original = originalValue;
        New = newValue;
    }
}
```

Then we'd define our event like this:

```
public event EventHandler<NumberChangedEventArgs> NumberChanged;
```

This event would be raised like we saw earlier, usually in a method called **OnNumberChanged**:

```
public void OnNumberChanged(int oldValue, int newValue)
{
    if(NumberChanged != null)
        NumberChanged(this, new NumberChangedEventArgs(oldValue, newValue));
}
```

Methods that want to handle this event would then look like this:

```
public void HandleNumberChanged(object sender, NumberChangedEventArgs args)
{
    Console.WriteLine($"The original value of {args.Original} is now {args.New}.");
}
```

You're not restricted to using any of these delegates (events can use any delegate you want) but most scenarios won't actually require you to build a custom delegate type for an event if you don't want to.

The Relationship between Delegates and Events

It's a common misconception among C# programmers that events are just delegates that can be attached to multiple methods, or that an event is just an array of delegates. Both of these ideas are wrong, though it's an easy mistake to make.

In the vast majority of cases, delegates are not used to call more than one method at a time, while events quite often are. So many C# programmers don't see delegates that reference more than one method at a time, and make the incorrect assumption that they can't handle it at all.

A more accurate way to think of it is more along the lines of an event being a property-like wrapper around a delegate. Specifically, what we've seen up until now is similar to an auto-implemented property. Let's look back at our earlier example with our **NumberChanged** event:

```
public event EventHandler<NumberChangedEventArgs> NumberChanged;
```

The compiler expands this into code that looks something like this:

```
private EventHandler<NumberChangedEventArgs> numberChanged; // The wrapped delegate.

public event EventHandler<NumberChangedEventArgs> NumberChanged
{
    add { numberChanged += value; }    // Defines behavior when a method subscribes.
    remove { numberChanged -= value; } // Defines behavior when unsubscribing.
}
```

Wrapping the delegate like this prevents people from outside of the class from invoking the delegate directly (in other words, you can't raise an event from outside of the class that it exists in) as well as from mucking with the methods that are contained in the delegate chain.

Interestingly, the code above is actually completely legal code. If you don't like the default implementation of an event, you can write code that looks like the previous sample and do something different with it. In practice, it's rare to actually need to deviate from the standard pattern, but it is allowed.

One complication with explicitly implementing the **add** and **remove** parts for an event like this is that you can no longer invoke the event directly. Instead, you have to invoke the delegate that it wraps (**numberChanged** instead of **NumberChanged**, in this specific case). That's because you've created custom behavior for what it means to add or remove a method to an event and the normal rules aren't guaranteed to apply. For instance, it's possible that the event doesn't even wrap a delegate at all anymore, or that it subscribes or unsubscribes from multiple delegates. Since the compiler can't guarantee what it means to raise the event anymore, the programmer must determine what it means.

Try It Out!

Delegates and Events Quiz. Answer the following questions to check your understanding. When you're done, check your answers against the ones below. If you missed something, go back and review the section that talks about it.

1. **True/False.** Delegates allow you to assign methods to variables.
2. **True/False.** You can call and run the method currently assigned to a delegate variable.
3. **True/False.** Events allow one object to notify another object when something occurs.
4. **True/False.** Any method can be attached to a specific event.
5. **True/False.** Once attached to an event, a method cannot be detached from an event.

Answers: **(1)** True. **(2)** True. **(3)** True. **(4)** False. **(5)** False.

Operator Overloading

In a Nutshell
- Operator overloading allows us to define how some operators work for types that we create.
- Operator overloading works for these operators: +, -, *, /, %, ++, --, ==, !=, >=, <=, >, and <.
- Operator overloading does not work for these operators: '&&' and '||', the assignment operator '=', the dot operator '. ', or the **new** operator (keyword).
- An example of overloading the '+' operator looks like this: **public static Vector operator +(Vector v1, Vector v2) { return new Vector(v1.X + v2.X, v1.Y + v2.Y); }**
- All operators must be **public** and **static**.
- The relational operators must be done in pairs. (== and !=, < and >, <= and >=.)
- Only overload operators when there is a single, unambiguous way to use the operation.

Throughout the course of this book, we've seen a lot of different operators. They all have built-in functionality that does certain specific things. Mostly, these are defined by math, going back thousands of years. In a few cases, we've seen some not-so-normal uses for these operators, like using the '+' operator for concatenating (sticking together) two **string**s (as in **string text = "Hello" + "World";)**. In math, there's no way to add words together, but in C# we can do it.

When you create your own types, you can also define how some of these operators should work for them. For example, if you create a class called **Cheese**, you may define what the '+' operator should do, allowing you to add two **Cheese** objects together (Though if you do that, Pepper Jack and Colby better result in Colby-Jack!) This is called *operator overloading*, and it is a powerful feature of C#.

In a minute, we'll look at how to actually overload these operators, but let's start by discussing what operators you're even allowed to overload. Many but not all operators can be overloaded. The creators of C# tried to allow you to overload as many as possible, but some would be too dangerous allow. These operators can be overloaded: **+, -, *, /, %, ++, --, ==, !=, >=, <=, >,** and **<.** The compound assignment operators (**+=, -=, /=, *=, %=,** etc.) can't be directly overloaded, but overloading + allows **+=** to be used, overloading * allows ***=** to be used, and so on.

The relational operators must be overloaded in pairs—if you overload the == operator, you must also overload the != operator, and if you overload the > operator, you must also overload the < operator as well, and so on.

On the other hand, the following operators cannot be overloaded: the logical operators **&&** and **||**, the assignment operator (**=**), the dot operator (**.**), and the **new** operator. Being able to overload these operators would just be too dangerous and confusing to anyone trying to use them. Take the assignment operator, for example. We use it for things like **int x = 3**;. If you could make it do something else besides putting the value of 3 into the variable **x**, it could cause some serious issues.

Note that the array indexing operator (**[** and **]**) can be overloaded, but it is done using indexers, which we'll look at in the next chapter.

Unfortunately, you can't define your own brand new operator with operator overloading.

Overloading Operators

You can overload operators for any of your own types, but for the sake of simplicity, I'm going to pick a class that should make some sense for overloading operators. I'll show operator overloading for a **Vector** class, which stores an x and y coordinate. Vectors show up all over in math and physics, but if you're fuzzy on the concept, you can think of a vector as a point (in this case, a 2D point).

So let's start with the basic class as a starting point:

```
using System;
using System.Collections.Generic;
using System.Linq;
using System.Text;
using System.Threading.Tasks;

namespace OperatorOverloading
{
    public class Vector
    {
        public double X { get; set; }
        public double Y { get; set; }

        public Vector(double x, double y)
        {
            X = x;
            Y = y;
        }
    }
}
```

Let's say you want to add two vectors together. In math and physics, when we add two vectors, the result is another vector, but with the x and y components added together. For example, if you add the vector (2, 3) to the vector (4, 1), you get (6, 4), because 2 + 4 = 6, and 3 + 1 = 4.

To overload the **+** operator, we simply add the following code as a member of the **Vector** class:

```
public static Vector operator +(Vector v1, Vector v2)
{
    return new Vector(v1.X + v2.X, v1.Y + v2.Y);
}
```

So now your **Vector** class might look something like this at this point:

```
using System;
using System.Collections.Generic;
using System.Linq;
```

```
using System.Text;
using System.Threading.Tasks;

namespace OperatorOverloading
{
    public class Vector
    {
        public double X { get; set; }
        public double Y { get; set; }

        public Vector(double x, double y)
        {
            X = x;
            Y = y;
        }

        public static Vector operator +(Vector v1, Vector v2)
        {
            return new Vector (v1.X + v2.X, v1.Y + v2.Y);
        }
    }
}
```

All operator overloads must be **public** and **static**. This should make sense, since we want to have access to the operator throughout the program, and since it belongs to the type as a whole, rather than a specific instance of the type. We then specify a return type, **Vector** in this case. We use the **operator** keyword, along with the operator that we're overloading. We then have two parameters, which are the two sides of the **+** operator.

For a unary operator like **-** (the negation operator or negative sign) we only have one parameter:

```
public static Vector operator -(Vector v)
{
    return new Vector(-v.X, -v.Y);
}
```

Notice, too, that we can have multiple overloads of the same operator:

```
public static Vector operator +(Vector v, double scalar)
{
    return new Vector(v.X + scalar, v.Y + scalar);
}
```

Now you can add a vector and a scalar (just a plain old number). Though from a math standpoint, this has little practical value.

The relational operators can be overloaded in the exact same way, only they must return a **bool**:

```
public static bool operator ==(Vector v1, Vector v2)
{
    return ((v1.X == v2.X) && (v1.Y == v2.Y));
}

public static bool operator !=(Vector v1, Vector v2)
{
    return !(v1 == v2); // Just return the opposite of the == operator.
}
```

Remember that the relational operators must be overloaded in pairs, so if you overload **==**, you must also overload **!=**, as shown here.

If you look closely at these operator overloads, you can see that they just look like a method. (The only real difference is the **operator** keyword.) The C# compiler converts this to a method behind the scenes.

Overloading operators is done primarily to make our code look cleaner. It is what's called *syntactic sugar*. Anything that you can do with an operator, you could have done with a method. Overloading an operator is sometimes more readable though.

Just because you *can* overload operators, doesn't mean you *should*. Imagine that you overload an operator to have it do something totally unexpected. If it isn't clear what your overloaded operator does, you'll cause yourself and others lots of problems. It's for this reason that Java and other languages, erring on the side of being overly cautious, have chosen to not even allow operator overloading. The rule to follow is to only overload operators that have a single, clear, intuitive, and widely accepted use.

With our operators defined, we can use them with the same syntax that we've seen before:

```
Vector a = new Vector(5, 2);
Vector b = new Vector(-3, 4);
Vector result = a + b;            // We use the operator overload here.
// At this point, result is <2, 6>.
```

Try It Out!

3D Vectors. Make a **Vector** class like the one we've created here, but instead of just **x** and **y**, also add in **z**. You'll need to add another property, and the constructor will be a little different. Add operators that do the following:

- Add two 3D vectors together. (1, 2, 3) + (3, 3, 3) should be (4, 5, 6).
- Subtract one 3D vector from another. (1, 2, 3) - (3, 3, 3) should be (-2, -1, 0).
- Negate a 3D vector. For example, using the negative sign on (2, 0, -4) should be (-2, 0, 4).
- Multiply a vector by a number (scalar) so (1, 2, 3) * 4 should be (4, 8, 12).
- Divide a vector by a number (scalar) so (2, 4, 6) / 2 should be (1, 2, 3).

Additionally, write some code to run some tests on your newly created 3D vector class and check to see if everything is working.

Try It Out!

Operator Overloading Quiz. Answer the following questions to check your understanding. When you're done, check your answers against the ones below. If you missed something, go back and review the section that talks about it.

1. **True/False.** Operator overloading means providing a definition for what the built-in operators do for your own types.
2. **True/False.** You can define your own, brand new operator using operator overloading.
3. **True/False.** All operators in C# can be overloaded.
4. **True/False.** Operator overloads must be **public**.
5. **True/False.** Operator overloads must be **static**.

Answers: (1) True. **(2)** False. **(3)** False. **(4)** True. **(5)** True.

Indexers

In a Nutshell

- An indexer is a way to overload the indexing operator ([and]).
- Defining an indexer works like a cross between operator overloading and a property: **public double this[int index] { get { /* get code here */ } set { /* set code here */ } }**
- Indexers can use any type as a parameter.
- You can have multiple indices by simply listing multiple things where you define the indexer: **double this[string someTextIndex, int numericIndex]**.

In the previous chapter, we talked about how to overload operators. In this chapter, we'll talk about indexers, which are essentially a way to overload the indexing operator ([and]).

How to Make an Indexer

Defining an indexer is almost like a cross between overloading an operator and a property. It is pretty easy to do, so we'll just start with some code that does this. This code could be added as a member of the **Vector** class that we made in the last chapter, though this same setup works in any class as well.

```
public double this[int index]
{
    get
    {
        if(index == 0) { return X; }
        else if(index == 1) { returnY; }
        else { throw new IndexOutOfRangeException(); }
    }
    set
    {
        if (index == 0) { X = value; }
        else if (index == 1) { Y = value; }
        else { throw new IndexOutOfRangeException(); }
    }
}
```

We first specify the access level of the indexer—**public** in our case—along with the type that it returns. (Note that we don't have to use **public** and **static**, unlike overloading other operators.) We then use the **this** keyword, and the square brackets (**[** and **]**), which indicate indexing. Inside of the brackets we list the type and name of the indexing variable that we'll use inside of this indexer.

Then, like a property, we have a **get** and a **set** block. Note that we do not need to have both of these if we don't want. We can get away with just one. Inside of the **get** and **set** blocks, we can use our **index** variable, and like properties, we can use the **value** keyword in the setter to refer to the value that is being assigned.

In this example, I'm making it so that people can refer to the **x** and **y** components of the vector using the 0 and 1 index respectively. With this in place, we would now be able to do this:

```
Vector v = new Vector(5, 2);
double xComponent = v[0]; // Use indexing to set the x variable.
double yComponent = v[1]; // Use indexing to set the y variable.
```

This is much clearer than if we had been forced to do it with methods. (**xComponent = v.GetIndex(0);**)

Using Other Types as an Index

We're not stuck with just using **int**s as an index. We can use any type we want. For example, **string**s:

```
public double this[string component]
{
    get
    {
        if (component == "x") { return X; }
        if (component == "y") { return Y; }
        throw new IndexOutOfRangeException();
    }

    set
    {
        if (component == "x") { X = value; }
        if (component == "y") { Y = value; }
        throw new IndexOutOfRangeException();
    }
}
```

This code is very similar to what we just saw, except that we're using a **string** for indexing. If they ask for "x", we return the x-component. If they ask for "y", we return the y-component.

So now we'd be able to do this:

```
Vector v = new Vector(5, 2);
double xComponent = v["x"]; // Indexing operator with strings.
double yComponent = v["y"];
```

There's still more! We can do indexing with *multiple* indices. Adding in multiple indices is as simple as listing all of them inside of the square brackets when you define your indexer:

```
public double this[string component, int index]
{
    get
    {
        return 0; // Do some work here to return a value from the two indices 'component' and 'index'.
    }
    set
    {
        // Do the logic to assign the value passed in. `value` contains the value being set.
        components.Find(component).AtIndex(index) = value;
```

```
        }
    }
}
```

Indexers can be very powerful, and allow us to make indexing or data access look more natural when working with our own custom made types. Like with operator overloading, we should take advantage of it when it makes sense, but be cautious about overusing it.

Try It Out!

Creating a Dictionary. Create a class that is a dictionary, storing words (as a **string**) and their definition (also as a **string**). Use an indexer to allow users of the dictionary to add, modify, and retrieve definitions for words.

You should be able to add a word like this: **dictionary["apple"] = "A particularly delicious pomaceous fruit of the genus Malus.";**

You should be able to change a definition by reusing the same "key" word: **dictionary["apple"] = "A fruit of the genus Malus that often times rots and is no longer delicious.";**

You should also be able to retrieve a definition using the indexer: **string definitionOfApple = dictionary["apple"];**

Note that the .NET Platform already defines a **Dictionary** class, which uses generics and in the real world could be used to do what we're trying to do here, plus a whole lot more. But we're trying to get the hang of indexers here, so don't use that class while doing this challenge.

Index Initializer Syntax

We've talked throughout this book about a lot of ways to initialize things. In Chapter 18 we introduced the simple constructor, where you pass in parameters to get things set up (**new Vector(10, -5)**), there's object initializer syntax (Chapter 19) that additionally lets you assign values to the object's properties on the same line at the same time (**new Vector () { X = 10, Y = -5 }**), there's collection initializer syntax that is used for setting up an array (Chapter 13) or a collection (Chapter 25) (**new Vector[] { new Vector(0, 0), new Vector(10, 5), new Vector(-2, -8) }**) and now we'll introduce one final option.

If a class defines an indexer, you can use *index initializer syntax* (or an *index initializer*). Going off of the *Try It Out!* problem above, with your own custom dictionary class, you could fill it up like this:

```
Dictionary dictionary = new Dictionary()
{
    ["apple"] = "A particularly delicious pomaceous fruit of the genus Malus.",
    ["broccoli"] = "The 7th most flavorless vegetable on the planet."
    // ...
};
```

This gets translated into direct use of the indexer, so the above code could be written like the code below without using index initializer syntax:

```
Dictionary dictionary = new Dictionary();
dictionary["apple"] = "A particularly delicious pomaceous fruit of the genus Malus.";
dictionary["broccoli"] = "The 7th most flavorless vegetable on the planet."
// ...
```

Because index initializer syntax can be used any time the type defines an indexer, and because lots of classes define indexers, there are quite a few places this can be used. Sometimes index initializer syntax is more readable, while other times it's not. Choose the option that is most readable.

Extension Methods

In a Nutshell
- Extension methods let you define a method that feels like it belongs to a class that you don't have control over.
- Extension methods are defined as static classes as static methods. The first parameter of the method is the type of the class that you want to add the extension method to, and it must be marked with the **this** keyword: **public static class StringExtensions { public static string ToRandomCase(this string text) { /* Implementation here... */ } }**
- Once an extension method has been created, you can call it as though it is a part of the class: string **text = "Hello World!"; randomCaseText = text.ToRandomCase();**
- Extension methods are syntactic sugar to make your code look cleaner. The C# compiler rewrites into a direct call of the static method.

Let's say that you are using a class that someone else made. Perhaps one of the classes that comes with the .NET Platform, like the **string** type.

What if you're using that type, and you wish it had a method that it doesn't have? Particularly, if you don't have the ability to modify it? If it's one of your own classes, you can simply add it in. But if it's not one that you can modify, what then?

The **string** type has a **ToUpperCase()** method and a **ToLowerCase()** method, but what if we want to create a method to convert it to a random case, so each letter is randomly chosen to be upper case or lower case? (SomEtHIng LiKE tHiS.) Writing the method is relatively easy, but wouldn't it be nice if we could make it so that we can say something like **myString.ToRandomCase()** just like we can do with **myString.ToUpperCase();**? Without having access to the class, we wouldn't normally have the ability to add our **ToRandomCase()** method as a new method in the class.

Normally.

But there's a way in C#. It is called an *extension method*. Basically, we'll create a static method in a static class, along with the **this** keyword, and we can make a method that appears as though it were a member of the original class, even though it's technically not.

Creating an Extension Method

Creating an extension method is as simple as I just described; we'll make a **static** class, and put a **static** method in it that does what we want for the extension method.

We start by adding a new class file to your project (see Chapter 18). While it is not required, I typically call my class something like **StringExtensions** if I'm creating extension methods for the **string** class, or **PointExtensions**, if I'm creating extension methods for a **Point** class.

In addition, we want to stick the **static** keyword on our class, to make the whole class a static class. To start, our class will look something like this:

```
using System;
using System.Collections.Generic;
using System.Linq;
using System.Text;

namespace ExtensionMethods
{
    public static class StringExtensions
    {
    }
}
```

To define our extension method, we simply create a **static** method here. The first parameter must be of the type that we're creating the extension method for (**string**, in our case), marked with the **this** keyword:

```
public static string ToRandomCase(this string text)
{
    // The method implementation will go here in a second...
}
```

We can indicate a return type, and in addition to the first parameter that is marked with the **this** keyword, we could also have any other parameters we want.

Like with operator overloading and indexers, this is basically just syntactic sugar. The C# compiler will rework any place that we call our extension method. So when we're done, we'll be able to say:

```
string title = "Hello World!"
string randomCaseTitle = title.ToRandomCase();
```

But the compiler will rework the code above to look like this:

```
string title = "HelloWorld";
string randomCaseTitle = StringExtensions.ToRandomCase(title);
```

The extension method looks nicer and it feels like a real method of the **string** class, which is a nice thing.

But this can be a double-edged sword. The method *feels* like it is a part of the original class, but officially, it's not. For instance, you may move from one project to another, only to discover that what you thought was a part of the original class turned out to be an extension method written by someone else, and you can no longer use it.

Also, if your extension method is in a different namespace than the original class, you may have problems where the *actual* type is recognized, but the extension method can't be found. To get all of the pieces to come together, you may need to add in multiple **using** directives (Chapter 27).

Just be aware of the limitations an extension method has.

We can now finish up our example by completing the body of the **ToRandomCase** method:

```
string result = "";

for (int index = 0; index < text.Length; index++)
{
    if (random.Next(2) == 0) // We still need to create the random object.
        result += text.Substring(index, 1).ToUpper();
    else
        result += text.Substring(index, 1).ToLower();
}

return result;
```

This goes through the original string one character at a time, chooses a random number (0 or 1), and if it is 0, it makes it upper case. If it is 1, it makes it lower case. So we end up with a random collection of upper and lower case letters, giving us the desired result.

So our complete code for the extension method class is this:

```
using System;
using System.Collections.Generic;
using System.Linq;
using System.Text;

namespace ExtensionMethods
{
    public static class StringExtensions
    {
        private static Random random = new Random();

        public static string ToRandomCase(this string text)
        {
            string result = "";

            for (int index = 0; index < text.Length; index++)
            {
                if (random.Next(2) == 0)
                    result += text.Substring(index, 1).ToUpper();
                else
                    result += text.Substring(index, 1).ToLower();
            }

            return result;
        }
    }
}
```

As we mentioned earlier, if your program is aware of the extension method, you can now do this:

```
string message = "I'm sorry, Dave. I'm afraid I can't do that.";
Console.WriteLine(message.ToRandomCase());
```

We can now use the extension method as though it is a part of the original type.

Try It Out!

Word Count. Create an extension method for the **string** class that counts the total number of words in the **string**. You can make use of the **Split** method, which works like this: **text.Split(' ');**. This returns an array of **string**s, split up into pieces using the character passed in as the split point.

For bonus points, take this a step further and split on all whitespace characters, including space (' '), the newline character ('\n'), the carriage return character ('\r'), the tab character ('\t'). For even more bonus points, ensure that words of length 0, don't get counted.

Try It Out!

Sentence and Paragraph Count. Following the example of the Word Count problem above, create additional extension methods to count the number of sentences and paragraphs in a string. You can assume that a sentence is delimited (ended/separated) by the period ('. ') symbol, and paragraphs are delimited with the carriage return symbol ('\n').

For tons of bonus points, put together a simple program that will read in a text file (see Chapter 29) and print out the number of words, sentences, and paragraphs the file contains.

Try It Out!

Lines of Code. Going even further, let's make a program that will count the number of lines of code a program has.

It is often interesting to know how big a particular program is. One way to measure this is in the total lines of code it contains. (There is some debate about how useful this really is, but it is always fun to know and watch as your program grows larger.)

Create a simple program that, given a particular file, counts the number of lines of code it has. For bonus points, ignore blank lines.

If you're up for a real big challenge, modify your program to start with a particular directory and search it for all source code files (*.cs) and add them all up to see how big an entire project is.

Lambda Expressions

In a Nutshell
- Lambda expressions are methods that appear "in line" and do not have a name.
- Lambda expressions have different syntax than normal methods, which for simple lambda expressions makes it very readable. The expression: **x => x < 5** is the equivalent of the method **bool AMethod(int x) { return x < 5; }**.
- Multiple parameters can be used: **(x, y) => x * x + y * y**
- As can zero parameters: **() => Console.WriteLine("Hello World!")**
- The C# compiler can typically infer the types of the variables in use, but if not, you can explicitly provide those types: **(int x) => x < 5**.
- If you want more than one expression, you can use a statement lambda instead, which has syntax that looks more like a method: **x => { bool lessThan5 = x < 5; return lessThan5; }**
- Lambda expressions can use variables that are in scope at the place where they are defined.
- Expression syntax can be used to define normal, named methods, properties, indexers, and operators as well: **bool AMethod(int x) => x < 5;**

The Motivation for Lambda Expressions

Lambda expressions are a relatively simple concept. The trick to understanding lambda expressions is in understanding what they're actually good for. So that's where we're going to start our discussion.

For this discussion, let's say you had the following list of numbers:

```
// Collection initializer syntax (see Chapter 25).
List<int> numbers = new List<int>(){ 1, 7, 4, 2, 5, 3, 9, 8, 6 };
```

Let's also say that somewhere in your code, you want to filter out some of them. Perhaps you want only even numbers. How do you do that?

The Basic Approach
Knowing what we learned way back in some of the early chapters about methods and looping, perhaps we could create something like this:

```
public static List<int> FindEvenNumbers(List<int> numbers)
{
    List<int> onlyEvens = new List<int>();

    foreach(int number in numbers)
    {
        if(number % 2 == 0) // checks if it is even using mod operator
            onlyEvens.Add(number);
    }

    return onlyEvens;
}
```

We could then call that method and get back our list of even numbers. But that's a lot of work for a single method that may only ever be used once.

The Delegate Approach

Fast forward to Chapter 32, where we learned about delegates. For this particular task, delegates will actually be able to go a long way towards helping us.

As it so happens, there's a method called **Where** that is a part of the **List** class (actually, it is an extension method) that uses a delegate. Using the **Where** method looks like this:

```
IEnumerable<int> evenNumbers = numbers.Where(MethodMatchingTheFuncDelegate);
```

The **Func** delegate that the **Where** method uses is generic, but in this specific case, must return the type **bool**, and have a single parameter that is the same type that the **List** contains (**int**, in this example). The **Where** method goes through each element in the array and calls the delegate for each item. If the delegate returns true for the item, it is included in the results, otherwise it isn't.

Let me show you what I mean with an example. Instead of our first approach, we could write a simple method that determines if a number is even or not:

```
public static bool IsEven(int number)
{
    return (number % 2 == 0);
}
```

This method matches the requirements of the delegate the **Where** method uses in this case (returns **bool**, with exactly one parameter of type **int**).

```
IEnumerable<int> evenNumbers = numbers.Where(IsEven);
```

That's pretty readable and fairly easy to understand, as long as you know how delegates work. But let's take another look at this.

Anonymous Methods

While what we've done with the delegate approach is a big improvement over crafting our own method to do all of the work, it has two small problems. First, a lot of times that we do something like this, the method is only ever used once. It seems like overkill to go to all of the trouble of creating a whole method to do this, especially since it starts to clutter the namespace. We can no longer use the name **IsEven** for anything else within the class. That may not be a problem, but it might.

Second, and perhaps more important, that method is located somewhere else in the source code. It may be elsewhere in the file, or even in a completely different file. This separation makes it a bit harder to truly understand what's going on when you look at the source code. It our current case, this is mostly solved by calling the method something intelligent (**IsEven**) but you don't always get so lucky.

This issue is common enough that back in C# 2.0, they added a feature called *anonymous methods* to deal with it. Anonymous methods allow you to define a method "in line," without a name.

I'm not going to go into a whole lot of detail about anonymous methods here, because lambda expressions mostly replaced them.

To accomplish what we were trying to do with an anonymous method, instead of creating a whole method named **IsEven**, we could do the following:

```
numbers.Where(delegate(int number) { return (number % 2 == 0); });
```

If you take a look at that, you can see that we're basically taking the old **IsEven** method and sticking it in here, "in line."

This solves our two problems. We no longer have a named method floating around filling up our namespace, and the code that does the work is now at the same place as the code that needs the work.

I know, I know. You're probably saying, "But that code is not very readable! Everything's just smashed together!" And you're right. Anonymous methods solved some problems, while introducing others. You would have to decide which set of problems works best for you, depending on your specific case.

But this finally brings us to lambda expressions.

Lambda Expressions

Basically, a *lambda expression* is simply a method. More specifically, it is an anonymous method that is written in a different form that (theoretically) makes it a lot more readable. Lambda expressions were new in C# 3.0.

> **In Depth**
> **The Name "Lambda."** The name "lambda" comes from lambda calculus, which is the mathematical basis for programming languages. It is basically the programming language people used before there were computers at all. (Which is kind of strange to think about.) "Lambda" would really be spelled with the Greek letter lambda (λ) but the keyboard doesn't have it, so we just use "lambda."

Creating a lambda expression is quite simple. Returning to the **IsEven** problem from earlier, if we want to create a lambda expression to determine if a variable was even or odd, we would write the following:

```
x => x % 2 == 0
```

The lambda operator (**=>**) is read as "goes to" or "arrow." (So, to read this line out loud, you would say "x goes to x mod 2 equals 0" or "x arrow x mod 2 equals 0.") The lambda expression is basically saying to take the input value, **x**, and mod it with 2 and check the result against 0.

You may also notice with a lambda expression, we didn't use **return**. The code on the right side of the **=>** operator must be an expression, which evaluates to a single value. That value is returned, and its type becomes the return type of the lambda expression.

This version is the equivalent of all of the other versions of **IsEven** that we wrote earlier in this chapter. Speaking of that earlier code, this is how we might use this along with everything else:

```
IEnumerable<int> evens = numbers.Where(x => x % 2 == 0);
```

It may take a little getting used to, but generally speaking it is much easier to read and understand than the other techniques that we used earlier.

Multiple and Zero Parameters

Lambda expressions can have more than one parameter. To use more than one parameter, you simply list them in parentheses, separated by commas:

```
(x, y) => x * x + y * y
```

The parentheses are optional with one parameter, so in the earlier example, I've left them off.

This example above could have been written instead as a method like the following:

```
public int HypoteneuseSquared(int x, int y)
{
    return x * x + y * y;
}
```

Along the same lines, you can also have a lambda expression that has no parameters:

```
() => Console.WriteLine("Hello World!")
```

Type Inference Failures and Explicit Types

The C# compiler's type inference is smart enough to look at most lambda expressions and figure out what variable types and return type you are working with, but in some cases, the type inference fails, and you have to fall back to explicitly stating the types in use, or the code won't compile.

If this happens, you'll need to explicitly put in the type of the variable, like this:

```
(int x) => x % 2 == 0;
```

Using explicit types in your lambda expressions is always an option, not just when the compiler can't infer the type. Most C# programmers will generally take advantage of type inference when possible in a lambda, but if you like the syntax better or if it makes some specific situation clearer, feel free to use a named type instead of just using type inference, even if it isn't required.

Statement Lambdas

As you've seen by now, most methods are more than one line long. While lambda expressions are particularly well suited for very short, single line methods, there will be times that you'll want a lambda expression that is more than one line long. This complicates things a little bit, because now you'll need to add in semicolons, curly braces, and a **return** statement, but it can still be done:

```
(int x) => { bool isEven = x % 2 == 0; return isEven; }
```

The form we were using earlier is called an *expression lambda*, because it had only one expression in it. This new form is called a *statement lambda*. As a statement lambda gets longer, you should probably consider pulling it out into its own method.

Scope in Lambda Expressions

From what we've seen so far, lambda expressions have basically behaved like a normal method, only embedded in the code and with a different, cleaner syntax. But now I'm going to show you something that will throw you for a loop.

Inside of a lambda expression, you can access the variables that were in scope at the location of the lambda expression. Take the following code, for example:

```
int cutoffPoint = 5;
List<int> numbers = new List<int>(){ 1, 7, 4, 2, 5, 3, 9, 8, 6 };

IEnumerable<int> numbersLessThanCutoff = numbers.Where(x => x < cutoffPoint);
```

If our lambda expression had been turned into a method, we wouldn't have access to that **cutoffPoint** variable. (Unless we supplied it as a parameter.) This actually adds a ton of power to the way lambda expressions can work, so it is good to know about.

(For what it's worth, anonymous methods have the same feature.)

Expression-Bodied Members

Lambda expressions were introduced to C# in version 3.0, and as I mentioned earlier, one of the big draws to it is that the syntax is much more concise. That's great for short methods that would otherwise require a lot of overhead to define.

C# 6.0 extends this a little, allowing you to use the same expression syntax to define normal non-lambda methods within a class. For example, consider the method below:

```
public int ComputeSquare(int value)
{
    return value * value;
}
```

Now that we know about lambda expressions and the syntax that goes with them, it makes sense to point out that this method could also be implemented with the same expression syntax:

```
public int ComputeSquare(int value) => value * value;
```

This only works if the method can be turned into a single expression. In other words, we can use the expression lambda syntax, but not the statement lambda syntax. If we need a statement lambda, we would just write a normal method.

This syntax is not just limited to methods. Any method-like member of a type can use the same syntax. So that includes indexers, operator overloads, and properties (though this only applies to read-only properties where your expression defines the getter and the property has no setter). The following simple class shows all four of these in operation:

```
public class SomeSortOfClass
{
    // These two private instance variables are used by the methods below.
    private int x;
    private int[] internalNumbers = new int[] { 1, 2, 3 };

    // Property (read-only, no setter allowed)
    public int X => x;

    // Operator overload
    public static int operator +(SomeSortOfClass a, SomeSortOfClass b) => a.X + b.X;

    // Indexer
    public int this[int index] => internalNumbers[index];

    // Normal method
    public int ComputeSquare(int value) => value * value;
}
```

Lambdas vs. Local Functions

In all cases where you might use a lambda, you could also use a local function, which was introduced in Chapter 28. The scenarios in which you might use a lambda are also good fits for local functions, and the two can even be combined together, using an expression-bodied local function. To illustrate, consider the following three methods which are all equivalent in terms of functionality:

```
public static IEnumerable<int> FindEvenNumbers1(List<int> numbers)
{
    return numbers.Where(x => x % 2 == 0); // Plain lambda expression.
}

public static IEnumerable<int> FindEvenNumbers2(List<int> numbers)
{
    bool IsEven(int number) // Local function.
    {
        return number % 2 == 0;
    }

    return numbers.Where(IsEven);
}

public static IEnumerable<int> FindEvenNumbers3(List<int> numbers)
{
    bool IsEven(int number) => number % 2 == 0; // Expression-bodied local function.

    return numbers.Where(IsEven);
}
```

Each of the three above options are functionally equivalent, but with rather different syntax. The first is a plain lambda expression. This is probably the most concise of the three, and for somebody comfortable with lambda expressions, is quite readable.

The second is a local function. It isn't nearly as concise, but has the advantage of giving a name to the functionality.

The third is a local function with an expression body. This is something of a compromise of the two.

Each of the above can be the best option in different scenarios. All have their place. Pick the one that produces the most readable code for any given situation.

Try It Out!

Lambda Expressions Quiz. Answer the following questions to check your understanding. When you're done, check your answers against the ones below. If you missed something, go back and review the section that talks about it.

1. **True/False.** Lambda expressions are a special type of method.
2. **True/False.** A lambda expression can be given a name.
3. What operator is used in lambda expressions?
4. Convert the following to a lambda expression: **bool IsNegative(int x) { return x < 0; }**
5. **True/False.** Lambda expressions can only have one parameter.
6. **True/False.** Lambda expressions have access to the local variables in the method they appear in.

Answers: (1) True. **(2)** False. **(3)** Lambda operator (=>). **(4)** x => x < 0. **(5)** False. **(6)** True.

Query Expressions

> **In a Nutshell**
> - Query expressions are a special type of statement in C# that allows you to extract certain pieces from a collection of data and return it in a specific format or organization.
> - Query expressions are made of multiple clauses:
>   - A **from** clause indicates the collection that is being queried.
>   - A **select** clause indicates the specific data that is to be returned.
>   - A **where** clause performs filtering in the query.
>   - A **let** clause allows you to give a name to a part of a query for later reference.
>   - A **join** clause allows you to combine multiple collections together.
>   - An **orderby** clause allows you to choose the order of the results.
>   - A **group** clause allows you to group or partition a set of data into related chunks.
>   - An **into** clause continues the query when it otherwise would have terminated.
> - All queries can be done using query syntax or with normal method calls instead.

A common programming task that you'll have is one where you must take a collection of data, extract certain parts, and return it in a certain shape or organized in a specific way. This data extraction and transformation is often called a *query*.

Here are some sample queries:

- In a real estate system, you might need to find houses that cost less than $300,000 but that also have at least two bathrooms and at least three bedrooms.
- In a project management tool, you might need to search through all tasks in a certain project to find ones assigned to people who are on a specific team.
- In a video game, you might need to find all objects in the game world within a certain distance of an explosion that can take damage.

LINQ Queries and Declarative Programming

The syntax of C#'s query expressions is inspired by SQL, which is a database query language. C#'s query syntax is called a *Language Integrated Query*, or *LINQ* for short. It's actually quite different from a lot of the rest of C#'s syntax. Nine keywords are used for LINQ queries that aren't used elsewhere.

But LINQ queries are not complicated. Indeed, the syntax makes queries easy to read and understand.

The primary difference between query expressions and other C# code is that query expressions are declarative, rather than procedural. With the procedural programming that we've gotten used to, we specify step-by-step how something should be done. With declarative programming, we don't specify how—we simply state ("declare") what we want and let the computer figure out how it gets it on its own.

Anything we might want to do with a query expression could have also been done procedurally with loops and **if** statements. But query expressions are often far more readable than their procedural counterparts.

IEnumerable<T> is the Starting Point for Queries

All LINQ queries operate on collections of data. It's important to point out that when we say "collections" here, we're referring specifically to the **IEnumerable<T>** interface that was introduced in Chapter 25. Virtually all container types implement this interface, making it so that query expressions can operate on virtually any data collection. This includes arrays, **List<T>**, even **Dictionary<K, V>**, and many others.

For the purposes of this chapter, when I say "collection" or "sequence," I'm referring to any type that implements **IEnumerable<T>**.

Query expressions always produce an **IEnumerable<T>** as output. If you store the results of a query expression in a variable, it will need to be of type **IEnumerable<T>**.

In the event that you need the results in an array or a **List<T>**, the **IEnumerable<T>** interface has a couple of extension methods called **ToArray()** and **ToList()** that will convert it to a **T[]** or a **List<T>** respectively.

The Structure of a LINQ Query

A query expression is composed of multiple *clauses*. A clause is a chunk of syntax smaller than a full expression that has meaning, but requires other clauses around it to be complete.

The structure of a LINQ query is this:

- All LINQ queries start with a **from** clause.
- This is followed by any number of **where**, **join**, **orderby**, **let**, and additional **from** clauses.
- A LINQ query terminates with either a **select** clause or a **group** clause.
- A LINQ query that would otherwise be terminated can be continued with an **into** clause, allowing you to go back to the beginning.

We'll get into the specifics of each of these clause types through the rest of this chapter.

Sample Classes

Before we dive in, it's worth defining a few sample classes to use with our queries. The following three classes give us some sample data to play with through this chapter. You might find some classes like this in a video game. The **GameObject** class might serve as a base class for other specialized objects to derive from (like the stubbed-out **Ship** class), while the **Player** class defines some basic properties of a player in a multi-player game.

```
public class GameObject
{
    public int ID { get; set; }
    public double X { get; set; }
    public double Y { get; set; }
    public double MaxHP { get; set; }
    public double CurrentHP { get; set; }
    public int PlayerID { get; set; }
}
```

```
public class Ship : GameObject { }

public class Player
{
    public int ID { get; set; }
    public string UserName { get; set; }
    public string TeamColor { get; set; } // A Color class might be better than string here.
}
```

As you explore the topics in this chapter, you might find it useful to recreate these classes in your own project. Create a **List<GameObject>** and a **List<Player>** and fill the lists with some sample data. This will give you something to run queries on to compare and explore the results. The following might serve as a starting point for that:

```
List<GameObject> gameObjects = new List<GameObject>();
gameObjects.Add(new Ship { ID = 1, X = 0, Y = 0, CurrentHP = 50, MaxHP = 100, PlayerID = 1 });
gameObjects.Add(new Ship { ID = 2, X = 4, Y = 2, CurrentHP = 75, MaxHP = 100, PlayerID = 1 });
gameObjects.Add(new Ship { ID = 3, X = 9, Y = 3, CurrentHP =  0, MaxHP = 100, PlayerID = 2 });

List<Player> players = new List<Player>();
players.Add(new Player { ID = 1, UserName = "Player 1", TeamColor = "Red" });
players.Add(new Player { ID = 2, UserName = "Player 2", TeamColor = "Blue" });
```

From Clauses

All queries start with a **from** clause. A **from** clause is a generator of sorts, which creates a range variable over the elements in a sequence (any **IEnumerable**).

There's nothing too exciting about them, other than defining a source of information to query.

A **from** clause is always used to start a query expression and can be used in the middle of a query to introduce additional sources of information. But a lonely **from** clause doesn't form a complete query expression. The following doesn't compile, but it serves the purpose of illustrating the structure of a simple **from** clause:

```
from o in gameObjects
```

A **from** clause introduces a *range variable*. This is a local variable that can be accessed throughout the rest of the query. In many ways, a range variable is like the variable in a **foreach** loop. The variable will take on each value in the sequence, one at a time, as the query is evaluated.

A **from** clause is composed of the **from** keyword, followed by the name of the range variable, followed by the **in** keyword, and then finally the sequence that the range variable belongs to—the data set that will be looked at in this query.

In this **from** clause, the range variable will have the same type as the collection. So if **gameObjects** is a collection of **GameObject**, then the range variable **o** will also be of type **GameObject**.

There is another variation for a **from** clause where you can specify the type of the range variable like this:

```
from Ship s in gameObjects
```

This type can be a more base type or a more derived type as the collection itself. So for example, we could have done **from object o in gameObjects**. That would simply mean we don't care about any **GameObject** specific code, and are OK falling back to a base class.

But as you can see in the example above, we can also specify a more derived type; we've used **Ship** instead of **GameObject**. This will actually work correctly up until the point where the execution of the query encounters something that isn't a **Ship**. So even if **gameObjects** is a **List<GameObject>** or an **IEnumerable<GameObject>**, this code only has problems if it encounters something that isn't a **Ship**.

A **from** clause gets the query expression started, but isn't a full query expression on its own. So let's continue on to the **select** clause, and start putting together full query expressions.

Select Clauses

A **select** clause is one of two ways to end a query expression (the other being a **group** clause). A **select** clause identifies the portion of an object (including the whole object) to be produced as the final results of a query expression.

A minimal (but rather useless) complete query expression combining our **from** clause with a simple **select** clause might look like this:

```
IEnumerable<GameObject> allObjects = from o in gameObjects
                                     select o;
```

This is about as simple as a query expression gets, resulting in our full **gameObjects** collection, completely unchanged. So let's do another example that is a bit more exciting:

```
IEnumerable<string> results = from o in gameObjects
                              select o.CurrentHP + "/" + o.MaxHP;
```

A **select** clause is a powerful tool on its own, allowing you to produce new values from existing ones.

Where Clauses

While we're able to make query expressions with just **from** and **select** clauses, another key type of clause is the **where** clause. A **where** clause is used to filter elements in a collection, based on some condition. Consider the **where** clause we've introduced below, which makes it so we filter to only objects that are "alive" (their **CurrentHP** is greater than 0):

```
IEnumerable<GameObject> aliveObjects = from o in gameObjects
                                       where o.CurrentHP > 0
                                       select o;
```

A query statement must start with a **from** clause and must end with a **select** clause (or a **group** clause) but in the middle, you can have any number of **where** clauses.

Multiple From Clauses

A query statement must start with a **from** clause, but is also allowed to contain additional **from** clauses anywhere in the middle as well. The effect of this is similar to two nested **foreach** loops and essentially produces a sub-query within the main query.

Consider the code below:

```
IEnumerable<string> intersections = from o1 in gameObjects
                                    from o2 in gameObjects
                                    where (o1.Intersects(o2)) // Assumes we have an Intersects method.
                                    select $"{o1.ID} intersects {o2.ID}.";
```

The **where** clause will be performed for each pairing of **o1** with each **o2**.

Multiple **from** clauses can use the same collection again, or pull in a second collection.

Let Clauses

A **let** clause is like a **select** clause in that it defines a new range variable, but does so by producing it from previous range variables. This makes it a "derived" range variable, computed from other range variables.

The primary purpose of a **let** clause is to allow you to define something that is used in multiple places later on in the query expression, or to give a name to a complex operation to make the code more readable. This can be used later in the query expression. For example:

```
IEnumerable<string> statuses = from o in gameObjects
                   let percentHealth = Math.Round(o.CurrentHP / o.MaxHP * 100)
                   select $"{o.ID} is at {percentHealth}%.";
```

Join Clauses

The **join** clause is a powerful tool that will allow us to combine two collections together, pairing them up based on a rule provided by the programmer.

The sample classes we defined earlier included a **gameObjects** and a **players** collection, which we can join together. The game objects themselves know the ID of the player they belong to, but not any other player specific data like the user name or color for a specific player. At some point, we might want to combine our **gameObjects** collection with our **players** collection, and a **join** clause does just that:

```
var objectColors = from o in gameObjects
              join p in players on o.PlayerID equals p.ID
              select new { o.ID, p.TeamColor };
```

A **join** clause is one of the more complex clauses in the LINQ world, but also one of the more useful ones.

A **join** clause is also a prime place to use an anonymous type, which we first looked at in Chapter 19. The example above is a good example of when an anonymous type might be useful. If these results don't have to be returned from the method, it is simple enough to just work with it as an anonymous type.

A **join** clause has some similarities with a **from** clause. It also introduces a range variable. But contrasted with using a second **join** clause, which simply produces all pairings of every item in one collection with every item in the other, a **join** will *only* produce the pairs that meet some criteria, specified by the **on X equals Y** portion of the **join** clause.

In order for a **join** to work at all, there must be some part of the two sequences that are equal to each other. (Note that the **equals** keyword translates to the **==** operator. If you have overloaded **==** for a given type, then you can use that type in a **join** clause.) You can't use another comparison operator like **<** or **>=**.

The placement of the two sides of the **equals** keyword is critical. The left side of the **equals** must reference an earlier range variable, while the right side may only reference the new range variable.

This is what database people call an *inner join*. In order for an object in either collection to show up in the results, there must be a match found for it in the other collection. If there is no player found for a specific game object, the game object will not be found in the resulting collection. Likewise, if a player has no corresponding game objects, you won't see the player in the resulting collection either.

Orderby Clauses

An **orderby** clause takes the given sequence and produces a new sequence that has been ordered in a particular way. For example, you could sort all **Player** objects using a simple **orderby** clause like this:

```
IEnumerable<Player> sortedPlayers = from p in players
                                    orderby p.UserName
                                    select p;
```

The default sort order is ascending order, though the ordering can be specified with either the **ascending** or **descending** keyword at the end of the clause.

```
IEnumerable<Player> sortedPlayers = from p in players
                                    orderby p.UserName descending
                                    select p;
```

Note that you don't have to just stick with the name of a property for an **orderby** clause. You can sort on the whole object (which makes more sense you're using a type that has a natural sorting order like **int** or **string**) or you can put in a more complicated expression in there as well.

You can also perform multi-level sorts by separating additional sort criteria with commas. For example:

```
IEnumerable<GameObject> sortedGameObjects = from o in gameObjects
                                            orderby o.PlayerID ascending, o.MaxHP descending
                                            select o;
```

This will sort by **PlayerID** first, from lowest to highest, then by **MaxHP** from highest to lowest.

Group Clauses

A **group** clause is another extremely powerful clause, though perhaps not quite as common. A **group** clause is one that allows you to take a single sequence and bundle the elements into groups based on criteria you supply. For example, the following query will take all game objects and separate them into groups based on the **PlayerID** that each object belongs to:

```
IEnumerable<IGrouping<int, GameObject>> groups = from o in gameObjects
                                                 group o by o.PlayerID;
```

This is the first query that we've seen that doesn't end with a **select** clause. A **group** clause is the other way to terminate a query expression. But you'll also notice that the variable type that we store these results in is quite a bit different, and quite a bit more complex than what we've seen before. (This nesting of generic types is one of the reasons some people like **var**, because they don't have to type all that out.)

Rather than a simple **IEnumerable<SomeType>**, our type is **IEnumerable<IGrouping<GroupType, ObjectType>>**. The **IGrouping<TKey, TElement>** interface defines what a group looks like. It is just a simple collection object that contains the items in the group, and also has a **Key** property that holds the group ID. So for example, in the previous code, each group's key would be the player ID that all items in the group had, and the items in the group would be all of the game objects that belonged to that particular player.

To illustrate how these groups are structured, the code below prints the groups from the previous sample:

```
foreach(IGrouping<int, GameObject> group in groups)
{
    Console.WriteLine(group.Key);
    foreach(GameObject o in group)
        Console.WriteLine("    " + o.ID);
}
```

The results of a **group** clause is essentially a collection of collections, where each collection can be identified by its key.

You won't get empty groups from a simple **group** statement.

Into Clauses

While a query expression ends with a **select** or **group** clause, it doesn't actually have to end when you encounter one. An **into** clause, sometimes called a *continuation clause*, allows you to take the results of a **select** or **group** clause and put the value into another range variable. This is a little like a **let** clause in that regard. Additional query clauses can follow an **into** clause:

```
var objectCountPerPlayer = from o in gameObjects
                           group o by o.PlayerID
                           into playerGroup
                           select new { ID = playerGroup.Key, Count = playerGroup.Count() };
```

You can see that the **into** clause above allows us to continue past the **group** clause and do more work.

In this particular example, because the **into** follows a **group** clause, the type will be some sort of **IGrouping**. We create another anonymous type that has an **ID**, based on the player that the group is for, and a **Count** property that is the total number of game objects that belong to each player.

An **into** clause can follow both **group** and **select** clauses.

Group Joins

There is one final type of clause, assembled from other clause keywords, that is both powerful and somewhat convoluted. This is the group join, which is something of a hybrid between a **group** clause and a **join** clause. (Bet you didn't see that coming!)

Similar to a **join** clause, a group join combines together two other sequences of data.

A normal **join** clause will take two collections and pair up elements that belong to each other, as defined by sharing some key. After the **join** clause, you are able to access the matching object from each collection together, at the same time. A caveat to this is that if an object in either sequence didn't match something in the other, then you will never see it as a result. A group join is a little different in this regard.

Similar to a **join**, a group join operates on two collections, and objects are matched together. But more precisely, with a group join, all items in the second collection are bundled together into a group that belongs to a single item in the first collection. This applies even if there were no items in the second collection that belonged to an item in the first collection (which results in an empty group).

With a normal **join** clause, what you have to work with is the two objects that matched. After a group join, you have the object from the first collection, followed by a (possibly empty) **IEnumerable** of the items that belonged to it from the second list.

A group join will make more sense with an actual example, so here is one:

```
var playerObjects = from p in players
                    join o in gameObjects on p.ID equals o.PlayerID into objectsOwnedByPlayer
                    select new { Player = p, Objects = objectsOwnedByPlayer };

foreach(var objects in playerObjects)
{
    Console.WriteLine(objects.Player.UserName + " has the following objects:");
    foreach(GameObject o in objects.Objects)
        Console.WriteLine($"    {o.ID} {o.CurrentHP}/{o.MaxHP}");
}
```

First thing's first: the syntax. A group join is performed by a somewhat normal **join** clause, followed immediately by an **into** clause.

After the group join, you can access the item from the first collection with the same name as before, and the matching items from the second collection through the name indicated by the **into** clause.

The above group join starts with all of the game objects and bundles them into groups based on IDs from the first collection (**players**). Each player ends up with a group, even if it is an empty group. (Game objects that didn't match with any player are left out of the results.) The code at the end iterates through the results and prints it out, to show how you might interact with data that comes out of a group join.

Query Syntax and Method Call Syntax

A key component of query expressions is that, in addition to the query syntax that we've been learning here, there is a second syntax for writing these queries. This second syntax is called *method call syntax*, and—surprise, surprise—it is done through simple method invocations.

For every type of clause we've seen above, there is a method that is available that does the exact same thing. All of these methods are extension methods (see Chapter 36) on the type **IEnumerable<T>**.

The following list outlines how the above clauses are turned into the method call syntax:

- **from** clauses turn into the collection object that you want to begin invoking methods on.
- **select** clauses turn into invocations of the **Select** method.
- **where** clauses turn into invocations of the **Where** method.
- **let** clauses do not have exact translations.
- **join** clauses turn into invocations of the **Join** method.
- **orderby** clauses turn into invocations of **OrderBy**, **OrderByDescending**, **ThenBy**, and **ThenByDescending**.
- **group** clauses turn into invocations of the **GroupBy** method.
- Group joins turn into invocations of the **GroupJoin** method.

These methods make heavy use of lambda expressions, which we saw in Chapter 37. As a simple example, the following code shows the same functionality in both query syntax and method call syntax:

```
IEnumerable<int> aliveIDs1 = from o in gameObjects
                            where o.CurrentHP > 0
                            select o.ID;

IEnumerable<int> aliveIDs2 = gameObjects.Where(o => o.CurrentHP > 0).Select(o => o.ID);
```

There are quite a few other query-related methods that exist on the **IEnumerable<T>** interface that have no query syntax equivalent. We won't go through those here, but taking a peek at them someday will probably be worth your time.

Queries are Lazy When Possible

It should be pointed out that queries (both syntaxes) are "lazy," meaning only the bare minimum is performed for any given result. For example, consider the following query expression and **foreach** loop:

```
IEnumerable<GameObject> aliveObjects = from o in gameObjects
                                       where o.CurrentHP > 0
                                       select o;

foreach(GameObject o in aliveObjects)
    Console.WriteLine($"{o.ID} is alive.");
```

After the query is built and assigned to **aliveObjects**, but before the **foreach**, absolutely none of the code in the query expression has been executed.

As the **foreach** loop begins looping over the items in **aliveObjects**, just enough of the query is executed to produce the next item.

For example, the first time through the **foreach** loop, only enough items from the original **gameObjects** collection will be looked at to find one where its **CurrentHP** is more than 0.

Lazy evaluation can be bad or good. On one hand, if you never actually walk through the entire result set, then the query doesn't have to process every single item. Since queries can get quite complicated and data sets can be very large, this can save a lot of time.

On the other hand, if you end up evaluating a query more than once, it can be quite costly. This can be solved by converting the results to an array or list, using the **ToArray()** or **ToList()** methods respectively. Either of these will cause the query to be evaluated fully once, but then caches the results in the array or list, preventing you from needing to reevaluate it again the second time.

Try It Out!

Full Health. Based on the **GameObject** class defined earlier in this chapter, you could say that a particular **GameObject** is at full health if its **CurrentHP** was equal to its **MaxHP**. Based on this definition of full health, write query expressions that return the following:

1. A collection of all game objects that have full health.
2. A collection of the IDs of all game objects that have full health.

Try It Out!

Percent Health. Write a query to produce game objects grouped by their owner (**PlayerID**) and ordered based on the percent health (**CurrentHP / MaxHP**).

Try It Out!

Back to Procedural Programming. Take the query expression below and rewrite it without using any LINQ methods or any LINQ keywords, just by using **if** statements and loops.

```
IEnumerable<GameObject> aliveObjects = from o in gameObjects
                                       where o.CurrentHP > 0
                                       select o;
```

Try It Out!

Query Expressions Quiz. Answer the following questions to check your understanding. When you're done, check your answers against the ones below. If you missed something, go back and review the section that talks about it.

1. What type of clause (or what keyword) is used to start a query expression?
2. What two types of clauses can terminate a query expression?
3. What clause is used to filter data?
4. **True/False.** You can order by multiple criteria in a single **orderby** clause.
5. What clause is used to combine two related sets of data together?

Answers: **(1) from** clause. **(2) select** and **group**. **(3) where** clause. **(4)** True. **(5) join** clause.

Threads

In a Nutshell

- Threading allows you to run sections of code simultaneously.
- Starting a new thread: **Thread thread = new Thread(MethodNameHere); thread.Start();**
- In the above code, the method must have a **void** return type with no parameters.
- Alternatively, **ParameterizedThreadStart** lets you pass in a parameter (**object**) to the method.
- You can wait for a thread to finish with the **Join** method: **thread.Join();**
- If you need to worry about thread safety (preventing problems when multiple threads are modifying the same data), you can use the **lock** keyword: **lock(aPrivateObject) { /* code in here is thread safe */ }**.

Back in the day, all computers had one processor. Nowadays, they usually have a lot more than one. (More specifically, this is usually done by having multiple cores that are all a part of the same processor chip.) I'm currently working on a computer with four processors, each of which is "hyper-threaded," making it appear that I have a total of eight processors. And this computer isn't even all that fancy. There are machines out there that have 16 or 32 processors, or even hundreds or thousands, all working together. (Turns out, they're kind of expensive.) You could even set up a program to hand off work to other computers across the network, giving you an unlimited number of processors at your disposal.

Computers have a lot of power, but unless you intentionally structure your code to run on multiple processors, it will only ever use one. Think of all of that raw computing power going to waste!

In this chapter, we're going to take a look at threading. The basic process of threading is that we can take chunks of code that are independent of each other and make them run in separate *threads*. A thread is almost like its own program, in that the computer will run multiple threads all at the same time on different processors. (For the record, a thread is *not* its own program. It still shares memory with the program/process that created it.)

When many threads are running, each processor will run a thread for a while, and then suddenly switch it out for a different one. The computer gets to decide when it is time to make the switch and which thread to switch to, but it does a pretty good job, so that's one less thing we need to worry about. This switching is called a *context switch*.

All threads will be treated fairly equally, but they *will* get switched around from time to time. It's something that you need to be aware of, and even write your code in a way that can handle it. If you fail to do it correctly, you can end up with strange intermittent errors that only appear to happen on Tuesdays where you ate tacos for lunch and the moon is waxing. We'll talk more about dealing with this in the section about Thread Safety.

There's a lot that goes into threading, and we simply don't have enough time to discuss all of the ins and outs of it here. So we won't. Instead, we'll take a look at the basics of threading, and I'll allow you to dig further into threading as you need it.

Threading Code Basics

We'll start out with a very simple example of how to start a new thread. To get started, let's say we have some work we want to do on a separate thread. This can really be anything, but let's say it is this:

```
public static void CountTo100()
{
    for (int index = 0; index < 100; index++)
        Console.WriteLine(index + 1);
}
```

To run this in a separate thread, you will need to create a new thread, tell it what method to run, and then start it. The following code does this:

```
Thread thread = new Thread(CountTo100);
thread.Start();
```

You'll also need to add a new **using** directive to get access to the **Thread** class (**using System.Threading;**) like we discussed back in Chapter 27.

The first line creates a new **Thread** object, but take a look at that constructor. We've passed in the method that we want it to run as a parameter. This is using a delegate. (Another good use of delegates!) This happens to be the **ThreadStart** delegate, which has a **void** return type and no parameters, so the method we use needs to match that.

After we call the **Start** method, a new thread will be created and will start executing the method we told it to run (**CountTo100**). At that point, we have two threads: the original thread, and the new one that running in **CountTo100**.

To have the original thread wait at some point for this new thread to terminate, we use the **Join** method:

```
thread.Join();
```

When a thread runs into this statement, it freezes and waits there until the other thread finishes up, effectively joining the execution of the two threads.

You can create as many threads as you want. As I mentioned earlier, they'll all get their fair share of the total processor time. (Though you don't want to have *too* many threads, because it takes time to create them all, and more threads means more frequent context switches, which take time.)

For example, here is some code that runs two threads and waits for them to finish:

```
using System;
using System.Threading;
```

```
namespace Threading
{
    class Program
    {
        static void Main(string[] args)
        {
            Thread thread1 = new Thread(CountTo100);
            thread1.Start();

            Thread thread2 = new Thread(CountTo100);
            thread2.Start();

            thread1.Join();
            thread2.Join();

            Console.ReadKey();
        }

        public static void CountTo100()
        {
            for (int index = 0; index < 100; index++)
                Console.WriteLine(index + 1);
        }
    }
}
```

Try running this code. There are two threads that are both going to print out the numbers 1 through 100. Typically, you'll see one thread active for a little while, and then the other active. So you might see the numbers 1-24 printed out, and then that thread will stop and the other thread will print out, say, 1-52, and then the first one will print out 25-87, and so on, until they both finish up.

You'll never get the exact same output the second time around. Things will be a little bit different because the operating system is doing context switches as it sees fit. That's an important point to remember about threads: the timing and ordering is unpredictable. This can be a big pain when you're trying to debug a problem in a multi-threaded program, and it is worth considering before you decide to run things on separate threads.

One other thing that I should point out is that you can make the current thread "sleep" for a certain amount of time. This is useful when you know one thread needs to wait a while for another thread to do something. To make the current thread sleep, you can call the static **Sleep** method in the **Thread** class:

```
Thread.Sleep(1000);
```

The parameter that you pass in is the amount of time to sleep for, measured in milliseconds. So 1000 is 1 second. The code above will cause the current thread to stop execution for one second, while other threads have a chance to run.

Using ParameterizedThreadStart

In the code we were using above, we used the **ThreadStart** delegate. This meant the method we ran could have no parameters, which meant that we couldn't pass any information to the method we were calling, which is somewhat limited.

There is an alternative that allows us to use methods that take a single parameter instead. To do this, we use the **ParameterizedThreadStart** delegate instead. This delegate has a return type of **void** and a single parameter of type **object**. Because the parameter is of type **object**, we can basically use it for anything, as long as we cast it correctly to the right type.

For example, consider this variation of our **CountTo100** method, which counts to any number you want:

```
public static void CountToNumber(object input)
{
    int n = (int)input;
    for (int index = 0; index < n; index++)
        Console.WriteLine(index + 1);
}
```

This has a parameter of type **object**, which we cast to an **int**, and use through the rest of our method.

Because this method matches the **ParameterizedThreadStart** delegate, we can create a new thread, with a reference to this method, and start it with a parameter, which gets passed along into our method:

```
Thread thread = new Thread(CountToNumber);
thread.Start(50);
```

Using **object** allows us to use any type imaginable, as long as we're willing to cast. It's unfortunate that there isn't a version of **ParameterizedThreadStart** that uses generics, but there isn't. Furthermore, while the **ParameterizedThreadStart** doesn't allow you to return information, you could easily construct an object that has a property that can store what would have been returned.

To illustrate, below is a simple little program that will do division on a separate thread (yeah, it's overkill):

```
using System;
using System.Threading;

namespace Threading
{
    public class DivisionProblem
    {
        public double Dividend { get; set; } // the top
        public double Divisor { get; set; }  // the bottom
        public double Quotient { get; set; } // the result (normally would be returned)
    }

    class Program
    {
        static void Main(string[] args)
        {
            Thread thread = new Thread(Divide);

            DivisionProblem problem = new DivisionProblem();
            problem.Dividend = 8;
            problem.Divisor = 2;

            thread.Start(problem);
            thread.Join();

            Console.WriteLine("Result: " + problem.Quotient);

            Console.ReadKey();
        }

        public static void Divide(object input)
        {
            DivisionProblem problem = (DivisionProblem)input;
            problem.Quotient = problem.Dividend / problem.Divisor;
        }
    }
}
```

> ## Try It Out!
>
> **Frog Racing.** Let's make a little simulator for a frog race. The idea is that there are multiple frogs that are lined up and competing against each other to jump across a finish line. In order to finish the race, a frog needs to jump a total of 10 times. Each frog runs on its own thread, and we'll have three total.
>
> To do this, create a method that matches the **ParameterizedThreadStart** delegate. As input, the object that is passed in will be the frog's number. Inside of that method, use a loop to print out "Frog #X jumped" and then use **Thread.Sleep** and a **Random** object to have the frog/thread sleep for a random amount of time between 0 and 1 seconds. When the frog/thread has jumped ten times and the loop ends, print out "Frog #X finished." (Generating random numbers is discussed in Chapter 16.)
>
> Start the frog race by creating three separate threads and starting them all with different numbers. Wait for each thread to finish using the **Join** method.

Thread Safety

We've covered the basics of threading, but it is worth looking at another, more advanced threading topic. Not all situations need to be worried about this, but some do, so it is worth knowing a little about.

In the examples that we've done so far, each thread has been working with its own data. But what if there was something that they had to share? Remember that threads get swapped out whenever the operating system decides, and a thread may actually be in the middle of something important when that context switch hits.

To help explain the concept of thread safety, I'm going to draw on a real-world example. Imagine you're driving your car down a road that has three lanes. You're on the outside lane (the black car), and another car is on the inside lane (the white car):

You want to change lanes to the middle. The normal process is that you look over into that other lane, make sure it is clear, and if so, you move over. But what if the white car was doing the same thing, without you knowing it? The other driver looked as well, saw that the lane was clear, and moved over. Unless one of you realizes the problem, you're headed for a crash.

Like with the cars, when you have multiple threads that are using any of the same resources, if you aren't careful, two threads can run into each other and cause problems.

Imagine even the simple problem of adding one to a variable. To do this, the computer will do the following steps:

- Read the current value from the variable.
- Do the math to figure out the result of adding 1 to the value.
- Store the new value back in the variable.

Now, imagine that two separate threads are both given the task of adding 1 to the variable. In a normal "happy" scenario, this variable should get incremented twice.

But let's see how things could go bad with multiple threads. Let's say our variable starts with a value of 1. In theory, both threads should increment the variable, and it should end up with a value of 3. But the following could happen as well:

- Thread #1 reads the current value from the variable (1).
- Thread #1 does the math to figure out the result of adding 1 to the value (2).
- Thread #2 reads the current value from the variable (which is still set to 1).
- Thread #2 does the math to figure out the result of adding 1 to the value (getting 2 also).
- Thread #2 stores the new value back into the variable (2 gets assigned back).
- Thread #1 stores the new value back into the variable (once again, 2 is assigned back).

Both threads did the work they were supposed to do, but because the two are running at the same time (or because of a context switch) things didn't turn out the way they should, and the variable is left with a value of 2, instead of 3 like it should be.

This example is kind of a toy problem, but the reality is that any time you have more than one thread modifying some specific data, you're likely to run into problems like this.

We want to be able to address this problem and make certain sections of code that we know might be problematic be *thread safe*, meaning that the code can prevent bad things like this from happening when multiple threads want to use it.

If we have a certain block of code that modifies data that could be accessed by other threads, we call that section a *critical section*. We will want to make it so that only one thread can get inside it at a time. This principle of only allowing one thread in at a time is called *mutual exclusion* and the mechanism that is used to enforce this is often called a *mutex*.

To enter a critical section, we require that the thread that is entering the section acquire the mutual exclusion lock for a specific object. When the thread has this lock, it can enter the critical section and execute the code. When it's done, it releases the lock, freeing it up for the next thread. If a thread shows up and tries to grab the lock that is already taken, the thread will be suspended until the lock is released.

Doing this in code is pretty simple. The first step is to create some sort of object that is accessible to anything that needs access to the critical section, which can act as the lock. Often, this is best done with a private instance variable in the same class as the data that is being modified:

```
private object threadLock = new object(); // Nothing special needed. Any object will do.
```

You could alternatively use a static variable instead of an instance variable if you need thread safety across all instances of the class.

To actually make a block of code thread safe, you simply add a block surrounding the critical section with the **lock** keyword:

```
lock(threadLock)
{
    // Code in here is now thread safe. Only one thread at a time can be in here.
    // Everyone else will have to wait at the "lock" statement.
}
```

That's the basics of threading in C#. There is a lot that goes on in multi-threaded applications, and there are entire books dedicated to the subject. We can only cover the basics here, but it should give you an idea of the fundamentals.

40

Asynchronous Programming

In a Nutshell
- Asynchronous programming is where you take a particular task or chunk of code and run it on a separate thread, outside of the main flow of execution.
- C# has used many ways of achieving asynchronous programming in the past.
- The Task-based Asynchronous Pattern (TAP) uses the **Task** and **Task<TResult>** class to represent a chunk of work that is running asynchronously.
- Tasks can be awaited with the **await** keyword (if the method is marked with **async**), allowing you simple syntax for scheduling additional work that happens once the task has been completed: **HighScores = await highScoreManager.LookupScores();**

In this chapter, we're going to continue what we started in the previous chapter, and introduce the best way to do most asynchronous things in C#. This uses the **async** and **await** keywords that were introduced into the C# language in C# 5.0.

Asynchronous programming is hard. There's not enough space in this chapter to cover every single detail and strange corner case. Rather, the goal of this chapter is to introduce you to the syntax surrounding calling code asynchronously, and get you to a point where it's not a deep, dark mystery, but something you feel comfortable with doing, while leaving some of the finer points of asynchronous programming for a later point in time.

In this chapter, we'll start by defining what asynchronous programming is and why you might use it. Then we'll take a look at how asynchronous programming has evolved in C# over time. We'll finally introduce the Task-based Asynchronous Pattern and the **async** and **await** keywords, which serve as the basis of modern asynchronous programming in C#.

What is Asynchronous Programming?

Asynchronous programming means taking a piece of code and running it on a separate thread, freeing up the original thread to continue on and do other things while the task completes.

The typical use case is when you start something that you know is going to take a while to happen. "A while" is measured in computer time, so we may be talking only a few milliseconds (or not). Some common scenarios include making a request to a server or a website, making requests to the file system, while running a particularly large or long running algorithm that you're using, or any other time where you know a particular piece of code is going to take some work to get done.

Modern computers have a lot of computational power, and users are expecting responsive user interfaces. Those two combined mean asynchronous programming is becoming more and more necessary and important to know.

The opposite of asynchronous programming (sometimes called "asynchrony") is synchronous programming, and it's what we've been doing up until now.

Approaches from the Early Days

There have been many approaches to doing asynchronous programming in C#'s past. While no longer recommended or preferred, those older approaches are worth mention because they illustrate the complexity of the problem, the beauty of the final solution, and the decade long journey it took to get there.

Throughout this section, we'll stick with a recurring example of getting a list of high scores for a game from a web server. This will help us see the trade-offs of the various approaches that we'll see.

A Synchronous Approach

Let's start by looking at how we might do this task (looking up high scores) using a traditional synchronous approach. That means blocking and waiting for the results to come back before moving on. Obviously, this defeats the purpose of what this chapter is talking about, but it is a worthwhile exercise anyway. The biggest thing we'll gain from this is an example of what "ideal" code looks like here. Synchronous requests are straightforward, and the method calls are clean and simple.

To do our high score lookup in a synchronous fashion, we might use code like this:

```
Score[] highScores = highScoreManager.LookupScores();
```

That's relatively straightforward. We just call the method directly, which returns the results upon completion, and we store them in an array.

I'm skipping the actual implementation of the **LookupScores** method. I know that is going to be a disappointment to some people, but it's irrelevant to the current discussion. The point is, it doesn't matter what the work is, just that it's some sort of long running task that we really don't want to sit around waiting for. (But if you're dying of curiosity, one possible way to do this might be with an HTTP request using C#'s **WebClient** class, which returns the results in a text stream of some sort, which could then be parsed and turned into a list of scores.)

While that code is short and easy to understand, it's not asynchronous.

Creating Threads Directly

Having seen a synchronous version of our high scores lookup problem, let's turn our attention to doing this in an asynchronous way.

Our first option is to create a thread like we did in the last chapter. It's using the most basic building block (starting a thread directly) but it certainly fits the definition of asynchronous programming.

Based on what we learned before, this might look something like this:

```
Thread thread = new Thread(() =>
{
    Score[] highScores = highScoreManager.LookupScores();
     // Do something with the results.
    HighScores = highScores;
});

thread.Start();
```

That code isn't so terrible. It gets the job done for sure. But as we'll soon see, there are better ways of structuring this code.

Using the ThreadPool

While directly creating a thread was our approach in the last chapter, it has long been discouraged. One obvious problem with this approach has been that it's pretty easy to end up with so many threads that you drown the CPU. You spend far too much of your time switching between threads, and far too little doing real work.

C# has the concept of a thread "pool", wrapped up in the **ThreadPool** class. The idea here is that the .NET runtime can provide a collection of threads that already exist (you don't need to create them yourself) that can then be reused to run any generic task. The **ThreadPool** class has the smarts to maintain the optimal number of threads.

When you have a chunk of work that you need done asynchronously, you can just hand it off to the thread pool. This is done by using the static **QueueUserWorkItem** method:

```
ThreadPool.QueueUserWorkItem(data =>
{
    Score[] highScores = highScoreManager.LookupScores();
    HighScores = highScores;
}, null);
```

This is pretty close to what we had in the previous iteration. This code uses a lambda statement. We could have used a named method instead, but this type of thing is a perfect use for lambda statements, so I went with that approach here in the sample code as well.

This gets us over the problem of not knowing when we should create new threads and when we should reuse an old thread, and we were also able to ditch the **Thread.Start** call.

You'll notice with this approach that the method required a parameter (**data**), which I filled in with **null**. This is more along the lines of the **ParameterizedThreadStart** that we talked about in the last chapter.

At any rate, this is a bit simpler than what we had before. Using the thread pool is preferable to not using it, but it's also still not our final solution. So let's keep looking.

Event-Based Asynchrony

The idea with the event-based asynchronous approach is that you call a method that is known to take a long time and it returns immediately. When the method completes asynchronously, an event on the class is raised.

Using Event-based asynchrony like this, we have to subscribe to the right event, and in most cases, the asynchronous method will end with the word **Async**:

```
HighScoreManager highScoreManager = new HighScoreManager();
highScoreManager.HighScoresLoaded += OnHighScoresLoaded;
highScoreManager.LookupScoresAsync();
```

And elsewhere we define our event handler method:

```
private void OnHighScoresLoaded(Score[] highScores)
{
    // Do something with the results.
    HighScores = highScores;
}
```

In the past, this has been a rather common approach to long running tasks. As you explore the .NET Standard Library that C# offers, you'll inevitably see methods that end with **Async** like this, which expect you to subscribe to a related event, and put your code for dealing with the results in the event handler.

While it works, it's definitely a little annoying that you've now separated your code into two separate pieces. You have the part that sets up and calls the method, and then in a different location, you have the method for dealing with the results. You'll see this same problem in the next few iterations as well.

A second problem we introduce with this is the event subscription. The second time we make this request, it's easy to forget that we may already have subscribed to the event (with the **+=**) and we may accidentally subscribe again. We can work around that but it does create more things you have to remember to do as a developer.

The AsyncResult Pattern

Moving along in our tour of asynchrony, our next option is the AsyncResult pattern. This approach is similar to various fast food restaurants and other places where you make your order or request, and you're given a ticket of some sort. When it's done, you can return the ticket to get your order (the results). Or you can take your ticket and stand at the counter waiting impatiently.

Using this pattern, you typically start with a synchronous method (let's call it **X**). You then add a **BeginX** method and **EndX** method to the mix. The **Begin** method starts the synchronous method running in an asynchronous way and returns your "ticket" in the form of an object that implements the **IAsyncResult** interface. You can use this object to periodically check if the asynchronous task is completed or not, or you can call the **End** method, passing in the **IAsyncResult** that you got from calling the **Begin** method, which will block, and cause the thread to do nothing else until the results come back.

This sometimes shows up in the form of three distinct named methods (**X**, **BeginX**, and **EndX**) but the easiest way to implement this is by using some functionality on the **Delegate** class:

```
HighScoreManager highScoreManager = new HighScoreManager();
Func<Score[]> scoreLookupDelegate = highScoreManager.LookupScores; // Synchronous version.

IAsyncResult asyncResult = scoreLookupDelegate.BeginInvoke(null, null);

HighScores = scoreLookupDelegate.EndInvoke(asyncResult);
```

In that second line, we store the **LookupScores** method in a delegate type. Remember from the chapter on delegates (Chapter 32) that we can usually get away with some variation of **Action** or **Func**, and that's what we've done in this case. (**Func<Score[]>** is a delegate for any method that has no parameters and returns an array of **Score**.)

Once stored in the delegate, we can start off the process by calling **BeginInvoke**. The two **null** values are for a callback method that should be called when the asynchronous task is completed, and a parameter that can be passed into the callback method.

If the method we were trying to make asynchronous had any parameters, we'd be able to list them in **BeginInvoke** before those two parameters.

In the last line of that code, we stop and wait for the task to complete with **EndInvoke**. That obviously defeats the purpose of making it asynchronous in the first place, but in a more realistic scenario, you wouldn't call **EndInvoke** immediately. Instead, you'd continue on to other things, and you could use the **IAsyncResult** that comes back to keep track of the asynchronous task's progress.

The best part about this delegate approach is that you can use it on any method. There are no limitations on it. It's a pattern that's infinitely reusable.

Unlike the event-based version, you don't have to worry about subscribing and unsubscribing correctly. There's no way to make that mistake with this approach.

At this point, you might be starting to feel like this async stuff just seems to be getting uglier and uglier, and more and more complicated. I definitely think that's the case so far. But let's keep going. It gets better from here.

Callback Methods

One of the cleanest ways we could structure an asynchronous call is to have our method run asynchronously, but include a parameter that allows the programmer to supply a method that will be called on completion. The method you pass in (in the form of a delegate) is called a callback method.

```
public void LookupScores(Action<Score[]> callbackMethod)
```

This can be called like this, using a lambda statement:

```
highScoreManager.LookupScores(scores => { HighScores = scores; });
```

We used a lambda here, but it could have been a normal named method as well.

This code is actually fairly readable. It's not quite as good as the original synchronous version, but it's the cleanest version we've seen so far. It probably seems strange that **LookupScores** has a parameter that's a delegate, until you realize that this is a callback method. We're definitely making progress though.

The Task-based Asynchronous Pattern

As you can see, asynchronous programming has been a mess in C# in the past. And it's not just C#. Every language and every programmer has struggled with this. Obviously we need a better solution that what we've seen so far.

C# 4.0 introduced yet another pattern for solving this problem: the Task-based Asynchronous Pattern (TAP). TAP doesn't magically solve our code clarity problems, but it lays the foundation for what came in C# 5.0, which does (for the most part).

TAP introduced two new classes: **Task** and **Task<TResult>**. **Task** represents a long running asynchronous chunk of work, while **Task<TResult>** is a generic variant that additionally serves as a promise of a resulting value when the task is completed. **Task** is used when the asynchronous task doesn't return a value or when you don't care to do anything with the returned value. When you care about the result, you would use the generic version, which has the option of grabbing the result from the task upon completion and doing something more with it.

Let's look at how we'd implement our high score lookup using the TAP approach:

```
public Task<Score[]> LookupScores()
{
    return Task.Run(() => {
        // Do the real work here, in a synchronous fashion.
        return new Score[10];
    });
}
```

Instead of directly returning the score array, we return a **Task** that contains it. More accurately, we return a task that promises to give us an array of scores when it completes. In this case, because we want to do something with the result, we want to use the generic version of **Task**, which promises a resulting value upon completion.

Outside of this class, we can handle a **Task** return value in a few different ways. The first way would be to just ignore it. If it were an asynchronous task that is "fire and forget," we could just ignore the return value.

The second option is to take the task and call **Wait()** on it:

```
Task<Score[]> scoresTask = highScoreManager.LookupScores();
scoresTask.Wait();
HighScores = scoresTask.Result; // Calling Result will actually also block, as though you had called Wait.
```

Wait causes the current thread to block, doing nothing else until the task finishes. This isn't the desired effect because it forces the main thread to suspend. It's not happening asynchronously anymore.

Which leads us to the third option: **ContinueWith**.

```
Task<Score[]> scoresTask = highScoreManager.LookupScores();
scoresTask.ContinueWith(task => HighScores = task.Result);
```

ContinueWith specifies a second method (another lambda expression in this case) that should execute when the task finishes. That code doesn't happen when the flow of execution reaches that line in the code. Rather, the continuation is only scheduled then, and executed when the task actually completes at some later point in time.

The 'async' and 'await' Keywords

We're now ready for the latest and greatest in asynchronous programming in C#. Building off of the TAP pattern, C# 5.0 made this far simpler and easy to read by integrating it into the language itself. It does this by adding two keywords to the language: **async** and **await**.

The **Task** and **Task<TResult>** classes still function as the core building block of asynchronous programming with these new keywords. You'll still create a new **Task** or **Task<TResult>** using **Task.Run**, like in the previous section. The real difference happens when you get a **Task** returned to you from a method, where you can do something when the task completes or do something with the result the task gives you upon completion:

```
Score[] highScores = await highScoreManager.LookupScores();
```

Before looking at what that code actually does, let's compare it to the synchronous version, right at the start of this chapter. Remember this guy?

```
Score[] highScores = highScoreManager.LookupScores();
```

It's *surprisingly* similar. And yet, it is asynchronous. While previous approaches to asynchronous programming have been convoluted, using **Task** or **Task<TResult>**, combined with the new **await** keyword, everything seems to fall in place and we get a clean solution.

So what does that **await** keyword do exactly?

Well let's start by rounding that piece of code out a little bit. I'm going to put some **Console.WriteLine** statements in there and wrap it in a method:

```
public async void GrabHighScores()
{
```

```
    // Preliminary work...
    Console.WriteLine("Initializing asynchronous lookup of high scores.");

    // Start something asynchronously.
    Score[] highScores = await highScoreManager.LookupScores();

    // Work to be done after completion of the asynchronous task.
    Console.WriteLine("Completed asynchronous lookup of high scores.");
}
```

Let's start there in the middle, with the **await** keyword, since it's the central point of this whole discussion. That **LookupScores** method returns a **Task<Score[]>**—an uncompleted task with the promise of having a **Score[]** when finished. Any time a method returns a task, you can optionally "await" it with the **await** keyword, which creates a situation similar to the **ContinueWith** that we saw in the previous section.

The preliminary code before the **await** happens immediately, by the thread that called the method.

Once an **await** is reached, the thread that called the method jumps out of the method and continues merrily on its way to something else. The asynchronous code will either happen on a separate thread (if you use **Task.Run**) or perhaps by no thread at all (if it's waiting for the network or file system to complete some work).

But everything after the **await** is scheduled to happen when the task finishes. The **await** effectively slices the method in two while still using syntax that is easy to understand.

You'll notice from the previous code sample that the **await** keyword also extracts the value out of the **Task<Score[]>**. We don't have to call **Task.Result** to get it. If a method returns a generic **Task<TResult>**, then the **await** keyword will do that for you. In other words, it extracts the promised value out of the task upon completion.

If a method returns just a **Task**, the non-generic version which doesn't have a promise value, you can still await it. It just has to be structured as a statement, rather than an assignment.

```
Console.WriteLine("Before await.");
await SomeMethodThatReturnsTask();
Console.WriteLine("After await.");
```

The **await** keyword can't be used just anywhere. It can only be called inside a method that is marked with the **async** keyword. You can see that I added that in the earlier code:

```
public async void GrabHighScores()
```

You can't put the **async** keyword on just any method. There are some limitations. The official rule is that you can put **async** on anything that has a **void** return type, or a valid "awaitable". The rules that define what a valid awaitable is are kind of complicated, so we'll skip the details here. In short though, you'll nearly always use either the non-generic **Task** class, the generic **Task<TResult>**, or more rarely, the generic **ValueTask<TResult>** struct. In the extremely unlikely event that none of these suit your purposes, you can look up the rules for making a custom awaitable, and make your own.

When do you use each of the four standard options?

- An **async** method with a **void** return type implies a fire-and-forget nature; you don't care when it finishes, just that it happens asynchronously.
- An **async** method with a **Task** for the return type implies you care about when it finishes, including scheduling stuff after the task completes (with **await**) but that the task itself doesn't return any meaningful data.

- An **async** method that returns the generic **Task<TResult>** implies the task returns a value (it promises a value upon completion) and allows you to grab it when it's done.
- **ValueTask<TResult>** is used in similar instances as **Task<TResult>**, with the difference being **ValueTask<TResult>** is a value type instead of a reference type like **Task<TResult>**. (**ValueTask** is not accessible out of the box. You must add a reference to the System.Threading.Tasks.Extensions NuGet package as described in Chapter 46.)

Asynchronous programming can be tricky. This chapter has hopefully demystified it to a large extent, but it takes a lot of time and practice to get good at asynchronous programming (in any language). But at least we've now gotten that particular adventure off on the right foot.

Try It Out!

Asynchronous Programming Quiz. Answer the following questions to check your understanding. When you're done, check your answers against the ones below. If you missed something, go back and review the section that talks about it.

1. Define *asynchronous programming*.
2. Indicate which of the following could benefit from asynchronous programming:
    a. A computationally expensive process like copying all pixels from one image to another.
    b. A small math operation, like an addition or multiplication.
    c. An operation that does little work of its own, besides waiting for a server to respond across the Internet.
3. What keyword is used to indicate that a method may complete some of its work asynchronously after returning?
4. What keyword is used to indicate that code further down the method should not be executed until an asynchronous task has finished?
5. Identify at least 3 return types that can be used with the **async** keyword.
6. **True/False.** Code is always faster when ran asynchronously.
7. **Matching.** Match the asynchronous return type on the left with the correct option on the right:

____ **void**

____ **Task**

____ **Task<TResult>**

A. You care when the task finishes, but it does not have a specific result to return.

B. You don't care when the asynchronous task finishes; fire-and-forget.

C. The asynchronous task has a specific result that it returns.

Answers: (1) Running code on a separate thread, usually to improve responsiveness or speed. **(2)** A: Yes. B: No. C: Yes. **(3)** async. **(4)** await. **(5)** void, Task, Task<TResult>, ValueTask<TResult>, etc. **(6)** False. **(7)** B, A, C.

Dynamic Objects

In a Nutshell
- Dynamic type checking happens at run-time, not compile time.
- The **dynamic** type tells the compiler to do dynamic type checking for the variable.
- Dynamic objects allow you to add and remove members at run-time.
- **IDynamicMetaObjectProvider** tells the dynamic language runtime how to look up members dynamically.
- **ExpandoObject** allows for simple, growable dynamic objects.
- Deriving from **DynamicObject** allows for greater control over dynamic members.

Types are a big deal in C#. We spend a lot of time defining what a new class or struct will look like. We worry about getting inheritance hierarchies right. We carefully cast to and from types, and make sure that everything is of the type it ought to be when assigning variables and calling methods.

Throughout the bulk of the C# world, types are considered "static" at run-time. (Not to be confused with the **static** keyword.) That is, you define a class, add properties and methods, and work with the class in the rest of your code. But the type can't change while the program is executing. Methods can't be added while the program is running. New properties can't be defined on the fly. This puts C# in the category of *statically typed* languages. Or it could be said that the compiler does *static type checking*.

There are some advantages and disadvantages to this. The primary advantage is that the compiler can guarantee that everything you do is "safe." If you attempt to call a method on an object, the compiler makes sure that the method exists. Reading a value from a property will work, because you know it will be there. Any errors of this nature are caught when you try to compile your program.

On the other hand, having the flexibility to add new methods, properties, and other elements at run-time is a powerful proposition. This is called *dynamic typing*, and a number of languages (Python, Ruby, JavaScript, Lua, etc.) allow this on any object. To be clear, with dynamic typing, the system still makes sure that the member is there when used; it just does so at run-time instead of at compile time. This is called *dynamic type checking*.

Back in C# 4.0, C# added the ability specify that certain variables should be checked at run-time instead of at compile time (dynamic type checking). It also added support for dynamic objects—objects where properties, methods, and other members could be determined or modified while running. This chapter covers how to utilize both dynamic type checking and dynamic objects in your C# code.

Dynamic Type Checking

With the familiar statically typed variables, you know its type, and can perform operations on it. The compiler can verify that operations that you do with it are safe at compile time. For example, in the following code, it can verify that the **string** type actually has a **Length** property, or that **Console** actually has a **WriteLine** method.

```
string text = "Hello World!";
Console.WriteLine(text.Length);
```

On the other hand, C# also has a **dynamic** type. Any variable or object can be stored in this type.

```
dynamic text = "Hello World!";
Console.WriteLine(text.Length);
```

Making something **dynamic** tells the compiler that it should not do static type checking. That is, it will not check to make sure that methods, properties, operators, etc. actually exist on the type at compile time, but rather, wait until run-time to check it. For example, look at the various operations that we attempt to do on the **text** variable in the following code:

```
dynamic text = "Hello World!";
text += Math.PI;
text *= 13;
Console.WriteLine(text.PurpleMonkeyDishwasher);
```

None of these are things that can be done with a **string**. Indeed, if we had left the type of text as **string**, this wouldn't compile. But when the variable is made **dynamic**, we are telling the compiler, "Don't verify that the methods we attempt to use on this actually exist at compile time. Wait until the program is running and you reach that code." Since **text** has a type of **dynamic**, this code compiles. But because **string** doesn't have the ability to add a **double**, multiply by an **int**, or have a **PurpleMonkeyDishwasher** property, any of these will fail at run-time with a **RuntimeBinderException**.

When there is a **dynamic** variable, the compiler won't fail just because it can't find a needed member of the type. Instead, it records some information about what is being requested in that particular spot (particularly the name of the member being used) so that at runtime, it can dig through that information and use it to figure out if the member exists or not.

While the code above shows that any object can be assigned to a **dynamic** variable (which we did with a **string**) doing so just isn't very practical unless the object is actually dynamic itself—that is, in some form or fashion, the type can either change at run-time, or you don't know what members it will have at compile time.

Dynamic Objects and the Dynamic Language Runtime

C# allows you to define objects that are modifiable or constructed while the program is actually running. Where this is the case, these objects are considered *dynamic objects*.

Dynamic objects were introduced in C# 4.0, when the *Dynamic Language Runtime* was added to the .NET platform. The Dynamic Language Runtime, or DLR for short, is a component that provides all of the tooling and infrastructure needed to enable dynamic typing and dynamic objects to the .NET platform.

The primary goal here was to allow dynamic languages such as Ruby (IronRuby) and Python (IronPython) to be able to run on the .NET platform itself. A side product of that was the introduction of the **dynamic** type and dynamic objects to C# as well.

Any type can be a dynamic object by implementing the **IDynamicMetaObjectProvider** interface. By implementing this interface, you can tell the DLR how it should look up dynamic properties, methods, and other members for a given type.

Unfortunately, **IDynamicMetaObjectProvider** is extremely low level, requiring you to do "metaprogramming," which requires your code to analyze other code and reason about it, and does so at the expression and statement level. This is both tedious and error prone.

Fortunately, you will almost never need to implement **IDynamicMetaObjectProvider** unless you're doing something crazy like adding another new dynamic language to the .NET Platform. Instead, there are two much simpler and more fun options: **ExpandoObject** and **DynamicObject**. We'll talk about both of these in some depth to illustrate how to use these, and skip the details of **IDynamicMetaObjectProvider** (which deserves its own book).

Emulating Dynamic Objects with Dictionaries

The first thing we should talk about is how we might get dynamic-like behavior without using actual dynamic objects. The reason for this is that is serves as a good frame of reference. All dynamic objects are actually implemented in a similar way to what we'll talk about here, just with better syntax.

If you wanted to emulate a dynamic object, where properties and methods can be added or removed on the fly, one option is to use the **Dictionary** class (Chapter 25). Specifically, a **Dictionary<string, object>** would allow us to add new data by name (much like a property name, just as a **string** instead).

For example:

```
Dictionary<string, object> poorMansDynamicObject = new Dictionary<string, object>();
poorMansDynamicObject["Name"] = "George";
poorMansDynamicObject["Age"] = 21;
```

By comparison, you could imagine having a normal class to represent the above with a **Name** and **Age** property. But on the other hand, using a dictionary like this allows us to add in any new "property" that we want on the fly. It doesn't have to be determined before compiling. That gives us a lot of flexibility.

You could also add something that resembles a method in a similar way using delegates:

```
poorMansDynamicObject["HaveABirthday"] = new Action(() =>
                    poorMansDynamicObject["Age"] = (int)poorMansDynamicObject["Age"] + 1);
```

(Note that we're using the **Action** type here, which we talked about in Chapter 32.) While the syntax is a bit awkward, you can invoke delegates directly. We could call this method like so:

```
((Action)poorMansDynamicObject["HaveABirthday"])();
```

In that code, we pull the **Action** object out of the dictionary, cast it to an **Action**, and then invoke it (the parentheses at the end).

Interestingly, with a dictionary, we could even remove elements dynamically using the **Remove** method.

These examples show how we could make something with dynamic-like features using a dictionary, though the syntax is quite awkward. We'll fix that by using *actual* dynamic objects, but keep in mind that behind the scenes is usually something similar to the dictionary approach we just saw.

ExpandoObject

The first option we have for true dynamic objects is a class called **ExpandoObject**. **ExpandoObject** is effectively just the **Dictionary<string, object>** that we just saw, but it also implements **IDynamicMetaObjectProvider** which means we get much better syntax for working with it.

Below is code that uses **ExpandoObject** to do the same stuff as the previous section with a dictionary:

```
dynamic expando = new ExpandoObject(); // Requires a 'using System.Dynamic;' directive in your file.
expando.Name = "George";
expando.Age = 21;
expando.HaveABirthday = new Action(() => expando.Age++);

expando.HaveABirthday();
```

You can that the syntax here is drastically improved. Adding properties is as simple as just assigning a value to them. Our method for incrementing age became far cleaner. And even our method call at the end is very readable, and looks like a normal method call.

This is all thanks to the magic of dynamic typing. **ExpandoObject** implements **IDynamicMetaObjectProvider**, and because of that, it defines how the dynamic type system should look up members like properties and methods at run-time, producing very clean syntax as shown above.

Interestingly, **ExpandoObject** actually implements **IDictionary<string, object>**, though it does so "implicitly." But that means if you cast an **ExpandoObject** to **IDictionary<string, object>** you can do some additional cool things like enumerate all members that an **ExpandoObject** currently has or even delete a member:

```
IDictionary<string, object> expandoAsDictionary = (IDictionary<string, object>)expando;

foreach(string memberName in expandoAsDictionary.Keys)
    Console.WriteLine(memberName);

expandoAsDictionary.Remove("Age"); // Remove the `Age` property.
```

After this code runs, if you attempt to access **Age** again, it will fail with a **RuntimeBinderException**.

This begins to illustrate the power of dynamic objects in general, and **ExpandoObject** specifically. Having an object where you can add and remove members like properties and methods is extremely powerful.

Extending DynamicObject

A second option for dynamic objects is to derive from the **DynamicObject** class. Contrasted with **ExpandoObject**, which is fairly light-weight, **DynamicObject** is a bit trickier, but gives you more control over the details. **DynamicObject** is a more powerful tool.

DynamicObject is an abstract class with a pile of virtual methods that can be overridden. While you can't create an instance of **DynamicObject** itself, you can derive a new class from **DynamicObject** and then override the methods it contains to add the functionality you want it to have.

Each of these methods allow you to do customize the behavior of one aspect of your dynamic type. For example, how it should retrieve property values, how it should set property values, how it should invoke methods, etc. The way **DynamicObject** is structured, you only have to override the methods that you care to have function.

The example below illustrates how you might override **DynamicObject** to support a supplied set of dynamic **string** typed properties:

```
public class CustomPropertyObject : DynamicObject  // Requires a 'using System.Dynamic;' directive.
{
    private Dictionary<string, string> data;

    public CustomPropertyObject(string[] names, string[] values)
    {
        data = new Dictionary<string, string>();

        for (int index = 0; index < names.Length; index++)
            data[names [index]] = values[index];
    }

    public override bool TryGetMember(GetMemberBinder binder, out object result)
    {
        if (data.ContainsKey(binder.Name))
        {
            result = data[binder.Name];
            return true;
        }
        else
        {
            result = null;
            return false;
        }
    }

    public override bool TrySetMember(SetMemberBinder binder, object value)
    {
        if (!data.ContainsKey(binder.Name))
            return false;

        data[binder.Name] = value.ToString(); // ToString(), in case it isn't already a string.
        return true;
    }
}
```

You can see that this type derives from **DynamicObject**, and overrides the **TryGetMember** and **TrySetMember** properties. These two pieces are the crux of making a **DynamicObject**-based implementation.

You can also see that—like with many things of a dynamic nature—a dictionary was used to store the existing properties and their values.

The constructor is relatively straightforward. It takes the two input arrays (the names of the properties and their values) and constructs a dictionary out of the pairings.

The overrides for **TryGetMember** and **TrySetMember** define how the dynamic runtime should handle property getters and setters. You can see a bit of a pattern there. Each has a **binder** parameter that defines what member is being looked at (**binder.Name**). In the getter, we use the name to look up the right value from the dictionary. In the setter, we update the dictionary with the new value.

In both cases, if the property being requested doesn't exist, we return **false**. This tells the dynamic runtime that the member being requested doesn't actually exist. At least with the setter, we could have added the new property and set it (dynamically adding the property, like what happens with **ExpandoObject**.) But in this particular sample, I chose to not do that. When **false** is returned, the DLR can do a number of things with a failed member access. In the C# world, this generally is going to result in a **RuntimeBinderException**.

There are many other methods that are a part of **DynamicObject** that can be overridden, depending on what you're trying to accomplish:

- **GetDynamicMemberNames**: Allows the dynamic object to list all dynamic members it contains.
- **TryUnaryOperation** and **TryBinaryOperation**: Allow you to overload operators.
- **TryConvert**: Allows you to include user-defined conversions.
- **TryGetIndex** and **TrySetIndex**: Let you provide an indexer for your type. There is also a **TryDeleteIndex**, but that doesn't work in the C# world, only other languages (like Python).
- **TryInvokeMember**: Allows you to provide dynamic methods.
- **TryInvoke**: Allows you to treat the object itself as a method, as though it were a delegate.
- **TryCreateInstance**: Allows you to create dynamic constructors, but this can't be done in C#.
- **TryDeleteMember**: Could be used to delete members, though no C# syntax for it.

Try It Out!

Dynamic CSV Importer. Review the section in Chapter 29 that describes the CSV file format, and how it was used there to store high scores.

Create a project that will use code similar to the previous **DynamicObject** code sample to read in data from a CSV file and produce dynamic objects with properties that match the headers in the file. Then write out the data to the screen in a format like, "[Player] had a score of [Score]."

When to Use Dynamic Object Variations

In this final section, we'll discuss when you should prefer each of the variations of dynamic objects.

To start, I should point out that dynamic objects should only be used when necessary. Static type checking is extremely useful, and you should only revert to dynamic type checking when you absolutely need either objects whose members can't be determined until run-time, or whose members can change at run-time. If you need this, then using dynamic objects is fine. Otherwise, stick to normal classes and structs.

You should also consider whether just using a dictionary to store your data would be a simpler option. Using dynamic objects requires a different thought pattern than the "normal" statically typed objects that C# programmers are accustomed to. In some situations, just using a dictionary will be easier than going with full-blown dynamic objects.

If you do need actual dynamic objects, then your options are using **ExpandoObject**, deriving from **DynamicObject**, and reimplementing **IDynamicMetaObject**.

ExpandoObject is perfect for simple scenarios where you need to be able to add properties (and less frequently methods) on the fly.

Deriving from **DynamicObject** is better for situations where there are rules that govern what properties, methods, and other members should exist for the type. The fact that you can program the rules into the object make it so you can't add things that shouldn't be there, which isn't the case with **ExpandoObject**. Additionally, **DynamicObject** allows you to customize virtually every aspect of your type, including operators and indexers, which **ExpandoObject** doesn't support.

You should generally avoid implementing **IDynamicMetaObject** from scratch. It is very difficult to do, hard to debug, and very error-prone. Unless you've become a dynamic object guru and need to optimize the tiny nuances of the dynamic language runtime, or are trying to add a new dynamic language to the .NET Platform, steer clear of implementing **IDynamicMetaObject**. Stick with **ExpandoObject** or **DynamicObject** instead.

Unsafe Code

In a Nutshell
- "Unsafe code" allows you to directly reference and manipulate memory locations.
- Unsafe code is primarily used for interoperating with native code.
- Avoid unsafe code when possible; most applications won't have any need for it.
- Unsafe code can only be used in unsafe contexts, determined by the **unsafe** keyword.
- Pointers allow you to reference a specific memory location.
- **fixed** can be used to "pin" managed references in place so a pointer can reference them.
- The **stackalloc** keyword allows you to define arrays whose data is stored on the stack.
- You can invoke native/unmanaged code using Platform Invocation Services (P/Invoke).

Before you read this chapter, I should warn you that you probably don't need this chapter at all, and should probably skip it. At least until it becomes clear that you do.

One of the key features of the C# language and the .NET Platform is that it manages memory for you. You don't have to manually allocate or free memory. Earlier languages like C and C++ didn't have this feature.

This is an extremely desirable feature, and one of the biggest selling points of C#. But sometimes, you find the need to interoperate with code that doesn't have this feature—code that does direct memory allocation and manipulation. Working with C and C++ code is a prime example of this. In these cases, you may find that you have to leave the managed memory world and enter the unmanaged, "unsafe" world.

If you aren't doing this in your projects, then I strongly advise skipping (or just skimming) this chapter.

Working with unsafe or unmanaged code can be tricky. There are many ways that you can shoot yourself in the foot. Going through the ins and outs of unsafe code deserves an entire book, and I can't do it justice here. But this gives you a starting point in the event that you find yourself diving into unsafe code.

Unsafe Contexts

Most C# code does not need to jump out of the realm of managed code and managed memory. However, C# does support certain "unsafe operations"—data types, operators, and other actions that allow you to directly reference, modify, and allocate memory when needed.

These unsafe operations can only be done in an *unsafe context*. This is done to ensure that programmers don't inadvertently use these unsafe operations unintentionally.

The name "unsafe" is somewhat misleading. Unsafe code doesn't mean the code is truly dangerous, just that the code is *unverifiable*—the compiler can't guarantee safety.

It is easy to make a chunk of code an unsafe context by wrapping it in an unsafe block like so:

```
public void DoSomethingUnsafe()
{
    unsafe
    {
        // You can now do unsafe stuff here.
    }
}
```

Inside of the unsafe block, you will be able to use pointer types (which we'll discuss soon) and other direct memory manipulation tasks. In effect, an unsafe context is a little like being able to write a small chunk of C or C++ code directly within your C# application.

You can make a whole method an unsafe context by adding the **unsafe** keyword to the method signature:

```
public unsafe void DoSomethingUnsafe()
{
}
```

A type such as a struct, class, or interface can be marked with the **unsafe** keyword as well, which makes it so every method inside is an unsafe context:

```
public unsafe class C
{
}
```

But creating an unsafe context is not quite enough. You also have to tell the compiler that you want to allow unsafe code in your project. This can be done by using the **/unsafe** compiler option on the command line, or by configuring your project to allow for unsafe code within Visual Studio itself.

To set up a project to allow unsafe code, follow these steps:

1. Right-click on the project in the Solution Explorer and choose Properties.
2. Select the Build tab on the left.
3. Check the box that says, "Allow unsafe code".

Without this, you will get the error "CS0227: Unsafe code may only appear if compiling with /unsafe."

Pointer Types

In an unsafe context, you can create variables that are *pointer types*. A pointer type is a variable that identifies a specific memory address where another object lives. This is conceptually similar to the reference types that we've been working with throughout this book, but has some huge differences on a practical level. While both pointers and references both direct you to some other object, a pointer contains a raw memory address, while a reference is indirect, and maintained by the garbage collector.

The garbage collector is the part of the CLR that is responsible for managing objects that are alive in RAM. This includes rearranging the data for efficiency and freeing up discarded objects to free up the memory. As the garbage collector moves data around, it also maintains references. But the garbage collector does not control pointers, so those are not updated.

You declare a pointer type with a ***** by the type:

```
int* p; // A pointer to an integer.
```

You can create a pointer to any of the numeric types, **bool**, enumerations, any pointer types (pointers to pointers) and any structs that you've made, as long as they don't contain references.

C# has borrowed three operators from C++ for working with pointer types: The address-of operator (**&**) for getting the address of a variable, the indirection operator (*) for dereferencing a pointer to access the object it points to, and the pointer member access operator, for accessing members such as properties, methods, etc. on a pointer type object. These are shown below:

```
int x;
unsafe
{
    // Address-Of Operator. Gets the memory address of something else and returns it.
    // This puts the address of `x` and puts it in pointerToX.
    int* pointerToX = &x;

    // Indirection Operator: Dereferences the pointer, giving you the object at the location pointed to
    // by a pointer. This puts a 3 in the memory location pointerToX points at (the original x variable).
    *pointerToX = 3;

    // Pointer Member Access Operator: Allows you to access members through a pointer.
    pointerToX->GetType();
}
```

Pointer types are the third and final major category of data types available in C#, next to value and reference types, completing our type hierarchy chart that we introduced in Chapter 6.

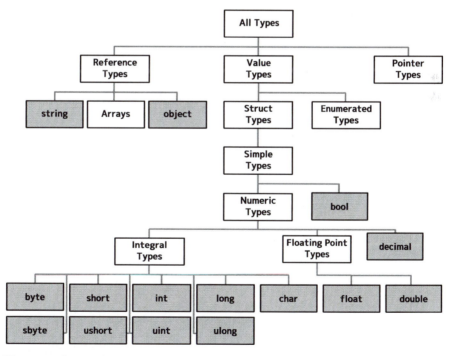

Stack Allocations

Because normal C# arrays are reference types, the array data is placed in the heap somewhere. An array variable stores a reference to it, rather than the data itself (see Chapter 16). Look at the following code:

```
public void DoSomething()
{
```

```
    int[] numbers = new int[10];
}
```

When this method is first called, a new frame is placed on the stack with enough memory allocated to store local variables—**numbers** in this case. This will be a reference to an array, so 4 bytes are allocated for this. When the **new int[10];** part is executed, the memory for the array contents is created in the heap (10 * 4 bytes for an int = 40 total bytes). When this is assigned to the **numbers** variable, the reference for this new memory is placed in the **numbers** variable itself.

When the method returns and the frame for it on the stack is removed, the 4 bytes for **numbers** is immediately cleaned up, but the 40 bytes in the heap remains for a while. If there are no other references to it in the system, the garbage collector will clean it up eventually.

This behavior is usually not just tolerable, but desirable. But sometimes, in order to interoperate with native code or if you just *have* to get that memory cleaned up the instant we return from the method, C# allows us to force the array contents to be placed in the stack itself with the **stackalloc** keyword:

```
public unsafe void DoSomething()
{
    int* numbers = stackalloc int[10];
}
```

Now when you call this method, the 40 bytes for the array are allocated on the stack, and not in the heap.

The garbage collector doesn't need to clean this up. When the method terminates, the method's stack frame is removed, along with all memory for it, which now includes the 40 bytes of data. The garbage collector doesn't have to deal with it, and it is immediately cleaned up.

stackalloc can only be used for local variables, and only in an unsafe context.

Fixed Statements

When working with unsafe code, one of the things you have to deal with is that in a managed environment, the garbage collector can move data around in memory to optimize it. When you're using a managed reference, those movements are abstracted away from you. It is OK if something moves on you because the reference is maintained, and will point to the new location as expected.

On the other hand, when we use pointers, we are using a raw memory address that aren't managed. If we are trying to work with a managed object in our unmanaged, unsafe code, it is possible that the object we're pointing at gets moved out from under us without us knowing. This would cause huge problems.

Fortunately, there's a way to tell the garbage collector to (temporarily) not move a specific object. Suppose we have a **Point** class defined with public instance variables like this:

```
public class Point
{
    public double X;
    public double Y;
}
```

If we want to get a pointer to an object's **X** field, we would want to make sure that the garbage collector doesn't try to move the **Point** object itself until we're done using it. To do this, you can use a **fixed** statement to "pin" a managed object in place as you're getting its address, like the following:

```
Point p = new Point();

fixed(double* x = &p.X)
{
```

```
    (*x)++;
}
```

Doing this will pin **p** in place for the duration of the **fixed** block.

A few minor points to mention with **fixed** statements:

- You must declare the pointer variable in the **fixed** statement. You can't use a pre-existing one.
- You can declare multiple pointer variables of the same type in a single **fixed** statement by separating them by commas.
- You can nest multiple fixed statements inside each other.
- Pointer variables created in a **fixed** block can't be modified to point to something else.
- After the fixed block, the pointer variable (**x** in the above code) is out of scope and can't be used.

Fixed Size Arrays

In C#, an array variable can reference arrays of different lengths during its lifetime:

```
int[] numbers = new int[10];
numbers = new int[1000];
```

In some languages like C and C++, this isn't possible; the array length is baked into the variable's type. If you are interoperating with code that expects fixed size arrays, the mismatch is a problem.

Fortunately, C# does allow you to declare arrays that are fixed size, to facilitate working with code that requires it. You can only declare them in a struct, but this limitation is not very limiting, as this is the exact scenario where you would want them anyway.

To shed a little more light on why you would even want fixed size arrays, consider the following struct:

```
public struct S
{
    public int Value1;
    public int Value2;
    public int[] MoreValues;
}
```

How many bytes will this struct be? If we try to pass this to native, unmanaged code, what would be sent?

This struct would be 12 bytes in size: 4 bytes for **Value1**, 4 bytes for **Value2**, and 4 bytes for the reference that is contained in **MoreValues**. The array data is not contained in a struct instance. A reference to the data is instead. (It is a reference type, after all.)

When you call native code that stores array data in place, normal C# arrays won't be compatible.

But C# allows you to declare fixed size arrays (sometimes called *fixed size buffers*) to facilitate working with native code that requires it. The following code sample illustrates making a fixed size array:

```
public unsafe struct S
{
    public int Value1;
    public int Value2;
    public fixed int MoreValues[10];
}
```

To make an array a fixed size array, you put the **fixed** keyword before the type. The size of the array goes at the end of the variable name inside of square brackets, and note that the type is **int** instead of **int[]**.

With this declaration, the struct itself will contain the data for the array, rather than a reference to data that lives elsewhere. This means that the size of this version of **S** will now be 48 bytes instead of 12: 4 for **Value1**, 4 for **Value2**, and then 4 * 10 = 40 for **MoreValues**.

A struct must be marked with the **unsafe** keyword in order to use fixed size arrays in it.

It is important to point out that the runtime does not perform any sort of index bounds checking on these. If you created an instance of **S**, you could access **MoreValues[33]** and access some other arbitrary memory location beyond the array, which is a dangerous toy to be playing with. (Which is why it can only appear in an unsafe context).

Calling Native Code with Platform Invocation Services

Platform Invocation Services, or *P/Invoke* for short, allows your managed C# code to call native code directly. This is powerful because there is a lot of native code out there that you can utilize, including native C or C++ libraries, operating system calls, or your own C++ code.

The managed C# world and the unmanaged world are quite different from each other. Conversions between managed references and unmanaged pointers and the nuances of marshalling the data across this boundary, means P/Invoke can get complicated.

A simple example is in order here. Let's assume that you have some C++ code that defines an **add** method to add two integers together. In your C++ code, you would make sure this method is exported from your DLL (a C++ topic for a different book). In your C# code, you would then be able to import this **add** method using the **DLLImport** attribute and the **extern** keyword:

```
public static class DllWrapper
{
    [DllImport("MyDLL.dll", EntryPoint="add")]
    static extern int Add(int a, int b);
}
```

When you use the **extern** keyword, you do not provide a body for the method. That is because the actual code for it is defined externally, in your native code library.

Additionally, all **extern** methods must also be **static**.

The **DllImport** attribute tells the compiler that it needs to transform calls to this method into a P/Invoke call. This attribute specifies the information needed to perform the correct P/Invoke call. At a minimum, the name of the DLL (**MyDLL.dll**) must be included. The **EntryPoint** (function name) must also be included if the two don't share the exact same name. **DLLImport** has some additional properties not shown here, which can be used to manage the nuances of calling the native code.

With this setup, calls to **DllWrapper.Add(3, 4)** will now jump over to the unmanaged DLL library and invoke the native **add** method, and return with the computed result.

This is a trivial example of calling native code, and real examples can get much more complicated. In particular, getting the signatures right and configuring the **DllImport** attribute properties correctly can be a huge headache. The website **http://www.pinvoke.net** can be very helpful in getting this just right.

Other Features in C#

In a Nutshell
- This chapter covers a large collection of random advanced topics. The purpose of this chapter is to ensure that you know they exist.
- **yield return** produces an enumerator without creating a container like a **List**.
- **const** and **readonly** define compile-time and runtime constants that can't be changed.
- Attributes let you apply metadata to types and their members.
- The **nameof** operator gets a string representation of a type or member.
- The **sizeof** operator returns the size of a type.
- The bit shift operators let you play around with individual bits in your data.
- Reflection allows you to inspect code while your program is running.
- **IDisposable** lets you run custom logic on an object before being garbage collected.
- C# defines a variety of preprocessor directives to give instructions to the compiler.
- Nullable types allow value types to take on a value of **null**.
- The **?.** and **?[]** operators let you perform succinct null checks: **a?.Property?.Method();**
- You can read in command line arguments from the command prompt.
- You can make your own user-defined conversions between types.
- The (dangerous) **goto** keyword allows you to instantly jump to another location in a method.
- Generic variance governs how a type parameter's inheritance affect the generic type itself.
- Checked contexts will throw exceptions when they overflow. Unchecked contexts do not.

In this chapter, we're going to cruise through a variety of features and tricks that we haven't talked about yet. Some of these are very useful but aren't big enough for their own chapter. Others are less useful, so we'll just cover their basics, and let you to explore it in depth if you feel the need.

There is a lot in this chapter and I don't expect you to become a master of it all overnight. Some of these topics are so big that it you could write books about it. Many of these topics may not ever apply to you.

There are two real purposes to this chapter. One is to open your eyes to the possibilities with C#. The other is to make it so that when you see these things, instead of being completely blindsided by it, you'll at least be able to say, "Hey, I remember reading something about this!"

You don't necessarily *need* the stuff in this chapter to write C# programs. Everything we've covered up until now will go a very long way. This chapter will help tie together some of the loose ends.

Iterators and the Yield Keyword

Way back in Chapter 13, we first introduced **foreach** loops. In Chapter 25 we introduced the **IEnumerable<T>** interface, and stated that anything that implements **IEnumerable<T>** can be used in a **foreach** loop. Remember, an **IEnumerable** is simply anything where you can examine multiple values in a container or collection, one at a time. This capability makes types that implement this interface *iterators*.

In addition to a direct **IEnumerable** implementation, you can additionally define an iterator using the **yield** keyword. This would look something like this:

```
class IteratorExample : IEnumerable<int>
{
    public IEnumerator<int> GetEnumerator()
    {
        for (int index = 0; index < 10; index++)
            yield return index;
    }

    IEnumerator IEnumerable.GetEnumerator()
    {
        return GetEnumerator();
    }
}
```

Much of this code should make sense by now. We're simply implementing the **IEnumerable<int>** interface, which requires us to have the **GetEnumerator** method that you see. And since the **IEnumerable<T>** interface is derived from the non-generic **IEnumerable** interface, we also need to define that second method, which just simply calls the first method.

The part that will likely seem strange to you is the **yield return**. As we're iterating, the method will be called multiple times, and each time, it will return the next item that is "yielded." Unlike a normal **return** statement, when we use **yield return**, we're saying, "pause what you're doing here and return this value, but when you come back, start up again here." That is very powerful. For example:

```
public IEnumerator<int> GetEnumerator()
{
    yield return 0;
    yield return 1;
    yield return 4;
    yield return 6;
}
```

Interestingly, the compiler isn't simply turning all yielded values into a list. It is happening one at a time. This means you could theoretically create an iterator that never ends:

```
public IEnumerator<int> GetEnumerator()
{
    int number = 0;
    while(true)
    {
        yield return number;
        number++;
    }
}
```

The calling code could keep calling the iterator forever, or stop when it has completed its job.

The **yield return** syntax cannot be used anywhere, just inside of methods that **return IEnumerator<T>** or **IEnumerable<T>** and their non-generic counterparts.

Named Iterators

There's a second way to do iterators. Instead of implementing the **IEnumerable<T>** interface and adding a **GetEnumerator** method, you can create a method that returns an **IEnumerable<T>.** You can then use this method in a **foreach** loop whenever you want. This approach lets you have multiple iterators for a single data collection class, and it lets you have parameters for those methods:

```
class Counter
{
    public IEnumerable<int> CountUp(int start, int end)
    {
        int current = start;
        while (current < end)
        {
            yield return current;
            current++;
        }
    }

    public IEnumerable<int> CountDown(int start, int end)
    {
        int current = start;
        while (current > end)
        {
            yield return current;
            current--;
        }
    }
}
```

You then call these iterators like this:

```
Counter counter = new Counter();

foreach (int number in counter.CountUp(5, 50))
    Console.WriteLine(number);

foreach (int number in counter.CountDown(100, 90))
    Console.WriteLine(number);
```

Constants

We've spent a lot of time talking about variables. True to their name, the contents of a variable can... well... vary. But there are times where we want to assign a value to something and prevent it from ever changing again. C# provides two ways of addressing this: the **const** and **readonly** keywords.

If you mark a variable with either of these, then you will not be allowed to change the value of the variable later on. The two are subtly different. Let's start with the **const** keyword. In this book, we've used **Math.PI** several times. If we made our own **Math.PI** variable, we could use the **const** keyword to define **PI** like this:

```
public const double PI = 3.1415926;
```

Adding in **const** tells the compiler that we're assigning it a value and it will never change. In fact, if we try to assign a value to it at some point in our program, we'll get a compiler error. If you have a value that you know will never change, it is a good idea to make it into a constant by adding the **const** keyword to it. That way, no one will mess it up on accident.

Anything marked with **const** is automatically treated as though it were **static**. Because this is assumed (and required) you don't need to (and can't) make it **static** yourself.

The **readonly** keyword is similar to this, but has an important difference. Anything that is marked **const** must be assigned a value right up front, when the program is being compiled. As such, they are often called *compile-time constants*. Things that are marked with **readonly** can still be assigned a value in a constructor or at the same place it is declared, and not after. These are called *runtime constants*.

A runtime constant isn't known at compile time, but once it has been assigned a value, it can't be modified. For example, we could create a **Point** class that stores an x- and y-coordinate in such a way that once it has been created, it is impossible to change the values.

```
public class Point
{
    private readonly double x;
    private readonly double y;

    public double X { get { return x; } } // We could have also just used a readonly property
    public double Y { get { return y; } } // for these, but this illustrates the point well.

    public Point(double x, double y)
    {
        this.x = x;
        this.y = y;
    }
}
```

We can then use this class, creating two point with different values, but both are unchangeable:

```
Point p1 = new Point(5, -2);
Point p2 = new Point(-3, 7);
```

This, by the way, is an excellent way of building immutable types like we discussed in Chapter 21.

Attributes

Attributes allow you to add metadata to an element of your code. They can be added to types that you create or their members. They can even be applied to a method's parameters and return types.

These attributes can be detected by the compiler, external code tools like unit testing frameworks, or even detected while your code is running, using reflection. (We'll talk about reflection in a second.)

There are hundreds of attribute types that come with the .NET Platform. We can't cover them all. When you learn a tool that uses attributes, they'll walk you through the attributes that you'll need to know.

But to illustrate the basics of how attributes are used, we'll look at one specific but simple attribute called the **Obsolete** attribute. You can use this to mark classes and methods that are out of date, and should no longer be used. To apply an attribute to a method, you put the attribute name in square brackets (**[** and **]**) above the element:

```
[Obsolete]
private void OldDeadMethod()
{
}
```

Depending on what namespace the attribute lives in, they may require an additional **using** directive.

The compiler uses this particular attribute to detect calls to obsolete methods and warn the programmer about it. If you use a method with this attribute on it, you'll see a warning in the Error List telling you so.

Many attributes have certain parameters that you can set as well, including the **Obsolete** attribute:

```
[Obsolete("Use NewDeadMethod instead.", true)]
private void OldDeadMethod()
{
}
```

In this case, the first parameter is text that will be displayed in the warning message, and the second indicates whether the compiler should treat the problem as an error rather than a warning.

Attributes are simply classes that are derived from the **Attribute** class, and you can make your own. When we use an attribute, we're essentially calling a constructor for that class.

Multiple attributes can be applied to an element:

```
[Attribute1]
[Attribute2]
[Attribute3]
public class MagicClass
{
}
```

When creating an attribute, people often put **Attribute** at the end of the name for their attribute (e.g. **ObsoleteAttribute**). In these cases, you can use either **[Obsolete]** or the longer **[ObsoleteAttribute]**.

For specific instructions on how to create your own attributes, see: **http://msdn.microsoft.com/en-us/library/84c42s56.aspx**.

The 'nameof' Operator

It's quite common to want to do something with the name of a property, method, type, or other bit of code. Among other things, this is useful in debugging and when you're doing data binding in a UI framework like WPF or Windows Forms, where property names are frequently used.

Let's consider a really simple example related to debugging, where we want to print out an object's properties and their values. Let's say we've got a **Book** class like the following:

```
class Book
{
    public string Title { get; set; }
    private string Author { get; set; }
    private int Pages { get; set; }
    private int WordCount { get; set; }

    public Book(string title)
    {
        this.Title = title;
    }
}
```

Let's say we want to override the **ToString** method to display the values of each of these properties:

```
public override string ToString()
{
    return $"[Book Title={Title} Author={Author} Pages={Pages} WordCount={WordCount}]";
}
```

This lets us see the details of a book either by writing it to the console window or in Visual Studio's debugger, revealing the values of all of the properties. It will appear like this:

```
[Book Title=There and Back Again Author=Bilbo Baggins Pages=118 WordCount=54386]
```

That's all fine and good, but what happens when we decide we want to change the name of something? For example, let's say we decide to rename **WordCount** to **Words** to mirror the **Pages** property. It's easy to refactor a property name like this (Ctrl + R, Ctrl + R), but in this case, our text remains unchanged. We'll still print out the same text, which is now misnamed.

This is where the **nameof** operator comes in. The **nameof** operator allows you to refer to a variable, type, or member, and the compiler will turn it into a string that matches the name. For example, consider the following uses of the **nameof** operator:

```
Book book = new Book("There and Back Again") { Author = "Bilbo Baggins", Pages = 118, WordCount = 54386 };
Console.WriteLine(nameof(Book));
Console.WriteLine(nameof(book));
Console.WriteLine(nameof(Book.Pages));
```

This results in the following output:

```
Book
book
Pages
```

Look carefully at how that works. Microsoft has gone out of its way to make sure it works in an intuitive way. For a type, it gives you the name of the type without the namespace. For the name of a variable, it gives you the name of the variable. When you access a property like **Book.Pages**, you get the name of the property. That syntax is special because you normally can't access a class's properties like that unless they're static properties (which this isn't).

If we update our **ToString** override from earlier in this section to use the **nameof** operator, we can make it much more resilient to changes in our code:

```
public override string ToString()
{
    return $"[{nameof(Book)} {nameof(Title)}={Title} {nameof(Author)}={Author} " +
           $"{nameof(Pages)}={Pages} {nameof(WordCount)}={WordCount}]";
}
```

Now any changes to variable, property, or class names will be reflected correctly in this code.

The 'sizeof' Operator

The **sizeof** operator is quite a bit like the **nameof** operator. To nobody's great surprise, it returns the size in bytes of a specific type.

For example, if you do **sizeof(int),** it will return 4, because the **int** type is four bytes big. This is actually a quick and convenient way to determine the size of any of the built-in types if you forget and don't have a handy reference (like the one in the tables in the back of this book).

This tends to be most useful when you are doing byte manipulation in your code, which doesn't apply to all applications you could make. But it does have its uses.

For example, the following code will create a byte array big enough to hold six integers:

```
byte[] byteArray = new byte[sizeof(int) * 4];
```

The **sizeof** operator is considered a constant value for most of the built-in types, with exceptions for **decimal** and **string**. (That is, **byte**, **short**, **int**, **long**, **sbyte**, **ushort**, **uint**, **ulong**, **float**, **double**, **char** and **bool** all have a known, pre-defined value and those values are swapped out at compile time.)

Any other type theoretically *can* be used with the **sizeof** operator, but the size is more complicated. For one, it is not a constant. That means it can't be placed in a **const**. It must be determined at runtime. And because of some optimizations done by the host machine at the last second, it may not always return the same value on every computer you run it on. It also must be done in an unsafe context, as we talked about earlier in Chapter 42.

The above limitations do make **sizeof** somewhat less useful, but if a calculation actually does require using the size of some datatype, using something like **sizeof(long)** is better than a hardcoded **8** because it conveys *why* it is that value.

Bit Fields

We usually work with variables at a relatively high level, thinking of them as containers for numbers, strings, or complicated classes. Behind the scenes, though, they are essentially little containers to store a pile of bits. Every type of data that we've talked about is represented as bits.

To illustrate, let's briefly look at how a **byte** stores its values. Remember, a **byte** can hold the values 0 to 255 in a single byte (8 bits). These values are stored using binary counting. So the number 0 is stored with the bits **00000000**, the number 1 is stored with the bits **00000001**, the number 2 is stored with the bits **00000010**, and so on.

There's a lot to know about counting in binary, and if you haven't had any exposure to it before, it is probably worth taking some time to learn how it works.

There are a few cases where we actually *want* to sort of fall back down to that low of a level, and work with individual bits and bytes. In fact, you may use this extensively in certain types of projects.

One of the popular ways of using the raw bits of data is a bit field. Let's start our discussion with a brief explanation of why people are even interested in bit fields. Let's say you're creating an online discussion board or a forum. You'll have lots of users, each with different permissions and abilities. Some people may be able to delete posts, edit posts, add comments, etc., while others may not.

Knowing what we've discussed before, we can easily imagine storing each of these values as a **bool**. And that gets the job done. But each **bool** variable takes up 1 full byte, and if you have dozens of settings per user, and millions of users, that adds up very quickly.

One popular solution to this is to have multiple Boolean values be packed into a single **byte**, or a single **int**. In one single byte, you can store eight Boolean values, with one in each bit. For each bit, a 1 represents a true value, and a 0 represents a false value. Something like this:

0	0	1	0	0	0	1	1
(Not used)	Account Suspended	Create threads	Delete others' posts	Edit others' posts	Vote on posts	Edit own posts	Create posts

Doing this kind of trick is actually very widespread, especially if you're talking about things like very large data sets, operating systems, and sending things across the network.

Even though we're treating our byte as a pile of Boolean values here, C# is going to want to present it to you as the **byte** type, with a single value for the entire collection. The bit field above will be shown to you as the number 35. Of course, since we don't care about it as a complete number, but as a collection of Boolean values or Boolean flags, we'll need some tools to help us work with the raw bits in a bit field. Fortunately, C# has those tools built in for us.

Bit Shift Operators

There are two operators that will take the bits in a **byte** or other integral type, and move them over a certain number of slots. These two operators are called bit shift operators. The left bit shift operator is two less than signs together (**<<**) while the right bit shift operator is two greater than signs together (**>>**). These operators look like little arrows that tell you which way the bits will be shifted.

To use the bit shift operators, you would do something like this:

```
int result = 0b00001101 >> 2; // Binary literal 13
```

In the above case, all of the bits get moved to the right two spots, giving us a result of **0b00000011** (decimal value of **3**). Notice that as things are shifted, some bits drop off one end, which are just gone, and 0's are added to fill in empty spots on the other end.

The left bit shift operator works the same way:

```
int result = 0b00001101 << 2; // Turns into 0b00110100 or 52.
```

Bitwise Logical Operators

Think back to when we first discussed the logical **&&** and **||** operators. Remember that **&&** evaluates to true if and only if both sides are true, and **||** evaluates to true if either side is true. There are a couple of related operators that work on bits themselves, and do a similar thing. As we look at this, think of 1 as being true, and 0 as being false.

The bitwise *and* operator is a single ampersand (**&**) and the bitwise *or* operator is a single vertical bar (**|**). These operators go down the bits, one at a time, and do an *and* or *or* operation on each bit. This will probably make more sense with an example. Imagine the two binary numbers:

```
01010101
11111111
```

If you use the bitwise *and* operator, the program will look at the first bit in each number. The top number has a 0, while the bottom one has a 1. That's like having a false and a true, which if they are combined together with *and* result in false, or a 0.

```
01010101
11111111
0
```

Then you look at the next value in each number. They are both 1, which is like having a true and a true, which when combined with *and*, would result in true, or a 1.

```
01010101
11111111
01
```

You continue down the entire sequence, doing this for each bit:

```
01010101
11111111
01010101
```

The bitwise *or* operator does the same thing, but combines the two numbers with *or* instead.

In code, these two operators look like this:

```
int a = 0b00000101;
int b = 0b00000011;
int combinedWithAnd = a & b; // results in 0b00000001, or 1.
int combinedWithOr = a | b;  // results in 0b00000111, or 7.
```

There's a third bitwise operator that is the *exclusive or* operator. (This is sometimes called *xor*, pronounced "ex-or.") The "normal" *or* operator returns true if either of the two parts are true. This still applies where both are true. The *exclusive or* operator is only true if *exactly one* is true. If they are both true, then it evaluates to false. The exclusive or operator is the caret symbol (^), which looks like this:

```
int combinedWithXor = a ^ b; // results in 0b00000110, or 6.
```

One final, similar operator is the bitwise complement operator (~), which is a little like the **!** operator we saw when we first looked at logical operators. This takes each bit and changes it to the opposite:

```
int number = 0b11001000;
int bitwiseComplement = ~number; // 0b00110111.
```

There is a compound assignment operator that you can use for all of these:

```
int number = 0b00001000;
number <<= 1;    // equivalent of number = number << 1;
number >>= 1;    // number = number >> 1;
number &= 32;    // number = number & 32;
number |= 32;    // number = number | 32;
number ^= 32;    // number = number ^ 32;
```

Enumeration Flags

While it is possible to work with the **byte**, **int**, or another type to accomplish what we've seen in this section, this kind of stuff is typically done with an enumeration in C#, to make the whole thing more readable. (Enumerations were introduced in Chapter 14.) Before we can use an enumeration for this, we must add the **Flags** attribute and assign the right values to each member of the enumeration:

```
[Flags]                         // Don't forget to add the Flags attribute.
public enum ForumPrivileges
{
    CreatePosts =       1 << 0, //  1 or 00000001
    EditOwnPosts =      1 << 1, //  2 or 00000010
    VoteOnPosts =       1 << 2, //  4 or 00000100
    EditOthersPosts =   1 << 3, //  8 or 00001000
    DeletePosts =       1 << 4, // 16 or 00010000
    CreateThreads =     1 << 5, // 32 or 00100000
    Suspended =         1 << 6, // 64 or 01000000

    // Note we can also add in "shortcuts" here:
    None = 0,
    BasicUser = CreatePosts | EditOwnPosts | VoteOnPosts,
    Administrator = BasicUser | EditOthersPosts | DeletePosts | CreateThreads
}
```

A Practical Example

Before you start thinking, "Well that's completely useless," let me show you why these are so useful. The **|** operator can be used to "turn on" a bit in the bit field:

```
ForumPrivileges privileges = ForumPrivileges.BasicUser;
privileges |= ForumPrivileges.Suspended; // Turn on the 'suspended' field
```

The **&** operator can be used to check if a particular flag is set, using some trickery:

```
bool isSuspended = (privileges & ForumPrivileges.Suspended) == ForumPrivileges.Suspended;
```

The trick is that if we do a bitwise and operation with something that only has one bit set to true, it will either become all 0's, which indicates that the field was not set. If the bit was set, we'll get back the value of the field we were checking for, turning all other fields to 0.

Using a combination of the **&** and the **~** operators, we can turn off a particular field:

```
privileges &= ~ForumPrivileges.Suspended;
```

You can also toggle a field using the ^ operator:

```
privileges ^= ForumPrivileges.DeletePosts;
```

Reflection

C# has the ability to inspect elements of executable code, and explore what types are in an assembly. They can see the methods, properties, and variables it contains, even while your program is running. The ability to have code analyze the structure of other code is called *reflection*.

The biggest use for reflection is when you want to look at an unknown assembly or object. Not every program has a use for this. Most won't. Doing this is always slower than directly accessing the code.

Having said that, there are still times where it is useful. To name a few examples, a unit testing framework might want to dig through an assembly to find any method that ends with the word "Test" or have a **Test** attribute applied to them, or a plugin system might want to find all classes in a DLL that implements a specific interface. Reflection can also be used to bend the rules, like calling a private method from outside the type it belongs to (a great way to shoot yourself in the foot).

The core class used in reflection is the **Type** class, which represents a compiled type like a class, struct, or enumeration.

For any given type, you can use the **typeof** keyword to get the **Type** object that represents it:

```
Type type = typeof(int);
Type typeOfClass = typeof(MyClass);
```

You can alternatively get a type from an object:

```
MyClass myObject = new MyClass();
Type type = myObject.GetType();
```

You can figure out what members a type has defined. For example:

```
ConstructorInfo[] contructors = type.GetConstructors();
MethodInfo[] methods = type.GetMethods();
```

If you're looking for a member of the type with a particular name and parameter list, you can do that too:

```
ConstructorInfo constructor = type.GetConstructor(new Type[] { typeof(int) });
MethodInfo method = type.GetMethod("MethodName", new Type[] { typeof(int) });
```

In all of these cases, if what you're looking for doesn't exist, an empty array or **null** will be returned.

Once you have the constructor, method, or whatever thing you asked for, you can execute that code with the **Invoke** method that they have. Doing so with constructors will return an object that was created by the constructor, and doing so with a method or property will return the result of the method (or **null** if the method's return type is **void**):

```
object newObject = constructor.Invoke(new object[] { 17 });
method.Invoke(newObject, new object[] { 4 });
```

Using Statements and the IDisposable Interface

Back in Chapter 16 when we first talked about the heap, we talked about garbage collection. One of the big things that the .NET runtime does for us is get rid of memory that we're no longer using. Our program's memory is managed for us. Occasionally though, the task we're trying to accomplish requires using unmanaged memory and resources. When we do this, we can no longer count on garbage collection to clean up those resources and memory.

There may be times where we create our own unmanaged memory, but it is more common to use a pre-existing type that uses unmanaged memory. As an example, when we open a file (Chapter 29) we need to access unmanaged memory to get to the file system. Back then, we simply used the **Close** method when we were done with a file to free unmanaged memory and resources, but there's a better way.

Typically, types that access unmanaged memory will implement the **IDisposable** interface. These classes have a **Dispose** method which cleans up any unmanaged memory the object is using. We could directly call this method (in fact, the **Close** method we used with files does that) but there are some tricky issues that come up. For instance, if an exception is thrown while the file is open, the **Close** method may not get called, leaving the file open. Using what we already know, it is possible to write code to handle this, but C# provides a simpler way to handle this: the **using** statement.

A **using** statement (not to be confused with a **using** directive) will look something like this:

```csharp
using (FileStream fileStream = File.OpenWrite("filename"))
{
    // Do work here...
}
```

When the ending curly brace is reached, the object inside of the parentheses in the using statement is disposed (the **Dispose** method is called) even if an exception is thrown in the middle of the block.

As you write code, be on the lookout for types that implement the **IDisposable** interface and dispose of them correctly when you're done using them. A **using** statement like this is a very readable and simple solution for doing this.

Preprocessor Directives

Many languages, including C#, give you the ability to include instructions for the compiler within your code. These instructions are called preprocessor directives. (The C# compiler doesn't have a preprocessor like some languages, but it treats these preprocessor directives as though there is.)

These preprocessor directives all start with the **#** symbol, which tips you off to the fact that something is a preprocessor directive.

#warning and #error

Two simple preprocessor directives are the **#warning** and **#error** directives, which give you the ability to make the compiler emit a warning or error with a specific message. While the compiler typically only generates errors or warnings when it detects a problem, this allows you to force it to happen.

You're probably wondering why you'd ever do that, and that's a great question. I sometimes will put in a **#warning** directive to remind myself that I need to still fix something. Because it shows up any time I compile, it's unlikely I'd forget about it. (There are plenty of other ways to do this, by the way.)

To add in a **#warning** or **#error** directive, you'd simply add something like this to your code:

```csharp
#warning Enter whatever message you want after.
#error This text will show up in the Errors list if you try to compile.
```

#region and #endregion

The **#region** and **#endregion** directives allow you to add little regions to your code, which Visual Studio then allows you to collapse and expand. This is one potential way to group related methods or instance variables (or anything else) within a type, and allow you to collapse and hide each group on the fly.

To add a region, you'd do something like this:

```
#region Any region name you want here
public class AwesomeClass
{
    // ...
}
#endregion
```

With a region defined, you can collapse and expand the entire region with the outlining feature in Visual Studio. This can be done by clicking the little '+' and '-' icons on the left hand side of your code:

```
namespace CreatingClasses
{
    #region Any region name you want here
    class Program
    {
        static void Main(string[] args)
        {
        }
    }
    #endregion
}
```

You can nest regions.

#if, #else, #elif, #endif, #define, and #undef

There is a whole collection of other useful compiler directives, but before I get into them, I need to discuss compilation symbols briefly. Compilation symbols are special names that can be defined (turned on) or undefined (turned off—the default). For example, there's a **DEBUG** symbol that is defined when you compile in debug mode, but not when you compile in release mode. You can define your own symbols, which I'll explain in a second.

The **#if**, **#else**, **#elif**, and **#endif** directives work very much like an **if** statement, except they're instructions for the compiler to follow, and don't end up in your final program. You could add the following to your program, and the parts between the **#if** and **#else** only get compiled if **DEBUG** is defined.

```
public static void Main(string[] args)
{
#if DEBUG
    Console.WriteLine("Running in debug mode.");
#else
    Console.WriteLine("Running in release mode.");
#endif
}
```

If you're running in debug mode, the compiled program would be equivalent to this:

```
public static void Main(string[] args)
{
    Console.WriteLine("Running in debug mode.");
}
```

And of course, if you're running in release mode, it's this:

```
public static void Main(string[] args)
{
    Console.WriteLine("Running in release mode.");
}
```

Despite this example, it is dangerous to have things run differently in the final release version than it does in testing, because you may not discover all of the bugs it has until the program has been released.

#elif is short for "else if" and can be used to chain together a sequence of conditional blocks.

You can use the **&&** and **||** operators with symbols as well.

You can also define a symbol with **#define**, and undefine it with **#undef**, right at the top of a file:

```
#undef DEBUG
#define MAGIC
```

This block would "undefine" or unset the **DEBUG** symbol, and define your own special **MAGIC** symbol. Since you can't determine the ordering of files, using **#undef** and **#define** only apply to a single file.

Alternatively, you can define a symbol for the entire compilation process (much like how **DEBUG** will be set in every file, unless you turn it off with **#undef**). To do this, right-click on your project in the Solution Explorer and choose Properties. Select the Build tab, and at the top, under Conditional Compilation Symbols, enter the list of symbols you wish to define for all files, separated by spaces.

Nullable Types

Value types are not allowed to be assigned a value of **null**. This is a fundamental feature of value types, but there are times where you wish you could bend the rules a little. For example, **bool** is a value type and can only store **true** and **false**. But occasionally, we have a need to represent **true**, **false**, or unknown.

The concept of nullable types addresses this. A *nullable type* is simply one that uses the **Nullable<T>** generic type:

```
Nullable<bool> nullableBool = true;      // We can assign true or false...
nullableBool = null;                     // but also null.
```

Even better, C# provides a shorthand way of doing this:

```
bool? nullableBool = true;
```

You can use the **HasValue** property to figure out whether the nullable type is **null** or contains a real value, and you can use the **Value** property to grab the value, assuming that **HasValue** is true:

```
if(nullableBool.HasValue)
    bool actualValue = nullableBool.Value;
```

You can use the *null-coalescing operator* (**??**) to assign a default or fallback value if a nullable type is **null**. (The null-coalescing operator works on null references as well.)

```
bool actualValue = nullableBool ?? false;
```

The **actualValue** variable will contain the value of **nullableBool** if it has a value, or if it's **null**, it will be false.

Nullable types can't be created from reference types, but that's OK because they already support **null**.

It is interesting to note that while **Nullable<T>** nominally makes value types be able to have a value of **null**, **Nullable<T>** is still a value type, and can't even contain a **null** reference itself. Instead, it associates an additional **bool** value with the rest of the data. If this is extra value is true, then the normal value is assumed to be good. If it's false, then **Nullable<T>** will throw exceptions when trying to access the data. The ability to treat it as though it can take on a **null** value is just compiler magic.

Simple Null Checks: Null Propagation Operators

C# 6.0 introduced another new feature called *null propagation*, *succinct null checking*, or the *null propagator operator* that is quite powerful. One of the greatest annoyances of programming in many programming languages, especially object-oriented languages like C# is null checking.

Let's say we have a **HighScoreManager** class that has a **Scores** property that contains an array of items in order from highest to lowest. Each score is represented with an instance of the **HighScore** class, which has a reference to the player that got the score, which has the player's name. (I know, that's kind of a mouthful.) To get the player's name that has the highest score, your code might look like this:

```
private string GetTopPlayerName()
{
    return highScoreManager.Scores[0].Player.Name;
}
```

That's all fine and good until you realize that there are five things in this statement that might be null. If any of those pieces are null, you'll get a **NullReferenceException**, which could bring your program to a crashing halt and veiled threats about sending you on a "vacation" to the Spice Mines of Kessel. (Some users take their crashes a little too seriously.)

The point is, checking for null in your code is a good idea. If there is any chance that something could be null, checking to make sure it's not is good defensive coding practice.

So what does that do to our code?

```
private string GetTopPlayerName()
{
    if(highScoreManager == null) return null;
    if(highScoreManager.Scores == null) return null;
    if(highScoreManager.Scores[0] == null) return null; // Could still fail if empty.
    if(highScoreManager.Scores[0].Player == null) return null;

    return highScoreManager.Scores[0].Player.Name;
}
```

Ouch. That's a ton of code just to make things safe for use. That's four whole lines of null checking!

C# 6.0 introduced two new operators called the *null propagator operators* (or simply, the *null propagators*) that makes it easy to do these null checks without causing your code to get ugly. These two operators are closely related, and are the conditional member access operator (**?.**) and the conditional indexer access operator (**?[]**). The following shows the conditional member access operator in action:

```
return highScoreManager?.Scores[0].Player.Name;
```

This operator checks if the thing before it was **null**. If it was, it simply evaluates to a **null** result. If not, it continues on and evaluates whatever is beyond the operator. You could say that this line of code turns into the following:

```
HighScoreManager manager = highScoreManager;
if(manager == null) return null;
return manager.Scores[0].Player.Name;
```

That's one null check down. Four more to go. We can string these together to get the result we want:

```
return highScoreManager?.Scores?[0]?.Player?.Name;
```

This shows us the conditional indexer access operator (the part that says **Scores?[0]**), and includes more conditional member access operators through the whole statement.

With all of these null propagators, if any of the objects involved (immediately before a null propagator) turn out to be null, the expression will short circuit and evaluate to null. Otherwise, it will keep going down the chain and evaluate the next part.

There are three nuances with these null propagators that deserve more discussion.

First, when you use a null propagator, it actually copies the object before it into a new variable. (The earlier code that shows what a null propagator turns into illustrates this by copying **highScoreManager** into the local **manager** variable.) This prevents situations where a value might become null after the null check, but before using it. This can happen in a multi-threaded application if the variable in question is shared by multiple threads. We make a local cached copy instead, and use that afterwards.

Second, when these operators "fail," they produce a **null** value. This is fine if you're working with a reference type, because those can handle a **null** value just fine. But it causes problems if we're using a value type. Imagine if we were trying to get the score (an **int**) instead of the name, as shown below:

```
int? score = highScoreManager?.Scores?[0]?.Score;
```

Because the null propagators might return null, this expression doesn't evaluate to a plain **int**, but rather a nullable **int**. (We discussed nullable types in the previous section.)

If we want to make sure it gets turned back into a non-null value, we would simply use the null-coalescing operator (**??**) from the previous section to turn nulls into some other specific value:

```
int score = highScoreManager?.Scores?[0]?.Score ?? 0;
```

In this case, we either get the score we wanted or we get the fallback value of 0 if we encounter any nulls.

The third point of note is that while there is a **?.** and a **?[]** null propagator, there is no **?()** operator. The following won't work:

```
Func<string, string> delegateMethod = null;
string resultOfMethod = delegateMethod?("3");        // Invalid...
```

The workaround is to invoke the delegate with the **Invoke** method, instead of directly invoking the object:

```
Func<string, string> delegateMethod = null;
string resultOfMethod = delegateMethod?.Invoke("3");    // Valid...
```

Here is a second example with an event:

```
public class SimpleClassWithAnEvent
{
    public event EventHandler<EventArgs> SomethingHappened;
    public void OnSomethingHappened()
    {
        SomethingHappened?.Invoke(this, EventArgs.Empty);
    }
}
```

This is actually a better and more concise way to write our event raising code than we learned about in Chapter 33, because it handles the situation where the event itself is just about to become null. (The **?.** operator makes a local copy to protect against that exact scenario.)

Command Line Arguments

Not all programs have a user sitting in front of them typing commands or pushing buttons. A second option is to allow the program to take command line arguments, supplied to the program at the time of launch. This allows you to put your program in scripts, and run it as a part of a larger automated task.

Let's say you have a program called Add.exe that adds two numbers together. Instead of asking the user to type in two numbers, as an alternative, the user can specify those numbers on the command line when they start the Add.exe program. From a command prompt, this might look like this:

```
C:\Users\RB\Documents>Add.exe 3 5
```

These values on the end are pulled into your program as command line arguments. If you look at your **Main** method, you'll see that it has a **string[] args** parameter. Command line arguments arrive in this:

```
static void Main(string[] args)
{
    int a = Convert.ToInt32(args[0]);
    int b = Convert.ToInt32(args[1]);

    Console.WriteLine(a + b);
}
```

User-Defined Conversions

Way back in Chapter 9, we looked at typecasting, which allows you to do things like convert a **float** into a **double**, or a **double** into a **float**, even though they're different types.

We briefly discussed implicit casting and explicit casting. Implicit conversions happen without asking, usually from a narrower type to a wider type. (For example, from **int** to **double**, because a **double** can store anything an **int** can store.) Explicit conversions do not happen automatically, but do allow for conversion between two types with the typecasting operator: **int a = (int)3.14;**

Casting works great for the built-in types. It also works well in an inheritance hierarchy. But C# also allows you to define conversions between types you've defined. Let's say you've got a simple class like the **MagicNumber** class below, where you have basically a number with an extra property:

```
public class MagicNumber
{
    public int Number { get; set; }
    public bool IsMagic { get; set; }
}
```

If you want to convert this to and from an **int**, you could always add methods to do this like this:

```
public int ToInt()
{
    return Number;
}

public static MagicNumber FromInt(int number)
{
    return new MagicNumber { Number = number, IsMagic = false };
}
```

This works, but isn't nearly as clean as we've seen with conversions between the built-in types. We can fix that by defining our own conversion operators:

```
public static implicit operator MagicNumber(int value)
{
    return new MagicNumber() { Number = value, IsMagic = false };
}
```

This is defined in essentially the same way as any other operator (Chapter 34). Like with all other operators, this must be **static** and **public**.

For a user-defined conversion, we must specify whether it is **implicit** or **explicit**. In this case, we've chosen **implicit**. The "name" of the operator will be whatever we are converting to. The body of the custom conversion does whatever work we need to do to produce the transformed value. With this added to our **MagicNumber** class, we can simply convert from **int**s to **MagicNumber**s:

```
int aNumber = 3;
MagicNumber magicNumber = aNumber;
```

We can also create an explicit cast in the same way. The following code defines an explicit cast from our **MagicNumber** type to **int**. (Any time we lose information in a conversion, we should always use an explicit cast.)

```
static public explicit operator int(MagicNumber magicNumber)
{
    return magicNumber.Number;
}
```

Now, elsewhere in our code, we can use this conversion, though this time, we'll need to use a typecast:

```
MagicNumber magicNumber = new MagicNumber() { Number = 3, IsMagic = true };
int aNumber = (int)magicNumber;
```

One gotcha with user-defined conversions is that they will always produce a new, separate instance. You can see the **new** keyword even popping up in our earlier implicit cast. The trick is that it's not always obvious that we've produced a new object, especially when the cast is implicit. For example:

```
TypeA a = new TypeA();
TypeB b = a; // Converted with an implicit user-defined conversion

b.DoSomething(); // Affects b, but not a, because b is a different object because of the implicit cast.
```

Because of weird errors like this, it may be easier to just use **ToWhatever()** methods (a la **ToString()**, which everything has). When you do this, it is much easier to see that you're working with a separate object:

```
TypeA a = new TypeA();
TypeB b = a.ToTypeB();
b.DoSomething();
```

User-defined conversions have their place, but it is always also worth considering if defining **ToWhatever()** methods or adding new constructors to do the conversion might be better in any particular case.

The Notorious 'goto' Keyword

C# has a **goto** keyword that allows the flow of execution to jump or "go to" an arbitrary other location in a method to continue execution. Before I go further, I should caution you that the second you mention using **goto**, you will literally have programmers crash through your wall yelling, "Don't use **goto**!"

Give it a try. When you're near some other programmers, look at your code studiously for a few seconds, scratch your chin, and say, "Maybe I'll use a **goto** here."

As we'll soon see, there are good reasons that programmers react so quickly and so harshly to **goto**. But if C# had hand grenades in it, I'd still want to teach you about C# hand grenades, so that if you stumble into a live one, you understand it well enough to react to it. For the same reason, I'm going to cover **goto** here.

How 'goto' Works

Conceptually, **goto** is pretty straightforward. It is a statement that causes the flow of execution to jump to another location, with some limitations.

A **goto** requires two parts:

1. A *label*, or a *labeled statement*. These are the targets for a **goto** statement.
2. A **goto** statement that identifies which label to jump to.

The following code is slightly complicated, but that's where you usually see **goto**. "Slightly complex" is **goto**'s natural habitat.

```
/// Look for one number in a multi-dimensional array of numbers.
public void FindNeedleInHaystack(int[,,] haystack, int needle)
{
    int locationX, locationY, locationZ;

    for(int x = 0; x < haystack.GetLength(0); x++)
    {
        for(int y = 0; y < haystack.GetLength(1); y++)
        {
            for(int z = 0; z < haystack.GetLength(2); z++)
            {
                if(haystack[x, y, z] == needle)
                {
                    locationX = x; locationY = y; locationZ = z;
                    goto Found;
                }
            }
        }
    }

    goto End;

    Found:
        Console.WriteLine($"Found at {locationX}, {locationY}, {locationZ}.");

    End:
        ;
}
```

This block of code illustrates all of the major mechanics of **goto**. In the heart of those nested loops is a **goto** statement, which identifies the label to jump to. (**Found**, in this case.) If that line is reached, the flow of execution will immediately leave where it is at and jump directly to the label it references: the **Found:** label towards the bottom.

This code also has a second **goto**. If the flow of execution never gets to that first **goto**, it will eventually complete the search and fall out of the loops normally. To skip the "Found at" message, the code includes another **goto** statement to skip past it to the end of the method.

Here are a few more of the finer points of **goto**:

- Labels can be any legal identifier. It has the same restrictions as any variable or method name.
- A label must always precede a statement. If nothing else, you can put an empty statement (a lonely semicolon) as shown after the **End** label.
- Encountering a label does not interfere with the flow of execution. **goto Something;** jumps you to the location of the label, but encountering a **Something** label does not.
- A **goto** can only take you up or down within the current scope (as is shown with **goto End;**), or up to a parent scope (as is shown with **goto Found;**). It cannot take you into a child scope, or into a different child scope of a parent (for example, out of one **for** loop and into another).
- A **goto** cannot take you between methods.

This code illustrates an example of where **goto** has potential value. Breaking out of multiple loops without a **goto** is not exactly trivial. That doesn't necessarily mean you *should* use it here. There are some definite good reasons to avoid **goto** here or anywhere. But if there were ever a time for a **goto** statement, this would be a good candidate.

Why You Should Avoid 'goto'

There is probably no programming concept that will evoke such an extreme negative reaction as using **goto**. But what makes it so bad?

The answer is that **goto** is that it has a profoundly negative effect on code readability and maintainability.

The earlier code sample is probably **goto** at its best. Here's an example of **goto** at its worst:

```
public void FindNeedleInHaystack(int[,,] haystack, int needle)
{
    int x = 0;

    Top:
    int y = 0;

    TryAgain:
    int z = 0;

    Next:
    if (z >= haystack.GetLength(2))
    {
        y++;
        goto TryAgain;
    }

    if (haystack[x, y, z] == needle) goto Found;

    z++;
    goto Next;

    y++;
    if (y < haystack.GetLength(1)) goto TryAgain;

    x++;

    if (x < haystack.GetLength(0)) goto Top;

    goto End;

    Found:
    Console.WriteLine($"Found at {x}, {y}, {z}.");

    End:
    ;
}
```

Pop Quiz: Does this code have the same functionality as before?

It is supposed to. I just unrolled the loops into **goto** statements, but in theory, kept the same functionality. But I'm having a hard time verifying that it still produces the correct results. And I wrote the thing!

The massive drop in readability is also a maintainability killer. Once a **goto** has been added, it tends to become impossible to extract. It's like a tick or a leech. One does not simply remove it.

Furthermore, **goto**s are contagious. One **goto** begets more **goto**s. In the original **goto** code, the mostly reasonable **goto Found;** produced a second less reasonable **goto End;**. This is commonplace with **goto**s.

The above code is an especially bad example, but once **goto** pops up, it morphs into this pretty quickly.

The reality is, by applying refactorings like extracting pieces into methods and just reorganizing confusing code, you can always rewrite **goto** code in a way that doesn't require **goto**. And nearly every experienced developer will tell you that taking this approach will save you a lot of pain in the long term.

Many teams will just simply forbid **goto** in their codebase. It's probably for the better.

At a minimum though, I would strongly recommend pretending **goto** doesn't even exist for at least the first year of your development life. That will get you practice with different (better) approaches and make you far wiser before you start unknowingly inflicting damage on your code quality.

Generic Covariance and Contravariance

When you have inheritance and you mix derived types with base types, the rule is that you can substitute the derived class any time the base class is expected. As a frame of reference for this discussion, let's assume we have the following two classes, which form a small inheritance hierarchy:

```
public class GameObject // Any object in the game world.
{
    public float X { get; set; }
    public float Y { get; set; }
}

public class Ship : GameObject
{
    public void Fire() { /* ... */ }
}
```

Recall that you can assign an instance of the derived class to a variable whose type is the base class:

```
GameObject newObject = new Ship();
```

Or consider the method below, which expects a **GameObject**:

```
void Add(GameObject toAdd) { /* ... */ }
```

You can invoke this with the derived object:

```
Add(new Ship());
```

The derived class can be used any time that the base class is expected, because the derived class is, in fact, *also* the base type. A **Ship** is a special type of **GameObject**, but that makes it a **GameObject** too.

Generics and the Type Hierarchy

This substitution relationship between derived and base classes is a useful one, but generics complicate the picture. While you can do this:

```
GameObject newObject = new Ship();
```

You cannot do this:

```
List<GameObject> newObjects = new List<Ship> { new Ship(), new Ship(), new Ship() };
```

While there is a relationship between **GameObject** and **Ship**, there is not an equivalent relationship between **List<GameObject>** and **List<Ship>**. The hierarchy relationship is not magically bestowed on generic types that utilize the types in the hierarchy. **List<T>** is instead derived from plain old **object**.

In fact, if this were allowed, it would cause serious problems. Consider the consequences of this code:

```
List<GameObject> objects = new List<Ship>();
objects.Add(new Asteroid());
```

That second line would seem reasonable (assuming **Asteroid** is another class derived from **GameObject**). We're simply adding an **Asteroid** to a collection that can hold any type of **GameObject**. Yet the actual **List** type being used is a list of **Ship**. You shouldn't be able to put **Asteroid** in a list of **Ship**.

But still, sometimes it could be nice to allow generic types to leverage the relationships of their type parameters.

Variance: Defining Hierarchy-Like Relationships with Generic Types

In C#, you actually have control over how the hierarchy relationship transfers over to a generic type that uses it. The rules that govern if and how this relationship is applied is called *variance*.

If you remember from Chapter 26, whenever you define a generic type, you specify a list of generic type parameters that can be used elsewhere in the class. For example, in the code below, we have a generic interface (called **IGeneric**) with two generic type parameters that called **T1** and **T2**:

```
public interface IGeneric<T1, T2> { /* ... */ }
```

For each of these generic type parameters, you can specify what form of variance you want it to use.

There are three variance options available.

The first is *invariance*, and is the default. This means that the type hierarchy relationship is ignored entirely. This is what we saw with how **List<Ship>** could not be supplied when **List<GameObject>** was required. When something is invariant, you must use the exact type specified.

The second is *covariance*. This means that the type hierarchy relationship is preserved. If you have a covariant generic type parameter, then you could assign a derived version when the base version is specified, which we might have hoped for with **List<T>**, had it not caused problems:

```
Covariant<GameObject> thing = new Covariant<Ship>();
```

Covariance only works if the generic type parameter is used solely as output from the class. That is, it is used as return values for methods (including property getters and indexers). It cannot be used as input to the class (the type of a method parameter or a setter for a property or indexer). This is exactly the reason why **List<Ship>** can't be stored in a **List<GameObject>**. The **Add** method requires passing in something of type **T**, so it can't be covariant.

On the other hand, **IEnumerable<T>** *is* covariant. **IEnumerable<T>** was introduced in Chapter 25. This is an interface that allows you to simply iterate over a collection, or run through a collection and view it, one item at a time. Because **IEnumerable<T>** doesn't define any methods that require the generic type as input, it can be covariant.

Also, since **List<T>** implements the **IEnumerable<T>** interface, the following is possible:

```
IEnumerable<GameObject> gameObjects = new List<Ship> { new Ship(), new Ship(), new Ship() };
```

A **List<Ship>** implements **IEnumerable<Ship>**, which is assignable to **IEnumerable<GameObject>**.

The third option is *contravariance*. While covariance preserves the type hierarchy relationship, contravariance actually inverts it. If a generic type parameter is contravariant, we can do this:

```
Contravariant<Ship> thing = new Contravariant<GameObject>();
```

This might seem strange at first, but it is related to the fact that contravariance can only work if the generic type argument is only used on inputs to the class.

The best practical example of contravariance is the **Action<T>** delegate type that we introduced in Chapter 32. **Action<T>** is a delegate type that matches any method that has a single parameter of the generic type **T** and a **void** return type. For example, if we had a delegate that looked like this:

```
Action<Ship> processShipDelegate;
```

We could assign either of these methods to it:

```
public void LogShip(Ship s) { /* ... */ }
public void DrawShip(Ship s) { /* ... */ }
```

But **Action<T>** is contravariant. That means that we could *also* assign these to it:

```
public void LogGameObject(GameObject o) { /* ... */ }
public void DrawGameObject(GameObject o) { /* ... */ }
```

The type isn't a perfect match, but contravariance allows **Action<GameObject>** (which these are) to be assigned to **Action<Ship>**.

But contravariance will only work if the generic type parameter is solely used for inputs.

Based on our earlier example, you can start to get a feel for how and why that works. If we assign **void DrawGameObject(GameObject o)** to that **processShipDelegate** variable, we can then turn around and invoke it with a **Ship**:

```
processShipDelegate = DrawGameObject;
processShipDelegate.Invoke(new Ship());
```

We're calling a method that expects the base type (**GameObject**) but passing in the derived type (**Ship**).

Specifying Variance in Code

We've covered how variance works at a conceptual level, as well as some examples of how to actually use covariant and contravariant generic type parameters. Now it's time to look at how to actually make something of your own creation covariant or contravariant.

Variance can be specified on generic interfaces and delegate types. (Notably not on generic classes.)

To specify variance, you simply put the **out** (for covariance) or **in** (for contravariance) keywords just before the generic type parameter where you define the type:

```
public interface IVariance<out TCovariant, in TContravariant>
{
    TCovariant ProduceAValue();
    void ConsumeAValue(TContravariant value);
}
```

While these keywords don't do a great job at helping you remember the terms "covariant" and "contravariant," they do a good job of helping you remember where they can be used.

If you've marked something as covariant with the **out** keyword, the compiler will enforce that it is only used as an output. If you attempt to use it as an input, it will not compile. The same applies with contravariance and the **in** keyword. If you make something contravariant, but then try to use it as a return value, the compiler will catch it.

Invariance is the default. If you leave **in** or **out** off, then the generic type parameter will be invariant. You will be able to use it as both an input and an output, at the cost of losing variance.

It is good practice to make types covariant or contravariant if the intent is to only use it as input or output.

Mixing and Matching

Every generic type parameter is allowed to have its own variance. You could have five generic type parameters, one of which is invariant, two of which are covariant, and two that are contravariant.

You don't have to look far in the Standard Library to find a type that does some mixing and matching. Recall that the **Func** family of delegates specifies some number of generic inputs and a generic return value. For example, there is this one:

```
public delegate TResult Func<in T1, in T2, in T3, out TResult>(T1 arg1, T2 arg2, T3 arg3);
```

The three generic type arguments that are used as inputs (**T1**, **T2**, and **T3**) all are marked with that **in** keyword, making them contravariant. The one that is used as an output (**TResult**) is marked with **out**, making it covariant.

To further illustrate the variance point, what this means is that if you have a variable that looks like this:

```
private Func<Ship, Ship, Ship, GameObject> shipMuxer;
```

You can assign it any of the following functions as a value:

```
private GameObject DoStuff(Ship a, Ship b, Ship c) { /* ... */ }
private Ship ReturnAShip(Ship a, Ship b, Ship c) { /* ... */ }
private GameObject ExpectGameObjects(GameObject a, GameObject b, GameObject c) { /* ... */ }
private Ship ExpectObjectsAndReturnAShip(object a, object b, object c) { /* ... */ }
```

Advanced Namespace Management

In Chapter 27 we discussed namespaces in depth. There are a few weird corner cases that we ignored in that chapter, simply because they have few practical uses. But since they are a part of the language, these corner cases are worth a brief mention here in this chapter.

In certain cases where names of classes and namespaces get reused, the C# compiler may get confused about what you're referring to. For example, while we're familiar with the **Console** class in the **System** namespace, imagine if you made a class called **System** that had a method called **Console** in it. At this point, **System.Console** is ambiguous.

The first rule here is, "Don't do that." Avoid name collisions between classes and namespaces whenever possible. It's not just confusing to the compiler, but to humans as well. So avoid it wherever possible.

On the other hand, sometimes the mess was caused by the exact wrong combination of third party libraries, and you have no choice.

To resolve these scenarios, use the **global** keyword with the namespace alias operator (**::**) shown below:

```
global::System.Console.WriteLine("Hello World!");
```

The **global::** indicates that the compiler should start searching for names (namespaces or type names) starting all the way up at the top of the system. (This top level is called the global namespace.)

On a related note, there are a few occasions in which you need to reference two versions of the same assembly or dependency. This, too, should be avoided whenever possible.

But when it's unavoidable, the way to deal with it is with an *extern alias*. An extern alias allows you to bring in the code in a DLL under a separate "root" namespace, alongside the global namespace, with a different name of your own choosing.

To do this, you must do two things. First, you must apply a namespace alias to the DLL that you're referencing. This is not hard to do:

1. In the Solution Explorer, in your project, under the References element, find the assembly that you want to give an alias to.
2. Right-click on it and select **Properties**.
3. Look for the property called **Aliases**. By default, this will say "global". Simply change this to another value. For example, "MyAlias".

In code files that want to use this alias, put code similar to the following at the very top of the file:

```
extern alias MyAlias;
```

Note that extern aliases *must* go before anything else in the file, including the rest of your **using** directives.

At this point, everything in your new aliased namespace is accessible like you're used to, with your alias prepended to the front. So you can add **using** directives for it, reference types in it with fully qualified names, etc.

Additionally, you can access stuff in this namespace using the namespace alias operator (**::**) as well: **MyAlias::My.Namespace.MyClass**. This helps illustrate that your extern alias is not under the global namespace, but is at the root level beside it.

Remember: these are situations that are best avoided. If you have a different way around needing to use the **global::** namespace reference or **extern alias**, you should. But it is good to know that things are in place to work through the problem if it becomes unavoidable.

Checked and Unchecked Contexts

In Chapter 9 we discussed overflow errors. To recap, when you do some math that causes your integral numbers to go beyond their allowed limits, you run into overflow. By default, the value is "truncated" and the number wraps around. For example, the following code outputs -2147483648, which is **int.MinValue**.

```
int x = int.MaxValue;
x++;
Console.WriteLine(x);
```

The code above, by default, wraps around when we exceed the maximum value. (Note that this does not apply to floating point numbers. They just become infinity instead.)

Most scenarios won't push you into overflow at all. If it's a threat, you upgrade to a larger data type, like using **long** instead of **int**, or **int** instead of **short**. In other cases, if you do wrap around, it's not that big of a deal. But in some cases, wrapping around causes *huge* problems. Suddenly the number goes from a big number to a small one. If that's the balance of your bank account, you're going to be sad that it changed like that without you even being told.

This is because by default, C# code runs in an *unchecked context*. That is a way of saying the runtime doesn't care if something overflows. It doesn't even check for it. It just allows the bits to be reinterpreted as the truncated value.

On the other hand, you can specify in your C# code that some math operation should be ran in a checked context instead.

```
int x = int.MaxValue;
checked
{
    x++;
}
Console.WriteLine(x);
```

If you do this, then instead of wrapping around, an **OverflowException** will be thrown. When this happens, you can optionally catch it and handle it however you feel you need to, as we discussed back in Chapter 30.

Likewise, you can also specify that a section of code should always be done in an unchecked context:

```
int x = int.MaxValue;
unchecked
```

```
{
    x++;
}
Console.WriteLine(x);
```

Unchecked is the default. So why have a keyword that specifies this?

It turns out you can set the entire application to be either checked or unchecked by default by setting an option on the compiler. If you have set up the application to be checked by default, then being able to specify that a certain computation must be unchecked is useful.

To specify that an application (or a single project) should be checked, you can either add the **/checked+** compiler command line argument (or **/checked-** to turn it off) or if you prefer to do this in the UI itself:

- Right-click on a particular project in your Solution Explorer.
- Choose **Properties**.
- Select the **Build** tab.
- Push the **Advanced** button.
- In the Advanced Build Settings dialog that comes up, check or uncheck the box that is labelled "Check for arithmetic overflow/underflow".

Whether something is checked or unchecked is not usually something you need to worry about. Usually you don't care because you won't run into a place where overflow can even happen or you don't care that it wraps around as the default behavior. But in cases where it matters, it is nice to know that you have options to control it.

Volatile Fields

In this section, we are going to talk about C#'s **volatile** keyword and some related concepts that help to paint a picture of what it does and why.

This topic is another one of those dark corners of C#, and of programming in general.

Program Order and Out-of-Order Execution

The first point of interest here is to describe two closely related concepts called *program order* of instructions and out-of-order execution. When you look at a chunk of source code like the following, you make the assumption that things will happen in the order you see it:

```
int x = 3;
x += 7;
int z = 10;
```

This is a key tenet of procedural programming. Things happen one after the next.

As it so happens, sometimes either the compiler or the hardware itself is able to see that it can get more things done faster if it can rearrange the order of some of the instructions, or run the instructions in parallel. The last line in the above code is a good example of this. The **int z = 10;** could actually be completed (or at least started) before the **x += 7** completes.

The value in allowing the hardware to rearrange instructions or interleave instructions is clearer when you recall that each line of C# code that you write tends to compile down to multiple binary instructions.

The ability for hardware to reorder instructions is called *out-of-order execution*. It is a key way that hardware can run code more quickly. When performing out-of-order execution, the hardware still guarantees that any changes it makes will still appear as though it were executed in program order.

Here's the catch: the hardware generally makes the assumption that only a single thread is running. When two or more threads (or processes) share memory, this out-of-order execution can occasionally cause problems. To illustrate, consider the following two chunks of code.

Thread #1 is running this:

```
value = 42;
complete = true;
```

And Thread #2 is running this:

```
while(!complete) { }
Console.WriteLine(value);
```

What will Thread #2 write out?

Under normal rules, you would assume that it prints 42. But because of out-of-order execution, it is possible that the ordering in Thread #1 could get reversed and something besides 42 could appear instead.

In this context, you may hear people talking about the results of one memory operation (a read or a write) being "visible" to other threads. You could say an operation is *visible* if, from the perspective of all threads that have access to the memory location, all changes to the memory it affects have completed.

In our code above, it's possible that setting **complete** to **true** might be visible before the change of **value** to **42**, at least from Thread #2's perspective.

Memory Barriers

Obviously, with a problem like what we're describing, you'd assume that there's a solution of some sort. The answer here is something called a *memory barrier*. A memory barrier is a special instruction at the hardware level that indicates that pending reads or writes must complete before continuing past the memory barrier. There are two ways that this can work:

1. **Acquire Semantics:** If an operation has acquire semantics, then it will be visible before later instructions.
2. **Release Semantics:** If an operation has release semantics, then earlier instructions will be visible before it.

Creating Volatile Fields

In C#, fields (both static fields and instance variables) can be marked with the **volatile** keyword. The **volatile** keyword is intended to help sort out issues that come up when multiple threads have access to the field, and you're not using another mechanism for thread safety (like a lock).

In particular, reading from a **volatile** field is a "volatile read," which means it has acquire semantics. It is guaranteed to occur before any references to memory that occur after it in program order.

Additionally, writing to a **volatile** field is a "volatile write," which means it has release semantics. It is guaranteed to occur after any references to memory that occur before it in program order.

If we defined our original **complete** variable like this:

```
private bool complete;
```

We could make it volatile like so:

```
private volatile bool complete;
```

This now means that when Thread #1 runs this code:

```
value = 42;
complete = true;
```

We can guarantee that **complete** won't be set to **true** until after **value = 42;** has completed, from the perspective of *any* thread. That fixes our issue.

So when should you use **volatile**?

If you only have one thread, you do not need **volatile**, and shouldn't use it for performance reasons. You also don't need it if the variable is always accessed through some other thread-safe mechanism.

But any time where two threads might access it without another thread-safe mechanism, you will likely want to make the field **volatile**.

Part 5

Mastering the Tools

In order to master C#, you need to thoroughly understand the development tools that you use. We've spent the bulk of this book looking at how to write C# code, but in order to truly understand how a program works, you'll need to learn the details of how C# and the .NET Platform function, and how to use Visual Studio effectively. In this section, we'll look in depth at how these things work, and we'll pay particular attention to how to debug your code and fix common problems.

We'll cover:

- The .NET Platform in more depth (Chapter 44).
- A detailed look at Visual Studio and useful features it has (Chapter 45).
- How to work with multiple projects and dependencies, including NuGet (Chapter 46).
- Dealing with common compiler errors (Chapter 47).
- How to debug your code (Chapter 48).
- A behind-the-scenes guide through the way Visual Studio organizes and manages your code and other assets in a project or solution (Chapter 49).

44

The .NET Platform

In a Nutshell
- The .NET Platform is the system on which C# runs.
- C# code is compiled to CIL instructions by the C# compiler, and to binary instructions at run-time by the JIT compiler.
- The Common Language Runtime is an application virtual machine that runs your program.
- The .NET Standard Library defines the collection of types that are available for you to reuse in your program.
- There are several stacks that you can utilize that run on different hardware platforms and operating systems:
    - The .NET Framework is the oldest and most popular, and runs on Windows devices.
    - The .NET Core is the newcomer, and can run on macOS, Windows, and Linux.
    - The Xamarin stack primarily targets mobile devices (iOS and Android).
- The .NET Platform also contains app models for creating specific application types (desktop apps, web, mobile apps, games, etc.).

The .NET Platform, often called the .NET Framework or simply ".NET", is the system that your C# applications run on. The .NET Platform has a lot of interconnected pieces with an interesting history. To make sense of this, we'll start with an overview of what the .NET Platform is. Then we'll cover a brief history of .NET, which shows how we got where we're at and shed some light on where it's heading. We will then go through the individual pieces that comprise the .NET Platform in more depth.

Overview of the .NET Platform

The .NET Platform, also called the .NET Framework (though we'll draw some distinctions between those two terms later) is a vast software platform, designed to make software development faster and easier. The goals is to let programmers focus on the unique aspects of their program, without needing to worry about "boilerplate" code that is common to all applications.

The .NET Platform architecture diagram below shows the current state of the .NET Platform. This has been evolving at a fast rate, and will continue to change in the future.

.NET PLATFORM

The .NET Platform can be thought of as three different layers. The bottom layer is a collection of shared infrastructure. This includes the languages themselves (the specification for each language) the compilers for the languages, the Common Intermediate Language (CIL) that the compilers emit, the Common Language Runtime (CLR) that runs .NET applications, along with supporting tools and components.

Built on top of that is the .NET Standard Library (often called the Base Class Library, though the two are subtly different). This is a vast collection of reusable code that takes care of common tasks or solves common problems, including things like networking, file system access, and collections. Your C#

application (or any other .NET language) can use anything in The Standard Library. It is common code that any type of application—web, desktop GUI, console, game—can utilize.

You can see that the top level is split into three different sections. Each of these can be called a different stack, flavor, or implementation of the .NET Platform. Sometimes, each of these are even called *a* .NET platform (contrasted with *The* .NET Platform with a capital 'P', which is the label I'm applying to the entire ecosystem, including all of the stacks).

The three stacks shown in the diagram are not meant to be a complete list of all possible flavors of .NET, though these are the three biggest and most widely used stacks. Each of these stacks represent a unique configuration of .NET. Some of the infrastructure pieces (like the Common Language Runtime or the C# compiler) are swapped out for compatible replacements. In different stacks, even the .NET Standard Library can be swapped for a completely different implementation.

Each stack is carefully crafted for different unique purposes. For instance, the .NET Framework is the biggest and oldest of the stacks. It's primarily suited to Windows machines. The .NET Core stack is much newer and much smaller, but can also target Linux and Mac. The Xamarin stack is aimed primarily at mobile development, including iOS and Android.

Each stack supports a number of different app models. An *app model* is primarily a library dedicated to building some specific type of application. For example, the Windows Presentation Foundation (WPF) app model is a framework for building desktop GUI applications. ASP.NET is a framework for building web applications (generally in conjunction with JavaScript, CSS, and HTML on the front-end). In addition to providing a library of code specific to a certain type of application, app models can also provide infrastructure as well: things like security models and deployment models.

Terminology: .NET Platform and the .NET Framework

The terminology here gets a little confusing. This is because of history. Out of all of the stacks, the .NET Framework was the first. Because of this, other stacks have also been frequently called implementations of the .NET Framework. You might hear people say, ".NET Core is an implementation of the .NET Framework that also runs on Linux and OSX." The term ".NET Framework" then basically has three definitions that depend on context:

1. A label applied to the entire ecosystem (what I'm referring to as the .NET Platform in this book).
2. The specific .NET Framework stack, excluding .NET Core, Xamarin, and other stacks.
3. A template of what a stack should look like, of which, .NET Core, Xamarin, etc. simply re-implement.

The Internet and other material will use all three of these definitions at different times. When you come across the term, you should stop and think about which of these definitions the author is referring to. In this book, I will always call #1 either ".NET" or "The .NET Platform", with a "The" at the front and a capital "P". When I say ".NET Framework", I'm always using definition #2: the specific .NET Framework stack. And if I mean #3, I will refer to them simply as stacks, or possibly .NET platforms, with a lowercase "p".

Specifications and Implementations

One important thing to point out about .NET is that it is a system of specifications and implementations. For many components, there is a specification of how it should work, and then one or more implementation of that specification. The C# compiler is a good example of this. The C# language itself has a specification about how it should work and what it should compile to. While there is a default, built-in compiler (the Roslyn compiler) that particular component can be replaced with another compiler in a different stack. As long as the compiler sticks to the specification, it is fine to replace it.

The .NET Standard Library is an even better example of this. The .NET Standard Library is actually not a shared, single implementation, but a specification. Each stack has a different implementation of this specification. The specification for this library is titled the *.NET Standard*. The .NET Standard defines what things should be in the shared class library available to all platforms, and each stack can have a different implementation that conforms to this standard. (Each stack additionally adds their own unique pieces to the library as well.)

The Common Language Runtime also has a specification, and each stack has its own implementation.

These specifications allow different stacks or variations of stacks to be able to swap pieces in and out for different implementations to get the behavior and structure they need. They can be tailored to fit their specific needs.

A Brief History of the .NET Platform

While the previous section focused on how the .NET Platform is currently organized, a different facet of the .NET Platform is its history, which is valuable because it sheds light on some of the reasons it is organized the way it is and also some of the confusing names that are floating around.

- **Early 2002:** The first version of .NET is released, which only included the .NET Framework stack. It includes the Base Class Library as its standard library. C# and .NET are mostly still what they were when first introduced.
- **Late 2002:** A second stack, the .NET Compact Framework, is released. This targets platforms such as phones that have storage, memory, and CPU constraints.
- **2004:** The Mono open source project is started as an alternate implementation of the .NET Framework intended to run on more platforms than just Windows. This is spearheaded by a company called Xamarin. This is the beginning of the Xamarin stack.
- **2004 - 2014:** The stacks continue evolving. New content is added to their respective class libraries, which begin to diverge from each other. New app models such as WPF (2006) continue to be added.
- **2012:** Portable Class Libraries are introduced in an attempt to make it easier to write code that works on different stacks.
- **2014:** Microsoft begins to work on a way to make ASP.NET run on Linux machines and Nano Server. This becomes .NET Core.
- **February 2016:** Xamarin is purchased by Microsoft, and becomes a subsidiary of Microsoft.
- **June 2016:** .NET Core 1.0 is released.
- **September 2016:** .NET Standard is introduced, replacing Portable Class Libraries as a solution to writing code that works on multiple stacks and in multiple app models. This defines how the middle layer of the .NET architecture diagram should function, giving motivation for the different stacks' class libraries to become more similar to each other instead of more different.
- **November 2016:** .Net Core 1.1 is released.

That brings us to the present—or at least to the time of publishing this book. The .NET Platform as a whole has grown and changed greatly over time, and the rate of change seems to be accelerating, not slowing down. More changes are certainly coming in the future.

Binary, Assembly, and Compilers

Now that we've outlined the high-level design of .NET and gone through a bit of its history, it's time to go back and revisit the components in the .NET Platform in greater depth. We'll start at the bottom and work our way upwards.

To do that, we should probably start with some conceptual topics first: binary languages, assembly languages, and compilers.

Computers can only understand binary: 1's and 0's. The instructions they follow are all coded in binary sequences, and the data the read and write is all stored in binary representations. For example, here is a sequence of three binary instructions:

```
00100100 00001000 00000000 00000010
00100100 00001001 00000000 00000010
00000001 00001001 01010000 00100000
```

Can you tell what that does? Turns out, it adds 2 and 2, and stores the result. While it is easy for a computer to understand this, humans can't easily make sense of it. But there was a time when humans controlled computers by manipulating individual bits like this. Of course, that era didn't last long; it's just too error prone and difficult to juggle in our brains.

So humans started building layers on top of binary. The first step to this is a low-level language called *assembly language*, or *assembler*, which can be thought of as a human-readable form of binary:

```
li $t0, 2
li $t1, 2
add $t2, $t0, $t1
```

Immediately, you'll see that this is far more readable than the earlier binary. For example, we can now actually see the 2's in there, and the **add** instruction on the last line. It's far clearer what's happening, and typos or logical mistakes are much easier to see.

Assembly code directly mirrors binary. Each line of assembly is turned into a single instruction in binary code (with a small handful of exceptions). You can think of assembly as a human-readable form of binary.

Of course, the computer isn't going to be able to directly run assembly code. We need a way to translate assembly into binary. This is what a compiler is: a program that translates from a higher-level language to a lower-level language. In this case, we simply need to create an assembly-to-binary compiler, and we never have to write in binary again!

But we're already running into a problem. Not every CPU is made the same. They don't all use the same set of 1's and 0's to represent the same instruction, and not all CPUs even have the same set of instructions available. This starts to become a problem for our compiler. This problem leads to the rise of multiple flavors of assembly, and multiple compilers for the different types of systems we might want to run on. The plot thickens!

Of course, there's no need to stop at assembly. It's more readable than binary, but it's still not *that* readable or concise. Simply doing 2 + 2 took three lines and 25 characters. There's obviously room for improvement. So we started making higher-level programming languages like FORTRAN and C++ where single statements could be translated into many lines of assembly or binary code. Each of these languages need their own compiler to translate from their own unique syntax to assembly or binary.

Different lines of thought, different use cases, and different users (the programmers) led to an explosion in the number of programming languages available, some general purpose (Java, C#, Python), some tailored to a specific task (R, MatLab), and others just plain weird (Ook).

Higher-level languages make life simpler for programmers because less code does more work. But we still have our original problem that every computer we want to run on is unique, with different instructions and representations of those instructions. The compilers can handle this, but it means a different executable .EXE (or equivalent) file for different target machines.

This organizational pattern is the traditional compilation model: Source code written in a particular language is turned to binary code by a compiler. The compiler must know and understand a lot about any targeted hardware platform in order to make instructions for that particular machine. This leads to either a large number of compilers, or to a large number of configurations for single, complicated compilers. The traditional compilation model has its problems, but it is a good model that has served many programming languages and many programmers well for decades.

Virtual Machines and the Common Language Runtime

More recently, a variation on traditional compilation has arisen. This alternate approach doesn't strictly replace traditional compilation; they both have their place. But this second approach has seen a surge in popularity, and is the approach C# and the .NET Platform takes.

This alternative approach is driven by two fundamental problems of traditional compilation. The first of these is the sheer number of compilers that need to exist to target each of the different hardware platforms and their nuances. The second is that compiler programmers need to be not just experts in their language, but also in every hardware platform they want their language to work on.

A solution to this problem is that of a *virtual machine*. The term "virtual machine" has a couple of meanings, depending on the context. In this context, we're referring to a *process virtual machine*, which is a software program that runs another software program (your program) in a way that is independent of the hardware itself. (This is in contrast to an *application virtual machine*, which is a software application that simulates an entire computer, including hardware, operating system, and multiple running applications.)

The .NET Platform's virtual machine is called the *Common Language Runtime*, or *CLR*. Like with many things in .NET, there is a specification for the CLR, and multiple implementations of it. Each different stack tends to have its own implementation. The CLR implementation for the main .NET Framework stack is simply called the CLR. The .NET Core's implementation is called CoreCLR, while Xamarin uses the Mono Runtime.

A real hardware machine can perform specific instructions, and has binary (and assembly) code that corresponds to it. similarly, a virtual machine like the CLR has its own instructions that it can perform.

If an application wants to target the CLR virtual machine, rather than compiling to instructions for any physical machine, it needs to compile to the instruction set that is supported by the CLR. The CLR then has the responsibility of turning those "virtual" instructions into the "real" instructions for the physical machine that it is running on.

Effectively, the compilation is split into two steps. The first step is to transform source code into this virtual instruction set. This is done by the language compiler. Then, as the program is running, the virtual machine (the CLR) has the responsibility of doing a final compilation step to transform the virtual instructions into ones that the underlying physical machine can execute. The CLR has its own compiler to do just this. This compiler is called the *Just-In-Time compiler* or the *JIT compiler*. Under normal scenarios, the JIT compiler translates methods (Chapter 15) one at a time, the first time they are called. This means nothing gets translated more than once and methods that are never used don't get JIT compiled.

This compilation pattern solves our two earlier problems. The compilers themselves are only concerned with one thing. The "main" compiler just has to translate from C# or another language to the virtual instruction set, and the JIT compiler doesn't need to care about the specifics of any language but the virtual instruction set and translating it to the hardware instructions. This also means that compiler programmers no longer need to be experts in many physical machine architectures, just in the CLR's instruction set.

Common Intermediate Language

The virtual instruction set that a virtual machine has is referred to as an *intermediate language*. It can be represented in a binary format as well as in a text-based format that is essentially the assembly language for the virtual machine.

For the .NET Platform, the intermediate language is called *Common Intermediate Language* (CIL). In the past, it was called *Microsoft Intermediate Language* (MSIL) and you still see that term used regularly.

Most Intermediate languages tend to be higher level than "normal" binary or assembly languages. For example, CIL instructions contain concepts about object-oriented programming (all of Part 3) such as casting, creating objects, and type checking. It also contains information about exception handling (Chapter 30).

The C# compiler only needs to convert C# source code into CIL instructions, disregarding the specifics of which computer you intend the application to run on. (It's targeting the virtual machine, after all.) When the CLR is running your code, the JIT compiler will convert the CIL instructions to their final form as binary instructions for the actual physical machine.

Advantages of a Virtual Machine

There are certain advantages and disadvantages to using a virtual machine like the CLR. This section and the next will dig a little into the good and bad.

Separation of Concerns

Probably the single most important benefit of using a two stage compilation process with a virtual machine in the middle is the idea of separating concerns. This has been touched on repeatedly in this chapter. By separating the hardware-specific concerns away from the language-specific concerns, you allow the C# compiler programmers to not have to worry about the details of many different hardware platforms, and you also allow the JIT compiler to not worry about any specific language.

Cross-Language Libraries

Because the code targets a virtual machine, you open up the door for any language that targets the virtual machine to be able to reuse the code without any additional work. For example, the entire .NET Standard Library is accessible by every language in the .NET Platform, including C#, VB.NET, F#, IronPython, and IronRuby. If you made your own language and compiled to CIL, you could get access to the Standard Library for free. And you can write a C# library that is works in all of these languages as well.

Memory Management

The CLR also performs memory management. C# and other .NET languages do not require you allocate memory for your objects, nor do you have to clean it up when you're done (in most cases). The CLR will manage what memory is used, and what isn't, and move things around to keep things organized. Memory management is like having a personal assistant whose job is to take care of these things for you, freeing you up to work on the interesting parts of your program.

There are a few times where you go beyond the bounds of the CLR's managed memory (Chapter 42), and when you do, you'll need to take extra care to clean things up correctly yourself.

Security

Because C# code is running on a virtual machine, it has a high level of control over what code can access the hard drive, the network, and other hardware. And because it is running inside a virtual machine, a program can't gain access to the memory of other programs. This prevents code from doing a whole slew of dangerous, virus-like activities.

The Drawbacks of Virtual Machines

Virtual machines are great inventions, but they don't come without a few strings attached. In many cases, the advantages outweigh the problems, but it is still important to understand these tradeoffs when it comes time to pick a language to use.

Performance

The primary drawback of a virtual machine is performance. Code running on a virtual machine is generally considered to be somewhat slower than code running without one.

But this isn't as bad as it seems.

For starters, in many applications, speed isn't an issue. Think about a GUI application, like a word processor or a web browser. As much as these applications do, the computer spends most of its time waiting for the user to press a key or click a button. The holdup is the user, not the computer. In these cases, a virtual machine won't hurt anything.

Additionally, it is technically possible for code running on a virtual machine to be faster. This may seem strange at first, knowing the overhead that the virtual machine needs, but it is possible. Without a virtual machine, the compiler makes the final decision about what machine instructions are actually going to be used. That happens on the developer's machine. With a virtual machine, the final compilation step happens at run-time, on the computer that will actually run it. The JIT compiler has more information to work with, so it has the potential to make better decisions about what to actually use. Despite this, in practice, .NET code does tend to run just a bit slower than its unmanaged counterpart.

Additionally, C# has the capacity to invoke unmanaged non-CLR code if needed (Chapter 42). This allows you to use C# code for the bulk of your application, and then call your own C or C++ code for the performance-critical pieces if needed.

Bad for Low-Level Coding

Obviously, there are just some things that can't be done in a virtual machine, because it has to run as an application on another computer. So you obviously aren't going to be writing an operating system using C#. Nor would you write something like a device driver to talk to actual hardware in C#. These things are just too low level. For things like this, you must use a different programming language, such as C or C++.

Your Code is More Visible

I occasionally hear people expressing concern about how compiled C# code is easier to decompile and reverse engineer than other languages. It's true that CIL code is higher level than raw binary or assembly. Because it is higher level, it is slightly easier to determine what the code is doing and reverse engineer it. But CIL is only *slightly* more readable than non-CIL assembly code. Plus, this can largely be solved by using a code obfuscator on your compiled projects before shipping them to customers.

The .NET Standard Library

We've now thoroughly dissected the bottom layer of the .NET Platform architecture, and we're going to move up to the next level: the .NET Standard Library. *The .NET Standard Library* is a vast collection of reusable code that can be utilized in any .NET application. While it is considered a "class library", that term is a general term; the .NET Standard Library contains not just classes, but structs, interfaces, delegates, enumerations, etc. that provide things that any type of application might want to leverage. This includes things like the primitive types (**int**, **string**, **double**, etc.), collections (lists, dictionaries, stacks, queues), networking, file system access, multi-threading, and much, much more.

While this book is more about C# as a language, and not the .NET Standard Library, many of the most important and useful types in the .NET Standard Library are covered throughout the book.

The .NET Standard Library is actually not just a single implementation. Like many things, it has a specification called the *NET Standard*, and each stack has its own implementation of this standard. The .NET Standard defines the Application Programming Interface (API) of the .NET Standard Library. This API specifies the types that need to exist and the members (methods, properties, events, etc.) that each type should have, as well as the expected behavior of those types and those members.

The .NET Standard is actually not a single standard, but consists of multiple tiers, specified as version numbers. Each version contains everything that lower version numbers contain, and then some.

For example, .NET Standard 1.0 includes the **Action** and **Func** types. .NET Standard 1.1 also contains these because the version number is higher. .NET Standard 1.1 contains additional types not included with .NET Standard 1.0. For example, it includes **ZipArchive**. If something only supports .NET Standard 1.0, then it won't include this.

The higher the version number, the more types and members it includes, but the harder it is to implement. Different individual stacks or platforms within the .NET ecosystem will support different levels of the .NET Standard. They're all striving to have as high of a version number as they can, but there's a lot to implement. New platforms in particular will take time to come online.

As of the time of publishing this book, there are 7 levels of the .NET Standard, comprising version 1.0, 1.1, 1.2, etc., up to 1.6. Version 2.0 is nearing completion. More versions in the future will inevitably come as well.

What this means for you, as a C# programmer, is that you can use more or less of the .NET Standard by choosing a .NET Standard version. The lower the number, the more broadly distributable your code will be. The higher the number, the more things you'll have available to you, but the narrower your distribution will be. Chapter 46 will discuss how to make your own libraries target the different versions of the .NET Standard Library.

The .NET Framework

We now move up to the top layer in the .NET Platform architecture diagram presented at the beginning of this chapter and discuss the different stacks and app models in more detail.

Our starting point is the stack that is the .NET Framework: the oldest, biggest, and most widely used stack of them all.

The .NET Framework itself includes quite a bit of additional code for you to leverage that isn't included in the .NET Standard. (.NET Standard 2.0 should cover much of this though, and as other stacks implement .NET Standard 2.0, they'll be mostly caught up.) This additional code is only available if you limit yourself to targeting just the .NET Framework. For example, if you're targeting .NET Core or Xamarin, you won't be able to use this additional code. (That goes in reverse for .NET Core or Xamarin specific things.)

The Base Class Library

Long before the .NET Standard was defined, the .NET Framework existed, and had the Base Class Library (BCL). You can think of this as the .NET Standard Library before there was a need for there to be any standardization at all. (Remember that the .NET Standard Library is a recent development, driven by the need for cross-platform libraries due to the rise of additional stacks like .NET Core and Xamarin.)

There have been many versions of the .NET Framework and its Base Class Library over the years. As of the time of publishing this book, the highest version number available is 4.6.2, released in late 2016. You will continue to see new versions of the .NET Framework come out in the future.

The Base Class Library is the .NET Framework stack's implementation of the .NET Standard, but because it actually pre-dates the .NET Standard (by well over a decade) it has a weird relationship to it. The .NET Standard is actually trying to catch up to the things currently included in the Base Class Library. This is in stark contrast to the other implementations of the .NET Standard Library, which are working to catch up to the .NET Standard.

The .NET Framework version 4.6.2 implements the .NET Standard 1.6. But it also contains a whole lot of additional reusable code as well. (Much more in line with the upcoming .NET Standard 2.0.) Earlier versions of the .NET Framework cover lower versions of the .NET Standard. For example, version 4.6.1 implements the .NET Standard 1.5 (along with a pile of other unique things). Version 4.6.0 implements .NET Standard 1.4 (plus unique things).

The fact that the .NET Framework's BCL contains things above and beyond the .NET Standard means you can also make your code target specific versions of the .NET Framework. This allows you to take advantage of the extra content in the BCL, but at the cost of losing portability to other stacks.

The Framework Class Library

Closely related to the Base Class Library, the Framework Class Library (FCL) is the total set of all reusable code that ships as a part of the .NET Framework. It includes the entirety of the Base Class Library (including everything in the .NET Standard Library and more) as well as the libraries for the various app models that exist in the .NET Framework stack, such as WPF and ASP.NET.

In some contexts, people use this term interchangeably with the Base Class Library to generally refer to reusable .NET Framework code, though the two names are technically different.

.NET Core

The .NET Core is the second stack that we'll look at here. This is a comparatively recent stack that is aimed at reaching macOS and Linux. Development on .NET Core was started in 2014, with version 1.0 coming out in June 2016, and 1.1 being released in November 2016. .NET Core is in heavy active development, so you should expect more updates to this.

The .NET Core stack supports the .NET Standard Library, and meets .NET Standard 1.6 at the time of publishing this book. Future versions should support .NET Standard 2.0 when it becomes available.

Contrasted with the .NET Framework stack, .NET Core doesn't have nearly as many unique APIs beyond the .NET Standard Library. (And beyond the app models it supports.)

Xamarin

The final stack that we'll discuss is the Xamarin stack, which targets mobile devices like iOS and Android.

This is a stack is built on the open-source Mono project, which is an open-source implementation of the .NET Framework. The Xamarin stack is designed primarily for mobile devices, especially for iOS and Android. This stack, as well as Mono itself, has largely been implemented by the company Xamarin, which was bought out by Microsoft in February of 2016, and is now a subsidiary of Microsoft.

This change has made Xamarin now a part of Visual Studio, which means that Xamarin development is now just a part of your Visual Studio license. If you're using Visual Studio Community, you get it for free. If you've paid for Visual Studio Professional or Visual Studio Enterprise, it is included there as well.

The Xamarin platform supports .NET Standard 1.5, and will support .NET Standard 2.0 in the future.

App Models

The .NET Platform supports a wide variety of app models. An *app model* is an additional library for creating a specific type of application. In addition to additional reusable code, app models tend to also provide additional infrastructure, such as security and deployment models as well.

While the .NET Standard Library contains code that is useful for all types of applications, the code contained in a specific app model is usually only relevant for a single specific type of application. Stated differently, while the .NET Standard Library is worth learning no matter what kind of work you're doing in C#, there's little value in learning the details of any specific app model besides the ones you are actually putting to use.

This book doesn't cover any of the app models in any great depth with the exception of console apps, which probably doesn't truly count as an app model. There are two reasons for this. First is just the sheer scope of the different app models. You could produce long tomes for each individual app model. (You don't have to look far to find books about WPF that are 1500+ pages long, and that assume you already know how to program in C#.) This book just simply can't do justice to any of the app models, much less *all* of the app models.

The second reason is that app models are compartmentalized. This book is intended to be useful for all C# programmers. You will probably eventually go on and learn about at least one app model in depth later on, but you almost certainly won't go learn all of the app models. For any specific app model, the majority of C# programmers will never need to use it.

GUI App Models: WinForms, WPF, and UWP

The .NET ecosystem supports a number of GUI applications (GUI being a "Graphical User Interface" with buttons, checkboxes, list boxes, etc.). The oldest of these is Windows Forms (WinForms) and was introduced in the very early days of .NET. Windows Forms is now in maintenance mode, meaning bug fixes are still being performed on it, but no new features are currently expected for Windows Forms.

Windows Presentation Foundation (WPF) is a newer GUI app model that is somewhat more complicated than WinForms, but significantly more powerful and flexible. Generally speaking, WPF (or UWP) is preferred to Windows Forms for new UI development.

The Universal Windows Platform (UWP) is a third GUI app model. It has a lot in common with WPF (most of the same controls and the same XAML markup language). UWP is perhaps not quite as powerful as WPF, but is designed to be able to target a wide variety of platforms (hence the "universal" part of its name) including Windows desktops, laptops, tablets, phones, the Xbox One, Internet of Things devices, and HoloLens. If you know you only need to target Windows PCs, then WPF might be a better choice for you. If you know you want to reach these other platforms, then UWP makes more sense.

Windows Forms and WPF are only available in the .NET Framework stack. UWP works in the .NET Framework as well as with .NET Core.

ASP.NET and ASP.NET Core

If you are making a web application with C#, then ASP.NET is probably the app model to look at. The ASP.NET app model is a part of the .NET Framework stack, but ASP.NET Core is an alternative implementation that runs on the .NET Core stack. The two have some small differences, but are currently becoming more aligned, rather than different.

ASP.NET allows you to do web development with C# on the backend, and JavaScript, HTML, and CSS on the frontend.

iOS and Android App Models

The Xamarin stack supports iOS and Android app models. These allow you to make C# code that runs on these devices. The Xamarin stack itself contains quite a bit of code beyond the .NET Standard Library that is Xamarin specific. This is done to reduce the amount of iOS or Android specific stuff in your mobile apps. But Xamarin's app models do allow for and support features unique to just Android and just iOS for making these specific app types.

Visual Studio Components and Project Types

The last item we should talk about here is a brief discussion on how to begin actually making applications using the different stacks or the different app models. This book doesn't get into the details of these different app models. But I do want to point out that in order to utilize them, you will need to get them installed (re-running the installer and look for the stack or app model in the list of components to install) and then create a project of the right type to begin working with a particular app model.

Installing every single stack and every single app model will take up a lot of space. If you've got the space, you can install everything. Otherwise, it makes more sense to just install the workflows and components that you are actually using.

Getting the Most from Visual Studio

In a Nutshell
- Outlines the windows that are visible in Visual Studio.
- You can exclude files that you do not want in a project without deleting them.
- You can show line numbers in your source code, which helps in debugging.
- Describes how to use IntelliSense.
- Outlines some basic refactoring techniques.
- Points out some useful and interesting keyboard shortcuts.

Visual Studio is a very sophisticated program. It is impossible to fit everything that is worth knowing about Visual Studio into a single chapter in a book. Like many other topics that we've talked about, you could write books about this. In this chapter, we'll cover some of the most important and most useful features of Visual Studio. There is a lot more to learn beyond what I describe in this and the next few chapters, but these things will get you started.

Windows

The Visual Studio user interface is essentially composed of a collection of windows or views that allow you to interact with your code in different ways. Each window has its own specific task, and there are lots of windows to choose from.

The Code Window

The main code window, where you have been typing in all of your code for all of your projects, is the most important window. This window has a lot of settings that you can customize, which I'll outline in the section below, about the Options Dialog.

```
Program.cs  ☐ ✕
C# CreatingClasses              ▾  ⁺C CreatingClasses.Program      ▾  ⁺C Main(string[] args)            ▾
    1 ⍟ ☐using System.Collections.Generic;
    2    using System.Linq;
    3    using System.Text;
    4    using System.Threading.Tasks;
    5
    6   ☐namespace CreatingClasses
    7    {
    8   ☐    class Program
    9        {
   10   ☐        static void Main(string[] args)
   11            {
   12            }
   13        }
   14    }
   15
   16
   17
   18
100 %  ▾
```

While this window is pretty straightforward, I want to point out that at the top of the window, just under the tabs to select which file to view, there are some drop down boxes that you can use to quickly jump to a specific type or member of a type in the current file. The middle drop down box lets you jump to a specific type within the file (you'll usually only have one) and the right one lets you jump to a member of the type, like a method or instance variable.

Speaking of jumping to a type or member, there are a few keyboard shortcuts that are well worth knowing here, as you work on code. If you select something and press **F12**, you'll automatically jump to where that thing is defined. If that happens to be in another file, that file will be opened.

Going the other way, if you press **Shift + F12**, Visual Studio will find all of the places in the code where the current selection is used. This works for any type, method, variable, or nearly anything else. These two shortcuts are convenient for quickly navigating through your code.

The Solution Explorer

This shows a high level view of how your solution and projects are organized. The Code Window and the Solution Explorer are the two most commonly used windows.

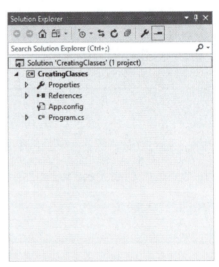

At the top of the Solution Explorer, you will see an item for your entire solution. A solution can contain multiple projects, but by default, when you create a new project you will get a solution with one project, and both will have the same name. You can always add more projects to a solution if you need.

Under each project, you'll see a Properties node, which you can use to modify a variety of properties about your project.

You'll also see that each project has its own References node, which you can use to manage the other projects or DLLs that the project needs access to. (This is described in detail in Chapter 46.)

Your code is typically organized into namespaces, which are usually placed in separate folders under your project, and each new type that you create is usually in its own .cs file.

The Properties Window

You can right-click on any item in the Solution Explorer and choose Properties to view properties of that file, project, solution, etc. Doing so will open up the Properties window.

The Properties window shows you various properties about what you have selected. As you select different things, the properties window will update to reflect the current selection.

This window becomes even more useful as you start to build GUI applications, because you'll be able to use a designer to lay out your user interface, and by selecting buttons, checkboxes, or other UI controls, you'll be able to modify various properties and settings that those items have.

The Error List

The Error List shows you the problems that occurred when you last compiled your program, making it easy to track down the problems and fix them.

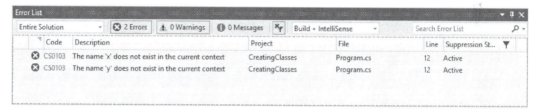

You can double click on any item in the list, and the Code Window will open up to the place where the problem occurred in your code. You can show or hide all errors, warnings, or messages at the top by clicking on the appropriate button.

Other Windows

Visual Studio has many other windows as well. To see what other views you can access, look for them under the View menu. Even the windows that are described above can be opened from here.

The Options Dialog

Visual Studio has tons of settings that you can modify. There are far too many to try to cover here, other than a few of the most popular ones. To get to these settings, on the menu, click on **Tools > Options**, which will bring up the Options Dialog. Like many other programs, these settings are organized into various pages, and the pages are organized by category in the tree on the left. Selecting different items in the tree will present different options to configure.

Including and Excluding Files

Sometimes you have a file that is not being used in your project. You may want to remove it from your project so that you don't keep seeing it in your Solution Explorer. One option is to simply delete the file (right-click on it and choose **Delete**) but sometimes, you don't actually want to delete the file, just stop it from being included in your solution.

To exclude a file from your project, simply right-click and choose **Exclude From Project**. When you do this, the file will disappear from your Solution Explorer, but it is not permanently deleted.

You can also add a file back in to your solution. This is also helpful if you create a file outside of Visual Studio and save it in your project directory. To do this, right click on your project (not the solution at the very top) and choose **Add > Existing Item...**. Browse to find the file you want to add and press Add. The file will now be included in your project.

Showing Line Numbers

Being able to see line numbers is very important. A lot of times, when something goes wrong, the error message will tell you what file and line number the problem occurred on, but if you have to manually count every line to get down to line 937, that information would be pretty useless.

Visual Studio has a way to turn on the display of line numbers. To do this, on the menu, choose **Tools > Options**. This opens the Options dialog box:

In the panel on the left, click on the node that is under **Text Editor > C#**. When you click on this, the panel on the right will show several options. At the bottom under Settings, check the box that says "Line numbers." Once you have done this, you will see line numbers on the left side of your code:

```
1    using System.Collections.Generic;
2    using System.Linq;
3    using System.Text;
4    using System.Threading.Tasks;
5
6    namespace CreatingClasses
7    {
8        class Program
9        {
10           static void Main(string[] args)
11           {
12           }
13       }
14   }
15
```

In my opinion, it is unfortunate that showing line numbers isn't the default, but it's not.

IntelliSense

Visual Studio has an incredibly powerful tool called IntelliSense (also called AutoComplete in other programs or IDEs) that makes typing what you want much faster, as well as providing you with quick and easy access to documentation about code that you are using. You have probably seen this by now. It usually pops up when you start typing stuff, like this:

```
class Program
{
    static void Main(string[] args)
    {
        C
    }
}
```

CLSCompliantAttribute
Comparer<>
Comparison<>
ConcurrentExclusiveSchedulerPair
Console
ConsoleApp1
ConsoleCancelEventArgs
ConsoleCancelEventHandler
ConsoleColor

IntelliSense will highlight the item in the list that is most recently used, making it so that you can simply press **<Enter>** to choose it. This means that even if you give a variable a long name, you may only need to type the first few letters and press **<Enter>**. This feature makes it easy to give things descriptive names without needing to worry about how hard it will be to type it all in later.

There are several things that cause IntelliSense to pop up automatically. This includes when you first start typing a word, when you type a "." (the member access operator) or parentheses. You can get IntelliSense to go away by pressing **<Esc>**, and you can bring up IntelliSense whenever you want it by pressing **<Ctrl> + <Space>**.

IntelliSense also shows you the comments that have been provided for any type or its members. This includes your own comments, so it is very helpful to write XML documentation comments for your code as we discussed in Chapter 15.

Basic Refactoring

Refactoring is the process of changing the way code is organized without changing how it functions. The idea with refactoring is to make it so that your code is better organized and cleaner, making it easier to add new features in the future. There are books written on the best way to refactor code, but it is worth pointing out that Visual Studio provides a small set of refactoring tools.

If you really want refactoring power, you should consider a Visual Studio add-on called ReSharper (http://www.jetbrains.com/resharper/). It's not cheap, but provides a massive amount of refactoring support among many other useful features.

Visual Studio has a few basic refactoring tools that are worth pointing out though. For starters, if you have something that you want to rename, rather than manually typing the new name everywhere, simply select it in the Code Window, right-click, and choose **Rename** (F2). Also, if you have a block of code that you want to pull out into its own method, you can select the code, right-click, and choose **Quick Actions**, then **Extract Method**.

Keyboard Shortcuts

Before finishing up here, there are several keyboard shortcuts that are worth pointing out.

- **F5:** Compile and run your program in debug mode.
- **Ctrl + F5:** Compile and run your program in release mode.
- **Ctrl + Shift + B:** Compile your project without attempting to run it.
- **Ctrl + Space:** Bring up IntelliSense.
- **Ctrl + . :** Show Quick Actions.
- **Ctrl + G:** Go to a specific line number.
- **Ctrl +]:** Go to the matching other curly brace (**{** or **}**).

- **F12:** Go to the declaration of a variable, method or class.
- **Shift + F12:** Locates all places where something is referenced, throughout the project.
- **Ctrl + R then Ctrl + R:** Rename an element of code.
- **Ctrl + R then Ctrl + M:** Extract selected code into its own method.
- **Ctrl + -:** Move back to the last place you were at.
- **Ctrl + Shift + -:** Move forward to the place you were at before moving back.
- **Ctrl + F:** Find in the current document.
- **Ctrl + Shift + F:** Find in the entire solution.
- **Ctrl + H:** Find and replace in the current document.
- **Ctrl + Shift + H:** Find and replace in the entire solution.

Dependencies and Multiple Projects

In a Nutshell
- A project can reference other projects that you have made, DLLs, or other parts of the .NET Platform. This gives you access to large piles of previously created code.
- You can add DLL references directly to a project.
- You can inter-link multiple projects within a single solution together.
- NuGet is a powerful and convenient way to reference 3rd party reusable packages of code.

Most of the projects that we've done in this book have been relatively small. All of the code can live together in a single place, and you don't intend on reusing any of it elsewhere. Furthermore, we haven't really done many things that require using code beyond your own, or the things that just come as a part of the .NET Standard Library. But that's not going to last forever.

Your source code is placed into various projects, which show up in the Solution Explorer in Visual Studio. Once compiled, all source code in a single project is placed together into a single compiled file called an *assembly* or sometimes called a *package*. These assemblies will either take the form of an EXE file (if the code has a defined entry/start point) or a DLL file (if it has no entry point, and is just meant for reuse).

Most of our code in this book will compile to an EXE file, but it is possible to organize reusable pieces into separate projects that compile to a DLL instead.

Perhaps more importantly, other people have *already* packaged up chunks of reusable code for you to reuse. You can use these libraries in your own projects so that you don't have to redo their work yourself.

When you write code that utilizes some other library, your code is said to "depend on" the other code. Or you could say that the other code is a *dependency* of your code.

This chapter will focus on how you can add dependencies to your own projects, including stuff that you've created in the past, as well as things others have created. We'll first talk about how to set up your project to reference other existing code. This comes in several different flavors:

1. Adding a reference to a plain DLL, including one of the .NET Platform DLLs.
2. Adding a reference to a NuGet package, which is the preferred way to package code for reuse, and the preferred way to reference this existing code (rather than directly referencing a DLL that you downloaded from the Internet or something).

You can also split a solution into multiple projects. This allows you group related code together into high-level sections. When you do this, you can reuse chunks of your code in other programs you make. This chapter will discuss how to add separate projects to your solution and then cross-reference them.

Adding DLL References

The starting point for adding any reference is the project's References node in the Solution Explorer:

Each project in your solution will contain a **References** node. You can expand this to see what your project is currently referencing. (There are a number of things that are referenced by default for each different project template.)

This node is the starting point for adding any type of reference to your project. Once something has been referenced, you will be able to start using it in your code.

To add a reference to a DLL, right-click on this **References** node and choose **Add Reference....** This will open a dialog window that will allow you to locate the DLL you are interested in adding as a dependency:

On the left side, you can pick from a number of categories of ways to add a reference. For example, if there is a library that you want to add that is a part of the .NET Platform itself, you can click on

Assemblies > Framework. This will display a list of .NET Platform components, which you can then check to add as a dependency for your project.

If you want to add a reference to a DLL that you have on your file system, you can hit the **Browse** button at the bottom of the dialog and hunt it down. Once you've chosen the dependency, you can click the **OK** button to close the dialog. If it was added correctly, the dependency will now show up under the **References** node in the Solution Explorer as a new item.

NuGet Packages

While the last section described how to add a reference to any DLL on your file system, this is typically not the preferred way to handle this in the .NET world. The better approach is to use NuGet packages instead.

The Dependency Management Problem

Copying around individual DLLs can create a lot of headaches for you. This is especially so when the DLLs you want to use have their own dependencies that they rely on. Your one single dependency might need 17 other DLLs in order to function. Or perhaps it only needs one, but that one has a dependency on one other thing, which has a dependency on one other thing, which has a dependency on one other thing. The dependency tree can be very wide, very deep, or both.

It gets worse when versions are added to the mix. When something is dependent on version 1.7.3 of another package, but you can only find 1.8.0.

This particular problem is lovingly called "dependency hell" or "DLL hell" by those who have faced it.

The NuGet Package Manager

To help solve this problem, many systems and frameworks utilize a tool called a package manager. A package manager is designed to work through these types of issues for you by arranging dependencies into packages with supporting metadata for it.

The package manager most commonly used by the .NET Platform is called NuGet. (It's a play on words! Like the candy confection nougat! Get it?). NuGet itself is a whole collection of tools, but the primary points of interest are a command line tool and a Visual Studio extension that ships with Visual Studio.

Most NuGet packages contain only a single DLL, though they aren't limited to that. A NuGet package could contain multiple DLLs, tools for the NuGet command line itself to run, random additional files that get added to a project, etc. But in general, most NuGet packages you might use will just be a single DLL.

NuGet has a ton of third party libraries that you can use in your program. If you think somebody else might have already made some code to do some particular task, it's always worth a quick search through the available NuGet packages to see if there isn't already something that you could reuse without having to write your own. The search can be done in Visual Studio itself (the next section) or on **nuget.org**.

Adding Dependencies with NuGet

In this section, I'll walk you through how to add a NuGet package to your project as a dependency.

Our discussion here could use any NuGet package, but I've chosen to walk through this with the System.ValueTuple package specifically. This package allows you to use the language-level support for tuples that C# 7 introduced. The details of value tuples are discussed in Chapter 28. Here we will focus solely on getting a NuGet package added as a dependency to your project.

The Visual Studio extension for NuGet makes it easy to add new NuGet packages to a project. Adding NuGet packages is done at the project level, not the solution level. (This is true of all dependencies, not just NuGet.) If multiple projects need the dependency, you will need to add it to each one.

1. In the Solution Explorer, right-click on the project that you want to add the NuGet package for.
2. Select **Manage NuGet Packages** from the context menu. This will open up a new window that will allow you to manage NuGet packages for this solution. (You would also come back here if you want to update or delete a dependency from a project.)

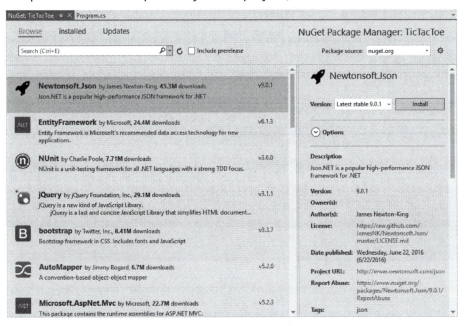

3. At the top of this window, you will see tabs for **Browse**, **Installed**, and **Updates**. Select **Browse**.
4. Search for the name (or keywords) of the NuGet package you are looking for. For our particular example, searching for "ValueTuple" should find the result you need.
5. In some cases, you may want to look for pre-release packages, not just ones that are considered official or final. If this is the case, check the box for it next to the search box.
6. As you begin typing, search results will begin to fill in left side of the panel.
7. Look for the NuGet package that you want to add (**System.ValueType** in our specific case.)

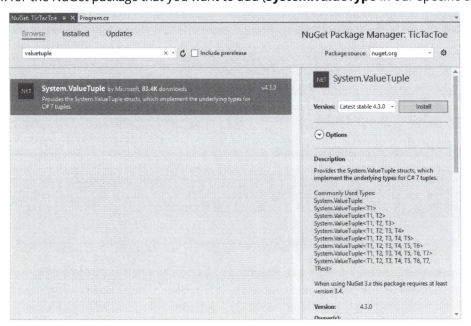

8. The panel on the right side will show you details for the selected NuGet package, including the license it uses (make sure it's compatible with what you want to do with it), a description, and any additional dependencies it may have. If it has other dependencies, NuGet will install those as well.

9. When you're ready to install your dependency into your project, click the **Install** button towards the top on the right side panel, and the dependency will be added to your project.

10. It might ask you to choose between the older packages.config and the newer PackageReference format for storing NuGet packages. Either one works, but the newer PackageReference version is probably better if your whole team is using Visual Studio 2017.

11. At this point, you can close this entire tab unless you want to add more NuGet packages.

12. You can verify that a package has been added by finding it under the References node for your project in the Solution Explorer. If you see it there, it has been added and you can start using it.

Creating and Referencing Multiple Projects

In this section, we'll talk about how to add extra projects to your solution, how to reference one project from another, and how to specify that a project should utilize a specific version of the .NET Framework or a specific level of the .NET Standard (Chapter 44).

Before we get into the specifics of how to do this, it's worth discussing why you would do this. Compiled code is grouped at the project level. Each project produces a single DLL or EXE file, regardless of how many source code files, folders, or namespaces there are in it. Separating code out into different projects, which results in different DLLs, allows you to reuse those pieces separately from the other pieces.

Imagine your company Wayne Enterprises is making a networked game called BatRPG that you want to run on PCs, the Xbox One, and iPhones. You might have quite a few projects for this game. For example:

- WayneEnterprises.BatRPG.Core: Contains the core functionality of the game. The server can run this, but so could a client that isn't playing online.
- WayneEnterprises.BatRPG.PC: The PC client for your game.
- WayneEnterprises.BatRPG.XboxOne: The Xbox One client for your game.
- WayneEnterprises.BatRPG.IPhone: The iPhone client for your game.
- WayneEnterprises.Physics: Contains the physics of your game, but is reusable in other games.
- WayneEnterprises.GUI: A GUI library that you've built yourself for your games.

Obviously this is just an example, not instructions on exactly how to structure your game, but it illustrates the point. This example has pulled out certain pieces that are meant for reuse in many games. And it separates the core of the game out into another project to be reused by many clients and the server.

Adding Additional Projects

Creating another project in your solution is not hard. Go to the Solution Explorer and right-click on the top-level solution node. Select **Add > New Project...** from the context menu. This will bring up the New Project dialog, which is what you also see when you create a brand new project and solution.

You can add any type of project that Visual Studio has. There are no limitations on mixing and matching. So add whatever you feel you need. But generally speaking, you will frequently be adding a separate class library to your solution. Class libraries are meant to be reusable, and not the primary executable.

Depending on what components you have installed in Visual Studio, you will have several different Class Library type projects to choose from. For example, you might have one called "Class Library (.NET Framework)", one called "Class Library (.NET Core)", and one called "Class Library (.NET Standard)". Recall from our discussion in Chapter 44 what these mean.

If you choose the .NET Framework class library, then it will have a dependency itself on the .NET Framework, which makes it not portable to other stacks. The same goes for the .NET Core class library. This is good and bad; it allows you to utilize code that only that stack has available, but comes at the expense of not being able to port it over to the other stacks.

On the other hand, if you choose the .NET Standard class library, you will be able to port the code across any stack, but only be able to utilize stuff in the .NET Standard.

It's not impossible to convert a class library from one thing to another, but it's not exactly trivial either. It's usually best to get it right in the first place.

After choosing the type of the project you want to add to your solution, give it a name at the bottom and click **OK** to add it to the solution. Once you do this, you should see your new project appear in the Solution Explorer, next to the original project.

Referencing Projects

Once your additional project has been added, you will need to reference it in order to use the things it contains in another project. Projects in a solution don't all automatically cross-reference each other. To make a project reference another, we'll return to our original approach for adding references to projects.

Right-click on the project that needs a new dependency and choose **Add > Reference** (or right-click on the References node and choose **Add Reference**). In the groups on the left, choose **Projects > Solution**. This will bring up a list of the other projects in the solution. You can check the box by any project that you need to add as a dependency, and then click **OK** when done.

Once you've done this, you will be able to utilize code in the dependency.

Namespaces and Using Directives

When you start putting code in another project, the namespace will likely be different than your main project. You can change namespaces manually, and you can also change the default namespace for a particular project, but the reality is, you do usually want a separate namespace for different projects. (And for other dependencies like NuGet and directly referencing a DLL, you won't even have the option of manually changing namespaces.)

As you start working with multiple projects, you will want to add in **using** directives for the namespaces that are contained in the library you're referencing. Chapter 27 covers this in detail.

If you want to change the default namespace for a new project, you can do so on the project's property page. This is accessible by right-clicking on the project and choosing **Properties**. On the **Application** tab, there is a box labeled **Default namespace** which you can change to whatever you want it to be.

Specifying API Levels

When you make a class library, you choose whether it is a .NET Standard class library, a .NET Framework class library, a .NET Core class library, etc.

But each of these stacks have different version numbers. You have the ability to choose which version or level you want your project to be.

This is especially important if your project is a .NET Standard class library, because the level directly determines how broadly distributable the library is. (The lower it is, the more broadly distributable it is. But the higher it is, the more classes and other types are available to your own code to utilize.)

Whether you are targeting the .NET Standard or one of the specific stacks, you can choose the API level by going to the project's properties (right-click on the project and choose **Properties**) and on the **Application** tab, look for the drop down labeled **Target framework**. For a .NET Standard class library, you will see the various .NET Standard versions: 1.0, 1.1, etc. For a .NET Framework class library, you will instead see versions of the .NET Framework (4.5, 4.5.1, 4.5,2, 4.6.2, etc.).

For a class library that is intended to be reused by other people, you will probably want to prefer the lowest value you can, without giving up useful classes that you want to leverage. This allows more people to be able to reuse it. (Don't just jump immediately to the highest level just because it is there.)

47

Handling Common Compiler Errors

In a Nutshell
- Outlines common compiler errors, what causes them, and how to fix them.
- Compiler errors are shown in the Error List window.
- If you don't know what a compiler error means, take the time to understand what it is telling you, fix what errors you do understand, and go to the web for help if all else fails.

As you are writing code, you're bound to write some that just doesn't compile. When this happens, C# will point out the problems that came up so you can fix them. There are hundreds of different types of errors, each with a variety of possible causes, so we clearly can't cover everything here (or anywhere). But it is worth taking some time to look at the most common errors. Additionally, we'll take a look at a few general guidelines for fixing these compiler errors.

Understanding Compiler Errors

When you compile your code before you run it, the compiler will need to work its way through your code and try to make sense of it, before it can turn it into IL code. If you made a mistake in your code, the compiler will notice the error and report it. This is called a *compiler error*, or a *compile-time error*.

Fortunately, this type of problem is relatively easy to solve. The compiler can tell you exactly what went wrong, and can often even point out how you might be able to fix it.

Compiler errors are shown to you in the Error List, which I described in Chapter 45. The Error List can be opened at any time by choosing **View > Error List** from the main menu.

Compiler Warnings

Instead of an error, sometimes you'll get a more minor problem called a warning. But warnings can sometimes be more dangerous than an error.

Errors mean that the compiler was completely unable to make sense of what you wrote, so it didn't finish compiling. When you get a warning, it means is that the compiler noticed something odd, but it still found a way to compile your source code. Sometimes, warnings are harmless. A lot of times they come up because you're only halfway done with a piece of code, and so things are naturally a little out of place.

But in general, a warning is an indication of a genuine problem in your code. But because the compiler still produces an executable program to run, it makes you think you can sneak by it. But if the compiler is pointing it out, it is almost always a real problem, and will eventually bite you, just at run-time instead of compile time.

Because of this problem, it is best to always try to treat compiler warnings as errors, and eliminate them as soon as you can. Don't let dozens (or hundreds) of warnings pile up. Fixing warnings up front will save you a great deal of trouble down the road.

Common Compiler Errors

We'll now take some time to look through some of the most common compiler errors, see what they mean, and look at how to fix them. Of course, we won't be able to cover *all* errors, so when we're through, I'll give you some basic principles for fixing other errors that we haven't been able to discuss.

"The name 'x' doesn't exist in the current context"

Sometimes, you'll get an error that says that a variable name doesn't exist in a particular context, meaning it either can't find the name anywhere, or if it can find it, it's in a different place, making it unusable in the spot it is currently at. One common time that this comes up is if you accidentally misspell a variable name. If so, that's an easy fix.

If it's not a spelling problem, then what this usually means is that you forgot to declare your variable. You'll see this if you do something like this:

```
static void Main(string[] args)
{
    int b = x + 7;
}
```

You've used the variable **x** without ever declaring it. This can be fixed by simply declare it first:

```
static void Main(string[] args)
{
    int x = 3;
    int b = x + 7;
}
```

There are times when you may think you've already declared a variable. In fact, you can even *see* the declaration! This is where that "in the current context" part comes into play. You may have declared it, but not in the context that you're using it.

This gets right down to the heart of variable scope, which I described in Chapter 18. If you're sure the variable has been declared and you're still getting this error, you'll want to make sure that the variable in question is still in scope at the place that you're trying to use it. This may mean moving the variable in question to a bigger scope.

One example in particular that I think is worth looking at is one where you have a variable that is declared at block scope, but you try to use it after the block (but still within the method) like this:

```
static void Main(string[] args)
{
    for(int index = 0; index < 10; index++)
```

```
    {
        // ...
    }

    index = 10; // Can't use this here. It has block scope, and doesn't exist after the loop.
}
```

Here, the variable **index** can't be used beyond the scope of the **for** loop. If you want to use this variable outside of the loop, you also need to declare it outside of the loop:

```
static void Main(string[] args)
{
    int index;

    for(index = 0; index < 10; index++)
    {
        // ...
    }

    index = 10; // You can use it here, now.
}
```

") expected", "} expected", or "; expected"

It is very common to see errors that say a parenthesis, closing curly brace, or semicolon is expected.

Interestingly, the solution isn't always to add **)**, **}**, or **;** at the spot that the compiler is complaining about. (Sometimes, but not always.) It just means that the compiler was unable to figure out where the end of a statement or block was.

In fact, the compiler sometimes thinks the error is in a location that is very different from where the problem actually lies! This is because the compiler only realizes there's a problem when it eventually runs into a place where it no longer makes sense to still think you're in the same block or statement.

It's kind of like driving down the road and missing your turn, only to discover the error ten minutes later when you see you're leaving the city limits. You don't know when you missed the turn specifically, just that at some point along the line, you went too far. That's exactly what the compiler does, and so you potentially get the error much later than when it actually occurred.

Take this code, for instance:

```
namespace Example
{
    class Program
    {
        static void Main(string[] args)
        {
            for(int index = 0; index < 10; index++)
            {
                // missing curly brace here...
        }
    }
} // error shows up here...
```

We're missing our closing curly brace for the **for** loop, which is pretty obvious when we've formatted the code this way. But the compiler doesn't care about whitespace, so it tries to match the next curly brace it sees with the end of the **for** loop, the one after that with the end of the **Main** method, and the last one for the end of the **Program** class. But then it reaches the end of the file, and it knows it should have come across one more curly brace. Adding the right missing curly brace, bracket, parenthesis, or semicolon will fix this problem, though sometimes you need to study your code a bit to find out where you went wrong.

It is also worth pointing out that sometimes, missing a single parenthesis, semicolon, or curly brace will cause a whole pile of errors to show up in the Errors List, because the compiler can't figure out where things begin and end. Simply fixing the one problem will often fix lots of errors.

Cannot convert type 'x' to 'y'

There's a category of data type conversion errors that you're bound to see at some point or another. This can come in one of several flavors, like these, below:

- Cannot implicitly convert type 'x' to 'y'.
- Cannot convert type 'x' to 'y'.
- Cannot implicitly convert type 'x' to 'y'. An explicit conversion exists (are you missing a cast?)

What this error means is that you are trying to take one type of data and turn it into another, and the compiler doesn't know what to do with it. If you fit in the category of that third error, and you are sure you want to change from one type to another, it is an easy solution. Just put in a cast to the correct type:

```
int a = 4;
short b = (short)a; // The cast tells the compiler you know what's happening here.
```

Whenever you're required to use an explicit cast, it means there's the potential to lose data, so you really should be sure of the explicit cast before doing it.

On the other hand, if you're running into one of the other errors, it means the C# compiler doesn't know of any way to get from the type you have to the type you want. If your intention was truly to convert between types, there are usually easy ways around that. In most cases, you can simply write a method that will convert from one type to another, passing in one type as a parameter, and returning the converted result from it.

Other times this means you made an entirely different mistake in your code. If you weren't intending to convert from one type to another, then this error means there was something else wrong here. For example, it may just mean you didn't finish typing all of the code you needed. For instance, if you have a **Point** class, with **X** and **Y** properties, casting is probably not what you wanted in this case:

```
Point p = new Point(4, 3);
int x = p;    // Fails because the compiler has no clue how to convert Point to int.
```

Instead, you want to just change your code to get the **X** property of the point:

```
Point p = new Point(4, 3);
int x = p.X;
```

So the true error may not be that the compiler can't convert from one type to another, but that you accidentally forgot a part of the code that left the compiler thinking you were trying to convert types.

"not all code paths return a value"

If you see an error that says something along the lines of **[Namespace].[Type]. MethodName(): not all code paths return a value**, it simply means that it is possible for the program to go through your code in a way that reaches the end of the method without ever returning anything.

The code below is perhaps overly simple, but it gets to the heart of what's going on:

```
public int DoSomething(int a)
{
    if (a < 10)
        return 0;
}
```

The method is supposed to return an **int**. If the value of **a** is less than 10, a value is returned (0). But if **a** is 10 or higher, it skips that **return** statement and gets to the end of the method without returning anything.

To solve this problem, you need to analyze your code to find what paths through your code are failing to return a value, and add it in. One possible way to fix the problem from the code above is this:

```
public int DoSomething(int a)
{
    if (a < 10)
        return 0;

    return a;
}
```

"The type or namespace name 'x' could not be found"

As soon as you start trying to use someone else's code or code in other projects that you've created, or even just putting things in different folders or namespaces, you're going to run into this error.

You'll see this error with something like this:

```
using System;
using System.Collections.Generic;
using System.Linq;
using System.Text;
using System.Threading.Tasks;

namespace Example
{
    class Program
    {
        static void Main(string[] args)
        {
            MissingClass c = new MissingClass(); // Error here
        }
    }
}
```

This means is that the compiler is running into a type name (**MissingClass**, in this case) that it can't find.

It's possible that you just misspelled something. Easy fix.

It is also possible that it is spelled correctly, and that the problem is a little deeper. When you get this error, you'll see that it also says "(are you missing a using directive or an assembly reference?)". The compiler is pointing you at the two most common causes of this problem.

It is either a missing **using** directive or a missing assembly/DLL reference. To tell the two apart, think about where the code is that you are trying to refer to. Is it something you wrote? Something in the project that you're currently working on? If so, then it is probably just missing a **using** directive. The details about what's going on with missing **using** directives and how to fix them are covered in Chapter 27, but in short, all you need to do is figure out what namespace the missing type is in and add a new **using** directive at the top of your file:

```
using System;
using System.Collections.Generic;
using System.Linq;
using System.Text;
using System.Threading.Tasks;
using BlackHole.CodeEatingGravity; // Add the appropriate namespace here

namespace Example
{
```

```
class Program
{
    static void Main(string[] args)
    {
        MissingClass c = new MissingClass();
    }
}
}
```

If you don't think the compiler knows where the code is because it is in a different project, DLL, or library that you haven't told it about, you'll need to add a reference to the missing assembly, which is discussed in Chapter 46. Even after you've added a reference to the project, you'll also need to add in a **using** directive to access the type in most cases.

"No overload for method 'X' takes N arguments"

If you see this error, it means that you're not calling a method with the correct number of arguments. Keep in mind that a method could be overloaded, meaning that there are multiple methods with the same name. You'll want to make sure you get the one you want. Double-check to see what parameters are needed for the method you are trying to call.

In some cases, you may also see this error if you've got parentheses in the wrong spot or if they're missing, so if you think you've supplied the right number of parameters, double-check your parentheses.

"The best overloaded method match for 'X' has some invalid arguments"

Like the previous error, this means you're not calling a method correctly. Unlike the previous error, this one means that you've got the right *number* of parameters, but they aren't the right *types*. Go back and check that the types of all of your parameters match.

Sometimes, to fix this problem, all you need to do is add in a cast to the correct type.

General Tips for Handling Errors

We can't cover all possible compiler errors here. There are just too many of them. Microsoft lists over 800 different compiler errors that could come up! And that doesn't even begin to look at the many root causes and possible fixes for those problems.

One of the key parts of making software is knowing how to find and fix your own problems. Think about it; you're making software that no one else has ever made before! That's cool, but that means you're going to run into problems that no one else has ran into before. So it is critical that you know how to deal with any and every error that comes up in your code.

So in this section, I'll outline a few guiding principles that should keep you going, even when you have no clue how to fix the problem.

Ensure that You Understand What the Error Says

Look at the error message. Does each word in the error make sense, or is there something there that you don't understand? Do you understand each of the phrases in the error? For instance, take the following error message:

```
Access modifiers are not allowed on static constructors
```

When you see this, stop and think: do you know what an access modifier is? (If not, see Chapter 18) Do you know what a static constructor is? (Also Chapter 18.) Once you know what all of the pieces mean, the solution is often pretty straightforward as well. This error is saying you need to remove the **public** keyword from this:

```
public static MyClass()
{
    // initialize the class here...
}
```

Fix the Errors You Do Understand

There are times that a single *actual* problem causes lots of errors to show up in the list. If you get a large pile of errors, look through the list and fix one or two that you understand and recompile. Doing so might get rid of *all* of the errors.

Compiling happens in parts. If the compiler can't get through one part because of an error and you fix it, it is also possible that when the compiler advances to the next part, additional errors are might come up. Because of this, don't worry if by fixing one error, extra errors appear to pop up. The error count shown to you doesn't necessarily show the actual number of problems in your code.

The Error May be in a Different Spot

Just because the error list takes you to a particular location, doesn't mean that the error is actually right there. When you double-click on an error in the Error List, it takes you to the place that it realized there's a problem. That does not necessarily mean that the error is actually on that line. Look around for other things that look out of place if nothing stands out to you.

Use Microsoft's Documentation

It used to be that documentation for programming languages and their code libraries were really cryptic and poorly done. But Microsoft has done an excellent job describing everything that they've done with C# and the .NET Platform. They're an excellent source for figuring out what your error means. Check it out here: **http://msdn.microsoft.com/en-us/library**

Use Other Programmers for Help

Programmers are usually willing to help each other when they run into problems. Programmers, by nature, like finding problems and fixing things. They're usually willing and interested in helping beginners (or pros) to learn, grow, and solve the problems they're running into.

I can't help but recommend **stackoverflow.com** as one of the best sites for overcoming software development problems. It's extremely well put together, and it is designed specifically for programming. In fact, in 99% of all cases, you won't even need to ask a question, because the question has already been asked. (Just be sure to read the FAQs before asking questions, because they sometimes throw a fit when you ask a question that isn't a "good fit.")

If all else fails, there's always the good old-fashioned Google search. Whatever problem you're running into, someone else out there has probably come across a similar problem before, and they've probably posted about it on the Internet. (Another thing programmers love doing.)

Debugging Your Code

In a Nutshell
- Debugging your code allows you to take a detailed look at how your program is executing. This gives you an easy way to see how things are going wrong.
- Describes the difference between running in debug mode and running in release mode.
- Describes how to analyze exceptions that occur while your code is running.
- Shows how to modify your code while you the program is running.
- Describes how to set breakpoints in your code, which suspend the program when reached.
- Outlines how to step through your code to see how things change.

Once you get through any compiler errors like we discussed in the previous chapter, you can run your program. Even though we've gotten rid of all of the compiler errors, sometimes things go horribly wrong while your program is running. This could be a crash, or just that your program isn't doing what you thought it would. These are called runtime errors, and we'll talk about how to deal with them here.

Visual Studio gives us the ability to dig into our program *while it is running* to see what's going on, so that we can fix it. This feature is called *debugging*.

Debugging is extremely powerful and useful when things are going wrong. Your program is unique, so no one else can tell you what's going wrong specifically, but I can show you how to use the debugging tools so that you can find the problems yourself.

Launching Your Program in Debug Mode

The first step is to make sure you start your program in debug mode. When the program is compiled and ran in debug mode (as opposed to "release" mode) it includes a whole lot of extra information in the EXE file. This extra information allows Visual Studio can keep track of what is currently being executed. This extra information slows down your program and makes the EXE file significantly larger, but it makes finding problems in your code much easier. Of course, when you're done constructing your program and you know it is bug free, you can build it in release mode and sell it!

Your program has to be compiled in debug mode or you won't be able to easily debug it.

When we first made a program back in Chapter 3, we discussed how you could start your program by pushing **F5** or **Ctrl + F5**. If you want to be able to debug your program, it will be important to use **F5**, or choose **Debug > Start Debugging...** from the menu. If you start it in release mode (**Ctrl + F5**) you won't be able to debug.

Viewing Exceptions

When your program is running in debug mode, if an unhandled exception is thrown, rather than dying, your program will pause and the computer will switch back to Visual Studio for you to take a look at it. You've probably seen this by now, but below is a screenshot that shows what this looks like:

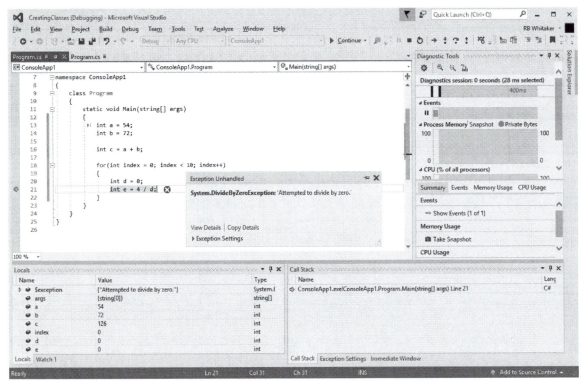

Visual Studio will mark the line that the exception or error occurred at in yellow, and it will bring up the Exception popup. On this popup, you'll see the specific name of the exception that occurred (**DivideByZeroException**, in the screenshot above) along with the text description of the problem. Ideally, this text would have a lot of useful details, but unfortunately, it's often kind of vague.

The dialog also gives you the option to View Details, which will allow you to dig through the actual Exception instance to see what it contains.

When the Exception dialog comes up, Visual Studio is giving you a chance to take a detailed look at the problem so that you can figure out what went wrong and fix it. All of the tools that are available in debug mode are there to assist you in doing this. Sometimes, you'll be able to edit your code while the program is still running, fix the problem, and continue on. In other cases though, once you reach this point, the computer won't be able to continue on and you'll need to restart to check your fixes.

Looking at Local Variable Values

When the program is stopped, you'll have the chance to see what state your program is currently in. One of the most useful features available is that you can hover over any variable and see its current value.

If the value is a composite type like a class or struct, you'll be able to dig down and look at all of the properties and instance variables that it has.

Note that this information is also available in the Locals Window. In many cases, this window will already be open for you, down towards the bottom, where the Error List is. If you don't see it anywhere in Visual Studio, you can open it up by going to **Debug > Windows > Locals**.

The Call Stack

The call stack is one of the most useful tools that you'll have to help you figure out what happened. The call stack tells you what method called the current method. And yes, this is directly related to the stack that we described in Chapter 16.

The problem is sometimes caused, not by the method that you are inside of, but by the calling method instead. You can use the Call Stack Window to see what methods have been called to get you to there.

The Call Stack Window is usually open by default when you're debugging, but it can be opened by choosing **Debug > Windows > Call Stack** from the menu. The Call Stack Window looks like this:

The method that you're currently in is at the top. (**DoSomethingElse**, in this case.) Each line below that shows the method that called it. (**DoSomethingElse** was called by **DoSomething**, which was called by **Main**.) You can click on one of those other lines and Visual Studio will jump to that method, allowing you to see what state your variables are in over there.

Editing Your Code While Debugging

In some cases, you will have the ability to edit your code while it is running and then continue running the program, exactly where you left off, with the edited code. I can't overstate how cool this is. This is like being able to change the tires of a car as you drive it down the road without even stopping.

But this doesn't work in all cases. For starters, if the problem occurred outside of the current method (on the top of the stack trace) you won't be able to edit that method and continue. You can only continue from changes made to the top method on the call stack.

Also, if you're doing a LINQ query when the exception occurs, you won't be able to edit.

In many other cases, you'll be able to edit your code while it's stopped. To edit your code, once the program has stopped and switched back to Visual Studio, just start editing your code like you normally would. If, in the process of editing, you introduce an error that prevents it from compiling, you won't be able to resume until you fix the compiler errors.

There are some types of edits that you won't be able to do. You won't be able to add a new **using** directive. And that means that the normal steps you may do to add a **using** directive just flat out won't show up in the menu. You won't be able to structurally modify a type, so no adding, deleting, renaming methods, properties, instance variables, or class variables. The way the debugger swaps out code just doesn't allow you to swap out structural changes like that, just changes to functionality. If you make a structural change, the change you made will be underlined in blue, and Visual Studio will tell you it needs to recompile and restart to allow the changes to take effect.

Breakpoints

Up until now, we've only about debugging code after your program runs into a problem. But you'll of course want to be able to occasionally analyze running code *before* there's a crash.

Whenever you want, you can set a breakpoint on a particular line of code in Visual Studio. A breakpoint is a way to mark a line of code so that when the program reaches that line during execution, the program will halt, allowing you to take a look at the program's current state.

To set a breakpoint, you simply locate the line you want to set the breakpoint at, and on the left side, click in the gray area, marked in the image on the left below:

When you do this, a red circle will appear in the left margin on the line you have selected, and the text on that line will also be marked in red. This looks like the image above on the right side.

You can set as many breakpoints as you want in your program. You can also add and remove breakpoints whenever you want, even if the program is already running. To remove a breakpoint, simply click on the red circle and it will go away.

Whenever your program is stopped at a breakpoint, you can press the Continue button (located on the Standard toolbar, taking the place of the Start button while your program is running) which will leave the breakpoint and continue on until another breakpoint is hit, or until the program ends and closes.

Stepping Through Your Program

While stopping your program in the middle of execution allows you to do everything you could before (looking at local variables, the call stack, etc.) it can do a whole lot more. After all, unlike before, the program hasn't run into a problem. You've stopped it before that happened.

To use these options, while your program is running, find the Debug toolbar among the various toolbars at the top of Visual Studio. The Debug toolbar looks similar to this:

If you don't see it, go to **View > Toolbars > Debug** to open it. This toolbar contains a collection of very useful tools for stepping through your code.

The debug toolbar may look a little different, depending on your settings and the specific version of Visual Studio that you have, but the items on the toolbar that we'll discuss should be available in all of them. If you feel like you're missing something useful, this toolbar (and all other toolbars) can be customized by clicking on the little down arrow at the end of the toolbar and choosing the items you want displayed.

Items on the Debug Toolbar

The first button on the Debug toolbar is the Break All button, represented by a pause icon. While your program is executing, you can press Break All, which will halt execution of your program immediately, and you can see where it's at. The computer runs your program so fast that this isn't useful for fine-grained control. (We'll see a better tool for that in a second.) Instead, this feature is usually more useful to figure out why your program is taking so long to do something. Usually, it is stuck in some infinite loop somewhere, and by hitting the pause button, you can track down where the problem is.

The second button is the Stop Debugging button. This terminates your running program. It is important to remember that as soon as you push this, you'll lose any debugging information you were looking at, so be sure you've got the information you need before hitting it.

The third button is the Restart button. This closes the current execution and starts over from the beginning. This is very convenient for the times that you've made a change and you want to restart to see if the changes are working.

There are three other buttons on the Debug toolbar which make it easy to slowly step through your code. These are the Step Into, Step Over, and Step Out buttons. The first two allow you to advance through your code one line at a time, giving you the ability to study what your code is doing. Step Into and Step Over both advance by one line, but there's a subtle difference between the two. The difference is most obvious when you are on a line of code that calls a method. If you use Step Into, the debugger will jump into the method that you're looking at, and the next line you'll see will be at the start of that method. You can then continue stepping through the code there. If you use Step Over, the debugger will "step over" the method call, running it entirely, and only pausing again when the flow of execution returns back to the current method.

If you are looking at a line of code that doesn't call a method, the two are identical.

On the other hand, if you're in a method and you know you're ready to just move back up to the method that called it, you can use the Step Out button. This will jump forward as many lines as it needs to until it is back up to the calling method.

There are two other tools that you may find handy for debugging as well, though these are buried away in a context menu. If you know you want to skip ahead to another specific line, you can click on the line you want to jump to, right-click, and choose **Run To Cursor**. This causes the program to run without pausing until it hits the line that you indicated. This is like setting a breakpoint on that line temporarily and hitting Continue. This makes it so you don't need to keep pressing the Step Over button repeatedly.

There's one other tool that is very powerful, but can also be a bit dangerous. Use it wisely. I'll point out the pitfalls that come with it in a second. But first, let me show you what the feature is.

At any point when you're debugging, you can right-click on a line elsewhere in the method that you're debugging and choose **Set Next Statement**. This is a very handy feature. To illustrate my point, take a look at the simple example code below, which simulates rolling a six-sided die:

```
public int RollDie(Random random)
{
    return random.Next(6);
}
```

In most cases, this will probably work fine. But if the object passed in for **random** was **null**, you'll get a null reference exception on that line when it tries to generate the number.

If you're debugging, the debugger will halt on that line of code and point out the problem to you. As I said earlier, in some cases, you can make edits to your code and continue. Perhaps you want to fix this by checking to ensure that **random** is not **null** before calling the **Next** method like this:

```
public int RollDie(Random random)
{
    if(random != null)
        return random.Next(6);

    throw new ArgumentNullException(nameof(random));
}
```

But after you've made these edits, if you try to continue executing, you'll still be on that line (now inside of the **if** statement). You could just restart the program, or you could use the Set Next Statement tool by selecting the **if(random != null)** line, then right-click and choose **Set Next Statement**, and then press the Continue button on the Debug toolbar. This will start your program running at the chosen line. Your program will check for **null** like you want, and you'll be able to move forward without needing to restart.

It's an extremely powerful tool, but there's a dark side to it as well. It is incredibly easy to misuse it and put your program in a weird state that it can't get into naturally. Take the code below, for instance:

```
static void Main(string[] args)
{
    int b = 2;

    if (b > 2)
        Console.WriteLine("How can this be?");

    b *= 2;
}
```

In the normal course of execution, we'd never be able to get inside of that **if** block. But, if you run this code and set a breakpoint at the closing curly brace of the method, then use Set Next Statement to move back up to the **if** statement, **b** will be 4, and the code inside of the **if** block will get executed.

It is very easy to accidentally get your program into an inconsistent state like this when you use the Set Next Statement tool, so it is important to keep this in mind as you use the feature. Even if you think you've fixed a problem, you'll still want to rerun the program from scratch again, just to be sure everything is working like it should.

Try It Out!

Debugging Quiz. Answer the following questions to check your understanding. When you're done, check your answers against the ones below. If you missed something, go back and review the section that talks about it.

1. **True/False.** You can easily debug a program that was compiled in release mode.
2. **True/False.** Debug mode creates executables that are larger and slower than release mode.
3. **True/False.** If an exception occurs in debug mode, your program will be suspended, allowing you to debug it, even if you haven't set a breakpoint.
4. **True/False.** In release mode, Visual Studio will stop at breakpoints.
5. **True/False.** In some cases, you can edit your source code while execution is paused and continue with the changes.

Answers: (1) False. **(2)** True. **(3)** True. **(4)** False. **(5)** True.

How Your Project Files are Organized

In a Nutshell

- Your solution structure looks like this:
  Solution Directory
  > **.sln** file: Describes the contents of your solution.
  > **.suo** file: User specific settings for a particular solution.
  > Project Directory (possibly multiple).
  > > **.csproj** file: Describes the contents of a project.
  > > **.csproj.user** file: User specific settings for a project.
  > > Code files and directories, matching various namespaces.
  > > **Properties** folder.
  > > **obj** directory: a staging area for compiling code.
  > > **bin** directory: finalized compiled code.

I once had a professor who hated Visual Studio. He explained that the reason why is because it's making programmers dumb. Students were turning in their assignments and they had no clue what they were even submitting, and they didn't know what to do when things went wrong with their submission.

Visual Studio has a bit of a bad habit of spewing lots of files all over the place. Some of these files are your **.cs** files, which contain your code. Others might be images, DLLs, or other resource files that you have. Those are all OK. But in addition, Visual Studio loves configuration files.

I personally don't think that this is a good reason to hate Visual Studio. In fact, this is evidence that Visual Studio is doing its job. (Though I do wish the contents of these files were simpler and perhaps less tied to the Visual Studio editor itself.) It hides all of the information needed to compile, run, and publish your program, and it does it while juggling flaming swords and singing a rock ballad about doing the Fandango. And the fact that people can get away with not knowing how it works means it's doing its job right.

Still though, I think it is worth digging into a project and seeing how things are organized and what everything is for. In this chapter, we'll take a look at the directory structure that Visual Studio creates and look at what is contained in each of the files we discover there.

> **Try It Out!**
> **Demystifying Project Files.** Follow along with this chapter by opening up any project of yours and digging around until you understand what every file you discover means.

> **In Depth**
> **Version Control.** Throughout this chapter, I'll be pointing out parts of your project's directory structure that should be placed in version control and parts that should not. While a full explanation of version control software is well beyond the scope of this book, it is worth a brief introduction. Version control software is a category of software that serves two primary purposes: the ability to share source code among team members, and the ability to track changes to that code over time, keeping a history of your software's development. SVN, Git, and Mercurial are all popular and free version control systems that you can use. (I'd recommend Git or Mercurial, as they are both "distributed" version control systems.)
>
> The general rule for what goes into version control are that user-specific project files don't belong in version control (everyone should have their own copy) and anything that can be rebuilt from other things (like compiled executable files) should be skipped as well. Everything else can go in your version control system.

Visual Studio's Projects Directory

Visual Studio will place each solution or project you create in its own directory. These project directories are all in the same place by default, though you can pick a different location when you create a project.

By default, these projects are all stored in **[Documents Directory]/Visual Studio 2017/Projects**, where [Documents Directory] is your 'My Documents' or 'Documents' directory.

If you've been putting all of your projects in the default location, you should be able to open that directory and see a folder for each of the projects that you've created. All projects have the same overall directory structure, so once you've figured one out, the others should make sense as well.

The Solution Directory

Solutions vs. Projects

The top level folder corresponds to a solution. Remember that a solution can be thought of as a collection of projects that are all related, and used together to accomplish a specific task.

You may remember that in the past, when you've been ready to start on something new, that you've chosen **File > New Project** from the menu. What you get is actually a new project, created inside of a new solution. In the past, when you've created a project, you've also creating a new solution to contain it.

Inside of the solution folder, you'll find three things. You'll see a **.sln** file, a folder for every project in your solution (only one if you've only got one project in your solution), and you may also see a **.suo** file. If you don't see the **.suo** file, it's probably still there, just hidden. If you don't see it, don't worry too much. It's not too critical that you can see it. It is just important to know that it is there.

The .sln File

The **.sln** file is your solution file. This file is very important. It contains information about what projects are contained in the solution, as well as solution specific settings like build configurations. The **.sln** file contains shared information that everyone will want to keep the same, and it should be included in your version control system if you have one.

The .suo File

The **.suo** file is the solution user options file. It contains various settings for the project that Visual Studio uses. Like I said earlier, it may be a hidden file, so you may not see it. This contains things like what files you had open when you last used the project, so they can get reopened when the project is reopened.

You could delete this file and nothing bad would happen.

Because this file contains user-specific information, this file shouldn't go into version control. Instead, everyone should have their own version of the file.

The Project Directories

In your solution directory, you should find that there is one folder for each project in your solution.

Let me clarify something that has confused many people in the past, including myself. By default, you'll have one project in your solution. This project is named the same thing as your solution. So if you created a new project called **LikeFacebookButBetter**, what you'll be looking at here is a folder called **LikeFacebookButBetter** inside of a folder called **LikeFacebookButBetter**. It can be confusing at first. The key to remember is that the top level one is the solution folder, and the lower level one is the project folder, and they represent two different things.

The Project Directory

Inside of a project directory, you'll see even more files. For starters, you will see a file ending with **.csproj**. You will also likely see another file ending with **.csproj.user**. You should also see a Properties folder. And you'll also probably find a pile of **.cs** files, or other folders than contain **.cs** files and other resources. You may also see a **bin** and an **obj** folder.

The .csproj File

This is one of the more important files that Visual Studio creates. This file essentially defines your project. It identifies what files are included in your project, as well as listing other assemblies, libraries, or other projects that this project uses. This file does for projects what the **.sln** file does for solutions.

Again, if you're using version control, this one belongs in the repository.

The .csproj.user File

This file, like the **.suo** file, contains user-based settings, but for your project instead of the solution. Like the **.suo** file, every user gets their own copy, so it should not go into version control.

The bin and obj Folders

You may or may not see folders called **bin** and **obj**. If you don't see them, open the project and compile it and these folders will appear. These are both used for building and storing executable versions of your projects and solutions (EXE and DLL files).

The difference between the **obj** folder and the **bin** folder is that when the program is compiling, at first it will place stuff in the **obj** directory. The stuff in here is not necessarily complete, and can be thought of as a staging area for the final executable code, which will get put into the **bin** folder. If you're going to hand off the EXE to anyone, or attempt to run the EXE from here, you should go with the one in the **bin** folder, not the one in the **obj** folder.

If you open up either of these directories, you'll likely see a folder in there called **Debug** or **Release**. Dig down further and you'll end up seeing the EXE file (or possibly a DLL file if the project is a class library) along with a random assortment of other files. You'll get a **Debug** or **Release** folder depending on how you've built your program. If you've told it to run in debug mode, you'll see a debug directory. If you've told it to run in release mode, you'll get a release directory.

Both the **obj** and the **bin** directories should be kept out of the version control repository, if you're using it. And if you're submitting an assignment for a class, or handing off your code to another programmer, these directories do not need to be included, because they can be rebuilt. (In fact, doing so is a good idea if you're giving it to someone else who has the capacity to compile it themselves. It reduces the total size of what you're sending and eliminates the executable files, which many email systems block.)

The Properties Folder

The **Properties** folder contains properties and resources that you've added to your project. For a large project, this can be quite large.

At a minimum, you'll probably see an **AssemblyInfo.cs** file in the Properties folder of the project. This file contains information about your project, including versioning information. This file is also quite important, and it is a shared file, so you should put it in version control.

You can open the file and see what it contains, but it is worth pointing out that everything in this file can be edited through Visual Studio by right-clicking on your project in the Solution Explorer and choosing **Properties**, and then on the **Application** tab click on the **Assembly Information...** button, where you can specify the information you want.

Source Files and Everything Else

At this point, we have covered everything except your actual code and other folders and files you may have added directly to your project in Visual Studio. If you look around, you're bound to find a bunch of **.cs** files, which are your C# code. Any directories that we have not discussed are directories that you have made yourself in Visual Studio, and each folder that you see likely represents a different namespace. This is the default behavior, but you can change your namespaces to be something else entirely. I wouldn't recommend doing that though, as it is very handy to have your namespaces match up with the folder structure that the files are in.

Part 6

Wrapping Up

In this final part, we're going to wrap up everything that we've been doing throughout this book, in more ways than one. Part 6 will cover the following:

- Give you several larger *Try It Out!* Problems for you to tackle, to help you be sure you've learned the things you needed to (Chapter 50).
- Discuss where you can go next, now that you've learned C#, including C#-based websites and web applications, desktop applications, and even video games (Chapter 51).

Try It Out!

In a Nutshell
- The best way to learn how to program is to do it. No amount of reading will make you learn.
- This chapter contains a variety of interesting problems that you can try out to help you learn. If you don't find any of these problems interesting, feel free to pick your own.
- This includes the following challenge problems to try out:
  Message from Julius Caesar: Encryption using the Caesar cipher.
  Reverse It!: A simple game that gives you practice with arrays and indexing.
  Pig Dice: A simple multiplayer game involving randomness and dice.
  Connect Four: Remake the classic game of Connect Four.
  Conway's Game of Life: An exploration of a zero-player game.

The best way to learn to program is by programming. That's why I've included the *Try It Out!* sections throughout this book. It's also the reason why there's homework.

In this chapter, I'm going to present a collection of tasks that will hopefully be interesting to you, and give you something to work on that will help you be sure that you've learned the things you needed to.

Of course, if you've got your own project that you want to work on, you should go for that instead. As interesting as these projects are, if you've got one of your own in mind, that's a better choice for you to work on. You'll get the best results and learn more from something that you've personally chosen and are excited about.

I should point out that these challenges are not necessarily easy. They're like the final boss of a video game, where you'll use all of the tools and tricks that you've learned throughout the game. It may take hours of coding, maybe even spread out over days or weeks, to get the right answer. (Or not.) Many of these are based on the projects that I did while learning to program that I thought were the most interesting, fun, or memorable.

Each of these problems can be kept to a very simple minimum, or you can add extra features to make them more detailed and more interesting. Feel free to keep going with an idea until you get tired of it.

By the way, like all of the other *Try It Out!* problems throughout this book, I'm posting answers to each of these on the book's website and you can go there to see a complete working solution. See **http://www.starboundsoftware.com/books/c-sharp/try-it-out/**

Message from Julius Caesar

Encryption is the process of taking data and turning it into a form that is no longer readable. This keeps the information protected, so that people who aren't supposed to read it can't. Of course, the person who is *supposed* to read it needs to be able to decrypt it and recover the message.

When encryption is performed, the algorithm used to encrypt stuff usually uses a special value called a key to perform the encryption. If a person has the key, they can usually decrypt the message as well.

The Caesar cipher is one of the simplest encryption schemes, and it is possibly something you used to send coded messages to friends when you were younger. It is an encryption method that supposedly Julius Caesar occasionally used when he wrote personal letters.

The basic idea is that for every letter in your message, you shift it down the alphabet by a certain number of letters. The amount you shift is the key for the algorithm. If you are using a key of 3, A would become D, B would become E, etc. Once you get to the end of the alphabet, it wraps back around, so Z would be C.

For example, with a key of 4, the message below is encrypted to look like this:

```
Plain text: EXPERIENCE IS THE TEACHER OF ALL THINGS
Encrypted:  IBTIVMIRGI MW XLI XIEGLIV SJ EPP XLMRKW
```

Write a program that will read in a message from a file (or from the user) and encrypt it, writing out the encrypted message to another file (or back to the console window). Don't overwrite the original file. Ideally, your program will ask for the name of a file to read, and a key (a number) to use in the encryption.

Anything besides a letter (punctuation, numbers, etc.) can either be skipped or passed along to the output without encrypting it.

Also create code that will do the reverse, decrypting a message given a decryption key.

If you want an extra challenge, try this. The Caesar cipher is really easy to crack. In fact, it is so basic that it provides little real protection in modern usage. Much more sophisticated algorithms are used now to encrypt data. To prove the point that the Caesar cipher can be cracked, we're going to try a "brute force" approach to crack the following code:

```
UX LNKX MH WKBGD RHNK HOTEMBGX
```

With the Caesar cipher, there are only 26 possible keys. Try each one, one at a time, until the decrypted message makes sense. The simple approach for this is to have a human (you) visually inspect the decrypted message to see if it makes sense. While it is more work, it is possible to have the computer figure out if the message has been decrypted by using a dictionary file (containing all or the words in the English language) and checking to see if all or most of the decrypted words are in it. A high percentage typically indicates a successful decryption.

Reverse It!

In this task, we're going to make a simple array-based game. We'll start by making an array that can hold 9 integer values, and we'll randomly put the numbers 1 through 9 in the array. Make sure you don't have any duplicates. Each number should appear exactly once.

The array will be printed out to the user like this:

```
5 3 8 6 4 1 2 9 7
```

Allow the user to type in a number 1 through 9. Whatever the user types in, we're going to reverse that many numbers, starting at the front. So from the randomized starting position shown above, if the user typed in the number 4, we'd end up reversing the first four numbers, and the resulting array would be:

```
6 8 3 5 4 1 2 9 7
```

The player can keep typing in numbers, and you will keep reversing the indicated part of the array until the array is in ascending order:

```
1 2 3 4 5 6 7 8 9
```

When this happens, the player has won the game, and the game ends. Before closing, show the number of moves it took the player to win.

Can you figure out an optimal strategy for this game? It is possible to win this game in no more than 16 moves, regardless of the starting arrangement.

Pig Dice

In the game of Pig Dice, players take turns rolling two six-sided dice. On a player's turn, they can roll the dice repeatedly until they either choose to hold (stop rolling) or roll a 1. As long as the player keeps rolling without getting a 1 on either die, the numbers on the dice are added to the player's turn score. At any point, a player can hold, which takes their turn score and permanently adds it to their overall score. If they roll a 1 on either die, they lose all of the points they had collected in their turn score, nothing extra is added to their overall score, and it becomes the next player's turn. When a player's overall score reaches 100, the game ends, and they have won.

To illustrate, let's say Alice (player #1) rolls a 3 and a 4. That gives her a turn score of 7. Alice chooses to roll again, getting a 2 and a 6. That gives her an extra 8 points, for a total turn score of 15 points. Alice then chooses to hold, and her current turn score is added to her overall score. Alice now has 15 points overall, and it is now Wally's turn (player #2). Wally rolls a 2 and a 3, giving him a turn score of 5. Wally chooses to roll again, but this time, gets a 1 and a 5. Since he rolled a 1, he loses his turn score (which was 5) leaving him still with 0 overall points, and it becomes Alice's turn again.

Our goal is to create a computer version of Pig Dice. On each player's turn, allow them choose to either hold or roll. When a player rolls, generate two random numbers between 1 and 6, and program the game to follow the logic described above. Between rolls, display the current status of the game, showing both player's overall score, and the current player's turn score. When a player gets up to 100, end the game and show who won. For an extra challenge, make the game playable by three or more players.

Connect Four

The game of Connect Four is a simple and interesting game played on a grid with six rows and seven columns. Two players take turns taking tokens and dropping them into one of the seven columns, where it falls down to either the bottom if the column is currently empty or to the top of the pile if it is not.

The goal of the game is to get four of your tokens in a row, up and down, side to side, or diagonally, before the other player does. Your task is to make a game where two alternating players can select a row (numbers 1 through 7) to place their token on and play the game of Connect Four.

There are a few pieces to this game that might be challenging. One will be writing the code to take a row and add a token to the top of it. On a related note, it may also be tricky to ensure that if a row is full, the game doesn't crash, but instead, notifies the player that the move they wanted to make was an illegal move, and give them another chance. Also, after each move, you'll want to check to see if that move caused the player to win.

By the way, while many games like this tend to look great with a GUI the game can still easily be made to look good by printing out the right things to the console window, as shown below:

```
. . . . . . .
. . . . . . .
. . . . . . .
. . . o . . .
. . . x . . .
. x . x o . .
```

Conway's Game of Life

In 1970, British mathematician John Conway invented a "zero player" game called the Game of Life. This is not the Milton Bradley board game called LIFE, but rather a mathematical game that simulates life.

The game is "played" on a grid, where the game advances in generations, with cells becoming alive or dying, based on certain conditions.

If a particular cell in the grid is empty (dead) then it can come to life if the following conditions are met:

- Exactly three neighbors that are alive.

If a particular cell in the grid is alive, then it dies in the following generation if any of the following are true:

- It has more than three neighbors. (Overcrowding.)
- It has 0 or 1 neighbors (Loneliness, I guess...)

For example, look at the little grid below:

In the next generation (round) the top cell that is alive will die, because it only has one neighbor. The one in the middle will stay alive, because it has two neighbors. The one on the bottom will also die, because it only has one neighbor. Additionally, just off to the left and the right of the three "alive" cells, there is a cell with three neighbors, both of which will become alive. After one generation, this will turn into the following:

Interestingly, if you look at this and follow it through to the next generation, you'll end up back where you were initially. This happens to create what is called an oscillator in the Game of Life. It will keep repeating forever.

These simple rules for determining when cells in the grid come to life or die create very interesting results that are much more interesting to see than to read in a book.

Because of this, we're going to take upon ourselves the challenge of creating the Game of Life as a computer program.

There are several key parts to this. For one, we will need to store the current grid. There are lots of ways to do this, but one might be a two dimensional array of **bool**s.

We will also need a method for drawing our current grid. Again, it would look nice with a fancy GUI, but we can get away without needing to go beyond the console. If you're sticking with the console, your best bet is to use 40 columns in your grid, and have each cell take up two characters (an "X" or "." depending on if it is alive or dead, plus an empty space) because on the console, characters are twice as tall as they are wide, and there are 80 columns by default. Using 40 columns with two characters per column gives you nice, square shaped cells. About 12 rows fit on the console window by default, but you can go up to 20 rows pretty easily and then drag the console window to resize it and make it taller.

Additionally, you will need to create a mechanism to update the grid using the rules described earlier for cell death and generation. It is important to work with a copy for the next generation or updating one cell will mess up the calculation in another cell.

Finally, you'll need to put it all together in a loop that repeats forever, updating the grid, drawing the grid, and waiting for a while in between, to animate the game and let you see what's happening. For this, you might find the **Thread.Sleep** method useful. We talked about this method in Chapter 39. You will need to add a **using** directive to the top of your code for **System.Threading** to get access to this, as discussed in Chapter 27. You might also find it useful to be able to clear the console window before you draw the new grid, using **Console.Clear();**

The most interesting part about the Game of Life is being able to start with different starting configurations and watching it evolve. To make this happen, make it so you can load in initial configurations in a file. The specifics of the file format are up to you, but one possibility is to make them look like this:

```
. . . . . . . . . . . . . . . . . . . . . . . . . . . . . . . . . . . . . . . .
. . . . . . . . . . . . . . . . . . . . . . . . . . . . . . . . . . . . . . . .
. . . . . . . . . . . . . . . . . . . . . . . . . . . . . . . . . . . . . . . .
. . . . . . . . . . . . . . . . . . . . . . . . . . . . . . . . . . . . . . . .
. . . . . . . . . . . . . . . . . . . . . . . . . . . . . . . . . . . . . . . .
. . . . . . . . . . . . . . . . . . . . . . . . . . . . . . . . . . . . . . . .
. . . . . . . . . . . . . . . . . . . . . . . . . . . . . . . . . . . . . . . .
. . . . . . . . . . . . . . . . . . X . . . . . . . . . . . . . . . . . . . . .
. . . . . . . . . . . . . . . . . . X . . . . . . . . . . . . . . . . . . . . .
. . . . . . . . . . . . . . . . . . X . . . . . . . . . . . . . . . . . . . . .
. . . . . . . . . . . . . . . . . . . . . . . . . . . . . . . . . . . . . . . .
. . . . . . . . . . . . . . . . . . . . . . . . . . . . . . . . . . . . . . . .
. . . . . . . . . . . . . . . . . . . . . . . . . . . . . . . . . . . . . . . .
. . . . . . . . . . . . . . . . . . . X . . . . . . . . . . . . . . . . . . . .
. . . . . . . . . . . . . . . . . . . . X . . . . . . . . . . . . . . . . . . .
. . . . . . . . . . . . . . . . . . . XXX . . . . . . . . . . . . . . . . . . .
. . . . . . . . . . . . . . . . . . . . . . . . . . . . . . . . . . . . . . . .
. . . . . . . . . . . . . . . . . . . . . . . . . . . . . . . . . . . . . . . .
. . . . . . . . . . . . . . . . . . . . . . . . . . . . . . . . . . . . . . . .
. . . . . . . . . . . . . . . . . . . . . . . . . . . . . . . . . . . . . . . .
```

You can create these files in any text editor, like Notepad.

When your game is up and running, try loading the following patterns and watch what happens:

Blinker: Glider: Pulsar:

Diehard:

There are tons of interesting patterns that show up in the Game of Life, so when you get your game working, experiment with various configurations, and look online and see what other interesting patterns exist.

What's Next?

In a Nutshell
- Your next step might include learning app models like WPF, UWP, ASP.NET, or Xamarin development, or maybe even game development tools like MonoGame or Unity.
- It is also worth your time to learn software engineering, as well as data structures and algorithms if you haven't already done so while learning another language.
- The best way to learn C# is to program in C#.
- You can get more information from MSDN, Stack Overflow, and this book's website.

As you finish learning everything this book has to offer, you may be wondering where you're supposed to go next. And it really depends. I want to take a little time and give you some pointers on where your next steps might take you.

Other Frameworks and Libraries

If you've gone through this book sequentially, you already know all of the basic things you need to know about the C# language. Much of the rest of your learning in the C# world will be more about playing with the different .NET stacks and app models, and learning useful libraries for building different types of programs. Below are some of the most useful ones.

Desktop Application Development

The .NET Platform includes a number of GUI desktop application frameworks, including Windows Forms, Windows Presentation Foundation (WPF) and the Universal Windows Platform (UWP). We talked about each of these different app models in depth in Chapter 44. Windows Forms is in maintenance mode, but is still quite popular. WPF is the most mature and powerful option, but is only supported on Windows desktops, laptops, and tablets. UWP is the newcomer, and supports a broader set of hardware platforms.

Web Development with ASP.NET

If you're more interested in making web-based software, ASP.NET is the next step. ASP.NET allows you to run C# code on the server side, in place of alternatives like PHP, Java (Java Server Pages), Python, or Perl. ASP.NET is supported in both the .NET Framework stack, as well as the .NET Core stack (ASP.NET Core).

Mobile Development with Xamarin

The Xamarin stack is built with a focus on mobile app development. If you want to make phone apps with your C# skills, this is the destination for you. Xamarin is designed to make it easy to make Android and iPhone apps, and allows you to make code that is largely sharable between the two versions.

Game Development

I've saved my personal favorite for last. C# is a very popular choice for game development, and you have a wide variety of options for doing so in C#. While none of the following are "official" app models from Microsoft, they all have large communities around to help you.

Unity is a powerful game engine that can target almost any platform you can dream up, and is a popular choice for C# programmers. Unity isn't the only full-fledged game engine on the market though. Xenko and Delta Engine are another two. And the list goes on....

MonoGame is another excellent option. It's not quite a game engine like Unity is. It doesn't provide as much framework for you, but at the same time, it gives you greater control into how you approach things. You don't have to do things "the Unity way" but can craft your own way. MonoGame can also target pretty much every platform out there, and is an open source port of Microsoft's old XNA framework.

If you want to get *really* close to the metal, there's always the option of using SharpDX, a very thin wrapper around DirectX, or one of a number of C# OpenGL bindings to make your game.

C# has no shortage of game development options.

Other Topics

In addition to learning other frameworks, it is also important to learn things like the best way to structure your code, or various algorithms and data structures to use. If you are studying C#, and you're getting started with formal education at a university, you'll learn things like this in a software engineering class, or a data structures and algorithms class. Most universities require you to take these classes, but if it is optional, don't skip it. It will be worth it.

If you aren't at a university, you'll still want to learn these things. Take the time to learn software engineering practices. It will be worth the time. You'll know much better how to organize code into classes and how to make classes interact effectively. Doing it the right way makes it easier to make changes as your plans for your program change and grow over time. You'll learn things like how to best test your code to make sure it is bug free and working like it should. And you'll get a basic idea of how to manage your projects to finish things on time.

Also, be sure to learn about data structures and algorithms for things like sorting and searching. Making software is a whole lot more than knowing how to write lines of code. And to make truly awesome software, you'll need to understand how things will work at a higher level, and how to get the fastest results, or when to maximize for speed vs. memory usage.

Of course, if you've been programming for a while, especially if you had formal education in things like this, then you probably already know most of this stuff. Generally speaking, the best practices that you learned in other languages will carry over to the C# world.

Make Some Programs

By far the best thing you can do now is make some programs. Nothing will launch you into the C# world faster than making a real program. Or several. You'll quickly see what topics you didn't fully grasp (and you can then go back and learn them in depth) or you'll figure out what extra little pieces you'll need to learn still, and you'll be able to quickly hunt down those things on the Internet.

Of course, that's why I've included the *Try It Out!* chapter (Chapter 50), to give you some interesting problems to work through while testing your knowledge of various aspects of programming.

The programs you choose to work on do not need to be limited to the basics of C# that we've discussed in this book. If you want to try tackling something that also uses WPF, ASP.NET, UWP, or game development, go for it. There's no better way to learn to program than by programming.

Where Do I Go to Get Help?

The best part about making software is that you're creating something that has never been done before. It is as much a creative process as it is mathematical or analytical. You're not just manufacturing the exact same thing over and over again. As such, you're going to run into problems that have never been encountered before. You're bound to run into trouble sooner or later, and so before we part ways, I want to point out to you a few meaningful things you can do to solve your problems when they come up.

First, obviously, a Google search will go a very long way. That's always a great place to start.

Second, make sure you fully understand what the code you are working with is doing. If you're having trouble with a particular class that someone else created (like the **List** class, for instance) and a method isn't doing what you thought it should, take the time to make sure you understand every piece that you're working with. I've learned over the years, that if you're running into a problem with code you don't quite understand, you're not likely to figure the whole problem out until you've figured out how to use all of the individual pieces that are in play. Learn what each parameter in a method does. Learn what exceptions it might throw. Figure out what all of its properties do. Once you truly understand the things you're working on, usually the problem solves itself.

Along those lines, the Microsoft Developer Network (MSDN) has tons of details about every type that the .NET Standard Library has, with plenty of examples of how to use them. It's a great resource if you're trying to learn how a specific type works. (http://msdn.microsoft.com/library/)

I probably don't need to say this, but if you're stuck, and you've got team members that might know the answer, it is always a good idea to talk to them.

If you don't have team members who can answer the question, Stack Overflow is one of the best sites out there for programming Q&A. (http://stackoverflow.com/) Stack Overflow covers everything from the basics up to some very specific, very detailed questions, and you're likely to get good, intelligent responses from people. Just be sure to do a Google search to make sure the answer isn't obvious, and search on the site as well, to make sure the question hasn't already been asked. (Because it probably has.)

Parting Words

You've learned the basics of C#, and ready to take the world by storm. There's so much that you can do with your new knowledge of C#. It truly is an exciting time!

From one programmer to another, I want to wish you the best of luck with the amazing software that you will create!

Glossary

.NET Core
A newer.NET Platform stack that is designed to be more cross-platform friendly, and primarily targets Linux and macOS. (Chapter 44.)

.NET Framework
The oldest (original) most popular, and most complete stack within the .NET Platform. Aimed primarily at Windows computers. This term is frequently used to refer to the entire .NET ecosystem, though this book makes a distinction between these two, and calls the entire system the .NET Platform. (Chapters 1 and 44.)

.NET Platform
The platform C# is built for and utilizes. The term used in this book to describe the entire .NET ecosystem, including all stacks (the .NET Framework, .NET Core, Xamarin, etc.), all app models, the entire .NET Standard Library, the compilers, CLR runtime, CIL language, and other tools. This is also sometimes called simply ".NET" and also frequently called the .NET Framework, though this book makes a distinction between the two. (Chapters 1 and 44.)

.NET Standard
A specification that defines a vast collection of reusable types (classes, interfaces, structs, enums, etc.) that exist across multiple stacks within the .NET Platform. The .NET Standard allows you to reuse code and produce code that can be migrated from stack to stack. It allows you to write code that runs on the original .NET Framework, as well as .NET Core, Xamarin, and other stacks. The .NET standard has many different levels or version numbers. Higher version numbers include more reusable material. Lower version numbers allow you to target more diverse stacks. (Chapters 1 and 44.)

.NET Standard Library
See .NET Standard.

Abstract Class
A class that you cannot create instances of. Instead, you can only create instances of derived classes. The abstract class is allowed to define any number of members, both concrete (implemented) and abstract (unimplemented). Derived classes must provide an implementation for any abstract members defined by the abstract base class before you can create instances of the type. (Chapter 23.)

Abstract Method
A method declaration that does not provide an implementation or body. Abstract methods can only be defined in abstract classes. Derived classes that are not abstract must provide an implementation of the method. (Chapter 23.)

Accessibility Level
Types and members are given different levels that they can be accessed from, ranging from being available to anyone who has access to the code, down to only being accessible from within the type they are defined in. More restrictive accessibility levels make something less vulnerable to tampering, while less restrictive levels allow more people to utilize the code to get things done. It is important to point out that this is a mechanism provided by the C# language to make programmer's lives easier, but it is not a way to prevent hacking, as there are still ways to get access

to the code. Types and type members can be given an access modifier, which specifies what accessibility level it has. The **private** accessibility level is the most restrictive, and means the code can only be used within the type defining it, **protected** can be used within the type defining it and any derived types, **internal** indicates it can be used anywhere within the assembly that defines it, and **public** indicates it can be used by anyone who has access to the code. Additionally, the combination of **protected internal** can be used to indicate that it can be used within the defining type, a derived type, or within the same assembly. (Chapters 18 and 22.)

Accessibility Modifier
See *Accessibility Level*.

Anonymous Method
A special type of method where no name is ever supplied for it. Instead, a delegate is used, and the method body is supplied inline. Because of their nature, anonymous methods cannot be reused in multiple locations. Lambda expressions largely supersede anonymous methods and should usually be used instead. (Chapter 37.)

Anonymous Type
A type (specifically a class) that does not have a formal type name and is created by using the new keyword with a list of properties. E.g., **new { A = 1, B = 2 }**. The properties of an anonymous type are read-only. (Chapter 19.)

App Model
A component of the .NET Platform that allows you to easily create a specific type of application. This primarily consists of a library of reusable code for creating applications of that type, but also contains additional infrastructure such as a deployment model or a security model. (Chapter 44.)

Argument
See *parameter*.

Array
A collection of multiple values of the same type, placed together in a list-like structure. (Chapter 13.)

ASP.NET
An app model for building web-based applications using the .NET Framework or .NET Core stacks. This book does not cover ASP.NET in depth. (Chapter 44.)

Assembly
Represents a single block of redistributable code, used for deployment, security, and versioning. An assembly comes in two forms: a process assembly, in the form of an EXE file, and a library assembly, in the form of a DLL file. An EXE file contains a starting point for an application, while a DLL contains reusable code without a specified starting point. See also *project* and *solution*. (Chapter 44.)

Assembly Language
A very low level programming language where each instruction corresponds directly to an equivalent instruction in machine or binary code. Assembly languages can be thought of as a human readable form of binary. (Chapter 44.)

Assignment
The process of placing a value in a specific variable. (Chapter 5.)

Associativity
See *Operator Associativity*.

Asynchronous Programming
The process of taking a potentially long running task and pulling it out of the main flow of execution, having it run on a separate thread at its own pace. This relies heavily on threading. (Chapters 39 and 40.)

Attribute
A feature of C# that allows you to give additional meta information about a type or member. This information can be used by the compiler, other tools that analyze or process the code, or at run-time. You can create custom attributes by creating a new type derived from the **Attribute** class. Attributes are applied to a type or member by using the name and optional parameters for the attribute in square brackets immediately above the type or member's declaration. (Chapter 43.)

Base Class
In inheritance, a base class is the one that is being derived from. The members of the base class are included in the derived type. A base class is also frequently called a superclass or a parent class. A class can be a base class, and a derived class simultaneously. See also *inheritance*, *derived class*, and *sealed class*. (Chapter 22.)

Base Class Library
The .NET Standard Library implementation that is a part of the .NET Framework. It is the most expansive and most widely use implementation of the Standard Library (Chapter 44.)

BCL
See *Base Class Library*.

Binary Code

The executable instructions that computers work with to do things. All programs are built out of binary code. (Chapters 1 and 44.)

Binary Instructions

See *Binary Code*.

Binary Literal

A literal that specifies an integer in binary, and is preceded by the marker "0b": 0b00101001. (Chapter 6.)

Binary Operator

An operator that works on two operands or values. Many of the most common operators are binary, such as addition and subtraction. (Chapter 7.)

Bit Field

The practice of storing a collection of logical (Boolean) values together in another type (such as **int** or **byte**) where each bit represents a single logical value. Enumerations can also be used as a bit field by applying the **Flags** attribute. When working with a bit field, the bitwise operators can be used to modify the individual logical values contained in the bit field. (Chapter 43.)

Bitwise Operator

One of several operators that operate on the individual bits of a value, as opposed to treating the bits as a single value with semantic meaning. Bitwise operators include bitwise logical operators, which perform operations like **and**, **or**, **not**, and **xor** (exclusive or) on two bits in the same location of two different values. It also includes bit shift operators, which slide the bits of a value to the left or right. In C#, the extra spots are filled with the value 0. (Chapter 43.)

Boolean

Pertaining to truth values. In programming, a Boolean value can only take on the value of true or false. Boolean types are a fundamental part of decision making in programming. (Chapter 6.)

Built-In Type

One of a handful of types that the C# compiler knows a lot about, and provides special shortcuts for to make working with them easier. These types have their own keywords, such as **int**, **string**, or **bool**. (Chapter 6.)

Breakpoint

While debugging, a line of code may be marked with a breakpoint, and when the program reaches that point, the program will pause and switch back to the Visual Studio debugger, allowing you to take a look at the current state of the program. (Chapter 48.)

C++

A powerful all-purpose programming language that C# is largely based on. C++ is generally compiled to executable code, and is not run on a virtual machine. (Chapter 44.)

Casting

See *Typecasting*.

Checked Context

A section of code wherein mathematical overflow will throw an exception instead of wrapping around. An unchecked context is the default. (Chapter 43.)

CIL

See *Common Intermediate Language*.

Class

One of several categories of types that exist in the C# language that can be custom designed. A class defines a set of related data that belongs to a single type or category of objects in the real world, or representation of a concept in the domain model, along with the methods that are used to interact with or modify that data. A class is as a blueprint for objects or instances of the class, defining what they store and what they can do. All classes are reference types. See also *struct*, *type*, and *object*. (Chapter 17.)

CLR

See *Common Language Runtime*.

Code Window

The main window, usually in the center of the screen, which allows you to edit code. The window can show multiple code files tabbed together. Any hidden window can be opened up through the **View** menu, or the **View > Other Windows** menu. (Chapter 45.)

Command Line Arguments

When a program is started, arguments may be provided on the command line of a program, which are passed into the program's main method where it can use them. These parameters are command line arguments. (Chapter 43.)

Comment

Additional text placed within source code that is designed to be read by any humans that are working with the code. The C# compiler ignores comments entirely. (Chapter 4.)

Common Intermediate Language

A special high-level, object-oriented form of assembly code that the CLR is able to execute. It includes instructions for things like type conversion, exceptions, and method calls. (Chapter 44.)

Common Language Runtime

A virtual machine that any .NET language including C# is built to run on. The Common Language Runtime, often called the CLR, converts CIL code that the C# compiler created into binary instructions for the computer to run on the fly. (Chapter 44.)

Compile-Time Constant

See *Constant*.

Compiler

A special program that turns source code into executable machine code. (Chapters 1 and 44.)

Compound Assignment Operator

An operator that combines a normal math operation with assignment, as in **x += 3;** (Chapter 7.)

Conditional Operators

The operators && (*and* operator) and || (*or* operator), which are used to perform checks for multiple conditions. (Chapter 10.)

Constant

A special type of variable that, once set, cannot be modified. Constants come in two variations. Compile-time constants are created when the program is compiled, using the **const** keyword. These are treated as global constants and cannot be changed without recompiling your program. Run-time constants, created with the **readonly** keyword, are variables that cannot be modified once assigned to. However, they can be assigned while the program is running. For instance, a type may have read-only instance variables, allowing instances of the type to be created with different values, but forcing the variables to be immutable. (Chapter 43.)

Constructor

A special type of method that initializes an instance of a type. The role of a constructor is to ensure that the new instance will be initialized to a valid state. Like a method, a constructor's definition may include any number of parameters. A constructor must have the same name as the type and no return type. A type may define multiple constructors. When creating a new instance of a type, a constructor is called, along with the **new** keyword. If a type does not explicitly include a constructor, the C# compiler will automatically generate a default parameterless constructor. (Chapters 17 and 18.)

Contravariance

See *Generic Variance*.

Covariance

See *Generic Variance*.

Critical Section

A block of code that should not be accessed by more than one thread at once. Critical sections are usually blocked off with a mutex to prevent multiple simultaneous thread access. (Chapter 39.)

Curly Braces

The symbols **{** and **}**, used to mark blocks of code. (Chapter 3.)

Debug

The process of working through your code to find and fix problems with the code. (Chapter 48.)

Declaration

The process of creating something, specifying the important information about it. This is typically used to refer to variable declaration, but it is also applied to methods and type definitions. (Chapter 5.)

Decrementing

Subtracting 1 from a variable. See also *Incrementing*. (Chapter 9.)

Delegate

A way to treat methods like objects. A delegate definition identifies a return type and a list of parameter types. A delegate is created in a way that is similar to declaring a variable, and can be assigned "values" that are the names of methods that match the return type and parameter list of the delegate. The delegate can then be called, which will execute whatever method is currently assigned to the delegate and return the result. (Chapter 32.)

Dependency

A separate library (frequently a DLL) or resource that another project references and utilizes. The project is said to "depend on" the referenced library. (Chapter 46.)

Derived Class

In inheritance, the derived class extends or adds on to another class (the base class). All members of the base class, including instance variables, methods, and events also exist in the derived class. Additional new members may also be added in a derived class. In the case of multiple levels of inheritance (not to be confused with multiple inheritance) a class may act as both a base class and a derived class. A derived class is also sometimes called a subclass. See also *base class* and *inheritance*. (Chapter 22.)

Digit Separator

An underscore character ('_') placed between the digits of a numeric literal, used to organize the digits more cleanly, without changing the meaning of the number. E.g., 1_543_220. (Chapter 6.)

Divide and Conquer

The process of taking a large, complicated task and breaking it down into more manageable, smaller pieces. (Chapter 15.)

Division by Zero

An attempt to use a value of 0 on the bottom of a division operation. From a math standpoint, it is meaningless and isn't allowed. In programming, it often results in your program crashing. (Chapter 9.)

DLL

A specific type of assembly that contains no specific entry point but rather a collection of code that can be reused by other applications. See also *assembly* and *EXE*. (Chapter 46.)

Dynamic Object

An object whose members (methods, properties, operators, etc.) are either changeable at run-time or whose members are not known until run-time. A dynamic object should be stored in a variable of type **dynamic**, so that dynamic type checking can be done. (Chapter 41.)

Dynamic Type Checking

The act of checking that members such as methods, properties, operators, etc. that are invoked on an object exist at run-time, instead of earlier at compile time. This is necessary for dynamic objects, which can change their members at run-time or whose members are not known at run-time. This is contrasted with static type checking, which happens at compile time. Most C# objects are checked dynamically type checked, with the exception of variables of type **dynamic**. (Chapter 41.)

E Notation

A way of expressing very large or very small numbers in a modified version of scientific notation (e.g., 1.3×10^{31}) by substituting the multiplication and 10 base with the letter 'E' (e.g., "1.3e31"). In C#, **float**, **double**, and **decimal** can all be expressed with E notation. (Chapter 6.)

Enum

See *Enumeration*.

Error List

A window in Visual Studio that displays a list of compiler errors and warnings. Any hidden window can be opened up through the **View** menu, or the **View > Other Windows** menu. (Chapter 45.)

EXE

A specific type of assembly that contains an entry point which can be started and run by the .NET Platform. See also *assembly* and *DLL*. (Chapter 44.)

Enumeration

A specific listing of the possible values something can take. In C#, enumerations are used to represent a type of data where there is a known, specific, finite set of options to choose from. (Chapter 14.)

Event

A delegate-based mechanism that allow one part of the code to notify others that something specific has occurred. Event handlers are methods which match a particular delegate and they can be attached or removed from the event, allowing it to start or stop receiving notifications from the event. (Chapter 33.)

Exception

An object that encapsulates an error that occurred while executing code. The object is "thrown" or passed up the call stack to the calling method until it is either handled ("caught") or is thrown from the Main method, causing the program to crash. (Chapter 30.)

Explicit

A term frequently used to mean something must be formally stated or written out. The opposite of "implicit." (Chapter 9.)

Extension Method

A special type of static method that appears to be a part of a class but is actually defined outside of it. This allows you to create methods for types that are sealed or that you do not have access to the source code for. (Chapter 36.)

FCL

See *Framework Class Library*.

Field

See *instance variable*.

Fixed Size Array

An array variable that is always the same size, and whose bytes are allocated as a part of the struct it belongs to, instead of elsewhere in the heap. Also called a "fixed size buffer." Used primary for interoperating with non-managed code. (Chapter 42.)

Fixed Statement

A statement that causes a normal reference to be "pinned" in place, barring the garbage collector from moving it temporarily. This is only allowed in an unsafe context, and allowing it to access managed objects. (Chapter 42.)

Floating-Point Type

One of several built-in types that are used for storing real-valued numbers, such as fractional or decimal numbers. (Chapter 6.)

Framework Class Library

A massive collection of reusable code that is a part of the .NET Framework. This includes all of the Base Class Library, plus additional code, including all of the app models in the .NET Framework stack. (Chapter 44.)

Fully Qualified Name

The full name of a type, including the namespace that it belongs in. (Chapter 27.)

Function

A chunk of reusable code that does some specific task. A function is identified by a name, and indicates the inputs provided to the function (parameters) and the values it produces as a result (return values). Nearly all functions in C# are methods (owned by a class) with the exception of local functions. The terms "function" and "method" frequently used interchangeably in C# programming. (Chapter 15.)

Garbage Collection

The process of removing objects on the heap that are no longer accessible. Garbage collection in C# is automated. It makes it so that you do not need to worry as much about memory leaks, and you do not need to manually deallocate memory for your program, in most cases. See also *managed memory*. (Chapter 16.)

Generic Variance

A mechanism for specifying hierarchy-like relationships among generic types. While one class is derived from another, **Generic<Derived>** has no association to **Generic<Base>**. Generic variance allows you to set up rules for how the generic class can be used in hierarchy-like relationships, but is dependent on how the generic type parameter is used inside of the generic class. If a type is only used as an output from the generic type, it can be made covariant, which makes **Generic<Derived>** substitutable for **Generic<Base>**. If a type parameter is only used as input to the generic type, then it can be made contravariant, which makes **Generic<Base>** substitutable for **Generic<Derived>**. If the generic type is used as both input and output, it must remain invariant, and **Generic<Base>** and **Generic<Derived>** will have no substitution relationship. (Chapter 43.)

Generics

A mechanism that allows you to create classes that are type safe, without having to commit to specific types at compile time. Rather than creating something that can work with only a specific type (and then creating a very similar version for other types) and instead of using a very generalized type (like **object**) and casting to and from that to the wanted type, generics can be used to specify that at run-time, a certain specific type will be used, but it is currently unknown, and may be different in different instances. (Chapters 25 and 26.)

Global Namespace

The root level namespace. If your code is not placed in a namespace block, then it will live in the global namespace. In some instances where name conflicts occur, you can reference a name by starting at the global namespace by starting with **global::** followed by the fully qualified name of a namespace or type. (Chapter 43).

Heap

One of two main parts of a program's memory. The heap is unstructured, and any part of the program can access the information on the heap as needed. Because the heap is unstructured, memory allocation and deallocation must be handled carefully. The CLR manages the heap (see managed memory) using garbage collection. See also *stack* and *reference type*. (Chapter 16.)

Hexadecimal

A base-16 numbering scheme, popular in computing because of its ability to represent the contents of a byte using two characters, which uses 16 total digits, instead of the 10 that is used in a normal decimal system. These characters are 0 through 9, then A through F. (Chapter 6.)

Hexadecimal Literal

A literal that specifies an integer in hexadecimal, and is preceded by the marker "0x": 0xac915d6c. (Chapter 6.)

IDE

See *Integrated Development Environment*.

IL

See *Common Intermediate Language*.

Implicit

A term frequently used to mean something happens without needing to be specifically stated. The opposite of "explicit." (Chapter 9.)

Incrementing

Adding 1 to a variable. See also *Decrementing*. (Chapter 9.)

Indexer

An indexer is a part of a type that defines what the indexing operator should do for the type. Indexers can use any number of parameters, and can use any type—they're not just limited to integers. (Chapter 35.)

Inference
See *Type Inference*.

Inheritance
The ability of one class to include all of the members that another class has, and add on additional members. Inheritance is designed to mimic an *is-a relationship*, or an *is-a-special-type-of* relationship—in other words, things where one type is a special type of another. For example, an octagon is a special type of polygon, and so an **Octagon** class may inherit from, or be derived from, a **Polygon** class. C# does not allow for inheritance from more than one base class (multiple inheritance) but a similar effect can be accomplished by implementing multiple interfaces. Inheritance can be many levels deep. Every type in C# is ultimately derived from the **object** type. Note that structs do not support inheritance. (Chapter 22.)

Instance
See *object*.

Interface
A listing of specific members that a type that implements the interface must have. It defines a specific contract that a type needs to present to the outside world. A type may implement multiple interfaces. All members defined in any interface that a type implements must be defined in the type. (Chapter 24.)

Integer Division
A special kind of division, used when working with only integral types, in which any remainder or fractional part of the result is dropped. Using integer division, 7 / 2 is 3. (Chapter 9.)

Integral Type
One of several built-in types that are used for storing integers. (Chapter 6.)

Integrated Development Environment
A program that is built for the purpose of making it easy to create programs. It typically includes a source code editor and a compiler, along with many other features to assist with things like project management, testing, and debugging. (Chapters 1 and 45.)

IntelliSense
A feature of Visual Studio that performs auto-completion of various tasks such as name completion, but also provides a convenient way to view the XML documentation comments of types and their members. IntelliSense is brought up automatically when the dot operator (member access operator) is used, but it can also be brought up any time by using **Ctrl + Space**. (Chapter 45.)

Internal
See *accessibility level*.

Invariance
See *Generic Variance*.

Immutability
A feature of a type (or sometimes, just a member of a type) that prevents it from being modified once it has been created. In order to make changes to an instance, a new instance must be created with the desired changes. Immutability provides certain benefits, including simplicity, automatic thread safety, usable as keys in a dictionary or hash table, and you do not need to make defensive copies when returning them from a method or property. Value types should be made immutable in most cases. Classes should be immutable when possible. (Chapter 21.)

Implicitly Typed Local Variable
Using type inference, a local variable's type does not need to be specified in some cases. Instead, the **var** keyword is used to indicate that type inference should be used. Only local variables can be implicitly typed. It is important to remember that implicitly typed local variables actually do have a specific type (they're not loosely typed) but that type is determined by the compiler instead of the programmer. (Chapter 6.)

Instance Variable
A non-static variable that is declared as a member of a type. As such, it is available throughout the type, and depending on its accessibility level, it may be accessible from outside the type as well. Contrasted with a static class variable, where all instances of the type share the same variable, each instance of the type will have its own variable that functions independently of the variable with the same name in other instances. It is good practice to make sure instance variables are not accessible from outside of the type to adhere to the principle of encapsulation. (Chapters 17 and 18.)

Iterator
A mechanism for visiting or looking at each item in a collection of data. A **foreach** loop can "iterate" over (or loop over) items in any type that provides an iterator. (Chapter 43.)

Jagged Array
An array of arrays, where each array within the main array can be a different length. (Chapter 13.)

Java

A high-level, all-purpose programming language similar to C#. Like C#, it also runs on a virtual machine. (Chapter 1.)

JIT Compiler

See *Just-in-Time Compiler*.

Just-in-Time Compiler

The process of converting IL code to executable code right before it is first needed. The CLR uses Just-in-Time compiling (JIT compiling) as it runs C# code. (Chapter 44.)

Keyword

A special reserved word in a programming language. (Chapter 3.)

Lambda Expression

An anonymous method that is written with a simplified syntax to make it easy to create. Lambda expressions are powerful when used where a delegate is required. If a lambda expression becomes complicated, it is usually better to pull it out into a normal method. (Chapter 37.)

Language Integrated Query

A part of the C# language that allows you to perform queries on collections within your program. These queries involve taking a set of data and then filtering, combining, transforming, grouping, and ordering it to produce the desired result set. Often called LINQ (pronounced "link"). LINQ can be done with a special query syntax or with simple method calls. (Chapter 38.)

Left Associativity

See *Operator Associativity*.

LINQ

See *Language Integrated Query*.

Literal

A direct representation of a value in source code. For example, in the line **int x = 3;** the 3 is an integer literal. The built-in types generally can all be created with a literal, rather than by use of the **new** keyword. (Chapter 6.)

Local Function

A function that is contained directly in another function or method. It is given a name, parameters, and return type, but is only accessible from within the function that contains it. (Chapter 28.)

Local Variable

A variable that is created inside of a method, and is only accessible within that method. Some local variables may have scope smaller than the entire method. A local variable that is declared inside of a loop, **if** statement, or other block will only have block scope, and cannot be used outside of that block. (Chapter 15.)

Loop

To repeat something multiple times. C# has a variety of loops, including the **for**, **while**, **do-while**, and **foreach** loops. (Chapter 12.)

Managed Memory

Rather than requiring you to allocate and deallocate or free memory on the heap, the CLR keeps track of this for you, freeing you to concentrate on other things. Memory that is no longer used is cleaned up by the garbage collector. The CLR also rearranges memory to optimize space. (Chapter 16.)

Member

Anything that can belong to a type, including instance variables, methods, delegates, and events. (Chapter 17.)

Memory Barrier

A hardware instruction that indicates that pending memory reads or writes must complete before passing the memory barrier. Memory barriers are important when multiple threads access the same data in a way that isn't otherwise thread-safe (for example a lock). Access to a specific piece of data can be protected with a memory barrier by using the **volatile** keyword on the variable. (Chapter 43.)

Method

A type of function that is a member of a type (a class, struct, etc.) Nearly all functions in C# are methods, with the exception of nested functions, and the two terms are largely interchangeable. (Chapter 15.)

Method Body

See *method implementation*.

Method Call

Going from one method into another. When a method is called, data may be sent to the method by passing them in as parameters to the method. When a method call is finishing, information may be sent back or "returned" from the method. A method may call itself (recursion). Method calls are kept track of on the stack. As a new method is called, a new frame is placed on the stack. As the flow of execution returns from a method call, the top frame, representing the current method is removed, returning execution back to the calling method. (Chapter 15.)

Method Call Syntax

Contrasted with *query syntax*, method call syntax allows you to perform LINQ queries using normal methods and lambda expressions, rather than the context-dependent keywords. (Chapter 38.)

Method Implementation

The actual code that defines what the method should do. This is enclosed in curly braces right below the method declaration in most cases. A method without an implementation is an abstract method, and can only be made in an abstract class. (Chapter 15.)

Method Signature

The name of the method and types of parameters that a method has. This does not include its return type or the names of the parameters. This is largely what distinguishes one method from another. Two methods in a type cannot share the same method signature. (Chapter 15.)

Mutex

See *Mutual Exclusion.*

Mutual Exclusion

Setting up code so that only one thread can access it at a time. The mechanism that forces this is often called a mutex. (Chapter 39.)

Named Parameter

When passing values into a method, the name of the parameter they go with can be explicitly named, allowing the parameters to be given out of order. (Chapter 28.)

Namespace

A collection of related types, grouped together under a common label. Namespaces often represent broad features of a program, and contain the types that are needed to implement the feature. The types in a namespace are typically placed together in a single folder in the directory structure. (Chapters 3 and 27.)

Name Collision

A situation where two different types use the same name. At compile time, the compiler will be unable to determine which of the two types is supposed to be used. To resolve a name collision, you must either use fully qualified names or an alias to rename one or both of the types involved in the collision. (Chapter 27.)

Name Hiding

When a variable in method or block scope has the same name as an instance variable or static variable, making the instance variable or static variable inaccessible. The instance variable or static variable may still be accessed using the **this** keyword. (Chapter 18.)

NaN

A special value used to represent no value. It stands for "Not a Number." (Chapter 9.)

Nesting

Placing one statement or block of statements inside of another block. (Chapter 10.)

NuGet Package Manager

A tool for making it easy to work with many 3rd party packages and libraries in your code. NuGet is built into Visual Studio. It is the most common tool for working with references to other code libraries. (Chapter 46.)

Null Reference

A special reference that refers to no object at all. (Chapter 16.)

Nullable Type

A mechanism in C# for allowing value types to additionally be assigned **null**, like a reference type. A nullable type is still a value type. A nullable type is simply one that uses the **Nullable<T>** struct, but the C# language allows for a simplified syntax, by using the type, followed by a '?'. For example: **int? a = null;** (Chapter 43.)

Object

Objects are instances of a type (often a class) and represent a specific instance or occurrence of a defined type. This is contrasted with the class (or other type definition) itself, which defines what kinds of data objects of that type will be able to keep track of and the methods that operate on that data. (Chapter 17.)

Object-Oriented Programming

An approach to programming or programming languages where code is packaged into chunks of reusable code that have data and methods that act on that data, bundled together. C# is an object-oriented programming language. (Chapter 17.)

Operator

A calculation or other work that is done by working with one, two, or three operands. Many of the C# operators are based on math operators, such as addition (**+**) or multiplication (*****). (Chapter 7.)

Operator Associativity

The rules that determine how operations of the same precedence are evaluated when used together in a single expression. Left-associative (or left-to-right associative) operators are evaluated starting from the left side. Right-associative (or right-to-left associative) operators are evaluated starting from the right side. For example, in the expression 5 – 3 – 1, the operations are evaluated like (5 –

3) – 1, because subtraction is left-associative. (Operators Chart, page 370 and Chapter 7.)

Operator Overloading

Within a type, providing a definition for what a particular operator (**+**, **-**, *****, **/**, etc.) should do. Not all operators are overloadable. Operators should only be overloaded if there is an intuitive way to use the operator. (Chapter 34.)

Optional Parameter

When a parameter is given a default value, allowing calling methods to not provide a value for the parameter if desired. (Chapter 28.)

Operator Precedence

The rules that determine which operator is evaluated first in an expression where multiple operations are used. Operators with higher precedence will be evaluated before operators with lower precedence. For example, multiplicative operations such as *****, **/**, and **%** will be executed before additive operations, such as **+** and **-**. Operator precedence can be overruled by placing pieces of the expression in parentheses. (Operators Chart, page 370 and Chapter 7.)

Order of Operations

See *Operator Precedence*.

Out-of-Order Execution

For the purposes of optimization, the CPU may run multiple instructions in parallel or in an order different from program order. This is called out-of-order execution. From the perspective of a single thread, all operations will always function as though the operations were executed in order. (Chapter 43.)

Overflow

When the result of an operation exceeds what the data type is capable of representing. In a purely mathematical world, this doesn't happen, but on a computer, since all types have a certain size with set ranges and limits, overflow is when those bounds are surpassed. (Chapter 9.)

Overloading

Providing multiple methods with the same name but different parameter list. Not to be confused with overriding, an overload creates an entirely different method, though usually, the purpose is to do similar things with different inputs or parameters. For overloading operators, see *operator overloading*. (Chapter 15.)

Overriding

Taking a method, property, or indexer in a base class and providing an entirely different implementation of it in a derived class. In C#, in the base class, the method must be either **virtual** or **abstract**, and in the derived class, the method must be marked with **override** in order to override the member. (Chapter 23.)

P/Invoke

See *Platform Invocation Services*.

Package

A set of resources (typically a single DLL file) along with some additional metadata, that makes it easy to reference and leverage a piece of code. In the .NET ecosystem, packages are typically referenced and managed using the NuGet Package Manager. (Chapter 46.)

Parameter

A type of variable that has method scope, meaning it is available from anywhere inside of a method. Unlike other local variables, the value contained in a parameter is determined by the calling method, and may be different for different method calls. (Chapter 15.)

Parent Class

See *base class*.

Parentheses

The symbols **(** and **)**, used for order of operations, the conversion operator, and method calls. (Chapters 7 and 15.)

Parse

The process of taking something and breaking it down into smaller pieces that have individual meaning. Parsing is a common task when reading data in from a file, or from user input. (Chapter 29.)

Partial Class

A class that is defined in multiple files. This can be done to separate a very large class into more manageable pieces, or to separate a class into parts that are maintained by separate things, such as the programmer and a GUI designer tool. (Chapter 22.)

Pattern

A syntactic element that allows for conditional execution of some code. It is composed of four parts. An *input*, which is supplied to the pattern, a *rule* which is applied to the input and is either "matched" (the rule returns **true**) or unmatched, and if matched, an *action* is performed that produces an *output* from the input. Patterns were introduced to C# 7. Patterns can be used in **switch** statements and with the **is** keyword. (Chapter 31.)

Pinning
See *Fixed Statement*.

Platform Invocation Services
A mechanic whereby your C# code can directly invoke unmanaged code that lives in another DLL that your project references. (Chapter 42.)

Pointer
Contrasted with a reference, a pointer is a raw "link" to a memory address. Pointers can only be used in unsafe contexts. C# pointers are similar to pointers in other languages such as C++. Pointers are generally only used when interoperating with code that requires it. Generally speaking, pointers should be avoided in favor of normal reference types. (Chapter 42.)

Polymorphism
In C#, a class may declare a method or property, including optionally providing an implementation for it, which can then be overridden in derived classes in different ways. This means that related types may have the same methods implemented with different behavior. This ability to have the same method that does different things when done by different types is called polymorphism. The term comes from Greek, meaning "many forms," which reflects the fact that these different types can behave differently, or do different things, by simply providing different implementations of the same method. (Chapter 23.)

Public
See *accessibility level*.

Precedence
See *Operator Precedence*.

Preprocessor Directive
Special commands embedded in source code that are actually instructions for the compiler. (Chapter 43.)

Primitive Type
See *Built-In Type*.

Private
See *accessibility level*.

Procedure
See *method*.

Program Order
When referring to out-of-order execution, program order is the order in which statements appear in the source code. For optimization purposes, the CPU may not always execute code in program order, but (assuming a single thread) the effects will always be as though the instructions were executed in program order. See also *Out-of-Order Execution* and *Volatile Fields*. (Chapter 43.)

Project
In Visual Studio, a project represents the source code, resource files, and settings needed to build a single assembly (in the form of an .EXE file or a .DLL file). See also *solution* and *assembly*. (Chapter 45.)

Property
A member that provides a way for the outside world to get or set the value of a private instance variable, providing encapsulation for it. This largely replaces any **GetX** or **SetX** methods, providing simpler syntax, without needing to publicly expose the data. The instance variable that a property sets or returns is called a backing field, though not all properties need a backing field. Properties do not need to provide both a get and a set component, and when they do, they do not need the same accessibility level. Auto-generated properties can be used for very simple properties that require no special logic. (Chapter 19.)

Protected
See *accessibility level*.

Query Expression
A special expression in C# that allows you to make SQL-like queries on data within a C# program. Query expressions are a fundamental part of LINQ. Query expressions are composed of a variety of context-specific keywords and structured into clauses that each manipulate, filter, combine, or rearrange data sets to produce a final set of results for the query (Chapter 38.)

Query Syntax
One of the two flavors of LINQ (contrasted with method call syntax) that uses query expressions to perform queries against data sets. (Chapter 38.)

Rectangular Array
A special form of multi-dimensional arrays where each row has the same number of values. (Chapter 13.)

Recursion
Indicates a method that calls itself. Care must be taken to ensure that eventually, a base case will be reached where the method will not be called again, or you will run out of space on the stack. See also *recursion*. (Chapter 15.)

Refactor
The process of tweaking or modifying source code in a way that doesn't affect the functionality of the program, but improves other metrics of the code such as readability and maintainability. (Chapter 45.)

Reference

A unique identifier for an object on the heap, used to find an object that is located there. This is similar to a pointer, used in other languages, which is a memory address pointing to the object in question. However, a reference is managed, and the actual object may be moved around in memory without affecting the reference. (Chapter 16.)

Reference Semantics

When something has reference semantics, the identity of the object is considered to be the object, rather than the data it contains. When assigned from one variable to another, passed to a method, or returned from a method, while the reference is copied, it results in a reference to the same object or data. This means both variables are ultimately referencing the same data, and making changes to one will affect the other. In C# all reference types have reference semantics. See also *reference type* and *value semantics*. (Chapter 16.)

Reference Type

One of the two main categories of types in C#. Reference types are stored on the heap. A variable that stores a reference type will actually contain a reference to the object's data. Reference types have reference semantics, and as they are passed into a method or returned from a method, a copy of the reference is made. The copy still points to the same object. Modifying the object inside of the method will affect the object that was passed in. Classes are all reference types, as are the **string** and **object** types, as well as arrays. See also *value type*, *pointer type*, and *reference*. (Chapter 16.)

Reflection

The ability of a program to programmatically inspect types and their members. This includes the ability to discover the types that exist in an assembly and the ability to locate methods and call them. Reflection allows you to sidestep many of the rules that the C# language provides (such as no external access to private variables or methods) though performance is slower. (Chapter 43.)

Relational Operators

Operators that determine a relationship between two values, such as equality (**==**), inequality (**!=**), or less than or greater than relationships. (Chapter 10.)

Return

The process of going from one method back to the one that called it. It is also used to describe the process of giving back a value to the method that called it, upon reaching the end of the method. In this sense, it is said to "return a value" from the method. (Chapter 15.)

Right Associativity

See *Operator Associativity*.

Run-Time Constant

See Constant.

Scientific Notation

The representation of very large or very small numbers by expressing them as a "normal" number between 1 and 10, multiplied by a power of ten. E.g., "1.3×10^{31}." In C# code, this is usually expressed through E Notation. (Chapter 6.)

Scope

The part of the code in which a member (especially a variable) or type is accessible. The largest scope for variables is class or file scope, and it is accessible anywhere within the type. Instance variables or class variables have class scope. Method scope is smaller. Anything with method scope is accessible from within the method that it is used in, but not outside of the method. Parameters and most local variables have method scope. The smallest scope is block scope, which is for variables that are declared within a code block such as a **for** loop. Variables in block scope or method scope may have the same name as something in class scope, which causes name hiding. (Chapter 18.)

Sealed Class

A class that cannot be used as a base class for another class. This is done by adding the **sealed** keyword to the class definition. (Chapter 22.)

Signed Type

A numeric type that includes a + or - sign. (Chapter 6.)

Solution

In Visual Studio, a solution represents a collection of related projects, and keeps track of how they reference each other and other external assemblies. See also *project*, *assembly*, and *Solution Explorer*. (Chapter 45.)

Solution Explorer

A window in Visual Studio that outlines the overall structure of the code that you are working on. At the top level is the solution you are currently working on. Inside of that, any projects included in the solution are listed, and inside of that are any files that the project uses, including source code files, resource files, and configuration files. Any hidden window can be opened up through the View menu, or the **View > Other Windows** menu. (Chapter 45.)

Source Code

Human-readable instructions that will ultimately be turned into something the computer can execute. (Chapters 1 and 44.)

Square Brackets

The symbols **[** and **]**, used for array indexing. (Chapter 13.)

Stack

One of two main parts of a program's memory. The stack is a collection of frames, which represent individual method calls and that method's local variables and parameters. The stack is structured and is managed by adding frames when a new method is called, and removing frames when returning from a method. See also *heap* and *struct*. (Chapter 16.)

Stack Allocation

Arrays are typically stored on the heap. A stack allocation allows an array to be allocated on the stack instead, which reduces pressure on the garbage collector, though the array must be fixed size in this case. This can only be done in an unsafe context, and only with local array variables. (Chapter 42.)

Static

A keyword that is applied to members of a type to indicate that they belong to the class as a whole, rather than any single instance. A static member is shared between all instances of the class, and do not need an instance to be used. A type may define a single, parameterless static constructor, which is executed just before the first time the class is used. This static constructor provides initialization logic for the type. If a type is static, all of its members must be static as well. (Chapter 18.)

Static Type Checking

The act of verifying that members of a type that the code uses exist at compile time. This ensures that incorrect or invalid members such as methods, properties, and data will exist or be caught at compile time. Catching type errors at compile time is usually better than waiting until the application is running, but this fails for dynamic objects that change their members at run-time or whose members aren't known until run-time. Aside from variables that have the dynamic type, all variables use static type checking in C#. Static type checking is contrasted with dynamic type checking, which happens at run-time. (Chapter 41.)

String

A sequence of characters. In programming, you can usually think of strings as words or text. (Chapter 6.)

Struct

A custom-made type, assembled from other types, including methods and other members. A struct is a value type, while a class is a reference type. Structs should be immutable in most cases. (Chapter 21.)

Subclass

See *derived class*.

Superclass

See *base class*.

Subroutine

See *method*.

TAP

See *Task-based Asynchronous Pattern*.

Task-based Asynchronous Pattern

A pattern for achieving asynchronous programming (doing other things while you wait for a long-running task to complete) using tasks, primarily in the form of the **Task** class and the generic variant **Task<TResult>**. (Chapter 40.)

Ternary Operator

An operator that works on three operators. C# only has one ternary operator, which is the conditional operator. (Chapter 10.)

Thread

A lightweight "process" (contained within a normal process) which can be given its own code to work on, and run on a separate core on the processor. Depending on what you're trying to do, running your code on multiple threads may make your program run much faster, at the cost of being somewhat more difficult to maintain and debug. (Chapter 39.)

Thread Safety

Ensuring that parts of code that should not be accessed simultaneously by multiple threads (critical sections) are not accessible by multiple threads. (Chapter 39.)

Tuple

A simple data structure that stores a fixed number of ordered (presumably related) items. There are two sets of types in C# that allow you to use tuples. The **Tuple** classes are reference types, and the **ValueTuple** structs are reference types. **ValueTuple** is also used to leverage C# 7's syntax for returning multiple values from a method, which is transformed into a **ValueTuple** behind the scenes. (Chapters 28 and 46.)

Type

A specific kind of information, as a category. A type acts as a blueprint, providing a definition of what any object or instance of the type will keep track of and store. C# has a number of built-in types, but custom-made value or reference types can be defined with structs or classes respectively. (Chapters 5 and 6.)

Typecasting

Converting from one type to another using the conversion operator: **int x = (int)3.4;** (Chapter 9.)

Type Inference

The ability of the C# compiler to guess the type involved in certain situations, allowing you to leave off the type (or use the **var** type). (Chapter 6.)

Type Safety

The ability of the compiler and runtime to ensure that there is no way for one type to be mistaken for another. This plays a critical role in generics. (Chapter 25.)

Unary Operator

An operator that works with only a single value, such as the negation operator (the – sign in the value "-3"). (Chapter 7.)

Unchecked Context

A section of code wherein mathematical overflow will wrap around instead of throwing an exception. An unchecked context is the default. (Chapter 43.)

Underflow

With floating point types, when an operation results in loss of information, because the value was too small to be represented. (Chapter 9.)

Universal Windows Platform

An app model designed to support GUI applications in the .NET Framework and .NET Core stacks. Sometimes abbreviated UWP. (Chapters 44 and 51.)

Unsafe Code

Unsafe code is not fully managed by the CLR, giving you some added abilities like better performance or calling native code, at the cost of giving up some of the benefits of the CLR. Pointer types can only be used in an unsafe context. Unsafe code is only rarely needed. (Chapter 42.)

Unsafe Context

An unsafe context is a region of code (a type, a method, or a section of a method) where unsafe code can be performed. This allows you to leave the CLR's managed memory framework and work more directly with memory addresses, etc. This is generally only used in the context of interoperating with external, non-C# code (like C or C++). (Chapter 42.)

Unsigned Type

A type that does not include a + or - sign (generally assumed to be positive). (Chapter 6.)

User-Defined Conversion

A type conversion mechanism that is defined by the programmer instead of the language. C# allows you to create implicit and explicit conversions for your types, but it is recommended that you use them sparingly, as they have a variety of complications that often arise from using them. See also *typecasting*. (Chapter 43.)

Using Directive

A special statement at the beginning of a C# source file, which identifies specific namespaces that are used throughout the file, to make it so you do not need to use fully qualified names. (Chapters 3 and 27.)

Using Statement

Not to be confused with **using** directives, a **using** statement is a special way of wrapping up an object that implements the **IDisposable** interface, which disposes of the object when leaving the block of code that it wraps. (Chapter 43.)

Value Semantics

Something is said to have value semantics if its value is what counts, not the thing's identity. When something has value semantics and is assigned from one variable to another, passed to a method as a parameter, or returned from a method, the value is copied, and while the two variables or sides will have the same value, they will be copies of the same data. Modifying one will not affect the other, because a copy was made. In C#, all value types have value semantics. See also *value types* and *reference semantics*. (Chapter 16.)

Value Type

One of two main categories of types in C#. Value types are stored on the stack when possible (when not a part of a reference type). Value types follow value semantics, and when they are passed to a method or returned from a method, are copied. Structs are value types, as are all of the built-in types except **object** and **string**. See also *reference type* and *pointer type*. (Chapter 16.)

ValueTuple

See *Tuple*.

Variable

A place to store data. Variables are given a name, which can be used to access the variable, a type, which determines what kind of data can be placed in it, and a value, which is the actual contents of the variable at any given point in time. Once a variable is created, its name and type cannot be modified, though its value can be. Variables come in a number of different varieties, including local variables, instance variables, parameters, and static class variables. (Chapter 5.)

Virtual Machine

A special piece of software that can run executable code. The CLR is the virtual machine that .NET uses. Virtual machines usually provide controlled hardware access to the software that they are running and perform a number of useful features for the code that it runs, including a security model and memory management. Virtual machines are also usually responsible for the task of JIT compiling code to machine code at run-time. (Chapter 44.)

Virtual Method

If a method is virtual, derived classes are allowed to override the method and provide a new definition for it. To mark a method as virtual, the **virtual** keyword should be added to it. See also *abstract method* and *overriding*. (Chapter 23.)

Visual Basic.NET

A programming language that is very different from C# in syntax, but has almost a 1-to-1 correspondence in keywords and features, because both were designed for .NET. (Chapter 44.)

Visual C++

See *C++*.

Visual Studio

Microsoft's IDE, designed for making programs in C# and other programming languages. (Chapters 2 and 45.) The latest version of Visual Studio is Visual Studio 2017.

Visual Studio 2017 Community Edition

A member of the Visual Studio 2017 family that is free and has identical features to Professional. It allows commercial development as long as you have no more than 5 developers, you don't have more than 250 computers, and your company doesn't gross more than $1,000,000 in revenue. There are additional exceptions that allow you to use this free, including for educational use and open source use. This is the version that most new C# developers will start with.

Visual Studio 2017 Professional

A member of the Visual Studio family that has identical features to 2017 Community, but comes at cost. If you have more than 5 Visual Studio users in your company, you have more than 250 computers in the company, or the company has gross revenue in excess of $1,000,000, then the company will have to find the money to pay for this.

Volatile Field

An instance variable that has been protected with memory barriers by using the **volatile** keyword. This is used to ensure that data accessed by multiple threads, but not protected by some other thread-safe mechanism will be accessed in a way that won't have any unintended consequences from out-of-order execution at the hardware level. (Chapter 43.)

Windows Forms

An older app model designed for creating GUI applications. This app model has largely been replaced by Windows Presentation Foundation. (Chapters 44 and 51.)

Windows Presentation Foundation

An app model designed for creating GUI applications. It is a part of the .NET Framework stack. This is frequently abbreviated WPF. This is generally preferred to Windows Forms. (Chapters 44 and 51.)

Xamarin

A .NET Platform stack designed primarily for mobile development (specifically iOS and Android). (Chapter 44.)

XML Documentation Comment

A special type of comment, placed immediately above a type or member of a type to define what it does and how it is used. These comments are started by using three forward slashes (///). The format can include certain XML tags. XML documentation comments are used by automated tools to generate documentation that can be displayed on websites for anyone else who uses your code. It is also used by Visual Studio to create IntelliSense for your code. (Chapter 15.)

Tables and Charts

Operators

Name	Syntax	Description	Category	Page	Overloadable?	Associativity	Arity
Member Access	x.y	Accesses members of an instance, type, namespace, etc.	Primary Operators (These Happen First)	84	No	Left-to-Right	2
Null Conditional Member Access	x?.y	Member access with a null check first		284	No	Left-to-Right	2
Function Invocation	x(y)	Invoking or calling a method		88	No	Left-to-Right	2
Aggregate Object Indexing	a[x]	Accessing items in a collection		78	Indexers	Left-to-Right	2
Null Conditional Indexing	a?[x]	Collection access with a null check first		284	Indexers	Left-to-Right	2
Postfix Increment	x++	Adds 1 to a variable (original value returned)		58	Yes	Left-to-Right	1
Postfix Decrement	x--	Subtracts 1 from a variable (original value returned)		58	Yes	Left-to-Right	1
Type Instantiation	new	Creates new objects by invoking a constructor		78	No	Right-to-Left	1
Typeof	typeof(T)	Produces a Type object from the name of a type		280	No	Right-to-Left	1
Checked	checked	Switches to a checked context for overflow		287	No	Right-to-Left	1
Unchecked	unchecked	Switches to an unchecked context for overflow		287	No	Right-to-Left	1
Default	default(T)	Produces the default value of a given type		171	No	Right-to-Left	1
Delegate	delegate	Defines delegate types or produces a new empty instance		206	No	Right-to-Left	1
Sizeof	sizeof(T)	Produces the size of a given type		276	No	Right-to-Left	1
Pointer Dereference	x->y	Member access through a pointer (unsafe context)		266	No	Left-to-Right	2
Unary Plus	+x	Produces the same value as the operand	Unary Operators	45	Yes	Right-to-Left	1
Unary Minus/Numeric Negation	-x	Produces the negative of the operand		45	Yes	Right-to-Left	1
Logical Negation	!x	Produces the Boolean inverse of the operand		65	Yes	Right-to-Left	1
Bitwise Complement	~x	Produces the bitwise complement of the operand		278	Yes	Right-to-Left	1
Prefix Increment	++x	Adds 1 to a variable (incremented value returned)		58	Yes	Right-to-Left	1
Prefix Decrement	--x	Subtracts 1 from a variable (decremented value returned)		58	Yes	Right-to-Left	1
Type Casting	(T)x	Specifies a cast or type conversion		55	User-Defined Conversions	Right-to-Left	1
Await	await	Awaits asynchronous tasks		256	No	Right-to-Left	1
Address Of	&x	Produces the address of a variable (unsafe context)		266	No	Right-to-Left	1
Dereferencing/Indirection	*x	Declare pointer types and dereference pointers		266	No	Right-to-Left	1
Multiplication	x * y	Multiplies two values	Multiplicative Operators	43	Yes	Left-to-Right	2
Division	x / y	Divides the first value by the second		43	Yes	Left-to-Right	2
Remainder/Modulus	x % y	Produces the remainder of a division operation		44	Yes	Left-to-Right	2
Addition	x + y	Adds two values	Additive Operators	43	Yes	Left-to-Right	2
Subtraction	x - y	Subtracts the second value from the first		43	Yes	Left-to-Right	2
Left Shift	x << y	Bitwise shifts a value a number of bits leftward	Shift Operators	278	Yes	Left-to-Right	2
Right Shift	x >> y	Bitwise shifts a value a number of bits rightward		278	Yes	Left-to-Right	2
Less Than	x < y	Returns whether x is less than y		63	Yes	Left-to-Right	2

Name	Syntax	Description	Group	Page	Overloadable	Associativity	Operands
Greater Than	x > y	Returns whether x is greater than y	Relational and Type Testing Operators	63	Yes	Left-to-Right	2
Less Than Or Equal	x <= y	Returns whether x is less than or equal to y		63	Yes	Left-to-Right	2
Greater Than Or Equal	x >= y	Returns whether x is greater than or equal to y		63	Yes	Left-to-Right	2
Is	is	Determines if a value is a certain type or matches a pattern		146	No	Right-to-Left	1
As	as	Type conversion, returns null where (T)x throws an exception		147	No	Right-to-Left	1
Equality	x == y	Returns whether x exactly equals y	Equality Operators	63	Yes	Left-to-Right	2
Inequality	x != y	Returns whether x does not equal y		63	Yes	Left-to-Right	2
Logical AND	x & y	Performs bitwise AND between two values	Logical AND Operator	278	Yes	Left-to-Right	2
Logical XOR	x ^ y	Performs bitwise XOR between two values	Logical XOR Operator	278	Yes	Left-to-Right	2
Logical OR	x	y	Performs bitwise OR between two values	Logical OR Operator	278	Yes	Left-to-Right	2
Conditional AND	x && y	Returns whether both x and y are true	Conditional AND Operator	66	No	Left-to-Right	2
Conditional OR	x || y	Returns whether either x, y, or both are true	Conditional OR Operator	66	No	Left-to-Right	2
Null Coalescing	x ?? y	Returns x unless it is null, otherwise returns y	Null Coalescing Operator	283	No	Right-to-Left	2
Conditional/Ternary	t ? x : y	If t is true, produces x, otherwise y is produced	Conditional Operator	67	No	N/A	3
Assignment	x = y	Assigns the value of y to the variable x		46	No	Right-to-Left	2
Addition Assignment	x += y	Shorthand for x = x + y		47	Indirectly	Right-to-Left	2
Subtraction Assignment	x -= y	Shorthand for x = x - y		47	Indirectly	Right-to-Left	2
Multiplication Assignment	x *= y	Shorthand for x = x * y		47	Indirectly	Right-to-Left	2
Division Assignment	x /= y	Shorthand for x = x / y	Assignment and Lambda Operators (These Happen Last)	47	Indirectly	Right-to-Left	2
Remainder Assignment	x %= y	Shorthand for x = x % y		47	Indirectly	Right-to-Left	2
AND Assignment	x &= y	Shorthand for x = x & y		278	Indirectly	Right-to-Left	2
OR Assignment	x |= y	Shorthand for x = x	y		278	Indirectly	Right-to-Left	2
XOR Assignment	x ^= y	Shorthand for x = x ^ y		278	Indirectly	Right-to-Left	2
Left Shift Assignment	x <<= y	Shorthand for x = x << y		278	Indirectly	Right-to-Left	2
Right Shift Assignment	x >>= y	Shorthand for x = x >> y		278	Indirectly	Right-to-Left	2
Lambda Declaration	=>	Defines a lambda		230	No	Left-to-Right	2

Keywords

Name	Reference
abstract	154
add ♦	218
alias ♦	293
as	147
ascending ♦	240
async ♦	256
await ♦	256
base	147, 153
bool	36
break	74
by	241
byte	32
case	68
catch	196
char	33
checked	294
class	112
const	273
continue	74
decimal	34
default	68, 171
delegate	206
descending ♦	240
do	73
double	34
dynamic ♦	260
else	62
enum	83
event	212
explicit	286
extern	270
false	36
finally	199
fixed	268
float	34
for	73
foreach	81
from ♦	238
get ♦	125
global ♦	293
goto	287
group ♦	241
if	61
implicit	286
in	81
in (generics)	292

Name	Reference
int	31
interface	157
internal	121
into ♦	242
is	146
join	240
let	240
lock	249
long	32
nameof	275
namespace	16
new	78
null	101
object	148
operator	219
orderby ♦	240
out	183
out (generics)	292
override	151
params	182
partial (method)	149
partial (type)	149
private	114
protected	148
public	114
readonly	273
ref	183
remove ♦	218
return	89
sbyte	32
sealed	148
select	239
set	125
short	32
sizeof	276
stackalloc	267
static	120
string	36
struct	138
switch	68
this	117
throw	197
true	36
try	196
typeof	280
uint	32

Name	Reference
ulong	32
unchecked	294
unsafe	265
ushort	32
using	16
value ♦	125
var ♦	40
virtual	151
void	89
volatile	296
where (query clause) ♦	239
where (generics) ♦	169
while	71
yield ♦	272

♦ = Contextual Keyword, only reserved in certain contexts.

Built-In Types

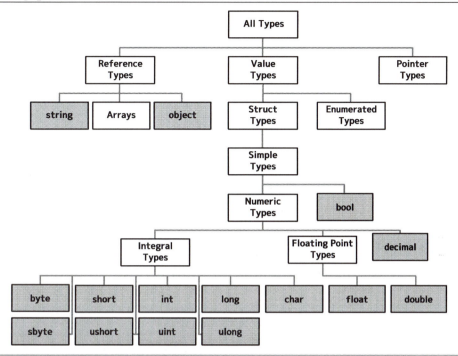

Type	Category	Size (Bytes)	Range	Precision
byte	Value	1	0 to 255	
short	Value	2	-32,768 to +32,767	
int	Value	4	-2147,483,648 to 2,147483,647	
long	Value	8	-9,223,372,036,854,775,808 to 9,223,372,036,854,775,807	
sbyte	Value	1	-128 to +127	
ushort	Value	2	0 to 65,535	
uint	Value	4	0 to 4,294,967,295	
ulong	Value	8	0 to 18,446,744,073,709,551,615	
float	Value	4	$\pm 1.0e\text{-}45$ to $\pm 3.4e38$	7
double	Value	8	$\pm 5e\text{-}324$ to $\pm 1.7e308$	15-16
decimal	Value	16	$\pm 1.0 \times 10e\text{-}28$ to $\pm 7.9e28$	28-29
char	Value	2	U+0000 to U+ffff (All Unicode characters)	
bool	Value	1	true/false	
object	Reference		Any type of data	
string	Reference	Size of content varies. References are 4 bytes.	Text of any length	
class	Reference		Custom reference type	
arrays	Reference		Collection of any other type	
enum	Value	Same as underlying type (default 4)	Listed enumeration members	
struct	Value	Size of content varies.	Custom value type	
pointer	Pointer	4	Pointers to other types	

Index

X